ARMENIANS AND LAND DISPUTES IN
THE OTTOMAN EMPIRE, 1850–1914

Edinburgh Studies on the Ottoman Empire
Series Editor: Kent F. Schull

Published and forthcoming titles

The Ottoman Canon and the Construction of Arabic and Turkish Literatures
C. Ceyhun Arslan

Migrating Texts: Circulating Translations around the Ottoman Mediterranean
Edited by Marilyn Booth

Ottoman Translations: Circulating Texts from Bombay to Paris
Edited by Marilyn Booth and Claire Savina

Death and Life in the Ottoman Palace: Revelations of the Sultan Abdülhamid I Tomb
Douglas Scott Brookes

Ottoman Sunnism: New Perspectives
Edited by Vefa Erginbaş

Ethnic Cleansing in Western Anatolia, 1912–1923: Ottoman Officials and the Local Christian Population
Umit Eser

Jews and Palestinians in the Late Ottoman Era, 1908–1914: Claiming the Homeland
Louis A. Fishman

Governing Migration in the Late Ottoman Empire
Ella Fratantuono

Spiritual Vernacular of the Early Ottoman Frontier: The Yazıcıoğlu Family
Carlos Grenier

The Politics of Armenian Migration to North America, 1885–1915: Sojourners, Smugglers and Dubious Citizens
David Gutman

The Kizilbash-Alevis in Ottoman Anatolia: Sufism, Politics and Community
Ayfer Karakaya-Stump

Çemberlitaş Hamami in Istanbul: The Biographical Memoir of a Turkish Bath
Nina Macaraig

Hagia Sophia in the Long Nineteenth Century
Edited by Emily Neumeier and Benjamin Anderson

The Kurdish Nobility in the Ottoman Empire: Loyalty, Autonomy and Privilege
Nilay Özok-Gündoğan

Armenians and Land Disputes in the Ottoman Empire, 1850–1914
Mehmet Polatel

Nineteenth-Century Local Governance in Ottoman Bulgaria: Politics in Provincial Councils
Safa Saraçoğlu

Prisons in the Late Ottoman Empire: Microcosms of Modernity
Kent F. Schull

Ruler Visibility and Popular Belonging in the Ottoman Empire
Darin Stephanov

The North Caucasus Borderland: Between Muscovy and the Ottoman Empire, 1555–1605
Murat Yaşar

Children and Childhood in the Ottoman Empire: From the 14th to the 20th Centuries
Edited by Gülay Yılmaz and Fruma Zachs

edinburghuniversitypress.com/series/esoe

ARMENIANS AND LAND DISPUTES IN THE OTTOMAN EMPIRE, 1850–1914

Mehmet Polatel

EDINBURGH
University Press

Edinburgh University Press is one of the leading university presses in the UK. Publishing new research in the arts and humanities, EUP connects people and ideas to inspire creative thinking, open new perspectives and shape the world we live in. For more information, visit www.edinburghuniversitypress.com.

© Mehmet Polatel, 2025

Edinburgh University Press Ltd
13 Infirmary Street, Edinburgh EH1 1LT

Typeset in Jaghbuni by
Cheshire Typesetting Ltd, Cuddington, Cheshire

A CIP record for this book is available from the British Library

ISBN 978 1 3995 2860 3 (hardback)
ISBN 978 1 3995 2862 7 (webready PDF)
ISBN 978 1 3995 2863 4 (epub)

The right of Mehmet Polatel to be identified as author of this work has been asserted in accordance with the Copyright, Designs and Patents Act 1988 and the Copyright and Related Rights Regulations 2003 (SI No. 2498).

Contents

List of Illustrations	viii
Abbreviations, Acronyms and Non-English Terms	ix
Note on Transliteration	x
Acknowledgements	xi

Introduction: The Political and Economic Aspects of the Land
    Question   1
    The Geographical Spread of the Problem   3
    Land as a Factor of Production   4
    Land, Politics and Sovereignty   6
    The New Territorial Turn and Land Policies around the World   7
    The Structure of the Book   9

1. Law, Land and Politics: The Transformation of the Ottoman
    Land Regime   17
    The Ottoman Land Tenure System before the Nineteenth Century   18
    Legal Changes and the Transformation of the Ottoman Land
        Regime from Tanzimat to the First World War   21
    Territoriality, Nationalism and the New Significance of Land   35
    Conclusion   40

2. Peasants versus Notables: The Emergence of the Armenian Land
    Question (1850–80)   50
    The Early Disputes and the Emergence of the Land Question   51
    The Armenian Community and Land Disputes   58
    The Ottoman Government's Approach   64
    The Armenian Question as an International Issue   66
    Conclusion   73

3. Mass Violence and Mass Seizures (1880–1908)	82
The Historical Context	83
Mass Seizures and the Transformation of the Land Question	85
The Means of Property Transfer in the Hamidian Period	96
Conclusion	105
4. Controlling Outcomes: The Hamidian Government and Land Disputes	117
The Activities of the Reform Commissions	118
Emigration Policies and Regulations	120
The Ban on the Sale of Immovable Property to Armenians	126
The Settlement of Muslim Immigrants	132
Conclusion	134
5. Revolution, Resolution and Resistance (1908–12): The Land Question under the Young Turks	142
The Constitutional Regime and Early Regulations	143
The Changes in the Government's Approach	152
The Local Ottoman Officials' Approach to Land Disputes	163
The Armenian Political and Religious Elite's Initiatives for the Resolution of the Land Questions	167
Conclusion	180
6. The Reforms and the Land Question after the Outbreak of the Balkan Wars	191
The Historical Context	192
Ottoman Attempts at Reform after the Outbreak of the Balkan Wars	194
The Armenians' Demand for Reform and the Internationalisation of Reform Debates	196
The Ottoman Government's Attempts to Domesticate the Prospects of Reform	199
Reform Questions at the International Level	206
The Yeniköy Conference and Negotiations between Germany and Russia	211
Conclusion	214
7. The Land Question on the Eve of the First World War	221
The Armenian Political and Religious Elite and the Land Question	222
Kurdish Reactions to the Reform Plans	225

Contents

The Situation in the Eastern Provinces	230
Regulations and Policies Regarding the Resolution of Land Disputes on the Eve of the First World War	240
Conclusion	248
Conclusion: The Armenian Genocide and the Land Question	256
Bibliography	262
Index	287

Illustrations

Figure

3.1 The distribution of seized agricultural lands larger than 100 *dönüm*s (10 hectares) or worth more than 100 liras   88

Maps

3.1 Geographical distribution of forcefully seized lands larger than 100 *dönüm*s or worth more than 100 liras   90
3.2 The geographical distribution of seizures with communal effects   94
3.3 The number of seized or destroyed church and monastery buildings   97
3.4 The number of properties seized for debts   100

Abbreviations, Acronyms and Non-English Terms

Abbreviations and Acronyms

ANA	Armenian National Assembly
ARF	Armenian Revolutionary Federation (Hay Heghap'okhaganneri Tashnagts'ut'iwn)
BOA	Başkanlık Osmanlı Arşivi (Ottoman Archive of the Presidency)
CUP	Committee of Union and Progress (İttihat ve Terakki Cemiyeti)
SKMAP	Society for Kurdish Mutual Aid and Progress (Kürt Teavün ve Terakki Cemiyeti)
TNA	The National Archives of the United Kingdom
VHA	USC Shoah Foundation, Visual History Archive

Glossary of Non-English Terms

Dönüm	measure of land, 940 m^2, about ¼ acre
Ferâğ	cession of property, transfer
Hafir	illegal protection tax
Kıyye	okka, about 1,300 grams
Kile	bushel, 36½ kilos
Mahlul	escheated (property), vacant
Miri land	lands of which the ownership rights (*raqaba*) belong to the state
Sened-i 'âdî	unofficial sale document
Takrir	memorandum, official note
Tapu	title deed
Tasarruf senedi	deed of possession

Note on Transliteration

I have followed the Library of Congress's Western Armenian transliteration system for transliterating Armenians words with diacritical marks. Names and titles in Eastern Armenian are transliterated based on this system.

All translations in the book are mine, unless stated otherwise. In the transliteration from Ottoman Turkish, the diacritical marks of ʿ*ayn* and *hamza* are retained throughout the text, with the addition of circumflexes to indicate lengthened vowels.

The Hicri and Rumi dates (corresponding to the lunar and Julian calendars) cited in the book are presented with Gregorian equivalents. The dates of archival documents are the dispatchment dates.

All place names in the archival documents are presented with their contemporary equivalent in parenthesis, except for those I was not able to locate.

Acknowledgements

Turning a research project into a book is not a solitary journey. I am deeply grateful to the many individuals, institutions and archives that have supported this project and provided insights, making this work possible.

First and foremost, I would like to express my gratitude to Seda Altuğ, my former advisor, for her valuable comments, literature suggestions and critical reading, which helped me give my research its final form. Additionally, I would like to extend my thanks to Şevket Pamuk, Çağlar Keyder, Yücel Terzibaşoğlu, Nadir Özbek and Selim Deringil for their comments and suggestions.

Ever since I began my graduate studies, the History and Sociology Departments of Koç University have played a significant role in my academic growth. I am deeply thankful to Yonca Köksal and Dilek Barlas, who have always supported me and played an essential role in my development as a scholar. The Atatürk Institute has also been instrumental in my scholarly journey, and I am grateful to all the faculty members who contributed to my growth.

Another institution that has played an essential role in my life during these years is the Hrant Dink Foundation. They always welcomed me – sometimes as a colleague, sometimes as a friend, sometimes as a volunteer. I am incredibly grateful to Delal Dink, who has supported me as a friend and a colleague for more than a decade.

I am deeply grateful for the Manoogian Postdoctoral Fellowship at the Center for Armenian Studies at the University of Michigan, Ann Arbor, which provided me with the time and resources essential to completing this book. I am deeply indebted to Ronald G. Suny for his unwavering guidance and encouragement. Since becoming a part of my dissertation committee, his insightful feedback on my research became instrumental in shaping this work. I am also thankful to Armen Abkarian, Hakem Al-Rustom,

Armenians and Land Disputes in the Ottoman Empire

Kathryn Babayan, Kevork Bardakjian, Haydar Darıcı, Dzovinar Derderian, Fatma Müge Göçek, Gottfried Hagen, David Leupold, Arakel Minassian, Michael Pifer, Vahe Sahakyan, Anoush Suni and Naira Tumanyan for their friendship and support during my stay in Ann Arbor.

I am immensely thankful to the Junior Postdoctoral Research Fellowship at the USC Shoah Foundation Center for Advanced Genocide Research (now the USC Dornsife Center for Advanced Genocide Research) for providing me with crucial time, resources and a supportive community. I am deeply indebted to Wolf Gruner, Martha Stroud and Badema Pitic for helping me the most of my stay. I would like to extend my sincere thanks to my friend and colleague Manuk Avedikian for his tireless help with my research in the oral history and testimony collections at the foundation's Visual History Archives. I am also thankful to the Ararat-Eskijian Museum and its director Marguerite Mangassarian Goschin. I also thank Richard E. Antaramian, Sedda Antekelian, Sebouh D. Aslanian, Ohannes Kulak Avedikian, Seta Korkor Kulak Avedikian, Crispin Brooks, Sevan Derbedrosian, Salpi Ghazarian, the late Richard G. Hovannisian, Nora Kayserian and Gabor Toth for their support.

For this study, I conducted research in several archives, including the Ottoman Archive of the Presidency in Turkey, the National Archives of the United Kingdom, the AGBU Nubarian Library in Paris, the National Archives of Armenia, the Armenian National Library and the USC Shoah Foundation Visual History Archive. I am thankful to the archivists and staff of these institutions for their expertise and assistance. I would also like to express my gratitude to the Calouste Gulbenkian Foundation, which provided funding for part of my archival research.

I am deeply grateful to Boris Adjemian, the director of the Nubarian Library, for helping me locate the necessary documents during my short-term visit. I would also like to express my sincere appreciation to Raymond H. Kévorkian for his kind help and feedback throughout my research at the Nubarian Library. Additionally, I am thankful to David Davidian, Thomas J. Samuelian, Hovhannes Asryan and Nişan Güreh for their invaluable assistance during my research visit to Yerevan. Finally, I would like to acknowledge and thank the staff of the libraries of Boğaziçi University and Koç University for their support.

While working on a book about seized Armenian properties, I had the privilege of collaborating with Uğur Ümit Üngör. Through our friendship and collaboration, I gained valuable insights that significantly contributed to the development of the book.

During a series of academic meetings in Switzerland, I had the privilege of discussing various topics explored in this study with distinguished

Acknowledgements

academics. I am grateful to Hans-Lukas Kieser for providing me with this opportunity. His perspective and suggestions were invaluable in refining the arguments presented here. I would also like to thank Thomas Schmutz for our collaborative work, which helped me to gain a better understanding of reform debates.

Thanks are due to Bedross Der Matossian, a cherished friend and colleague whose extensive knowledge and generous help were indispensable to the completion of this project. Apart from helping me find several books and documents, his valuable insights and comments have profoundly influenced my thinking throughout these years.

I would like to express my gratitude to my editor and the publishing team at Edinburgh University Press for their valuable expertise and guidance throughout the publication process. Kent Schull, the series editor, and Rachel Bridgewater, the Senior Commissioning Editor, have been supportive since I submitted my proposal, and their feedback and suggestions have been immensely helpful in shaping this book. I would also like to thank Isobel Birks for her assistance in the finalisation of the publication. Additionally, I am grateful to the Series Advisory Board and the two anonymous reviewers for their outstanding feedback and constructive criticism. Their thoughtful comments helped me to improve the manuscript. Finally, I would like to thank Nina Macaraig for copy-editing the manuscript.

My access to many of the documents and books examined in this study has been possible thanks to the help of several friends. I am thankful to Ayhan Aktar, Y. Tolga Cora, Sait Çetinoğlu, Matthew Ghazarian, Chris Gratien, Edip Gölbaşı, Onur Günay, Hagop Hachikian, Vahakn Keshishian, Yener Koç, Rober Koptaş, Khatchig Mouradian, Zakarya Mildanoğlu, Ara Sarafian, Ali Sipahi, Vahé Tachjian and Kenan Yenice. They were not only kind enough to share books and documents with me, but they also contributed to shaping my approach with their valuable comments on various topics. I would like to thank Vahan Ohanian for giving me permission to use the image on the book cover. I thank Özgür Leman Eren for her support and friendship, especially for helping me prepare the maps used in this book. I am also thankful to Margaret Lavinia Anderson, who was kind enough to read and comment on my work and Stephan Astourian, who invited me to various academic meetings to present parts of this research.

In my experience, Armenian is not an easy language to learn. I am extremely thankful to my amazing teacher, Şuşan Özoğlu, who has been incredibly patient and helpful in guiding me on this journey. I also thank her and Nayat Muradyan for their friendship and support.

During the research and writing process of this book, the support of several friends has sustained me. I thank Özkan Akpınar, Serhat Arslan, Damla Barın, Uğur Bayraktar, Serhat Bozkurt, Adnan Çelik, Çetin Çelik, Haki Dere, Şerif Derince, Namık Kemal Dinç, Gülseren Duman, Pakrat Estukyan, Murat Gözoğlu, Uygar Gültekin, Ayhan Işık, Alp Kanzık, Nayat Karaköse, Ayşenur Korkmaz, Nora Mildanoğlu, Can Nacar, the late Sarkis Seropyan, Zeynep Sungur, Osman Şahin, Adom Şaşkal, Zeynep Taşkın and Altuğ Yılmaz for their friendship and support.

Since our time in the master's program, Harun Ercan has helped me develop my approach to the subject-matter of this book. Apart from his intellectual contribution, Harun has been more than a friend to me – he has been like a brother. I am truly grateful for his unwavering support and invaluable friendship.

I thank my family for supporting me on my academic journey. I am indebted to my mother Zayime, my father Sefer and my brother Semih. I would also like to thank my mother-in-law Ayten, my late father-in-law Ayvaz and my sister-in-law Nermin for their support.

This book would not have been realised without my wife, Nazife Kosukoğlu, who has been a constant source of inspiration and motivation. Her critical reading of my works, challenging questions and emotional support have been precious to me. I am grateful for her unwavering love and encouragement.

To Nazife

Introduction: The Political and Economic Aspects of the Land Question

In the early 1870s, Abraham and Melkon, two friends from a village called Dağ Marnik (Çubuklu), took to the road to Istanbul. Their small village, located on top of a mountain in Muş, was far from the capital. This was a long journey, and they had to walk for weeks. In their bundles, they carried something valuable – something that gave them the power to begin this difficult undertaking. This special and powerful thing was a stack of papers issued by a governor,[1] documenting that the lands on which they had toiled belonged to them. These were documents of hope, of subsistence and of a bright future. Armed with them, the two mountain villagers themselves would knock on the door of the *Bâb-ı Âlî*.

The events that brought them to Istanbul began with the Tanzimat, among the ruins of an ancient Armenian village abandoned since the Safavid attacks of the sixteenth century.[2] In the 1830s, a couple of Armenian families decided to revive this village and make it a home for themselves. They built houses, cleared the roads, worked the lands and paid their taxes. For thirty years, no one raised a competing claim. Then, one day, the villagers found one of the most powerful men of Muş against them. The mufti of Muş, Hüseyin Efendi, claimed that his family was the rightful owner of all lands in the village.[3] The mufti occupied a very significant post, was well-connected and held a seat on the administrative council of the city. However, these were novel times. The governor of Erzurum, İsmail Pasha, had just decided to put the Tanzimat into practice and to make 'a showcase of Ottomanism'.[4] For this purpose, he established a commission to investigate the troubles of the Armenians in Muş. He handed the mountain-dwellers those precious papers, stating that they indeed were the rightful owners of these lands. However, time proved that this was a short-lived victory. Using his clout and power to make threats and promises, the mufti managed to receive an administrative council decision in his favour. The villagers protested, saying that 'they were not, nor could they become, the serfs of Hussein Effendi'.[5] Hence, Abraham and Melkon started their journey.

For years, they struggled to get by in the big city, sleeping in *hans* and coffeehouses. They applied to the Armenian Patriarchate and the Council of State. At last, a final decision was made. Their claims were in line with the framework of the Tanzimat. However, the Council of State decided in favour of the mufti.[6] Abraham and Melkon returned to their village in despair. Their hopes, sparked by İsmail Pasha's showcase of Ottomanism, were completely crushed by the reality of power.

In the 1910s, there were thousands like Abraham and Melkon. The number of land disputes between Armenians and Muslims reached massive heights. In some places, more than half of all arable land in the province was disputed. By then, these disputes had evolved into a distinct political problem and begun to be called the 'Armenian Land Question' (*Haygagan Hoghayin Harts'ě*). This book will examine the emergence and transformation of this question and the effects and implications of its evolution.

The long nineteenth century was an era of agrarian questions – and, in some cases, land wars – in many countries. From the Oklahoma Land Rush in the US (1889) to the Land Wars in Ireland (1879), land was at the centre of many conflicts and episodes of mass violence worldwide.[7] The Ottoman Empire was no exception in this regard. Especially in the second half of this long century, land disputes erupted in almost every corner of the empire. Muslim refugees fleeing from lost territories, nomads trying to or being forced to settle, as well as small and large landholders attempting to adapt to the changes in the Ottoman economy all took part in these disputes fuelled by modern state formation and the encroachment of capitalism. The Armenian Land Question emerged and transformed within and as a particular part of this broader agrarian question in the Ottoman Empire. One of the major contentions of this book is that it emerged as a particular social problem, both because of the extent to which it was politicised and because of the scale into which it evolved after the massacres of the 1890s.

Tracing the evolution of the Armenian Land Question from the mid-nineteenth century to the outbreak of the First World War, I will show that there existed a complicated relationship between mass violence, ethno-religious tensions and competition over resources such as land. On the one hand, underlining that the massacres of the 1890s radically changed the scale and characteristics of land disputes concerning Armenians, this book will document the transformative power of mass violence and its impact on socio-economic life and structures. The formation of modern

Introduction

states and markets were violent processes in Europe.[8] In this book, I will argue that this was also the case for the Ottoman Empire and show that mass violence constituted a very important factor in shaping the relations between state, land and people in the empire. On the other hand, this study will also highlight the potential effects of competition over resources on the escalation of tensions among different communities, the erosion of trust and the outbreak of further violence. Especially when they transform into such massive social problems affecting the subsistence, enrichment or livelihood of hundreds of thousands, disputes over natural sources may poison intercommunal relations and pave the way for the rise of intractable conflicts.

One of the main arguments of this book posits that the transformation of land disputes involving Armenians into the Armenian Land Question was embedded in the new territorial turn that started to change the relationship between sovereignty and territoriality in the mid-nineteenth century worldwide. Over time, Armenian, Turkish and Kurdish nationalisms all developed strong territorial aspects. As land was the tie that connected people to territories and as land ownership and population became the primary means of raising claims to sovereignty, independence and autonomy, land disputes involving Armenians became increasingly politicised. By the 1910s, for many Turks, Armenians and Kurds, what was at stake in these disputes was ethno-national dominance, political sovereignty and the future of the homeland. Thus, these disputes over land had in fact transformed into disputes over territories linked to competing nationalist projects.

The Geographical Spread of the Problem

From its inception to its escalation, the Armenian land question predominantly concerned rural lands in the Ottoman East.[9] Land disputes concerning Armenians occurred not only in this region but also in Cilicia, in the form of sizable land seizures. However, most of these were concentrated in the Ottoman East. Some key Ottoman policies, such as the exclusion of Armenians from the land market in the late 1890s, were also geographically specific and targeted this particular region.

This region – located on the border between the Ottoman, Russian and Persian empires – was populated by ethnically and religiously diverse groups. Kurds, Armenians and Turks constituted the bulk of the population, which included Muslims, Christians, Jews and Yazidis. There was also considerable diversity in terms of life-styles and forms of living. The Armenian population was exclusively settled at the beginning of the nineteenth century, while Kurdish tribes were mostly nomadic or semi-nomadic.[10] This situation would change in later decades, and forced and voluntary settlement would exacerbate the pressure on land. Another important group in the region consisted of Muslim immigrants, whose numbers in these parts of the country gradually increased.[11]

Until the nineteenth century, political life in the Ottoman East was marked by a considerable degree of autonomy. Local Kurdish *mir*s ruled many parts of the region. With the abolition of the emirates in the early nineteenth century, the central authority tried to enhance its power in the region.[12] However, in later decades, local powerholders continued to have considerable power on the ground. As in many other parts of the empire, the state carried out reforms depending on the co-optation and cooperation of local notables.[13] This was not always guaranteed, and the capacity of the state declined 'as one moved away from the imperial capital to the provinces'.[14]

Land as a Factor of Production

Land is an elementary factor of production which makes economic activity possible. Without land, neither agriculture nor manufacturing can take place.[15] While land continues to carry a crucial significance in the contemporary world, it was even more significant in the nineteenth century, especially in the Ottoman Empire, since its economy largely depended on agricultural production. At the end of this century, at least 80 per cent of the Ottoman population made a living through agriculture.[16] In a world where agriculture was the major economic activity, land was an extremely valuable possession. Gaining or losing even a small strip of land could drastically change one's living conditions. What rendered the land disputes between Armenians and Muslims so contentious was partly this predominance of agriculture in the Ottoman economy. These land disputes were important because land itself held such great significance.

Apart from this general situation, several specific factors heightened the economic importance of land ownership in the nineteenth century. One of them was the accelerated integration of the Ottoman economy into the world economy. The empire became a semi-periphery in the global economic system, especially following the signing of the Anglo-Ottoman Treaty of 1838, which ended monopolies and allowed open-market policies.[17] In this period marked by economic liberalism, agricultural production in Anatolia began to transform. Market-oriented production started to take hold, first in Western Anatolia, then on the Black Sea Coast and in the Adana region. The central parts of Asia Minor were connected

Introduction

to the capital at the end of the century, facilitating grain transport and market-oriented grain production.[18] This process was very slow in the Ottoman East. However, capitalism also made inroads into this region, especially towards the end of the century.[19] Overall, the expansion of market-oriented agricultural production increased the demand for land and enhanced its economic significance.

Another factor that made land more important was the transformation of the Ottoman land regime. Following the adoption of the Land Code of 1858, land gradually became a commodity that could be bought, sold and mortgaged, and ownership rights increasingly began to be defined in exclusionary terms. These legal developments paved the way for the emergence of mass disputes between different groups of people who were using the same lands. For example, nomads who claimed an ancient right to passage found themselves in conflict with agriculturalists who wanted to block their access. Thus, the transformation of the legal regime also affected the significance of land and land disputes.

Another factor consisted of the influx of Muslim immigrants from the lost territories of the empire and other countries, such as Russia. Between 1820 and 1914, the Ottoman population in the regions that today lie within Turkey rose from 9.4 to 16.5 million.[20] A significant part of this population increase was due to migration because around 4 million Muslims had immigrated to the centre of the empire in this period. And most of the refugees were agriculturalists. The influx of such a large group of agriculturalists awaiting settlement increased the pressure on land. In various places, Muslim immigrants were settled on officially unclaimed lands. Soon, it became clear that these lands were seasonally used by nomads. And this situation contributed to the eruption of land disputes across the country. Most of the refugees were settled in the western and central parts of Asia Minor. Partly due to the agreement between Russia and the Ottoman Empire, until the twentieth century there was minimal Muslim refugee settlement in the Ottoman East.[21] However, in Central Anatolia and beyond, immigrants made up a significant group involved in the Armenian land question.

A final factor that increased the demand for land in the nineteenth century was the voluntary and forced settlement of nomadic tribes. On many occasions, the centralising Ottoman state forced nomadic groups, which due to their mobility were difficult to control and tax, into settlement. One can also find cases where the tribes themselves wanted to change their life-style. In the Ottoman East, life had a traditional rhythm for nomadic and settled groups, which took the form of a symbiosis. Nomadic and semi-nomadic groups spent the winters with settled people, in return for payment.[22] This was an uneasy situation, but it made it possible for these three groups to live in the region simultaneously. When most of the population wanted to or was forced to settle, a land shortage emerged. As will be examined in this book, this settlement trend also affected the transformation of the Armenian land question because it escalated the pressure on land.

Land, Politics and Sovereignty

Territoriality is one of the basic components of human social organisation.[23] However, the characteristics of human territoriality and the importance attached to territoriality in the organisation of human groups are neither ahistorical nor universal but are bounded by time and space.[24] There emerged a marked change in the understanding and organisation of territoriality in Europe in the early modern period. This transformation was related to the development of geographical and statistical techniques and knowledge, on the one hand, and the transformation of the basic tenets of sovereignty and governmentality, on the other. The Treaty of Westphalia of 1648 came as a turning point in the emergence of the modern state system based on territorial sovereignty. In this particular mode of political organisation, sovereignty became a territorial rather than a social or relational concept. As underlined by Jordan Branch, the General Treaty of the Vienna Congress of 1815 was another turning point in the establishment of modern territorial sovereignty, because it represented 'the culmination of centuries of change' through which political rule began to be assigned 'as exclusive and complete sovereignty over a space defined by cartographic lines'.[25] As underlined by Andy Hanlun Li, the rise of modern territoriality was not only a European phenomenon. It was also experienced in other places, such as China.[26]

Another historical trend that accompanied the emergence of territorial sovereignty and the modern state system consisted of the rise of nationalism. In nationalist discourses, land is prefixed by 'the' and serves as a key element of political identification.[27] The importance of land, as the raw material of political space production or territoriality, became increasingly more pronounced with the rise of nationalism because nationalism is a territorial ideology. As underlined by Ernest Gellner, nationalism is 'primarily a political principle which holds that the political and national unit should be congruent'.[28] In this sense, land serves as the source of the material existence of a nation.

As underlined by Eric J. Hobsbawm, nationalism also had its own historical journey. In the 1870s, nationalisms began to change, and there occurred an upsurge of newly invented traditions in education, public rituals, public monuments and sports. In this period, ethnicity and language became the central, if not the only, criteria of nationhood. Moreover, there was 'a sharp shift to the political right of nation and flag'.[29] Thus, political sovereignty and territoriality became increasingly crucial for nationalist movements.

In the nineteenth century, land was increasingly seen as a means of establishing or maintaining ethno-national dominance. As underlined by Stanley L. Engerman and Jacob Metzer, the rise of such nationalist approaches to land ownership contradicted the liberal conception of land.[30] Absolute liberalisation of land requires abolishing all administrative barriers to entry into the land market and transforming land into alienable property. However, absolute nationalisation of land requires the exclusion of non-nationals or nationals not belonging to the dominant ethno-national group from the land market and their dispossession, since land is considered a part of the homeland belonging to nationals. Thus, there is a conflict between these two trends on a conceptual level. Engerman and Metzer have pointed out that, on a practical level, these two trends simultaneously affected land disputes and policies worldwide, to varying degrees, and that accommodations emerged between these two trends.[31] As shown by Yücel Terzibaşoğlu, tensions and accommodations between these two trends also shaped late Ottoman land policies and practices in Western Anatolia.[32] In this book, I will show that these two approaches and the conflicts and accommodations between them were critical for the transformation of the Armenian land question.

The New Territorial Turn and Land Policies around the World

With the rise of new imperialism,[33] which emphasised direct territorial control, and the rise of nationalist approaches to land, a new territorial turn happened in the nineteenth century.[34] In this period, liberalism reigned supreme in many regards. However, in terms of land policies and approaches to land ownership, one can observe a gradual move away from liberalism in many countries.

The traces of this turn can be found in the policies of the Russian Empire, especially in her policies towards Jewish and Polish populations and their property rights. As underscored by Ronald G. Suny, in the nineteenth century, the Russian Empire made 'vital distinctions between Russians and non-Russians' that was reflected on its 'discriminating and nationalizing policies'.[35] In the late 1880s, Russia made it almost impossible for foreigners to buy or lease land in her peripheries.[36] The property rights and freedom of movement of the Jewish population in Russia had already been very limited. Yet, these policies became even more draconian with the May Laws and other regulations adopted in the 1880s. As result, purchasing rural real estate became practically impossible for the majority of Jews. Such policies also targeted the Polish subjects of the empire. In the western provinces, a special tax increased their burden, and they could only acquire land by inheritance.[37] Russia also tried to strengthen its political claims to this region by encouraging Russian settlement.[38] Thus, the land regime in the Russian Empire included various discriminatory aspects devised to ensure Russian ethno-national dominance, and despite the abolition of serfdom the land market in Russia was anything but liberal.

Prussian land policies also exemplify this trend. The Prussian state established a settlement commission to strengthen the German element in Polish-inhabited territories through settlement, land purchase and later confiscation. As an exclusionist approach replaced an assimilationist approach, the Prussian state sought to displace the Polish population under its rule.[39] The Poles resisted these attempts, establishing land banks and socially excluding those who sold their lands to the commission. Ultimately, the state failed to 'buy its way to a German population majority'.[40] Moves away from liberal land policies were also influential in Western Europe. Especially after the Franco-Prussian War of 1870, restrictions concerning the property rights of aliens became widespread.[41] Such policies and confiscation initiatives marked the land regimes in many European countries during the First World War.[42]

There also existed radicalisation in terms of land policies in colonised countries. As underlined by A. Dirk Moses, land rather than labour and dispossession rather than proletarianisation were critical for capital accumulation in the colonies.[43] However, throughout the nineteenth century, some changes transformed the land policies in the colonies. For instance, in Namibia, Europeans began to amass land in 1883, alienating thousands yearly.[44] In the early 1900s, tensions arising from this situation contributed to the outbreak of the Herero and Nama war of resistance, which was followed by a genocide and expropriation of all tribal lands by the German colonial administration.[45] In Ireland, tensions caused by agrarian conflicts escalated in the late 1870s, leading to the outbreak of the Land War of 1879–82.[46] In the US, new tribal lands were opened to settlement, accelerating the dispossession of indigenous people and the emergence of what is known as the Land Rush of 1889.[47]

The Ottoman Empire, too, was caught up in this global moment, defined by the tensions between liberal and nationalist approaches to land.[48]

Introduction

The case to be examined in this book was part of this world-historical trend. Thus, by focusing on the Armenian land question, this book will provide an account of the new territorial turn as it was experienced in the Ottoman Empire.

The Structure of the Book

The first chapter will look at the trends that shaped the emergence of the Armenian land question in the 1850s. After examining the legislative framework and the economic and legal impacts of the empire's intensifying integration into the world economy and the rise of the central administrative state, the chapter will then provide an overview of the eruption of land disputes in different parts of the empire. A second development followed from the first: the significance of land began to take on a new and threatening political dimension.

Chapter 2 will scrutinise the earliest land disputes, which consisted of struggles between the land's current occupants – that is, lowly Armenians, primarily peasants and share-croppers – and those who coveted the same land, mostly local powerholders – namely, *bey*s and *agha*s. However, these disputes acquired a political dimension through the reactions of Armenian intellectuals, who petitioned the Ottoman authorities in the capital and sought to involve traditional Armenian institutions, such as the Patriarchate. It shows that Istanbul ignored most of the demands for restitution, except in cases involving thousands of people, thus having the potential to disrupt the social order. However, two developments in the 1870s – the shifting focus of Armenian nationalism from culture to territory and the emergence of the Armenian question as an international problem – led to a significant change in the government's perceptions, transforming the land issue in new ways. Armenian intellectuals such as Raffi and institutions such as the Armenian Patriarchate and the Armenian National Assembly began to see their grievances as systemic, more so than the sum of individual land disputes. At the same time, the government became more alert to the need for some structural resolution. This new awareness failed to produce any tangible results. The best that could be said was that some government officials recognized the need for some kind of intervention that would eventually be required to resolve the problem.

In the third chapter, the narrative will move from a conflict resembling a class struggle to the onset of mass violence against Armenians *qua* Armenians. With the consolidation of Sultan Abdülhamid II's regime in the late 1870s, which coincided with painful territorial losses in the Russo-Ottoman War of 1877–78, concern over the future demography of the empire began to shape Ottoman policy. Seeking to strengthen the sultan's ties with his Muslim subjects, the government armed some Muslim tribes, mainly Kurds, recruiting them into regiments bearing the sultan's name: 'Hamidian'. In the years from 1894 through 1897, these regiments, local Muslims, as well as several other tribes, massacred thousands of Armenians in the central and eastern parts of the empire, forcing thousands to flee, 'abandoning' their homes. This catastrophe, which this book will investigate through more than 7,000 land dispute cases by tracking their geographical distribution, not only transformed the dimensions of the Armenian land question but also fundamentally changed its character and significance for the Ottoman state. It was no longer a struggle in which men of means seized the property of peasants: now, large estate-owners, if they were Armenian, might be targeted for dispossession, while the usurpers, although always Muslim, also included ordinary people and impoverished immigrants.

The Hamidian government was neither an indifferent by-stander to these clashes nor a fall guy, haplessly reacting to events as they unfolded. Chapter 4 will examine the role of the government in land disputes and how it tried to control the outcomes of the land seizures and dispossession affecting Armenians. The chapter will show that the government intervened actively, working to shape the massacres' demographic and political consequences, and not least its property 'transfers'. It adopted new policies, such as settling Muslim immigrants on property belonging to Armenians, banning the sale of immovable properties to Armenians and, through legislation and international agreements, preventing the Armenian refugees' return to their homes.

Ottoman politics changed significantly when the Young Turks seized power in 1908 and reinstated the constitutional regime. The land question immediately became a much-discussed political issue, as Armenian intellectuals and institutions demanded a solution, or at least a resolution. The fifth chapter will examine the policies and regulations that the new leaders adopted to manage the issue, the way in which these policies were implemented – and resisted – locally, as well as the ongoing negotiations between the Armenian Patriarchate, Armenian political organisations and Armenian intellectuals such as Krikor Zohrab, Kegham Der Garabedian, A-Tō and Adom, on the one hand, and the traditional Ottoman political elite, the radical Committee of Union and Progress (CUP) and the local Kurdish powerholders and intellectuals, on the other. The government's initial response was to try to resolve land disputes through administrative channels, and soon some properties in the East began to be returned to their Armenian owners. This policy, however, was met with protests

Introduction

and strong resistance by Kurdish leaders. The CUP soon changed its approach, cancelling its initial measures and resuming the sultan's policy of settling Muslim immigrants on lands formerly held by Armenians. The CUP-Kurdish rapprochement resulted in a new wave of violence against Armenians.

With the outbreak of the Balkan Wars in 1912, Istanbul's policy towards 'Armenian' lands changed yet once again. Ottoman vulnerability during a succession of military losses had encouraged Armenians to commend their grievances (now formulated in demands for broad reforms in the eastern provinces) to the agendas of the Great Powers and international diplomacy. Chapter 6 will discuss the implications of these developments. Ottoman officials and CUP members began treating agrarian disputes as a political bargaining chip. Accordingly, for the duration of the reform negotiations, they blocked the mechanisms introduced to circumvent the courts and swiftly resolve disputes through administrative channels.

The last chapter will present the state of land disputes before the First World War, focusing on the approach of the Armenian and Kurdish political and religious elite to the reform and especially to the Armenian land question. Armenians, aware of the importance of ethnic demographics, now made the resolution of existing land disputes and the prevention of new seizures a priority. Among the Kurdish intellectuals and power-holders – such as Abdürrezzak Bedirxan, Musa Bey, Haydaranlı Hüseyin Pasha and Sheikh Selim – some of whom were developing nationalist aspirations, the reaction to the prospect of reform and restitution was swift and strong: protests to the press, petitions to the government and, in some places, rebellion. Before the entry of the Ottoman Empire into the war, tensions were high, trust was lost on all sides, and some local governors were trying to resolve the disputes in their provinces as soon as possible, by implementing plans that would equally displease every contending party.

Notes

1. BOA: ŞD 2871/47, petition by Abraham and Melkon from the village of Dağ Marnik to the Sublime Porte, 24 Teşrin-i Evvel 1288 (5 November 1872).
2. Murat Alanoğlu, 'Osmanlı Döneminde Muş (1515–1700)', in *Muş Tarihi*, ed. Murat Alanoğlu et al. (Istanbul: Ideal, 2021), 148.
3. BOA: ŞD 2874/46, a petition by Abraham and Melkon, 4 Safer 1290 (3 April 1873).
4. Yaşar Tolga Cora, 'Transforming Erzurum/Karin: The Social and Economic History of a Multi-Ethnic Ottoman City in the Nineteenth Century' (PhD diss., University of Chicago, 2016), 291.

5. *Reports on Provincial Oppressions* (London: Gilbert and Rivington, 1877), 12.
6. Ibid; BOA: ŞD 2874/46, a note, 17 Rabiulevvel 1290 (15 May 1873).
7. Paul Frymer, '"A Rush and a Push and the Land Is Ours": Territorial Expansion, Land Policy, and US State Formation', *Perspectives on Politics* 12, no. 1 (March 2014): 119–44; David A. Chang, *The Color of the Land: Race, Nation, and the Politics of Landownership in Oklahoma, 1832–1929* (Chapel Hill: University of North Carolina Press, 2010), chap. 3; Philip Bull, 'Irish Land and British Politics', in *The Land Question in Britain, 1750–1950*, ed. Matthew Cragoe and Paul Readman (London: Palgrave Macmillan UK, 2010), 126–45.
8. Karl Marx, *Capital: A Critique of Political Economy*, vol. 1, Reprinted in Penguin Classics (London: Penguin, 1992), 875; Charles Tilly, *Coercion, Capital, and European States, AD 990–1992* (Cambridge, MA: Blackwell, 1992); Onur Ulaş İnce, 'Between Equal Rights: Primitive Accumulation and Capital's Violence', *Political Theory* 46, no. 6 (December 2018): 885–914.
9. For this definition and for a detailed analysis on the region, see Y. Tolga Cora, Dzovinar Derderian and Ali Sipahi, 'Introduction: Ottoman Historiography's Black Hole', *The Ottoman East in the Nineteenth Century: Societies, Identities and Politics* (London: I. B. Tauris, 2016), 1–18.
10. Yener Koç, 'Celali Aşireti: Üç İmparatorluğun Sınırında', in *Kürt Aşiretleri: Aktör, Müttefik, Şakî*, ed. Tuncay Şur and Yalçın Çakmak (Istanbul: Iletişim, 2022), 299–316.
11. Reşat Kasaba, *A Moveable Empire: Ottoman Nomads, Migrants, and Refugees* (Seattle: University of Washington Press, 2009).
12. Martin van Bruinessen, *Agha, Shaikh, and State: The Social and Political Structures of Kurdistan* (London, Atlantic Highlands: Zed Books, 1992); Metin Atmaca, 'Resistance to Centralisation in the Ottoman Periphery: The Kurdish Baban and Bohtan Emirates', *Middle Eastern Studies* 55, no. 4 (4 July 2019): 519–39.
13. Gülseren Duman, 'Reformları Müzakere Etmek: 19. Yüzyıl Muş Sancağı'nda Eski Elitler, Yeni Düzen', in *Osmanlı Devleti'nde Yurtluk-Ocaklık ve Hükümet Sancaklar*, ed. Erdal Çiftçi et al. (Istanbul: Tarih Vakfı Yurt Yayınları, 2022), 355. See also Nilay Özok-Gündoğan, *The Kurdish Nobility in the Ottoman Empire: Loyalty, Autonomy and Privilege* (Edinburgh: Edinburgh University Press, 2022); Uğur Bayraktar, 'Yurtluk-Ocaklıks: Land, Politics of Notables and Society in Ottoman Kurdistan, 1820–1890' (PhD diss., Boğaziçi University and École des Hautes Etudes en Sciences Sociales, 2015).
14. Fatma Müge Göçek, *Denial of Violence: Ottoman Past, Turkish Present, and Collective Violence against the Armenians, 1789–2009* (Oxford: Oxford University Press, 2015), 80.
15. Simon Winchester, *Land: How the Hunger for the Ownership Shaped the Modern World* (New York: HarperCollins, 2021).

Introduction

16. Şevket Pamuk, *Türkiye'nin 200 Yıllık İktisadi Tarihi: Büyüme, Kurumlar ve Bölüşüm* (Istanbul: Türkiye İş Bankası Yayınları, 2014), 127; Donald Quataert, 'Ottoman Reform and Agriculture in Anatolia, 1876–1908' (PhD diss., University of California, 1973).
17. Roger Owen, 'The 1838 Anglo-Turkish Convention: An Overview', *New Perspectives on Turkey* 7 (1992): 7–14.
18. For a general overview of this process, see Şevket Pamuk, *The Ottoman Empire and European Capitalism, 1820–1913: Trade, Investment, and Production* (Cambridge: Cambridge University Press, 1987); Reşat Kasaba, *The Ottoman Empire and the World Economy: The Nineteenth Century* (Albany: State University of New York Press, 1988).
19. Şevket Pamuk, 'Agriculture and Economic Development in Turkey, 1870–2000', in *Agriculture and Economic Development in Europe since 1870*, ed. P. Lains and V. Pinilla (London: Routledge, 2008), 375–96; Tevfik Güran, *19. Yüzyıl Osmanlı Tarımı* (Istanbul: Eren Yayınları, 1998); Veli Yadırgı, *The Political Economy of the Kurds of Turkey: From the Ottoman Empire to the Turkish Republic* (Cambridge: Cambridge University Press, 2017). On the development of transportation networks, see Fulya Özkan, 'A Road in Rebellion, a History on the Move: The Social History of the Trabzon-Bayezıd Road and the Formation of the Modern State in the Late Ottoman World' (PhD diss., Binghamton University, 2012).
20. Pamuk, *Türkiye'nin 200 Yıllık İktisadi Tarihi*, 131.
21. Ellinor Morack, *The Dowry of the State? The Politics of Abandoned Property and the Population Exchange in Turkey, 1921–1945* (Bamberg: University of Bamberg Press, 2017), 58. Vladimir Hamed-Troyansky, in his recently published book, has argued that, because of the stipulation of the Treaty of Berlin of 1878 guaranteeing security of Armenians against Circassians and Kurds, the Ottoman government became hesitant to settle North Caucasian refugees in Armenian-populated provinces, but that the government discreetly settled them to increase the Muslim presence in provinces such as Erzurum and Muş. See Vladimir Hamed-Troyansky, *Empire of Refugees: North Caucasian Muslims and the Late Ottoman State* (Palo Alto: Stanford University Press, 2024), 81.
22. Chris Gratien, *The Unsettled Plain: An Environmental History of the Late Ottoman Frontier* (Palo Alto: Stanford University Press, 2022); Zozan Pehlivan, 'Beyond "the Desert and the Sown": Peasants, Pastoralists, and Climate Crises in Ottoman Diyarbekir, 1840–1890' (PhD diss., Queen's University, 2016).
23. Robert D. Sack, 'Human Territoriality: A Theory', *Annals of the Association of American Geographers* 73, no. 1 (1983): 55.
24. Edward W. Soja, 'The Political Organization of Space', *Association of American Geographers*, research paper no. 8 (1971): 30.
25. Jordan Branch, *The Cartographic State: Maps, Territory, and the Origins of Sovereignty* (Cambridge: Cambridge University Press, 2014), 5. For a

discussion on sovereignty, see James J. Sheehan, 'The Problem of Sovereignty in European History', *The American Historical Review* 111, no. 1 (February 2006): 1–15.
26. Andy Hanlun Li, 'From Alien Land to Inalienable Parts of China: How Qing Imperial Possessions Became the Chinese Frontiers', *European Journal of International Relations* 28, no. 2 (June 2022): 237–62.
27. David M. Smith, 'Introduction: The Sharing and Dividing of Geographical Space', in *Shared Space, Divided Space: Essays on Conflict and Territorial Organization*, ed. Michael Chisholm and David M. Smith (London: Unwin Hyman, 1990), 1–21; Colin Williams and Anthony D. Smith, 'The National Construction of Social Space', *Progress in Human Geography* 7, no. 4 (1983): 502–18.
28. Ernest Gellner, *Nations and Nationalism* (Oxford: Blackwell Publishers, 1983), 1.
29. Eric J. Hobsbawm, *Nations and Nationalism since 1780: Programme, Myth, Reality*, 2nd ed. (Cambridge: Cambridge University Press, 2012), 102. See also Eric Hobsbawm, 'Mass-Producing Traditions: Europe, 1870–1914', in *The Invention of Tradition*, ed. Eric Hobsbawm and Terence Ranger (Cambridge: Cambridge University Press, 1992), 263–307; Benedict R. Anderson, *Imagined Communities: Reflections on the Origin and Spread of Nationalism*, rev. ed. (London: Verso, 2006); Michael Billig, *Banal Nationalism* (London: Thousand Oaks, 1995).
30. Jacob Metzer and Stanley L. Engerman, 'Some Considerations of Ethno-Nationality (and Other Distinctions), Property Rights in Land, and Territorial Sovereignty', in *Land Rights, Ethno-Nationality, and Sovereignty in History*, ed. Stanley L. Engerman and Jacob Metzer (London: Routledge, 2004), 10.
31. Ibid.
32. Yücel Terzibaşoğlu, 'Land Disputes and Ethno-Politics: Northwestern Anatolia, 1877–1912', in Metzer and Engerman, *Land Rights*, 153–80.
33. Christian Fuchs, 'Critical Globalization Studies: An Empirical and Theoretical Analysis of the New Imperialism', *Science and Society* 74, no. 2 (2010): 215–47.
34. Charles S. Maier, 'Consigning the Twentieth Century to History: Alternative Narratives for the Modern Era', *The American Historical Review* 105, no. 3 (June 2000): 815. For more detailed analysis of territoriality, see Maier's book, *Once within Borders: Territories of Power, Wealth, and Belonging since 1500* (Cambridge, MA: The Belknap Press of Harvard University Press, 2016); John Breuilly, 'Modern Territoriality, the Nation-State, and Nationalism', in *Spatial Formats under the Global Condition*, ed. Matthias Middell and Steffi Marung (De Gruyter, 2019), 149–80.
35. Ronald Grigor Suny, 'The Empire Strikes Out: Imperial Russia, "National" Identity, and Theories of Empire', in *A State of Nations: Empire and Nation-Making in the Age of Lenin and Stalin*, ed. Ronald Grigor Suny and Terry Martin (Oxford: Oxford University Press, 2001), 52.

Introduction

36. Hans Rogger, 'Government, Jews, Peasants, and Land in Post-Emancipation Russia: The Pre-Emancipation Background; Stirrings and Limits of Reform', *Cahiers Du Monde Russe et Soviétique* 17, no. 1 (1976): 189.
37. Theodore Weeks, 'Managing Empire: Tsarist Nationalities Policy', in *The Cambridge History of Russia, Vol. 2: Imperial Russia, 1689–1917*, ed. Dominic Lieven (Cambridge: Cambridge University Press, 2006), 38.
38. Timothy Snyder, 'Ukrainians and Poles', in Lieven, *The Cambridge History of Russia: Vol. 2*, 177.
39. Róisín Healy, 'From Commonwealth to Colony? Poland under Prussia', in *The Shadow of Colonialism on Europe's Modern Past*, ed. Róisín Healy and Enrico Dal Lago (London: Palgrave Macmillan, 2014), 117.
40. Scott M. Eddie, 'The Prussian Settlement Commission and Its Activities in the Land Market, 1886–1918', in *Germans, Poland, and Colonial Expansion to the East: 1850 Through the Present*, ed. Robert L. Nelson (New York: Palgrave Macmillan US, 2009), 56.
41. Daniela L. Caglioti, 'Waging War on Civilians: The Expulsion of Aliens in the Franco-Prussian War', *Past & Present* 221, no. 1 (1 November 2013): 161–95.
42. Daniela L. Caglioti, 'Property Rights in Time of War: Sequestration and Liquidation of Enemy Aliens' Assets in Western Europe during the First World War', *Journal of Modern European History / Zeitschrift Für Moderne Europäische Geschichte / Revue d'histoire Européenne Contemporaine* 12, no. 4 (2014): 523–45. See also Uğur Ümit Üngör and Eric Lohr, 'Economic Nationalism, Confiscation, and Genocide: A Comparison of the Ottoman and Russian Empires during World War I', *Journal of Modern European History / Zeitschrift Für Moderne Europäische Geschichte / Revue d'histoire Européenne Contemporaine* 12, no. 4 (2014): 500–22. For a new understanding of territoriality in terms of the Franco-Prussian War, see Burak Kadercan, *Shifting Grounds: The Social Origins of Territorial Conflict* (New York: Oxford University Press, 2023), 101–6.
43. A. Dirk Moses, *The Problems of Genocide: Permanent Security and the Language of Transgression* (Cambridge: Cambridge University Press, 2021), 248.
44. Wolfgang Werner, 'A Brief History of Land Dispossession in Namibia', *Journal of Southern African Studies* 19, no. 1 (March 1993): 137.
45. Ibid., 138–46. On the genocide, see Dominik J. Schaller, 'From Conquest to Genocide: Colonial Rule in German Southwest Africa and German East Africa', in *Empire, Colony, Genocide*, ed. A. Dirk Moses (Berghahn Books, 2022), 296–324; Jürgen Zimmerer, *From Windhoek to Auschwitz? Reflections on the Relationship between Colonialism and National Socialism* (Berlin: De Gruyter Oldenbourg, 2024).
46. Michael J. Winstanley, *Ireland and the Land Question 1800–1922* (London: Methuen, 1984); Terence Dooley, 'Land and the People', in *The Oxford Handbook of Modern Irish History*, ed. Alvin Jackson (Oxford: Oxford

University Press, 2014), 106–25; Rachael Walsh and Lorna Fox O'Mahony, 'Land Law, Property Ideologies and the British–Irish Relationship', *Common Law World Review* 47, no. 1 (March 2018): 7–34.
47. Stuart Banner, *How the Indians Lost Their Land: Law and Power on the Frontier* (Cambridge, MA: Belknap Press of Harvard University Press, 2005), chap. 8.
48. Terzibaşoğlu, 'Land Disputes', 153–80; İpek Yosmaoğlu, *Blood Ties: Religion, Violence, and the Politics of Nationhood in Ottoman Macedonia, 1878–1908* (Ithaca: Cornell University Press, 2014); Janet Klein, 'The Kurds and the Territorialization of Minorityhood', *Journal of Contemporary Iraq and the Arab World* 14, no. 1 (1 June 2020): 13–30.

Chapter 1

Law, Land and Politics: The Transformation of the Ottoman Land Regime

Land, so Karl Polanyi has written, is 'an element of nature inextricably interwoven with man's institutions', and the formation of a market for it was in fact a very strange undertaking.[1] The transformation of land into a commodity, freed from the many rights and obligations that shaped its use prior to commodification, was a crucial process for the rise of capitalism and its globalisation. It was also a painful and violent process.[2] It changed the dynamics of life, as well as production and the relationship between people and nature, oftentimes forcefully.

This chapter concerns the unfolding of this process in the Ottoman Empire and its entanglements with the territorial turn that changed the political significance of land ownership. In this chapter, I lay out the two background trends into which the Armenian land question was embedded: the commodification and nationalisation of land. On the one hand, beginning with the nineteenth century, all Ottoman lands became commodities that could be bought, sold and mortgaged, being gradually freed from the rights and obligations that had once conditioned their use. In other words, land ownership and use were increasingly regulated in reference to market principles. On the other hand, due to the territorial turn that affected almost every country in the world, land ownership began to be seen as a key issue for nationalist projects. Especially because of the largely agrarian nature of many nineteenth-century economies, including the Ottoman economy, land ownership became a battleground for competing nationalist claims. As will be examined in the following chapters, clashes and accommodations between these two background trends would shape the emergence and transformation of the Armenian land question in the nineteenth and twentieth centuries. Examining the characteristics of these two trends and their development, along with the changes in the legal framework and land disputes across the empire, this chapter will situate the Armenian land question in its context.

The Ottoman Land Tenure System before the Nineteenth Century

Agricultural production was the most significant socio-economic activity for the majority of the Ottoman population. Thus, land served as the primary means of production from which surplus value was derived. The land regime in the empire was primarily based on state ownership of the land, and the government held two critical concerns. One of these was controlling the surplus value for the needs of the state. During the classical period, the land regime helped to maintain a significant part of the country's military force through the granting of fiefs (*tımar*) to *tımar* holders. In exchange for these fiefs, *tımar* holders were required to provide a specific number of cavalry soldiers (*sipahi*s) during times of battle. The state's primary objective, as noted by historian Halil İnalcık, was to secure fief revenue to address its military and financial needs.[3]

The second concern that shaped the organisation of the land regime was maintaining social order and the state's role as the dispenser of justice. As noted by several authors, the Ottoman dynasty tried to prevent the accumulation of land and power by other dynasties or individuals.[4] The basic tenets of the land regime served this purpose. State ownership of land (*miri*) hindered the emergence of potential rivals to the central authority and prevented the evolution of local powerholders into feudal landlords as well as the transformation of the relations of production. Therefore, it contributed to the maintenance of social order. The small peasantry was one of the essential elements of this social order. Çağlar Keyder has underscored the importance attached to the small peasantry in the classical land regime and noted that this regime established 'a unit of land based on the ploughing capacity of a pair of oxen', which would be 'in the inalienable possession of a peasant family'.[5] Huri İslamoğlu has pointed out the role of practices and rules inherent in the land regime in the legitimisation of the social order and Ottoman rule. She has noted that the state was concerned with ensuring the subsistence of peasants, preventing land accumulation and guaranteeing the provision of city-dwellers. As she has underlined, these concerns reflected a paternalist approach which emphasised 'the role of the state as dispenser of justice and perpetrator of eternal order'.[6]

Tımar lands in the classical Ottoman land regime were a subset of *miri* lands, the ownership rights of which belonged to the state. However, the rights of cultivators on *miri* lands were also recognized. The cultivators of these lands held inheritable usufruct rights (*tasarruf*) which were guaranteed by deeds issued for a fee by the local administrator.[7] The cultivators could use the land as long as they paid taxes and did not abandon cultivation for more than three years.[8]

Another important category of land in the classical land regime was the freehold (*mülk*). According to Ömer Lütfü Barkan, the rights of *mülk*-holders were absolute. They could sell, transfer or donate the *mülk* lands in their possession. While claiming that the rights of *mülk*-holders were absolute, Barkan has also noted that the ownership rights with regard to *mülk* or *waqf* lands did not entail the transfer of *raqaba* (absolute ownership of lands, which lay with the state) to individuals or pious foundations. The ownership rights to *mülk* or *waqf* lands did not give owners the right to use the lands however they wished. What property owners could have as absolute property was the sum of taxes that could be taken from the land and those living on it.[9] İslamoğlu has underscored the significance of this distinction and claimed that freehold did not equal private ownership. It meant entitlement to tax revenue and the income derived from the land, including from the trees and buildings erected on those lands.[10] The situation was different for *miri* lands because their holders were not entitled to the fruits of the land. Another difference between *miri* and *mülk* lands concerned the responsibility for the cultivation of the land. Like the cultivators of *miri* lands, *mülk*-holders were also obliged to cultivate lands in their possession and to pay taxes. If the lands were not cultivated or the landholders failed to pay taxes, the lands could be leased or even sold to third parties. Martha Mundy and Richard Saumarez Smith have noted that in similar cases concerning *miri* lands, 'should the cultivator's lot remain uncultivated and no one else be found to take it on, since it was treasury property, the land could not be sold. Rather, the cultivator was to be returned to the lot'.[11]

Another category of land within the Ottoman land regime consisted of *waqf* properties. *Waqf*s were either pious or private endowments. *Mülk* lands could be donated to these endowments. *Waqf*s were also responsible for securing the continuous cultivation of lands in their possession. As shown by Michael Nizri, ownership rights to *waqf* lands were not absolute. Deeds of formal possession granted by the sultan (*temlikname*s) regarding *waqf* lands had to be confirmed by each new sultan, and in some cases sultans declined to renew the *temlikname*.[12] In these cases, lands that had been in the possession of a *waqf* were returned to state control.

Another important category of the Ottoman land regime was the *yurtluk-ocaklık* (hereditary estate).[13] As the Ottoman Empire expanded eastward, it began to grant differing degrees of political and socio-economic autonomy to Kurdish powerholders in the region. Most notable among these powerholders were *emir*s. This process brought about the emergence of a new category of land, the *yurtluk-ocaklık*, which were hereditary family estates or properties. According to Uğur Bahadır Bayraktar, 'whether the lands in the *yurtluk-ocaklık* and *hûkûmet* districts constituted full property rights is a debatable question, [but] their freehold property status is beyond question'.[14] Nizri's analysis of the transformation of the Gönelü saltworks in Erzurum from a *yurtluk-ocaklık* to a *waqf* property of the Feyzullah Efendi Waqf supports the claim that land in *yurtluk-ocaklık*s had freehold property status. In that case, the property, located within a *yurtluk-ocaklık* held by the family of one Ali Bey, was purchased by the treasury before being allocated to the Feyzullah Efendi Waqf. The procedure followed in this case indicates that ownership rights of *yurtluk-ocaklık*-holders were very much recognized by the Ottoman authorities.[15]

The Ottoman land regime underwent a series of transformations starting at the end of the sixteenth century. Kemal Karpat has defined this process as the disintegration of the land system and argued that it was caused by economic and technological changes, such as the widespread adoption of fire-arms which diminished the importance of cavalrymen responsible for *miri* lands.[16] The spread of the tax-farming (*iltizam*) practice accompanied the decline of the *tımar* system. This practice entailed the sale of tax revenues by the Ottoman government.[17] In the seventeenth century, the government began to sell the tax revenues of some lands for life in return for a cash advance.[18] Lands, the tax revenues of which were sold under this condition, were called *malikane*s.

Karpat has noted that provincial notables, *ayan*, were interested in controlling the land for several reasons, including acquiring income, status and a leading position in the community.[19] By the end of the eighteenth century, *ayan* had become important powerholders and, in some cases, they had begun to challenge the control of the central authority.[20] The rise of *ayan* was a process by which powerholders in the Ottoman periphery began to increase their share of agricultural surplus. As noted by Dina R. Khoury, the tax-farming system and the lowering of barriers dividing the military from the rest of the population contributed to the ascendancy of *ayan* in the eighteenth century.[21] In many cases, however, the rise of provincial notables did not transform agrarian relations.[22] Haim Gerber has pointed out that the income and power of provincial notables depended on the shares that they derived from taxation rather than on direct control of lands. Even in cases where the provincial elite was able to control vast tracts of land, these lands retained their *miri* status.[23]

It should be noted that there exist different arguments regarding the effects of the rise of provincial notables on the land regime and patterns of land ownership in the Ottoman Empire. Some authors, such as Gerber, have argued that large land ownership was not a significant phenomenon before the Land Code of 1858.[24] Others, like Khoury, have pointed out that the commercialisation of agriculture led to the emergence of such a trend well before the nineteenth century in some regions of the Ottoman Empire.[25]

Legal Changes and the Transformation of the Land Regime from the Tanzimat to the First World War

The empire's land regime was radically transformed in the late Ottoman period. One of the most important factors that led to this transformation was the rise of a central administrative state. Beginning with the reign of Selim III, the central government initiated a series of reforms and tried to curb local powerholders. While local notables had succeeded in imposing their will on the central government in the wake of the political turmoil in 1808, Mahmud II renewed the efforts of the Ottoman centre to curb the power of local notables such as the *ayan* and *emir*s in the years that followed. Mahmud II adopted several strategies, including coercion and co-optation, to bring these powerholders under control and end the autonomy of *emir*s in the Ottoman East.[26] To increase central control over surplus value, Mahmud II also re-organised the regime of pious endowments and curtailed their financial autonomy. Another critical development in this regard was the implementation of a plan to terminate the *tımar* system, which had declined since the seventeenth century. In line with this plan, *tımar*-holders were stripped of their holdings.[27]

The reforms, which were necessary for revitalising the empire, required funds, and in a historical period in which income from conquests was lacking, the primary source of income for the treasury was tax revenues. Thus, the central government attempted to increase its control over the surplus value derived from agriculture. As noted by Nadir Özbek, the main objectives of the Ottoman bureaucrats in the Tanzimat period were to secure the transfer of tax revenues to the centre and to limit the role of intermediaries in this process. The rise of tax revenues in the nineteenth century indicates that the central government was successful in realising this objective.[28] Yet, the introduction of direct central taxation proved to be a failure for the treasury. Thus, a couple of years following the attempt to abolish *iltizam*, the Ottoman government reconciled with the local notables and recognized their role in the tax collection process. With this reconciliation, the central government recognized that local powerholders had a share in tax revenues.

In line with this development, the *iltizam* system continued to make up a part of the central tax regime.[29]

The rise of the central administrative state brought about a series of changes with regard to land tenure. In this process, the central government introduced a new regime emphasising individual and exclusionary rights to land. A series of regulations, including the Land Code of 1858, contributed to the commodification of land in the Ottoman Empire, a process by which land became something that could be sold, bought and mortgaged. The details of this transformation and its effects will be examined in the following section.

Another important factor that contributed to the transformation of the land regime and the increased demand for land was the settlement of nomads, semi-nomads and immigrants. To bring nomadic and semi-nomadic populations under control, the Ottoman government began to work towards their settlement. Several reasons were underlying the attempt of the central government to settle nomadic and semi-nomadic tribes.[30] First, the central government was unable to tax nomadic and semi-nomadic populations. Their settlement would contribute to the development of agriculture and to the treasury's income. Second, the government could not recruit soldiers among nomadic and semi-nomadic tribes. Once they had been settled, the men of these tribes could be conscripted. Third, several nomadic and semi-nomadic tribes were disrupting public order and hindering agricultural production. Some tribes raided areas inhabited by agricultural populations and looted their produce and animals.[31] The Ottoman authorities sometimes executed the settlement of these tribes by force. In some cases, the nomadic and semi-nomadic populations themselves preferred to settle. While some of these tribes were settled on vacant lands, opening up new areas to agriculture, others forcefully took over established villages in the eastern provinces in the 1890s. The government settled some nomadic and semi-nomadic tribes on lands that had been abandoned by Armenians during the massacres.[32]

In addition to the settlement of nomadic and semi-nomadic populations, the Ottoman government faced great difficulty settling Muslim immigrants. During this period, the Ottoman Empire experienced an influx of Muslim immigrants (*muhacirs*) that can be grouped into three categories. The first wave of immigrants came with the influx of Crimean Muslims, which began in the late eighteenth century and accelerated with the Crimean War of 1854. The second group were immigrants from the Caucasus, especially Circassians. The influx of this group also accelerated at the height of the Crimean War. Another group of immigrants consisted of Muslims from the Balkans. This group began to flee to territories under

Ottoman rule following the Russo-Ottoman War of 1877–78. Immigration from the Balkans took a new turn with the Balkan Wars of 1912–13. Some of these immigrants had fled to the empire from territories lost by the empire. Thus, their influx did not lead to a population increase per se, but it increased the population pressure, transformed the distribution of the population and increased the ratio of Muslims living under Ottoman rule. Immigrants who had fled to the empire from territories that had not been under Ottoman rule were recent additions to the Ottoman population. According to Donald Quataert, the total number of immigrants numbered between five and seven million.[33] Şevket Pamuk has underscored that, in estimating the number of immigrants, population growth within the Ottoman Empire should also be taken into consideration. According to Pamuk, the number of immigrants who came to the territories under Ottoman rule in each of the three waves of immigration totalled around a million to a million and a half.[34]

The Ottoman authorities faced a significant problem settling such a substantial number of people.[35] The central government tried to solve this problem by opening new lands to agriculture and distributing state-owned lands to immigrants. Several new villages in Central Anatolia were established as consequence of this settlement process.[36] Immigrants from the Caucasus were also settled on vacant lands in Eastern Anatolia and Syria.[37] The settlement of immigrants increased the demand for land and contributed to the escalation of land disputes. While they seemed vacant according to Ottoman records, some lands used for the settlement of immigrants were actually in use by others, such as nomads. This situation led to the eruption of disputes between those who were settled and those who claimed customary rights to these lands.[38] Land disputes concerning the settlement of immigrants accelerated after the 1890s.[39] In this period, the government began to settle immigrants on lands held by Armenians. These lands mostly belonged to those scattered after the massacres of 1894–97; however, the settlement of immigrants and the expansion of land disputes concerning Armenians were not confined to immigrants settled on lands which the government considered vacant or abandoned. There existed also cases in which immigrants themselves seized Armenian lands, to be examined in Chapters 2 and 3.

Another development that contributed to the transformation of the land regime can be found in the acceleration of the Ottoman economy's integration into the world economy and the commercialisation of agriculture.[40] This process was unevenly experienced in different regions of the Ottoman Empire and affected Ottoman cities on the Balkans and along coastlines first. The rise of market-oriented agricultural production proved integral to this process. Several factors contributed to the commercialisation of agriculture. First was the rise of internal and international demand for agricultural products. Developments in transportation and infrastructure facilitated the trade of agricultural products. While agricultural products were the predominant exports of the empire, internal demand was even more significant than external demand for such products, as three-fourths of agricultural production was consumed within the empire. Another factor that contributed to the commercialisation of agriculture consisted of the monetarisation of tax payments throughout the nineteenth century. As the burden on peasants increased and tax payments were increasingly demanded in cash, peasants increasingly saw themselves pushed to develop market-oriented production strategies. A final factor contributing to the commercialisation of agriculture was the peasants' demand for consumption goods.[41]

The effects of this process on patterns of landholding and land use varied from region to region. In Egypt, the rise of market-oriented production, which led to the expansion of cotton production to the extent that it became the dominant crop in the region, was accompanied by the rise of large land ownership. Through a series of regulations and administrative changes initiated by Mehmed Ali Pasha, the governor of Egypt, and his successors, a small number of elites came to possess a vast portion of the arable lands in Egypt.[42] Another region where the commercialisation of agriculture went hand in hand with the acceleration of large landholding was the Balkans, where the integration into the world economy moved faster than in the rest of the Ottoman Empire. Çukurova, where cotton production served as a crucial socio-economic activity for thousands of seasonal migrant workers from around the region, was another centre where large landholding accompanied the development of market-oriented agricultural production.[43]

Indeed, the commercialisation of agriculture did not automatically cause the rise of large landholdings in all regions of the Ottoman Empire. In Western Anatolia, the effects of the integration of the Ottoman economy into the world economy began to be felt starting in the early nineteenth century, and market-oriented production became highly developed.[44] However, large landholding remained a rare phenomenon in Western Anatolia, and small-scale peasantry continued to be the primary landholders in the region.[45]

Another factor that contributed to the transformation of the significance of land and land tenure is found in the rise of territorial concerns on the parts of the state and various religious and nationalist groups. This was a historical epoch in which great empires – such as the Ottoman Empire, the

Law, Land and Politics

Austro-Hungarian Empire and the Russian Empire – faced the difficulty of developing strategies for reformulating their legitimacy in the face of nationalist claims.[46] Land, in particular, and territory, in general, began to play an important part in struggles related to political authority and sovereignty. This development underscored the significance of land and attached a novel political significance to it, to be examined in the last part of this chapter.

REGULATIONS REGARDING THE LAND REGIME

Throughout the nineteenth century, the central government tried to extend its control over land. As noted above, Mahmud II introduced new regulations concerning *waqf* lands and curbed the autonomy of the *waqf*s. The central government continued to adopt regulations and laws in line with this objective throughout the century.

After the promulgation of the Tanzimat, the central government initiated a new programme. Based on their examination of imperial orders (*irade*s) in this period, Mundy and Smith have claimed that the government sought to 'encourage the generation of wealth through education, public works and a more equitable distribution of the tax burden' and demanded 'information concerning agriculture, the infrastructure of communication and exchange, and the forms and distribution of wealth'.[47] Referring to a regulation (*nizamname*) dated 1840, Dina R. Khoury has noted that the central government tried to renew its control over land and introduced changes to the land tenure system in the 1840s. This regulation 'sought to limit the property in revenue of real property (*malikane*) owners by ordering the reversion to the state of all land whose revenue collectors or cultivators had died'.[48] The heirs of the *malikane* owners could later receive title deeds (*tapu*s) for these lands and gain usufruct possession rights. The regulation allowed landholders to leave their lands to male and female heirs.

Another critical legal regulation regarding the land regime was the regulation of title deeds, issued in 1847. With this regulation, female heirs of landholders were given the right to inherit without paying the fee for a title deed.[49] Before this regulation, this had been a privilege reserved for male heirs. The transfer of landholdings via inheritance without the payment of the fee for a title deed to the sons and daughters of landholders also applied to the lands of mothers. Mundy and Smith have argued that the law recognized the unrestricted right of title deed holders to lease their land. Another novelty introduced by this regulation was the change of the authority that would issue title deeds for land. Before the regulation, title deeds were issued by courts or local administrators. The new regulation gave this authority to the district council.[50]

One of the most important developments regarding the land regime was the adoption of the Land Code of 1858.[51] The scope of this code was limited to *miri* lands. The code was a significant turning point in developing individual and exclusionary rights to *miri* lands. According to the code, all lands in a village or town would not be granted to the whole of the inhabitants or an individual or a few individuals chosen from amongst them. Each inhabitant would be given separate parcels of land and title deeds showing their possession (Article 8).[52] The Land Code restricted the common interest of villages. These common interests could include roads, places of worship, areas for cattle and carts, woodlands, threshing grounds and pasture lands, but not agricultural lands. In formulating relevant articles, the drafters of the code refrained from introducing legal definitions, instead referring to customs and customary practices.[53]

Several articles of the Land Code strengthened the individual and exclusionary use of *miri* lands and contributed to the development of individual ownership of land. For example, landholders were free to choose the crops which they would sow on the land (Article 9). The code stipulated that meadows from which grass was reaped *ab antiquo* and from which tithable produce was taken would be considered cultivated land. The usage rights of meadows were limited to the landholders who held the title deeds, and they could prevent others from profiting from the grass (Article 10). The code stipulated that title deed holders could leave the lands fallow under certain circumstances. They could prevent others from entering such lands and also keep animals belonging to others from entering and grazing on such lands (Article 11). Landholders who held title deeds could prevent others from trespassing without right (*mürur*) on their lands. However, they were not allowed to do so in cases where there was an *ab antiquo* right to passage (Article 13). The code stipulated that landholders were entitled to the fruit of trees naturally growing on their lands. Yet, neither strangers nor landholders were allowed to cut down or pull up these trees; if they did so, they would pay the cost of the tree to the treasury (Article 28).[54]

As seen in these articles, the Land Code of 1858 strengthened individual and exclusionary rights to land. Nonetheless, it did not grant absolute ownership rights to landholders. The code recognized several principles and claims without specific definitions and stipulations. For example, in Article 13, the exclusionary right of the landholder against trespassers was recognized, but so were the customary rights of third parties.

If an individual, family or group held an ancient (*kadim*) right to passage through a land, they could continue to pass through it. However, these customary rights were not defined in the code. This combination of old and new principles without specific definitions gave the code its flexibility.[55]

A number of articles in the code limited the rights of landholders. For example, except under certain conditions, land could not be left uncultivated (Article 9). Landholders were not allowed to plant trees or turn lands into gardens or vineyards without the permission of the authorities (Article 25). Landholders could not erect new buildings on *miri* lands without the permission of the authorities, which had the right to demolish buildings constructed without permission (Article 31). Furthermore, landholders who had meadows could only cultivate them with the permission of the authorities (Article 10). As noted by Barkan, most of these limitations reflect the state's concern about maintaining agricultural revenues and securing the income of the treasury.[56] Another stipulation of the code, which limited ownership rights to *miri* lands, concerns the terms of restitution in seizure cases. The code stipulated that the possessors of lands that had been taken and cultivated unlawfully or by violence and on which the taxes had been paid could not claim restitution from the occupiers – neither damages for depreciation nor an equivalent rent (Article 21). Thus, as long as the usurpers paid the taxes, landholders could not demand restitution or rent for the period during which the lands were occupied. The situation was different when it came to *mülk* holdings. In these cases, landholders were entitled to restitution for seized lands, regardless of whether the occupier paid the taxes.[57]

The code included several provisions aimed at securing the continuity of cultivation on *miri* lands. It stipulated that, if landholders left their lands uncultivated for more than three years without providing a valid excuse, the title deeds of the lands would have to be renewed. Lands in this situation were referred to as *müstehakk-ı tapu* (Article 68). In this case, the landholder could get the land back by paying its equivalent value. Otherwise, such lands would be put up for auction and sold to the highest bidder. Valid excuses specified in the law were leaving lands uncultivated for more than one or two years due to exceptional local circumstances, the necessity of leaving the land fallow until it re-acquired the capacity for cultivation after a flood, and non-cultivation due to being a prisoner of war. Another exceptional situation was specified in Article 72, stipulating that, if all or a part of the inhabitants of a village or town left their residence for a legitimate reason, their title deeds would not be invalidated (*müstahakk-ı tapu*). However, if the people left without a legitimate reason or did not return within three years of the day when the legitimate reason ceased to exist, then their title deeds would become invalid, and the state could issue new title deeds for their lands. There was also a special provision for soldiers: their title deeds could not be considered invalid unless their death had been proven (Article 73). If soldiers' lands were given to others, soldiers could take them back upon their return. The code also introduced a similar principle of punishment for leaving meadows unproductive. If meadows held by title deed and for the produce of which the holders paid tithe were not sown, and if the tithe had not been paid for three consecutive years, then the title deeds for these meadows would become invalid (Article 85).[58]

The code also recognized prescriptive rights. It stipulated that everyone who possessed and cultivated state or *mevkufe* lands for ten years without dispute would acquire prescriptive rights to such lands (Article 78). In such cases, the land would not be considered vacant (*mahlul*), regardless of whether the cultivator had a valid title deed or not, and the cultivator would be granted a new title deed for free. In cases where such possessors admitted and confessed that they had taken possession of the vacant lands without any legal right, they would have to pay the value of the title deed. Moreover, if the possessor did not assent to pay for the title deed, the lands would be put up for auction. These articles on cultivation and prescriptive rights were significant for land disputes involving Armenians. As Chapter 5 will show, after 1908 the Armenian political and religious leaders demanded that massacres and oppression committed during the Hamidian regime be considered a valid reason for leaving the land uncultivated.

The code also regulated the terms and conditions of rent, sale and mortgage of *miri* lands. While confirming the right of the holder to lease the land, the code did not specifically regulate the terms of rent. Sharecropping agreements, which formed the basis of agricultural production in various regions of the Ottoman Empire, were not regulated by the Land Code. According to Barkan, this was one of the code's most significant shortcomings.[59]

The code also regulated the transfer of *miri* lands (Articles 36–53). According to the code, the transfer of *miri* lands could only be carried out with the permission of the authorities. The code forbade the transfer of lands via coercion (Article 113). If someone in a position of power who could act out their threats secured the transfer of land to themselves through coercion, then the transfer would be considered void.

The Land Code's articles concerning the mortgaging of *miri* lands were a radical break from the classical Ottoman land regime. This was regulated in Articles 115, 116, 117 and 118. Although a creditor could not seize the lands of a debtor, the former could 'force the latter by taking the appropriate steps to sell it to another and discharge the debt out of the purchase money' (Article 115). A debtor could transfer lands in their possession to the creditor, on the condition that the latter would return them to the former whenever they settled the debt (Article 116). The debtor could also give the creditor the authority to sell the lands in question and to take their due from the sum of the sales price (Article 117).[60] As noted by Mundy and Smith, by lifting the limitations preventing cultivators from being dispossessed of their land for debts, these regulations represented a 'painful erosion of Ottoman legal tradition with regard to *miri* land'.[61] As will be examined in Chapter 3, this transformation shaped the unfolding of the Armenian land question because many Armenian peasants lost their lands due to debt.

After 1858, the conditions for mortgages were further liberalised, and the central government introduced the principle of forced sale for debt. This became an issue in the late 1850s regarding tax arrears, an issue not regulated in the code. Examining the matter, the Supreme Council (*Meclis-i Vâlâ*) prepared a report suggesting that the sale of *miri* lands could be forced in cases where landowners were indebted to the state, excluding 'the roof over the person's head and a basic amount of land required for survival'.[62] The forced sale of *miri* lands under these conditions was regulated in the decrees of 7 January 1861 and 29 September 1861.[63] The forced sale of *miri* lands was later extended to ordinary debts in the decree of 2 December 1869.[64] With these regulations, land became alienable property.

Another important regulation regarding the transformation of the land regime in the Ottoman Empire in the nineteenth century was the 'Law Giving Foreigners the Right to Possess Immovable Property in the Ottoman Empire', adopted on 10 June 1867.[65] With this law, foreign subjects were allowed to enjoy the right to possess immovable property, urban or rural, anywhere within the empire, except for the province of Hedjaz, with the same title as Ottoman subjects and without any other condition, upon submitting to the laws and regulations governing Ottoman subjects themselves. It should be noted that the law included a specific exception for Ottomans who had changed their nationality, stipulating that their situations would be regulated separately.[66]

As examined above, the Land Code introduced several limitations on the use of *miri* lands. Still, in a historical context where the *sipahi*s had disappeared, the state could not enforce these limitations in practice.[67] In this situation, usage rights to land de facto turned into individual ownership rights. Another critical turning point regarding the liberalisation of the land regime can be seen in the adoption of the decree law on immovable properties in 1913.[68] With this law, several limitations regarding the use of *miri* lands were abolished, and the rights of landholders to *miri* lands came close to individual ownership rights in absolute terms. The law stipulated that landholders were free to transfer, mortgage or lease these lands. They could turn gardens and vineyards in their possession into cultivated lands. Moreover, they could transform cultivated lands into gardens or vineyards by planting trees, or they could turn them into threshing grounds. With this law, landholders were also given the right to erect buildings on these lands, on the condition that they not form neighbourhoods or villages. In contrast to the Land Code, these acts were not tied to the condition of permission from the Ottoman authorities.[69] Another provision of this law, which eroded the differences between *mülk* and *miri* lands, related to seizures. According to Article 14 of this law, landholders could demand restitution (*ecr-i misil*) from those who unlawfully occupied and cultivated their lands. Thus, this law can be seen as the final point of a process by which individual, exclusionary and absolute ownership of land became the legal norm in the Ottoman Empire.

CHANGES IN THE LAND REGIME AND LAND DISPUTES

Regulations and laws adopted by the Ottoman Empire in the nineteenth century introduced a new regime of landholding which contributed to the commodification of land and emphasised individual and exclusionary rights to use land, on the one hand, and aimed to secure the continuity of cultivation and to protect small-scale cultivators, on the other. These changes contributed to the surge of land disputes and a significant increase in land prices in the nineteenth-century Ottoman Empire.[70] From Vidin to Basra, several regions under Ottoman rule witnessed rising disputes over usufruct and ownership rights to land.

In examining the transformation of agrarian relations in Britain, E. P. Thompson has challenged the assumption that law constituted a superstructure and noted that the law was not an instrument or tool of just the powerful in these struggles.[71] The transformation of the Ottoman land regime also demonstrates that the legal and administrative framework and procedures, which underwent substantial changes in the Tanzimat period, constituted the field in which disputes over usufruct, cultivation and ownership rights to land were played out by a variety of actors.[72] Parties to land disputes, cultivators and local powerholders alike often situated their cases within a discursive framework the outlines of which were determined by legal categories introduced by or preserved in the Ottoman legislation.[73]

While the agency of peasants has been minimised in some early studies on agrarian relations and the transformation of landholding patterns,[74] studies conducted in recent decades have shown that peasants in various regions of the Ottoman Empire were active agents who tried to register land in their own names and adopted several strategies to ensure this outcome.[75] Rather than replacing the set of rights to land that was recognized by the central authority with a completely new set of recognized rights, post-Tanzimat legislation provided room for negotiation and accommodated new and old categories and concepts.[76] While not being defined in the text of the Land Code of 1858, prescriptive rights and ancient rights were recognized in the new legal framework. These categories were commonly referred to in land disputes in the nineteenth century.

The inclusion of ill-defined principles, such as prescriptive and customary rights in the text of the code, provided for the role of local knowledge in land disputes in Western Anatolia. Disputing parties used various strategies, and when they raised claims based on customary or prescriptive rights, 'the conflict was brought into the field of oral tradition and local power relations', diminishing the significance of more centralised institutions, such as the courts and the Council of State.[77] In some cases, nomads and peasants tried to situate the disputes in this context and benefit from local custom and memory, while large landholders spent their efforts on the intervention of central agencies and the administration, 'thereby pulling the conflict to the arena of a more formal legal procedure'.[78]

The outcomes of the transformation of the land regime in the aftermath of legislative changes depended on several factors and were the results of contestation among different groups. While some authors have interpreted this as a failure of the Land Code,[79] others have emphasised the fact that the code itself was a flexible text designed to accommodate local practices, knowledge and dynamics.[80] Scholars in the latter group have underscored that these disputes often involved a series of confrontations, negotiations and accommodations among the state, local powerholders and cultivators. As noted by Terzibaşoğlu, nomads and settled peasants found themselves in disputes over lands across the western regions of the empire. Moreover, peasants, especially those who held positions in village councils, could use their positions and local knowledge to their advantage in the course of registration procedures and legal disputes over land in different regions of the Ottoman Empire.[81]

The Ottoman state also constituted an actor involved in these disputes. As noted by Linda Schatkowski Schilcher, the state participated as one of many contenders in the struggles over economic interests related to agrarian production and land ownership.[82] The role of the state in disputes over land ownership has been defined as a balancing act by Huri İslamoğlu. The dispute between cultivators and local landlords in Yanya shows that some state officials, such as Ahmed Cevdet Pasha, developed several means for managing land disputes. In this case, local powerholders acquired ownership titles to large tracts of land. Upon the protests of the cultivators, who were determined to defend their rights of use in opposition to the establishment of the individual, absolute ownership rights of estate holders (*ashab-ı alaka*), Governor Cevdet Pasha formed a commission consisting of representatives from both parties. In this process, cultivators accepted that they were tenants and gave up hereditary claims of ownership to the disputed lands. Nevertheless, the tenancy rights of cultivators were still open to debate and negotiation. The central government was concerned with securing the support of powerholders in politically sensitive territories on the Balkans, such as Yanya.[83] Thus, in the following years, the central authority proceeded with issuing special regulations for such regions and protected the ownership claims of local powerholders.

The policy that Mustafa Assim Pasha, governor of Damascus, adopted in 1889–90 represents a stark contrast to the Yanya case.[84] At that time, Mustafa Assim Pasha began to support the cultivation rights of peasants vis-à-vis a broad group of local powerholders including land inspectors, contractors and sheikhs. Using administrative rather than judicial channels, he pressed charges against the urban notables, accusing them of being usurpers. In line with this policy, he also disregarded land registration documents held by local powerholders. As underscored by Schatkowski Schilcher, this policy caused considerable resistance and was protested by local powerholders who adopted several strategies. The resignation of high-ranking local officials, the refusal of the Damascene Administrative Council to convene and the refusal of urban tax-farmers to deliver the taxes they had collected were some of the strategies that local powerholders employed to protest the policies of the governor.[85]

Land disputes in southern Basra also illuminate the tension between state agencies and local powerholders. These disputes were provoked by the local Title Deed Office's attempts to turn the lands, which were then occupied by local powerholders, over to the state, supporting the argument that the Ottoman authorities' approach to land disputes varied across time and space. In this case, which erupted after 1908, *miri* lands that had not been legally inherited by officially recognized heirs were occupied by local powerholders, including religious authorities such as *seyyid*s, who established large-scale holdings. These large landowners also held official documents of sale (*hüccet*) and mounted official protests against the attempts of the Title Deed Administration to return the lands to state control, by sending petitions signed by hundreds of notables. In their petitions, local powerholders underscored that the measures being attempted by the Title Deed Administration contradicted the principles of equity and justice enshrined in the newly promulgated Ottoman Constitution. The case was later brought before the Council of State, which brokered a compromise between the demands of local powerholders and the Title Deed Administration, ruling that the Title Deed Administration could not take all the lands back into state control and sell them at auction. However, the Council of State decided that some lands, the legal ownership of which was disputed, could be subjected to this procedure by the Title Deed Administration.[86]

Land disputes concerning *emir*s and owners of *yurtluk-ocaklık* lands demonstrate the agency of local actors and contestation at the local level. As noted by Nilay Özok-Gündoğan, in the Palu region, the question of what would happen to the lands taken from the *emir*s during the centralisation efforts of the state in the first half of the nineteenth century had evolved into a multi-faceted problem by the mid-nineteenth century. While the state considered these lands to be *miri* lands at its disposal, there were *agha*s who held titles issued by the *emir*s, indicating their possession of some such lands. Furthermore, peasants in the region were putting forward their claims to these lands by relying on customary and prescriptive rights. Thus, the outcomes of such disputes depended on negotiations at different levels, and rather than being ignorant or fearful, cultivators and peasants were active participants in such negotiations.[87]

In many places, local powerholders counted among the parties to land disputes. In examining the efforts of the Zirki Beys to reclaim their rights to land that had been their *yurtluk-ocaklık* in the Hazro district of Diyarbekir before the state's centralisation policy, Bayraktar has shown that in the period following the Tanzimat Decree, local notables such as the Zirki Beys managed to re-secure ownership of lands lost during the centralisation efforts, underscoring the agency of provincial notables.[88]

Another factor leading to variation among land disputes in the Ottoman Empire was the composition of actors and institutions involved. As noted above, these disputes mostly concerned the state, local powerholders and cultivators. But in some disputes, religious institutions such as patriarchates took an active role in the progression of the case. One example of church involvement in disputes over the distribution of agrarian surplus can be found in the Kisrawan rebellion on Mount Lebanon. In this case, Maronite cultivators rebelled against local landlords. The peasants did not make ownership claims with regard to land but demanded financial, social and juridical equality. As noted by Axel Havemann, the upper ranks of the clergy gave tacit support to the rebels in the initial phase of the rebellion.[89] While the support of the upper clergy was withheld in later phases, low-level clergy continued to play an essential role in the rebellion.

A limited number of studies has illuminated the role of the Greek Patriarchate and other religious institutions in land conflicts concerning Greeks. The dispute over the ownership rights to a plot of land in Burhaniye in 1910 suggests that Greek ecclesiastical councils at the local level took a direct interest in the course of certain land disputes.[90] However, it should be noted that, in this particular dispute, there stood a sacred shrine on the disputed plot, according to the ecclesiastical council. This might be the reason why the council approached the issue as a communal matter. Atilla Aytekin's examination of several disputes related to illegal taxation (*kesim*) and land ownership in Canik has also provided important insights regarding the role of Greek religious institutions in land conflicts concerning Greeks. In Canik, tax collectors and local powerholders, including members of the Haznedar family who had controlled large tracts of land before the centralisation measures of the Ottoman state, had managed to register dozens of villages in their names during the Tanzimat period. Moreover, members of the Haznedar family continued to extract surplus from agricultural production by levying an illegal tax called *kesim*. Using their position in the administrative councils, local powerholders managed the situation in line with their own interests, to the detriment of thousands of long-time cultivators. In the 1850s, the peasants began to refuse paying the *kesim* tax, and the rent was demanded by local powerholders who argued that the lands were theirs. In this case, the Greek Patriarchate acted as representative of the interests of the cultivators, tried to secure the involvement of central authorities and followed the progression of the case.[91] This case shows that the Greek Patriarchate became involved in a land dispute that did not concern communal lands, highlighting the possibility that Greek religious institutions might have played a role in the progression of conflicts concerning a great number of Greeks.

Finally, in some cases, disputes over the distribution of agricultural surplus and land ownership contributed to the polarisation of the involved parties along ethnic or religious lines. The overlap between socio-economic and material grievances and ethno-national polarisation has been underscored with respect to several cases in the Balkans. One of the best-known is the Vidin case, where Muslim local powerholders had formed large estates. According to Ottoman officials, these landlords, who demanded corvée labour from the peasants, had 'almost reduced the peasants into slavery'.[92] Christian peasants protested this situation by several means, including rebellion, but due to the concern of the central government that the lands in question remain under Muslim ownership, the peasants failed to realise their aims. Land disputes in Nish also proceeded similarly to Vidin. The long-term conflict between Christian peasants and Muslim land owners regarding taxation, corvée labour as well as communal rights to land led to an uprising in the 1840s.[93] As noted by Yücel Terzibaşoğlu and Alp Yücel Kaya, during these uprisings in Nish and Vidin, the peasants not only demanded the easement of taxation or an end to the corvée, but they also asked for the abolishment of the land tenure system called *gospodarlık* and the distribution of farm lands to the peasants.[94] This case also shows the ways in which the language introduced by the Gülhane Rescript (*Hatt-ı Hümayun*) of 1839 was adopted by the cultivators, who tried to establish their case against the demands from local landlords.[95]

Another well-known case in which conflicts over land ownership became entangled with ethno-nationalist politics was the Bosnia Rebellion of 1875. The demands of the rebels in Bosnia in the course of this crisis highlight the importance of problems related to land ownership. The first demand of the rebels was the distribution of at least one-third of the land to Christians.[96] Thus, land was a crucial element underlying the ethnic tension and political turmoil in Bosnia.

As indicated by this brief overview of land disputes in different regions of the Ottoman Empire, there existed considerable variation among the land disputes in the empire. There were differences with regard to landholding patterns, the approaches of the Ottoman authorities, the involvement of religious institutions and the overlap of disputes over land with ethno-religious differentiation. While some general developments, such as the transformation of the land regime, affected all these disputes, some particularities did indeed differentiate them.

Territoriality, Nationalism and the New Significance of Land

As noted in the Introduction, a critical turn in terms of territoriality and nationalism occurred in the years between 1870 and 1914.[97] In this period, territoriality became a crucial component of nationalisms around the world, and people who considered themselves to be nations began to make territorial claims at the level of international diplomacy. Another characteristic of this period can be found in the transformation of the nature of imperialism itself. The new imperialism brought about the territorialisation of imperial power relations and conflicts of interests among the Great Powers, the most explicit reflection of which was the scramble for Africa.[98]

This trend towards the territorialisation of political power and political imagination also affected the approaches of actors in the Ottoman state, and a new conceptualisation of Ottoman sovereignty – shaped by the notion of modern territoriality – came about in the late nineteenth century.[99] The transformation of the understanding, definition and contestation of geographical space in the Ottoman Empire can be traced in the transformation of cartography, 'the primary apparatus of territoriality'.[100] In examining mapping techniques in the early Ottoman Empire, Ahmet T. Karamustafa has noted that there existed no clear distinction between different forms of visual representation during the medieval era, including in Islamic regions, and that the processes of standardisation and specialisation only commenced during the modern era.[101]

Benjamin C. Fortna has argued that a significant change occurred in Ottoman cartography in the 1890s. The earlier maps, which depicted territory continent by continent and consequently undermined Ottoman sovereignty, were substituted with intentionally designed maps that presented 'all Ottoman land in a single frame with Anatolia at the centre'.[102] The preparation of such maps, which showed the empire in its entirety, was part of a transformation in the ways in which Ottoman territoriality was understood and projected. By insisting on maps that focused attention on the empire as a whole, as opposed to segments on three different continental maps, the late Ottoman state was reinforcing the notion of Ottoman territoriality in a fixed geographical space.[103]

Geography books in the Hamidian period provide important insights into the ways in which territorial sovereignty was understood and contested in the late-nineteenth-century Ottoman Empire. Özkan Akpınar has shown that, in this period, the subject of geography in Ottoman curricula was fundamentally shaped by the sultan's attempt to create a unified Ottoman territoriality and to legitimise his power and authority in this unified space.[104] The Ottoman government not only tried to disseminate its own imagery of a unified Ottoman space but also tried to remove the signifiers of alternative territorial and historical imaginations from the school curricula. In line with this territorial consciousness on the part of state actors, geography books containing information considered harmful to the interests of the state were collected and destroyed. Geography books in Armenian and Bulgarian received special attention from the government, due to the political sensitivity of the Armenian and Bulgarian questions. A book in Bulgarian stating that Van and Erzurum were located in Armenia, a book in Armenian referring to Erzurum as 'famous city of Armenia', and another book mentioning 'the region of Armenia' were considered harmful by the authorities, along with many others.[105]

Between 1870 and 1914, the imagination of collective identity promoted by the central government began to emphasise that Anatolia made up the core of Ottoman national space. The construction of Anatolia as the heart of Ottoman national space can be traced in the accounts of Ottoman intellectuals and the political elite.[106] With the rise of Turkish nationalism and the Ottoman Empire's territorial losses on the Balkans, this territorial emphasis became even more pronounced. What makes this point crucial for this study is the fact that the Armenian Question had the potential to destabilise the core of Ottoman national space. Unlike political struggles for territorial sovereignty on the Balkans, the geographical space that was contested with regard to the Armenian Question made up a crucial part of the Ottoman homeland.

It can be said that the trend towards the territorialisation of collective identity affected not only the policies and practices of the Ottoman state as well as the Turkish or Muslim intellectuals and political elite, but also the approaches and acts of Armenian institutions and politicians. In the 1870s, Armenian nationalism experienced a crucial territorial turn. The term *Hayasdan* (Armenia) entered the everyday vocabulary of the Armenian political elite. The territorialisation of Armenian nationalism can be traced to the mid-nineteenth century, when Armenian intellectuals began to construct historic Armenia as the Armenian homeland. However, the emphasis on Cilicia and the eastern provinces became part of the Armenian political struggle only after the 1870s.[107] The territorialisation of Armenian nationalism affected the ways in which Armenian interests were conceptualised, presented and contested by Armenian institutions, political organisations and political elites in this period.

Another issue regarding territoriality and collective identity between 1870 and 1914 can be seen in the rise of Kurdish territorial claims in the Ottoman East. One of the most significant developments in this regard was the rebellion led by Sheikh Ubeydullah, who aspired to establish a Kurdish state in the territories corresponding to the Ottoman East and Western Persia. As noted by Robert Olson, the prospect of the establishment of an Armenian political entity in the region, which became a topic in international diplomacy following the Russo-Ottoman War of 1877–78, formed a driving force behind this rebellion. Sheikh Ubeydullah promoted the idea that Kurdish interests in the region should be treated as more important than the interests of other groups and that Kurdish powerholders would not tolerate the territorial claims of Armenians.[108]

After suppressing the rebellion, the central government adopted a new policy to create a direct tie between the sultan and the Muslim subjects of the empire. With the establishment of the Hamidian Regiments and the

Hamidian Tribal School, the Ottoman government attempted to redesign the relations between the central authority and local powerholders. At the beginning of the twentieth century, Kurdish nationalists became influential actors in the contestation over the Ottoman East.[109]

On the eve of the First World War, different actors had conflicting geographical imaginations with regard to the Ottoman East. It was this political struggle over the same territory that led to the emergence of conflicting conceptualisations of the Ottoman East. In the accounts of Kurdish nationalist intellectuals, the region was Kurdistan. In the discourse of Armenian nationalist intellectuals, the region encompassing Cilicia and the eastern provinces was Armenia. In the official Ottoman discourse, the region was referred to as the six provinces, the eastern provinces, or the fourth and fifth sectors – that is, as administrative units rather than as a distinct geographical space with specific political, historical or demographic characteristics. The emergence of this new emphasis on territoriality affected land policies and practices. An example of this concerned Western Anatolia. In his examination of land disputes in this region, Terzibaşoğlu has shown that land ownership began to be seen as a means of establishing ethno-religious dominance by some actors in the Ottoman state, whose policies about land ownership and settlement were influenced by demographic concerns.[110]

Population policies and practices related to settlement and land ownership in the autonomous region of Eastern Rumelia between 1877 and 1886 also carried a territorial dimension. Anna M. Mirkova has demonstrated that these policies and practices formed an integral part of the development of territorial sovereignty by the Eastern Rumelian administration, which was predominantly run by Bulgarians.[111] Land ownership began to be seen as a means of establishing ethno-religious dominance and territorial sovereignty by the Bulgarian nationalist elite during the Russo-Ottoman War. The Russian authorities developed several policies and practices to strengthen the Christian element in the territories that they occupied. They 'allowed Christians to cultivate lands deserted by fleeing Muslims, and even settled Christian refugees in villages Muslims had abandoned'.[112] As a result of these policies, an extensive property transfer from Muslims to Bulgarians occurred during the war.

The Russian administration also issued ownership documents to cultivators who settled on the lands of Muslims and introduced administrative barriers to the restoration of such lands to their original owners, such as a mandate that returning Muslims had to prove their ownership rights to land in court with appropriate documentation. There also happened attempts to prevent the return of North Caucasian immigrants whom the

Ottoman Empire had settled there before the war. The Bulgarian government reserved their 'abandoned' lands to settle the new Bulgarian immigrants from the Ottoman, Russian and Habsburg empires.[113] Therefore, issues related to land ownership, land use and taxation were critical for the decimation of the Muslim population in the region; indeed, these issues were vital to the establishment of the territorial sovereignty of Bulgaria.

Sovereignty concerns and its links to land policies were also visible in conflicts in Ottoman Lebanon, Syria and Jordan. Land disputes played a major role in the eruption of sectarian violence in Lebanon in the mid-nineteenth century. Struggle over land and the question of who would control the territory turned other differences, such as class, into intercommunal tensions.[114] With regard to the land policies of the government in southern Syria, Nora Elizabeth Barakat has argued that the Ottoman state considered two priorities – namely, market and security. While some bureaucrats wanted to keep the lands in the hands of the state for the purpose of ensuring its sovereignty, others – most importantly, the Imperial Property Register Ministry – wanted to increase the revenue by auctioning off vacant lands.[115]

Zionist land amassment in Palestine illuminates the links between territorial claims, political struggles for sovereignty and land policies and practices. In the late nineteenth century, Zionist bodies established to promote Jewish settlement in the region began to amass large tracts of land. In this case, it was not a politically recognized body but a religious-political collectivity that initiated the change in land ownership patterns in a particular region. At the beginning of the twentieth century, the Ottoman political elite began to see Zionist land amassment in Palestine as a political and socio-economic problem.[116] As a result, Jews, including Ottoman Jews, were banned from acquiring property in the region.[117]

Overall, studies on land practices and policies in the Balkans, Anatolia and Syria indicate that the Ottoman government was not the only actor involved in shaping land disputes in different parts of the empire. In the case of Eastern Rumelia, a political body recognized by the Ottoman Empire, the Eastern Rumelia Administration, effectively shaped land disputes in a way that secured the decimation of the Muslim population in the region. In the case of Palestine, a religious-political organisation became one of the most critical actors shaping the land market and transforming patterns of land ownership. These cases illuminate that the transformation of the political significance of land ownership and the rise of modern territoriality affected not only the policies and approaches of Ottoman policymakers but also the approaches and operations of other actors who made alternative claims to territorial sovereignty over lands under Ottoman rule.

In sum, territoriality gained a new significance in the late nineteenth century in the Ottoman Empire and became an important component of Ottoman sovereign rule. While the Ottoman state tried to create an Ottoman national space and to disseminate the idea that the lands under Ottoman rule constituted a unified entity, alternative spatial imaginations challenged such projections. Studies focusing on land disputes and policies and demographic policies have indicated that various groups making territorial claims to lands under Ottoman rule began to see land ownership as a means of securing ethno-national dominance.

Conclusion

In the nineteenth century, there occurred major changes in the legal, socio-economic and political aspects of land ownership in the Ottoman Empire. On the one hand, there emerged a liberalisation process which continued in the twentieth century. In this process, land was gradually separated from the rights and obligations which had traditionally conditioned its use. With the establishment of individual and exclusive property rights, land became a commodity that could be bought, sold and mortgaged. Thus, the legal and socio-economic meaning of land and land ownership significantly changed through this process. With this transformation, an outbreak of land disputes arose across the entire Ottoman Empire. Moreover, a number of administrative and socio-economic changes – such as the acceleration of the Ottoman economy's integration into global capitalism, the rise of the central administrative state, the monetisation of taxation, the influx of Muslim immigrants and the settlement of nomads – increased the competition for land, adding fuel to the flames.

Another background trend that affected the transformation of land disputes concerning Armenians into the Armenian land question consists of the change in the political significance attached to land and land ownership by different actors with territorial concerns. The nineteenth century saw a shift in the international context and international politics with regard to the importance of territorial boundaries and claims. In this period, territoriality gained a new significance. This territorial turn also affected the ways in which Ottoman territoriality was imagined, projected and contested. Over time, various state and non-state actors started to see land as a means of establishing or maintaining ethno-national dominance, political sovereignty or autonomy. As will be examined in the succeeding chapters, this major turn also affected the course of land disputes concerning Armenians.

As has been discussed in this chapter, the outbreak of land disputes after the Tanzimat not only affected Armenians or the Ottoman East.

From Mount Lebanon to the Aegean Coast, from the Balkans to Central Anatolia, there arose conflicts over land ownership across the breadth and length of the Ottoman Empire. While all these disputes were embedded in these two background trends and affected by the tensions between them, they also demonstrated particularities and differences. This book focuses on one of them, which later turned into a political crisis and began to be seen as a distinct social problem and the main source of disagreement between Turks, Kurds and Armenians. As will be examined in the chapters that follow, a number of factors (such as mass violence, mass uprooting and the development of specific land policies targeting Armenians) would transform these disputes into the Armenian land question.

Notes

1. Karl Polanyi, *The Great Transformation* (Boston: Beacon Press Boston, 1957), 178.
2. Robert Nichols, *Theft Is Property! Dispossession and Critical Theory* (Durham: Duke University Press, 2020). See also Harry D. Harootunian, *The Unspoken as Heritage: The Armenian Genocide and Its Unaccounted Lives* (Durham: Duke University Press, 2019), chap. 4.
3. Halil İnalcık, 'Filāha', in *Encyclopaedia of Islam, Second Edition*, ed. P. Bearman, Th. Bianquis, C. E. Bosworth, E. van Donzel and W. P. Heinrichs. http://dx.doi.org/10.1163/1573-3912_islam_COM_0222.
4. Ömer Lütfü Barkan, 'Osmanlı İmparatorluğu'nda Kuruluş Devrinin Toprak Meseleleri', in *Türkiye'de Toprak Meselesi: Toplu Eserler 1* (Istanbul: Gözlem Yayınları, 1980), 281–90; Halil İnalcık, 'Land Problems in Turkish History', *The Muslim World* 45, no. 3 (July 1955): 221–28.
5. Çağlar Keyder, *State and Class in Turkey: A Study in Capitalist Development* (London: Verso, 1987), 11. See also Halil İnalcık, 'Osmanlılar'da Raiyyet Rüsûmu', *Belleten* 23 (1959): 575–610.
6. Huri İslamoğlu-İnan, 'Peasants, Commercialization, and Legitimation of State Power in Sixteenth-Century Anatolia', in *Landholding and Commercial Agriculture in the Middle East*, ed. Çağlar Keyder and Faruk Tabak (New York: State University of New York Press, 1991), 38.
7. Huri İslamoğlu, 'Property as a Contested Domain: A Reevaluation of the Ottoman Land Code of 1858', in *New Perspectives on Property and Land in the Middle East*, ed. Roger Owen (Cambridge, MA: Harvard University Press, 2000), 19.
8. Martha Mundy and Richard Saumarez Smith, *Governing Property, Making the Modern State: Law, Administration and Production in Ottoman Syria* (London: I. B. Tauris, 2007), 14.
9. Ömer Lütfi Barkan, 'İmparatorluk Devrinde Toprak Mülk ve Vakıfların Hususiyeti', in *Türkiye'de Toprak Meselesi*, 253. For the meaning of

'absolute' in ownership and property rights, see Joseph William Singer, *Property*, 3rd ed (New York: Aspen Publishers, 2010); Crawford B. MacPherson, ed., *Property: Mainstream and Critical Positions* (Oxford: Blackwell, 1978), chap. 1.
10. İslamoğlu, 'Property as a Contested Domain', 18.
11. Mundy and Smith, *Governing Property*, 14.
12. Michael Nizri, 'Defining Village Boundaries at the Time of the Introduction of the *Malikane* System: The Struggle of the Ottoman State for Reaffirming Ownership of the Land', *Journal of the Ottoman and Turkish Studies Association* 2, no. 1 (2015): 37–57.
13. Erdal Çiftçi, Veysel Gürhan and Mehmet Rezan Ekinci, *Osmanlı Devleti'nde Yurtluk-Ocaklık ve Hükümet Sancaklar* (Istanbul: Tarih Vakfı Yurt Yayınları, 2022).
14. Uğur Bayraktar, 'Yurtluk-Ocaklıks', 57.
15. Nizri, 'Defining Village Boundaries', 50–53.
16. Kemal Karpat, 'The Land Regime, Social Structure, and Modernization in the Ottoman Empire', in *Beginnings of Modernization in the Middle East: The Nineteenth Century*, ed. William R. Polk and Richard L. Chambers (Chicago: The University of Chicago Press, 1968), 71. On the effects of fire arms, see also Halil İnalcık, 'The Socio-Political Effects of the Diffusion of Fire-Arms in the Middle East', in *War, Technology and Society in the Middle East*, ed. V. J. Parry and M. E. Yapp (London: Oxford University Press, 1975), 195–217.
17. İnalcık, 'Filaha'; Karpat, 'Land Regime', 71.
18. Bruce McGowan, 'The Age of the *Ayan*s, 1699–1812', in *An Economic and Social History of The Ottoman Empire, vol. 2: 1600–1914*, ed. Suraiya Faroqhi, Bruce McGowan, Donald Quataert and Şevket Pamuk (Cambridge: Cambridge University Press, 1997), 713–14.
19. Karpat, 'Land Regime', 77.
20. McGowan, 'Age of *Ayan*s', 715–16; Ali Yaycıoğlu, *Partners of the Empire: The Crisis of the Ottoman Order in the Age of Revolutions* (Palo Alto: Stanford University Press, 2016), 167.
21. Dina Rizk Khoury, 'The Ottoman Centre versus Provincial Power-Holders: An Analysis of the Historiography', in *The Cambridge History of Turkey, vol. 3: The Later Ottoman Empire, 1603–1839*, ed. Suraiya N. Faroqhi (Cambridge: Cambridge University Press, 2006), 154.
22. Keyder, *State and Class*, 16.
23. Haim Gerber, *The Social Origins of the Modern Middle East* (Boulder: Lynne Rienner Publishers, 1987), 63.
24. Gerber, *Social Origins*; Ömer Lütfü Barkan, 'Türk Toprak Hukuku Tarihinde Tanzimat ve 1274 (1858) Tarihli Arazi Kanunnamesi', in *Türkiye'de Toprak Meselesi*, 291–375.
25. Dina Rizk Khoury, 'The Introduction of Commercial Agriculture in the Province of Mosul and its Effects on the Peasantry, 1750–1850', in Keyder and Tabak, *Landholding*, 155–71.

26. For detailed information on this period, see İlber Ortaylı, *İmparatorluğun En Uzun Yüzyılı* (Istanbul: Hil Yayın, 1983); Albert Hourani, 'Ottoman Reform and the Politics of Notables', in *The Emergence of the Modern Middle East* (Berkeley: University of California Press, 1981), 36–66.
27. Donald Quataert, 'The Age of Reforms, 1812–1914', in *An Economic and Social History of The Ottoman Empire, vol. 2: 1600–1914*, ed. Suraiya Faroqhi, Bruce McGowan, Donald Quataert and Şevket Pamuk (Cambridge: Cambridge University Press, 1997), 854–55.
28. Nadir Özbek, *İmparatorluğun Bedeli: Osmanlı'da Vergi, Siyaset ve Toplumsal Adalet (1839–1908)* (Istanbul: Boğaziçi University Publications, 2015), 22–23.
29. Ibid., 47.
30. For an examination of the settlement process in Central Anatolia in the Tanzimat period, see Yonca Köksal, 'Coercion and Mediation: Centralization and Sedentarization of Tribes in the Ottoman Empire', *Middle Eastern Studies* 42, no. 3 (2006): 469–91; Kasaba, *A Moveable Empire*, 84–122; Gratien, *Unsettled Plain*, chap. 2.
31. Abdul-Karim Rafeq, 'Land Tenure Problems and their Social Impact in Syria around the Middle of the Nineteenth Century', in *Land Tenure and Social Transformation in the Middle East*, ed. Tarif Khalidi (Beirut: American University of Beirut, 1984), 371–96; Kasaba, *A Moveable Empire*, 91. For the environmental reasons behind the conflict between pastoralist and sedentary communities, especially in the Ottoman East, see Zozan Pehlivan, 'Beyond the Desert'. It should also be noted that this does not mean that these tribes were not economically active. See Yonca Köksal and Mehmet Polatel, 'A Tribe as an Economic Actor: The Cihanbeyli Tribe and the Meat Provisioning of İstanbul in the Early Tanzimat Era', *New Perspectives on Turkey* 61 (November 2019): 97–123.
32. The government envisioned a modernist project for the settlement of nomadic and semi-nomadic tribes in order to improve agriculture and control the population, and it implemented extensive violence to forcibly settle them. However, the results were beyond the government's intended goals. As Chris Gratien has shown in the case of Cilicia, forced settlement led to social, economic, environmental and humanitarian catastrophe. See Gratien, *Unsettled Plain*.
33. Quataert, 'Age of Reforms', 793. For detailed information about this population movement, see Kemal H. Karpat, *Ottoman Population 1830–1914: Demographic and Social Characteristics* (Madison: University of Wisconsin Press, 1985), 60–77.
34. Pamuk, *Türkiye'nin 200 Yıllık İktisadi Tarihi*, 65.
35. For Muslim immigration, migrant settlement and the problems encountered by the state, see Kemal H. Karpat, 'The Status of the Muslim under European Rule: The Eviction and Settlement of Çerkes', *Institute of Muslim Minority Affairs. Journal* 1, no. 2 (1979): 7–27; Nedim İpek, *Rumeli'den*

Anadolu'ya Türk Göçleri (1877–1890) (Ankara: Türk Tarih Kurumu Basımevi, 1994); Ahmet Halaçoğlu, *Balkan Harbi Sırasında Rumeli'den Türk Göçleri (1912–1913)* (Ankara: Türk Tarih Kurumu Basımevi, 1994); Fuat Dündar, *İttihat ve Terakki'nin Müslümanları İskân Politikası (1913–1918)*, 3rd ed. (Istanbul: İletişim Yayınları, 2002); David Cameron Cuthell, 'The Muhacirin Komisyonu: An Agent in the Transformation of Ottoman Anatolia, 1860–1866' (PhD diss., Columbia University, 2005); Isa Blumi, *Ottoman Refugees, 1878–1939: Migration in a Post-Imperial World* (London: Bloomsbury, 2013); Hamed-Troyansky, *Empire of Refugees*; Başak Kale, 'Transforming an Empire: The Ottoman Empire's Immigration and Settlement Policies in the Nineteenth and Early Twentieth Centuries', *Middle Eastern Studies* 50, no. 2 (4 March 2014): 252–71.

36. Terzibaşoğlu, 'Land Disputes', 165–66.
37. Hamed-Troyansky, *Empire of Refugees*, 73–74.
38. Ibid., 31, 220–22; Terzibaşoğlu, 'Land Disputes', 169; Gratien, *Unsettled Plain*, 62–63.
39. For some examples of land disputes between resettled immigrants and local communities, see Vladimir Hamed-Troyansky, 'Imperial Refuge: Resettlement of Muslims from Russia in the Ottoman Empire, 1860–1914' (PhD diss., Stanford University, 2018), chap. 4.
40. Reşat Kasaba, Immanuel Wallerstein and Hale Decdeli, 'The Incorporation of the Ottoman Empire into the World-Economy', in *The Ottoman Empire and the World-Economy*, ed. Huri İslamoglu-İnan (Cambridge: Cambridge University Press, 1987), 88–97.
41. Donald Quataert, *Osmanlı İmparatorluğu, 1700–1922* (Istanbul: İletişim, 2000), 196–98.
42. Joel Beinin, *Workers and Peasants in the Modern Middle East* (Cambridge: Cambridge University Press, 2004), 51–54.
43. Meltem Toksöz, 'The Çukurova: From Nomadic Life to Commercial Agriculture, 1800–1908' (PhD diss., State University of New York at Binghamton, 2000); Stephan Astourian, 'Testing World-System Theory, Cilicia (1830s–1890s): Armenian-Turkish Polarization and the Ideology of Modern Ottoman Historiography' (PhD diss., University of California, 1996); Gratien, *Unsettled Plain*, chap. 3.
44. Sibel Zandi-Sayek, *Ottoman Izmir: The Rise of a Cosmopolitan Port, 1840/1880* (Minneapolis: University of Minnesota Press, 2012); Onur İnal, 'A Port and Its Hinterland: An Environmental History of Izmir in the Late Ottoman Period' (PhD diss., University of Arizona, 2015), chap. 4.
45. Şevket Pamuk, *Osmanlı'dan Cumhuriyet'e Küreselleşme, İktisat Politikaları ve Büyüme: Seçme Eserleri II* (Istanbul: İş Bankası Yayınları, 2008).
46. Selim Deringil, *The Well-Protected Domains: Ideology and the Legitimation of Power in the Ottoman Empire, 1876–1909* (London: I. B. Tauris, 1998), 16–44.
47. Mundy and Smith, *Governing Property*, 41–42.

48. Dina Rizk Khoury, *State and Provincial Society in the Ottoman Empire: Mosul, 1540–1834* (Cambridge: Cambridge University Press, 1997), 105.
49. 'Tapu hakkında icra olunacak nizamat', in *Tanzimat Sonrası Arazi ve Tapu* (Istanbul: Osmanlı Arşivi Daire Başkanlığı, 2014), 36–40.
50. Mundy and Smith, *Governing Property*, 44–45.
51. The imperial order was issued on 23 Şevval 1274 (6 June 1858). Sarkis Karakoç, *Arazi Kanunu ve Tapu Nizamnamesi, Tahşiyeli* (Istanbul: Cihan Biraderler Matbaası, 1340/1342), 175–254. For the Turkish transcription of the Code, see *Arazi Kanunnamesi*, trans. Orhan Çeker (Istanbul: Ebru Yayınları, 1985). For the English translation of the Land Code, see *The Ottoman Land Code*, trans. F. Ongley (London: William Clowes and Sons, 1892); Sir Stanley Fisher, *Ottoman Land Laws: Containing the Ottoman Land Code and Later Legislation Affecting Land with Notes and an Appendix of Cyprus Laws and Rules Relating to Land* (London: Oxford University Press, 1919). For a review of the literature on the Land Code, see E. Attila Aytekin, 'Hukuk, Tarih ve Tarihyazı: 1858 Osmanlı Arazi Kanunnamesi'ne Yönelik Yaklaşımlar', *Türkiye Araştırmaları Literatür Dergisi* 3, no. 5 (2005): 723–44.
52. *Arazi Kanunnamesi*, 20; Fisher, *Ottoman Land Laws*, 6.
53. Mundy and Smith, *Governing Property*, 46.
54. *Arazi Kanunnamesi*, 20–21, 25; Fisher, *Ottoman Land Laws*, 6–7, 12.
55. Eugene L. Rogan, *Frontiers of the State in the Late Ottoman Empire: Transjordan, 1850–1921* (Cambridge: Cambridge University Press, 1999), 83.
56. Barkan, 'Türk Toprak Hukuku', 340.
57. *Arazi Kanunnamesi*, 23; Fisher, *Ottoman Land Laws*, 10; Barkan, 'Türk Toprak Hukuku', 343.
58. *Arazi Kanunnamesi*, 44–50; Fisher, *Ottoman Land Laws*, 24–28.
59. Barkan, 'Türk Toprak Hukuku', 371. Gerber has explained this absence: landlord/tenant relations 'were rare in the years spanning the sixteenth and nineteenth centuries' (*Social Origins*, 71).
60. *Arazi Kanunnamesi*, 29–35, 64–66; Fisher, *Ottoman Land Laws*, 15–19, 37–39.
61. Mundy and Smith, *Governing Property*, 46.
62. Ibid., 47.
63. Karakoç, *Arazi Kanunu*, 257–60.
64. This decree was later amended on 28 December 1871. 'Deyn için emvâl-i gayr-ı menkûlenin fürûhtu hakkında nizamnâmedir', *Tanzimat Sonrası Arazi ve Tapu*, 152–54, 157–59; Fisher, *Ottoman Land Laws*, 61.
65. Fisher, *Ottoman Land Laws*, 57–59; United States, *Capitulations of the Ottoman Empire: Report of Edward A. Van Dyck, Consular Clerk of the United States at Cairo, upon the Capitulations of the Ottoman Empire since the Year 1150*, 2 v. in 1 (Washington DC: Govt. print. off., 1881), 104.
66. Fisher, *Ottoman Land Laws*, 57–59.

67. Barkan, 'Türk Toprak Hukuku', 340–41.
68. 'Emval-i gayr-i menkulenin tasarrufu hakkında kanun-ı muvakkat', 30 Mart 1329/12 Nisan 1913; Sarkis Karakoç, *Kavanin-i Cedide Külliyatı*, aded 9 (Istanbul: Matbaa ve Kütüphane-i Cihan, 1339–41), 708–24.
69. Halil Cin, *Mirî Arazi ve Bu Arazinin Özel Mülkiyete Dönüşümü* (Tarsus: Çağ Üniversitesi, 2005), 303.
70. Vedat Eldem, *Osmanlı İmparatorluğu'nun İktisadi Şartları Hakkında Bir Tetkik* (Ankara: Türk Tarih Kurumu Basımevi, 1994), 26.
71. E. P. Thompson, *Whigs and Hunters: The Origin of the Black Act* (London: Allen Lane, 1975), 261–65.
72. İslamoğlu, 'Property as a Contested Domain'; Terzibaşoğlu, 'Land Disputes'.
73. Yücel Terzibaşoğlu, 'Eleni Hatun'un Zeytin Bahçeleri: 19. Yüzyılda Anadolu'da Mülkiyet Hakları Nasıl İnşa Edildi?' *Tarih ve Toplum Yeni Yaklaşımlar* 4 (2006): 121–47; Özok-Gündoğan, *Kurdish Nobility*; Nilay Özok-Gündoğan, 'A "Peripheral" Approach to the 1908 Revolution in the Ottoman Empire: Land Disputes in Peasant Petitions in Post-revolutionary Diyarbekir', in *Social Relations in Ottoman Diyarbekir, 1870–1915*, ed. Joost Jongerden and Jelle Verheij (Leiden: Brill, 2012), 179–215; Mundy and Smith, *Governing Property*.
74. Doreen Warriner, 'Land Tenure in the Fertile Crescent in the Nineteenth and Twentieth Centuries', in *The Economic History of the Middle East, 1800–1914: A Book of Readings*, ed. Charles Issawi (Chicago: University of Chicago Press, 1966), 71–78. For a criticism of this approach, see Gerber, *Social Origins*.
75. Martha Mundy, 'Village Authority and the Legal Order of Property (The Sourthern Hawran 1876–1922)', in *New Perspectives on Property and Land in the Middle East*, ed. Roger Owen (Cambridge, MA: Harvard University Press, 2000), 63–92; Martha Mundy, 'The State of Property: Late Ottoman Syria, the Kaza of 'Ajlun (1875–1918)', in *Constituting Modernity: Private Property in the East and West*, ed. Huri İslamoğlu (London: I. B. Tauris, 2004), 214–47; Terzibaşoğlu, 'Eleni Hatun'; Özok-Gündoğan, *Kurdish Nobility*; Erden Attila Aytekin, 'Land, Rural Classes, and Law: Agrarian Conflict and State Regulation in the Ottoman Empire, 1830s–1860s' (PhD. diss., Binghamton University, 2006); Rogan, *Frontiers of the State*, 84; Nora Elizabeth Barakat, *Bedouin Bureaucrats: Mobility and Property in the Ottoman Empire* (Palo Alto: Stanford University Press, 2023), 140–42.
76. Huri İslamoğlu, 'Property as a Contested Domain', 3–62.
77. Terzibaşoğlu, 'Land Disputes', 158–59.
78. Ibid.
79. Karpat, 'Land Regime'.
80. İslamoğlu, 'Property as a Contested Domain'; Gerber, *Social Origins*; Rogan, *Frontiers of the State*; Mundy and Smith, *Governing Property*.
81. Terzibaşoğlu, 'Eleni Hatun', 129–31; Mundy, 'Village Authority', 63–92.

82. Linda Schatkowski Schilcher, 'The Grain Economy of Late Ottoman Syria and the Issue of Large-Scale Commercialization', in Keyder and Tabak, *Landholding*, 178.
83. İslamoğlu, 'Property as a Contested Domain', 36–39.
84. Linda Schatkowski Schilcher, 'Violence in Rural Syria in the 1880s and 1890s: State Centralization, Rural Integration, and the World Market', in Kazemi and Waterbury, *Peasants and Politics*, 64–65.
85. Ibid, 64–65. For another analysis that situates the disputes over agrarian production and land ownership in this region vis-à-vis the policy of Abdülhamid II towards the Arab populations of the Ottoman Empire, see Engin D. Akarlı, 'Abdülhamid II's Attempt to Integrate Arabs into the Ottoman System', in *Palestine in the Late Ottoman Period: Political Social and Economic Transformation*, ed. David Kushner (Jerusalem: Yad Izhak Ben Zvi Press, 1986), 74–89.
86. Burcu Kurt, 'II. Meşrutiyet Döneminde Basra Vilayeti (1908–1914)' (PhD diss., Marmara University, 2012), 254–61.
87. Özok-Gündoğan, *Kurdish Nobility*.
88. Bayraktar, 'Yurtluk-Ocaklıks'.
89. Axel Havemann, 'The Impact of Peasant Resistance on Nineteenth-Century Mount Lebanon', in *Peasants and Politics in the Modern Middle East*, ed. Farhad Kazemi and John Waterbury (Miami: Florida International University Press, 1991), 85–100.
90. Terzibaşoğlu, 'Land Disputes', 174–76.
91. Aytekin, 'Land, Rural Classes and Law', 14–35.
92. Halil İnalcık, 'The Emergence of Big Farms, *Çiftlik*s: State, Landlords, and Tenants', in Keyder and Tabak, *Landholding*, 31.
93. Mark Pinson, 'Ottoman Bulgaria in the First Tanzimat Period: The Revolts in Nish (1841) and Vidin (1850)', *Middle Eastern Studies* 11, no. 2 (1975): 103–46.
94. Yücel Terzibaşoğlu and Alp Yücel Kaya, '19. Yüzyılda Balkanlar'da Toprak Rejimi ve Emek İlişkileri', in *İktisat Tarihinin Dönüşü: Yeni Yaklaşımlar ve Tartışmalar*, ed. Ulaş Karakoç and Alp Yücel Kaya (Istanbul: İletişim, 2021), 49–106.
95. Halil İnalcık, *Tanzimat ve Bulgar Meselesi (Doktora Tezi'nin 50. Yılı), 1942–1992* (Istanbul: Eren, 1992).
96. Other demands raised by the rebels consisted of the withdrawal of Ottoman troops, the reconstruction of burnt churches and houses by the government, a three-year tax exemption and the implementation of reforms. Azlizan Mat Enh, 'The Phantom of the Bosnia-Herzegovina Revolt, 1875–1878', *Journal of International Studies* 4 (2008): 95.
97. Hobsbawm, *Nations and Nationalism*, chap. 4.
98. E. J. Hobsbawm, *The Age of Empire, 1875–1914* (New York: Vintage Books, 1989); Norrie MacQueen, *Colonialism* (London: Pearson, 2007), chap. 2. For a discussion on the involvement of the Ottoman Empire in this

process, see Mostafa Minawi, *The Ottoman Scramble for Africa: Empire and Diplomacy in the Sahara and the Hijaz* (Palo Alto: Stanford University Press, 2016).

99. Laura Robson, *The Politics of Mass Violence in the Middle East* (Oxford: Oxford University Press, 2020), 17. On the concept of sovereignty in the Ottoman Empire in that period, see Benjamin C. Fortna, 'Sovereignty in the Ottoman Empire and After', in *Sovereignty after Empire: Comparing the Middle East and Central Asia*, ed. Sally N. Cummings and Raymond Hinnebusch (Edinburg: Edinburgh University Press, 2011), 92–103; Lâle Can, *Spiritual Subjects: Central Asian Pilgrims and the Ottoman Hajj at the End of Empire* (Palo Alto: Stanford University Press, 2020); Michael Christopher Low, *Imperial Mecca: Ottoman Arabia and the Indian Ocean Hajj* (New York: Columbia University Press, 2020); Lâle Can, Michael Christopher Low, Kent F. Schull and Robert Zens, eds, *The Subjects of Ottoman International Law* (Bloomington: Indiana University Press, 2020).
100. Yosmaoğlu, *Blood Ties*, 83.
101. Ahmet T. Karamustafa, 'Introduction to Islamic Maps', in *The History of Cartography, volume 2, book 1: Cartography in the Traditional Islamic and South Asian Societies*, ed. J. B. Harley and David Woodward (Chicago: University of Chicago Press, 1992), 7.
102. Benjamin C. Fortna, 'Change in the School Maps of the Late Ottoman Empire', *Imago Mundi* 57, no. 1 (2005): 23.
103. Ibid., 30.
104. Özkan Akpınar, 'Geographical Imagination in School Geography during the Late Ottoman Period, 1876–1908' (Master's thesis, Boğaziçi University, 2010).
105. Ibid., 96–100.
106. Selim Deringil, 'From Ottoman to Turk: Self-image and Social Engineering in Turkey', in *The Ottomans, the Turks and World Power Politics: Collected Studies* (Istanbul: The Isis Press, 2000), 170–75.
107. For further reading on the territorialisation of Armenian nationalism, see Gerard Libaridian, *Modern Armenia: People, Nation, State* (New Brunswick, NJ: Transaction Publishers, 2011); Razmik Panossian, *The Armenians: From Kings and Priests to Merchants and Commissars* (London: Hurst and Company, 2006). Richard E. Antaramian has argued that the territorialisation of Armenian identity had not been articulated in this period; see his *Brokers of Faith, Brokers of Empire: Armenians and the Politics of Reform in the Ottoman Empire* (Palo Alto: Stanford University Press, 2020), 120.
108. Robert Olson, *The Emergence of Kurdish Nationalism and the Sheikh Said Rebellion, 1880–1925* (Austin: University of Texas Press, 1989), 1–7; Sabri Ateş, *The Ottoman-Iranian Borderlands: Making a Boundary, 1843–1914* (Cambridge: Cambridge University Press, 2013), 218.
109. On the emergence of Kurdish nationalism, see also Wadie Jwaideh, *The Kurdish National Movement: Its Origins and Development* (Syracuse:

Syracuse University Press, 2006); Djene Rhys Bajalan, 'Between Accommodationism and Separatism: Kurds, Ottomans and the Politics of Nationality (1839–1914)' (PhD diss., St Antony's College, University of Oxford, 2015).
110. Terzibaşoğlu, 'Land Disputes', 153–80.
111. Anna M. Mirkova, '"Population Politics" at the End of Empire: Migration and Sovereignty in Ottoman Eastern Rumelia, 1877–1886', *Comparative Studies in Society and History* 55, no. 4 (2013): 955–85. For more details on the transformation of the land regime in Bulgaria and its effect on inter-communal relations, see Mirkova's *Muslim Land, Christian Labor: Transforming Ottoman Imperial Subjects into Bulgarian National Citizens, 1878–1939* (Budapest: Central European University Press, 2017).
112. Ibid., 965.
113. Hamed-Troyansky, *Empire of Refugees*, 114.
114. Ozan Ozavcı, *Dangerous Gifts: Imperialism, Security, and Civil Wars in the Levant, 1798–1864* (Oxford: Oxford University Press, 2021), 248; Ussama Samir Makdisi, *The Culture of Sectarianism: Community, History, and Violence in Nineteenth-Century Ottoman Lebanon* (Berkeley: University of California Press, 2000), 63–67.
115. Nora Elizabeth Barakat, 'An Empty Land?' 35–40.
116. Jacob Metzer, 'Jewish Land – Israel Lands: Ethno-Nationality and Land Regime in Zionism and in Israel, 1897–1967', in Engerman and Metzer, *Land Rights*, 87–110.
117. Neville J. Mandel, 'Ottoman Policy and Restrictions on Jewish Settlement in Palestine, 1881–1908: Part I', *Middle Eastern Studies* 10, no. 3 (1974): 312–32; Louis A. Fishman, *Jews and Palestinians in the Late Ottoman Era, 1908–1914: Claiming the Homeland* (Edinburgh: Edinburgh University Press, 2020).

Chapter 2

Peasants versus Notables: The Emergence of the Armenian Land Question (1850–80)

One day in 1873, a few years after the Tanzimat reforms had started to be implemented in Van and its environs, a curious spectacle happened in front of the governor's office. Around two hundred Armenian peasants from the Şatak (Çatak) Mountains, who had walked eighteen hours to see the governor, were protesting the abuses of the *agha*s and local officials who had helped them. In the past, the same villagers had petitioned the government, complaining that the *bey*s from the Giravi tribe had expelled the Armenians from six villages and seized the fields of twelve other Armenian villages, killing many locals to have their way. A year before this demonstration, the government had sent a commission to the region to investigate these claims, and it had decided in favour of the peasants. However, thanks to a local official named Hacı İbrahimzade Reşit Bey, who was in charge of land registration, the *agha*s were able to register 'the richest Armenian fields' in their names.[1] Upon discovering this misdeed, the villagers decided to make some noise in the city and also to send a petition to Istanbul.

This case concerned a great number of people, and the villagers transformed it into a crisis, pushing for a response from the authorities at all levels of the state. They also got the Armenian Patriarchate involved. Upon the submission of a memorandum by the latter, the Sublime Porte equally became involved in the matter. In the end, 500 plots of land were registered in the names of the Armenian peasants, but the *agha*s soon resumed their attacks to compel them to renounce their ownership rights.

The march and demonstration of Şatak's peasants offers us a glimpse of the Tanzimat in action in the Ottoman East because this case, from the acts of the peasants to those of the *agha*s who tried to manipulate the mechanisms introduced by the reforms, was shaped by the language and legal framework of the Tanzimat. This chapter is about such instances and the emergence of the Armenian land question as a distinct social problem – especially after the territorial turn and the contextual shift of the late 1870s.

The first part of this chapter will examine the historical development of land disputes concerning Armenians before the 1880s. In this part, I will scrutinise the character of the expropriations and land conflicts in the period between 1850 and 1878, as well as the ways in which these conflicts were perceived by the different parties, including the Armenian Patriarchate, Armenian intellectuals and the Ottoman government. I will then discuss how these approaches changed under the pressures for reform, the territorialisation of Armenian nationalism and the rise of a new demographic concern at the Sublime Porte.

The Early Disputes and the Emergence of the Land Question

Land became a serious matter of dispute among Ottomans in the nineteenth century. As the land regime underwent a process of transformation that intensified after the adoption of the Land Code of 1858, Ottomans from different regions, classes, religions and ethnicities began to come forward with conflicting claims over ownership and usage rights to land. As noted by Terzibaşoğlu, in the late nineteenth century, the judicial workload of numerous Anatolian provinces was largely centred around land disputes.[2]

The rise of land disputes in the Ottoman Empire in the mid-nineteenth century was related to several factors. First came the transformation of the land regime. The Land Code adopted by the central government in 1858 aimed to standardise the norms and rules framing the issue of land ownership and tenure throughout the empire. As mentioned in the previous chapter, the code also promoted small landownership to increase agricultural revenue and the tax income of the government, but this led to different outcomes in different parts of the empire.[3] The commodification of land – by which land was stripped of various social obligations and became a thing that could be bought, sold and mortgaged – slowly took place in this context.

Another general factor that affected the rise of land disputes in Anatolia was the population pressure triggered by the influx of immigrants from the Caucasus, especially after the Crimean War of 1854.[4] This first wave of immigrants was followed by others after the Russo-Ottoman War of 1877–78 and the Balkan Wars. The influx of Muslims brought about concerns regarding their settlement and further increased demands for land. Another factor that complicated land disputes consisted of the settlement of nomads. In some cases, nomads were settled by the government directly. In other cases, the tribal leaders themselves took the initiative to settle their tribes.[5] All these developments contributed to the transformation of the significance and regulation of land, as well as of the social relations based on it.

Provinces with a high percentage of Armenian populations were not exempt from this trend of increasing land disputes. Further complicating land disputes in the Ottoman East was the fact that local power relations in the region also experienced a significant period of transformation in the mid-nineteenth century. Following the abolition of emirates in the first decades of the century, tribal leaders, sheikhs and local notables started to dominate local politics.[6] These local powerholders filled the gap left by the abolition of the emirates, increasing their influence in provincial politics. Some of these local powerholders were also incorporated into the new administrative structure established by the central government. This situation gave local powerholders leverage in conflicts with peasants. The socio-economic and political significance of land ownership in the Ottoman East began to change in line with these developments. Local notables such as *agha*s and *bey*s, who lost the feudal rights and privileges which they had possessed in the pre-Tanzimat period, started to acquire land in an attempt to maintain power. In these disputes, local powerholders and peasants from various ethnic and religious backgrounds found themselves in legal struggles with each other over land.[7]

An In-depth Analysis of the Armenian Patriarchate's Reports

In the mid-nineteenth century, Armenian political and communal life also underwent a significant process of transformation.[8] With the adoption of the Armenian Constitution, communal matters concerning the Armenian population began to be regulated through a new institutional framework that included a national assembly. A process called the 'Armenian Enlightenment' accompanied this institutional re-organisation.[9] Both traditional institutions, such as the Armenian Patriarchate, and new institutions, like the National Assembly, began to play vital roles in raising the issue of land disputes concerning Armenians in the 1870s.

In the 1870s, the Armenian Patriarchate prepared two reports titled 'Reports on Provincial Oppressions' (*Deghegakirk'Kawaragan Harsdaharut'eants*), to be submitted to the Sublime Porte.[10] These reports consisted of memoranda (*takrir*s) that the Patriarchate submitted to the Sublime Porte, summaries of the results of memoranda and lists of Armenian lands seized by *bey*s and *agha*s.[11] These reports prepared by special commissions and authorised by the Armenian National Assembly

(ANA) resulted from an initiative started by the Armenian Patriarch Mgrdich Khrimian, who was 'determined to use the National Constitution as a means of general reform, to alleviate the sufferings' of provincial Armenians who called him Hayrig (little father).[12] As noted by Gerard J. Libaridian, Khrimian launched an extensive investigation of the abuses of state officials, systemic discrimination and incidents of 'unpunished violation of rights and property'.[13] In order to prepare the reports, the commission relied on two sources. First, they received information from local prelates, which outlined the specific issues that they faced and proposed their solutions. Second, the commission conducted a thorough examination of the memoranda and petitions that had been sent to the Patriarchate since the 1850s.[14]

Another important figure who influenced this process was Krikor Odian.[15] Once the first report was finalised, the matter received discussion in the ANA. As noted by Lillian Etmekjian, Odian had several connections with the ruling elite of the time and told members of the assembly that 'the time was ripe for winning reforms'.[16] The first report was submitted by the ANA to the Sublime Porte on 23 April 1872 and covered the twenty-year period up to 1872.[17] The Sublime Porte did not respond to the first report. This was interpreted as a failure and, together with other criticisms and complaints, brought about the resignation of Patriarch Khrimian.[18] The second report, which was related to the oppression of the Armenian community between 1872 and 1876, was presented to the ANA on 29 September 1876.[19] The reports include fifty-eight cases related to taxation, religious fanaticism, forced conversion, seizure of lands and other agricultural problems such as forced labour, as well as murder. Twelve of the cases in the second report were related to land disputes and agrarian problems.

Land disputes concerning Armenians in this period were not limited to those detailed in the report. The report only mentioned cases brought to the attention of the Armenian Patriarchate. A general overview of the second report and the list attached to it reveals that the fields belonging to twenty-one monasteries as well as 363 villages and other properties had been appropriated in the 1870s. According to the report, among the actors who had seized these properties counted *bey*s, *agha*s, sheikhs, muftis and local officials. Those whose lands had been appropriated were exclusively peasants.[20] Most seizures had taken place in the eastern provinces, including Diyarbekir, Erzurum, Van and Bitlis, but the report also mentioned two cases in Ankara and Trabzon. A close examination of the cases in the report uncovers the nature and characteristics of land conflicts concerning Armenians before the Hamidian period.

The report mentioned one land dispute between the villagers of Dağ Marnik and the mufti of Muş, Hüseyin Efendi. An examination of this case, also mentioned in the Introduction, shows how relations between local notables and local officials affected the outcomes of land disputes.[21] According to the summary of a memorandum that the Armenian Patriarchate submitted to the Sublime Porte, the lands in the village of Dağ Marnik had been cultivated by Armenian peasants for more than forty years without any protest or claims. The Patriarchate claimed that, a few years earlier, the mufti of Muş, Hüseyin Efendi, had intervened with the aim of appropriating these lands. The peasants had argued that the lands in question belonged to them and emphasised that the Land Code recognized the prescriptive rights of cultivators. Despite the peasants' protests, the mufti forced them to give up their lands. During his visit to the region, İsmail Pasha, the governor of Erzurum, investigated the case and concluded that the mufti's claims were unjustified. Thus, İsmail Pasha decided to register these lands in the names of the peasants and issued them twenty-five temporary title deeds (*ilmuhabers*).

When İsmail Pasha was removed from his post, the mufti tried to reverse the decision and applied to the local council of Muş, arguing that 'all the lands and fields belonging to the said village were exclusively' his property and that 'the villagers were merely his tenants'.[22] According to the memorandum, he compelled a couple of villagers from Marnik to testify on his behalf before the council of Muş. Using his influence over the local council members, he achieved an annulment of the order of İsmail Pasha and acquired ownership rights to the disputed lands. Faced with these developments, the villagers argued that they were neither tenants nor serfs of Hüseyin Efendi. They chose two representatives, Abraham and Melkon, from among themselves, collected the provisional title deeds issued by İsmail Pasha along with a petition and other documents and sent these representatives to Istanbul. Upon the request of these representatives, the Patriarchate requested that the case be submitted to the Council of State. The villagers were unable to gain possession of the lands in question since the decision of the Council of State was in favour of Hüseyin Efendi.

The Marnik case illuminates the ways in which the vocabulary introduced by the Land Code was adopted by disputing parties. In the memorandum, the peasants' claims were grounded in prescriptive rights, and it was emphasised that the lands in dispute had been cultivated by the peasants for decades, without any claims from third parties. This case also shows that peasants were neither passive by-standers nor helpless victims, but actors who developed various strategies for the recognition of their rights to land. In this case, the peasants had sent representatives to Istanbul to secure their rights. Furthermore, this case illuminates that, in some cases, it was the peasants, rather than the local powerholders, who tried to get the central authorities involved in land disputes.

Another case cited in the report concerned the settlement of immigrants on the lands of Armenians. Abdurrahman Agha, the director (*müdir*) of Yarhisar in the district of Kangal, Sivas, had settled Circassian immigrants on fields that had long been cultivated by Armenian peasants.[23] The report, which underscored the prescriptive rights of the peasants, stated that two memoranda regarding the case had failed to produce results. The case was later examined by a special commission established by the Porte to investigate claims of oppression. According to the commission, the villagers cultivated 18,500 *dönüm*s of land, which was larger than what was written on their deed, and 300 *dönüm*s were allocated for the settlement of the Circassian immigrants. However, the latter cultivated 3,000 *dönüm*s, an area much larger than what they had been allocated, which the commission found unlawful. Thus, the commission decided that the claims of the Armenians were justified and suggested that, as the resettlement of the Circassian immigrants in another place would not be appropriate, 1,200 of the 3,000 *dönüm*s that they were using should be allocated to the Circassian immigrants. Additionally, the commission recommended parcelling out the remaining 15,500 *dönüm*s among the villagers according to their needs to satisfy them.[24] Finally, the Council of State decided to keep the Circassian immigrants on the disputed lands, …

> … alleging that those lands being over and above those mentioned in the title deeds held by the villagers, they belonged to the Government, without considering that the lands given to the Circassians had been for a long time past cultivated by Armenians, and according to law, have therefore become the property of the cultivators.[25]

Later on, the Sublime Porte sent an order for the removal of Abdurrahman Agha from his post as director. This order was not carried out by the governor of Sivas, who claimed that his removal could cause trouble in the region.[26] The wording of the decision of the Council of State indicates that the Armenian peasants held title deeds and managed to have their prescriptive rights recognized. It also suggests that, when they deemed it necessary, the Ottoman authorities underscored the fact that the *raqaba* (absolute ownership) of *miri* lands lay with the state, that they first and foremost belonged to the government, and that the government could disregard title deeds held by cultivators.

A dispute in the Sbargerd (Sürücüler) township in the district of Hizan, Bitlis, supports the argument that land disputes in this period were mostly related to conflicts between peasants and local notables who exploited their positions in local government. The memorandum sent by the Patriarchate to the Sublime Porte on 12 April 1874 claimed that, after becoming director of the district, the Kurdish chief Abdi Bey oppressed the villagers of Sbargerd, seized fields, lands and animals belonging to Armenian peasants and appropriated a church in the region. In this case, the Patriarchate noted that those subjected to oppression by Abdi Bey and other *agha*s and *bey*s in the region, 'being poor and without protection, did not venture to appeal to the local authorities'.[27] In this matter, the Patriarchate demanded improving security in the region and restoring the church to the villagers. Upon receiving this memorandum, the Sublime Porte sent an order for the resolution of these two problems.

Another important land dispute concerning Armenians before the 1880s involved disputed lands in the Çarsancak district of Mamuretülaziz.[28] The *agha*s in Çarsancak, led by İshak Bey, alleged that every kind of immovable property – including lands, houses, shops, vineyards and fields – belonged to them, and they compelled the Armenians 'to pay rent for the houses and shops, vineyards and gardens, to obtain the corn seeds from themselves, and to compensate them with half the produce'.[29] The Patriarchate noted that, since the late 1850s, several complaints about this situation had been issued to the Sublime Porte. For example, the Armenian Patriarchate had submitted a memorandum on 3 September 1862 regarding the lands belonging to Keshishoghlu and his brothers, Mardiros and Artin, in the village of Nelanezbey, Harput. These lands had been appropriated by Hacı İshak Agha. After evaluating this memorandum and other petitions submitted by local Armenians, the Supreme Council had ordered the district governor (*mutasarrıf*) of Harput to investigate the situation.[30] In the report submitted to the ANA in 1874, the Patriarchate noted that the Porte had responded to these petitions and complaints by sending orders to the local authorities, but the local authorities had not complied with these orders and sided with the *agha*s and *bey*s.

The Porte had then sent a commission of inquiry to the region.[31] The findings of this commission, together with other documents and memoranda presented by the Patriarchate, were examined by the Council of State, which had decided that the claims of the *agha*s and *bey*s were inadmissible. Thus, the Council of State 'ordered that the villagers should be recognized as the owners of the above fields and lands; it was also ruled that the interference of the *agha*s should be prevented and that title deeds should be filled out in the name of the villagers'.[32] The decisions of the Council of State were also confirmed by an imperial order. This turn of events following the decision of the Council of State and the imperial order shows the significance of the agency of actors, including provincial notables, in shaping the outcomes of land disputes. Upon receiving the decision of the Council of State, the provincial authorities declared that the decision was contrary to justice and equality and that they would not implement it. Preparing a report on the matter, the provincial authorities asked for a new resolution from the Council of State. At the same time, two *agha*s went to Istanbul to appeal to the Council of State. This time around, the Council of State determined that its former decision was unfair and that a new trial should take place at the provincial level. If the parties in dispute were dissatisfied with the decision of the provincial court, the case would once again be referred to the central government. The second decision of the Council of State was also confirmed by imperial decree. Upon this second decision, the Patriarchate submitted two memoranda to the Porte claiming, …

> … [that] the last order of the Council of State with regard to this long-pending question would prove injurious to the interests of the Armenian agriculturist; that the said order was given upon the protest of the Mussulman Aghas without hearing the other side; that it was contrary to justice for the Council of State to annul its previous decision without ascertaining which of its points was contrary to justice and equity; that the Armenians could not pretend to make their claims good against those powerful Aghas before the provincial authorities, and that the people could not be contended with any but the previous order.[33]

The memoranda submitted by the Patriarchate regarding the matter remained unanswered. The prolonged land dispute in Çarsancak shows that the central government tried to manage land disputes concerning a large number of people cautiously and that it performed a balancing act between disputing parties when the case had the potential to cause social strife.[34] While they did not want to alienate the *bey*s, neither did they want to cause mass discontent or trigger an uprising. And they opted for dragging out the case in order to avoid either of these outcomes.

Other significant sources of information regarding land disputes before the massacres of 1894–97 consist of the Patriarchate reports prepared after 1908, to be analysed in detail in the next chapter. The fourth volume of the Patriarchate reports on the issue of seized Armenian properties includes a chapter on those seized before the 1890s.[35] These cases involved seizures by force and the settlement of Muslim immigrants. These cases were related to seizures in the provinces of Erzincan, Van, Sivas, Kastamonu and Bitlis. It should be noted that most of the seizures mentioned were carried out in the 1870s and 1880s; however, cases dating back to the 1860s were also listed in this report.

The Armenian Community and Land Disputes

In the 1870s, the Armenian Patriarchate began to assume a new role with regard to land disputes concerning Armenians. A memorandum prepared by the Patriarchate and the Armenian Civil Council on 5 September 1874 clearly reflects this situation. In contrast to the Patriarchate's other memoranda concerning the oppression of Armenians and specific land disputes, this one was not related to specific disputes but concerned land disputes and agrarian problems in general. This memorandum noted that the majority of Armenians who lived in the Asiatic provinces of the Ottoman Empire were primarily occupied with agriculture and were under the pressure of 'self-constituted feudal lords'. It was also noted that these pressures were driving agriculturists to migrate and that this was the reason why many fertile lands remained uncultivated, 'to the great detriment of the Imperial revenues'.[36] The claim that pressure from the *agha*s and *bey*s hindered the development of agriculture and diminished the revenue of the state received emphasis at numerous points throughout the text. This shows that the Armenian political and religious elite were aware that increasing state revenue constituted an important concern for the Ottoman authorities and that they tried to point out this concern to make their case heard.

This memorandum provides important insights into how land disputes and Tanzimat reforms were perceived by Armenian institutions:

> Before the establishment of the *Tanzimat*, or the new regulations, when many of the district vilayets of Asiatic Turkey were administered in an irregular, illegal manner, a number of Beys and Aghas, through their power and influence, usurped a considerable number of fields and vineyards, and began to regard them as their *Yourdlouk*, *Odjaklik*, or feudal territory, and to consider the common husbandman as their mere slave. However, since the promulgation of the Tanzimat, Beys and Aghas of this description have been brought under subjection, the fields and lands they had appropriated were restored to the peasants according to the special rules and instructions which were issued for that purpose. The benevolent Government has tried everything to save the peasantry from the clutches of these oppressors and the chains of serfdom, but through the culpable oversight or indifference of the local officials, those interferences and tyrannies which occur in many localities of Asiatic Turkey are still allowed, and, as regards the question of their ownership of fields and lands, consequently the agricultural classes have reached the last stages of ruin and insolvency under these unrighteous exactions and oppressions.[37]

Thus, according to the Patriarchate and Armenian Civil Council, regulations introduced in the Tanzimat period aimed to strengthen cultivators' rights on land and to empower them vis-à-vis local powerholders.

The problem was not the regulations or the intentions of the central government but the ineffectiveness and indifference of the provincial authorities. According to the memorandum, despite the government's efforts to improve the 'condition of the oppressed and downtrodden people' and to end violent actions regarding the Armenian lands and fields, the local authorities prioritised the baseless claims of *bey*s and *agha*s who insisted that they owned those lands. Without conducting thorough investigations into these claims, they left the people's complaints and appeals unresolved.

According to the Patriarchate and Civil Council, if the Porte wanted to improve agriculture in the country, it should ensure the peace and wealth of the agricultural labourer, take measures to the effect that no one could 'interfere with his rights of proprietorship' and empower agriculturalists who had no lands of their own by giving them plots and fields. The authors of the memorandum also recommended the formation of a mixed commission to investigate these problems.

This memorandum, which elaborated on the characteristics of land conflicts, can be considered an early indication of an emerging trend: the rise of the issue of land disputes as a communal or national matter that, in the eyes of the Armenian political and religious elite, was more than the sum of the individual disputes. It was the first document in which land disputes concerning Armenian individuals were approached as a communal matter with a holistic approach. However, this did not mean that the Armenian political and religious elite in this period perceived land disputes as an exclusively Armenian matter. In this memorandum, the land question was formulated as a matter of class between 'self-constituted feudal lords' and 'agriculturalists' rather than as a religious or ethnic matter.

The Minister of Foreign Affairs, Arifi Bey, responded to this memorandum by underscoring that the main problem lay with local officials and functionaries. Arifi Bey noted that the Porte, 'with a view to improve this state of things and ensure the welfare of the people', had 'repeatedly issued orders to the provincial authorities', but that those orders, 'owing to the incapacity of the functionaries, remained fruitless'.[38] Arifi Bey also stated that the demand to form a mixed commission had been passed on to the Council of State, which required further information from the Patriarchate regarding the location of the disputed lands, the actors involved in the disputes and more detailed information in order to evaluate this demand.[39] Following this request for information, the Patriarchate presented another memorandum on 11 January 1875, which included a detailed list of cases requested by the Council of State. Following this correspondence, a special commission was established to investigate the cases cited on the list.

The list included the details of land conflicts concerning lands and fields belonging to 363 villages and twenty-one monasteries.[40] While the list and report provide details regarding neither the acreage nor the type of seized lands, the report shows that the alleged usurpers involved in these seizures were exclusively local powerholders such as *beys*, *aghas*, sheikhs and local officials. Moreover, it stated that, in contrast to the land disputes of the Hamidian era, the Armenians who claimed ownership and usufruct rights to disputed lands in this period were exclusively peasants and village communities. Additionally, large lands such as farms were not among the seized properties mentioned in the accounts of Armenian institutions.

On 21 June 1875, the Council of State sent an order about the memorandum and the list of the Armenian Patriarchate to the provinces of Erzurum, Diyarbekir, Ankara, Trabzon and Sivas. The provincial administrations and local councils cited on the list provided by the Patriarchate were ordered to investigate the cases on a just and egalitarian basis and to inform the central government about the results of the investigations to be carried out.[41]

RAFFI AND THE EARLY LAND DISPUTES

As noted above, the rise of land disputes concerning Armenians became an issue of communal concern in the 1870s. By the mid-1870s, the Patriarchate and the ANA began to assume a new role and started to approach land disputes concerning Armenians as a communal matter. In this period, the issue also began to attract the attention of Armenian intellectuals, who started to see them as a national matter. One Armenian intellectual, Hagop Mirzayants Melik Hagobiants, wrote an analysis of the Patriarchate's report, under the pen-name Raffi.[42] Raffi was an important intellectual of the period and played an essential role in public debates regarding what constituted the basis of the Armenian nation. As noted by Ronald G. Suny, Raffi had deployed the newly coined Armenian term *azgutyun* (nationality) in the 1870s and proclaimed that 'the idea of nationality is established not by religion but rather by (a nationality's) racial characteristics, among which language occupies the first place, which is and always remains the base for the preservation of the nation'.[43]

In evaluating the report, Raffi criticised the Patriarchate for ignoring the land question, which was a 'matter of life or death for the Armenian'.[44] Raffi's analysis illuminates the importance that some Armenian intellectuals in the late nineteenth century attached to land and can be considered one of the earliest reflections of the nationalisation of land disputes concerning Armenians. Thus, it is necessary to examine the arguments raised by Raffi in detail.

Raffi emphasised the significance of land ownership for Armenians in the Ottoman Empire, underscoring that land connected peasants to the lands of their forefathers:

> Bearing thousands of misfortunes and all kinds of wretchedness with patience, the Armenian in Armenia had only one comfort: he was the master of the land. It had been irrigated with the sweat of his forefathers. But he was deprived of that comfort, too. On the one hand, the Kurd forcibly took his land, while on the other the government, stealing it, gives it to the Muslims. So what is left?[45]

According to Raffi, the actions of the Patriarchate, which were limited to sending memoranda to the Sublime Porte, did not suffice, considering the significance of the issue for the agricultural classes. According to him, the seizure of lands was a significant problem; the Patriarchate was preoccupied with problems of a temporary nature but ignored what was vital for Armenians as a nation:

> The whole Report, as we recall, contains the record of 25 years of activity by the Patriarchate. In all of those 25 years, there was only one protest note issued by the Patriarchate about land extortion, and it was presented to the Sublime Porte on January 3, 1875. It too did not bring about any satisfaction, and the Patriarchate stayed silent on the subject thereafter. On the contrary, we see that Giragos' daughter has been raped or kidnapped by Muslims; that Mardiros' sheep were stolen; or that the Turks have hung a cross from some church around the neck of a dog they are parading through the streets; these scandals have become the subjects of years of negotiation between the Sublime Porte and the Patriarchate. We are not saying that they should not have been given as much importance as they have. These things are odd incidents, they may happen today but not tomorrow. But when the Muslims appropriate all the Armenian villages in a province – that is a crucial and vital matter, because it leads to a whole mass of people dying materially and morally, and subsequent generations are deprived of food and therefore their lives.[46]

Raffi's understanding of land disputes indicates that he attached particular significance to this social problem and saw the seizure of Armenian lands as a threat to the Armenian existence in the provinces inhabited by Armenians. Raffi interpreted land seizure as a new form of oppression used by Kurdish tribes, notables and the government, and he saw the Land Code as a legal instrument which would serve to dispossess the Armenians:

> The majority of Armenian-owned land is purloined by the government, which in turn is given to Muslims. So that its injustice takes a legal form, the

government created the fraudulent Tapou Law. On the basis of this law, every piece of land that has remained uncultivated for a number of years is considered mahloul or without an owner and therefore belonging to the state. This sort of land is taken by the government itself, and can then be registered to Muslims; for a very small fee, the Muslim can have an imperial certificate of ownership issued in his name. This is the reason Armenians are likely to lose the majority of their lands.[47]

The last point that Raffi raised about this matter was related to the seizure of lands belonging to those Armenians who had migrated to other parts of the empire, mainly Istanbul, or beyond its borders, to find employment.[48] According to Raffi, who stated that there were almost 45,000 immigrants in Istanbul alone, the oppression by Kurdish *bey*s and *agha*s, heavy taxes and the abuses of tax collectors had driven Armenians into migration and emigration.

The report of the British Consul J. G. Taylor supports the argument that oppression by Kurdish tribes was an important motivation for Armenians to leave their hometowns and villages. According to the consul, Kurds from Muş, Bulanık, Ahlat and Beyazıd were in the habit of pillaging Armenian villages and stealing their animals. He stated that this situation resulted in the impoverishment of the agricultural classes, leading them to emigrate to foreign countries.[49] However, it should be noted that fleeing oppression was not the sole motivation of Armenians who migrated or emigrated. As examined by Sinan Dinçer, the prospects of a better life and wealth were significant factors contributing to these trends, which accelerated in the last decades of the nineteenth century.[50] Another interesting point regarding Raffi's evaluation of land disputes and the transformation of the land regime concerns his interpretation of the Land Code. While it is true that the Land Code included an article according to which lands not cultivated for a certain period of time would be considered vacant (*mahlul*) and sold by the government, this was a general regulation that could be applied to all Ottoman subjects. However, Raffi's words indicate that it was perceived as a measure targeting Armenians.

In the first report of the Armenian Patriarchate, which covered those acts of oppression that occurred during the twenty-year period until 1872, there were no references to land disputes. According to Raffi, this was related to the absence of land disputes before the 1870s. He argued that the central government had decided to settle semi-nomadic and nomadic Kurds in the 1870s, accelerating competition for land. In Raffi's portrayal of the Ottoman East before the 1870s, the Armenians were the sole landowners in the region:

Peasants versus Notables

The Turkish central government, seeing that the barbarities perpetrated by the Kurds and other wild tribes arise from the nature of their nomadic life, has recently begun efforts to persuade them to leave their lives of wandering, leave shepherding, have settled homes and become farmers. It hopes in this way to subdue the Kurds and other wild tribes. The idea was not a bad one, but it was incorrectly implemented: instead of collecting the Kurds from the Armenian highlands and settling them in an area of Turkey that was unpopulated (such as the deserts of Mesopotamia or Assyria), the government allowed them to occupy areas in Armenia itself as settlement areas. How could this be? The land was in the hands of Armenians, left to them by their fathers and ancestors as inheritance. It was difficult for the Kurd to buy land from Armenians with money, as he was used to taking whatever he wanted from them by force. So he did the same again. It is from this land and property problem that a new form of oppression started. In the records contained in the Patriarchate's first Report – in other words, until 1872 – there were almost no land or property matters cited. This means that, until that year, the Armenians were the owners of their land and other property. This was the time during which the Kurds were still living nomadically and had not yet become concerned with land. But when, by government order, they gradually began to establish settled lives, the question of land was bound to arise.[51]

Although Raffi's point about the settlement of nomadic tribes and the rise of land disputes concerning Armenians is relevant, several documents, reports and secondary sources indicate that there occurred, in fact, several land conflicts in the region before 1872.[52] As examined at the beginning of this chapter, the land dispute in Çarsancak began in the middle of the nineteenth century. This case, which concerned a large group of peasants, had been brought before the Supreme Council by the Patriarchate by the 1860s.[53] Also, in the districts of Ahlat, Bulanık and Malazgird in the province of Bitlis, the Hasenanlı and Milikanlı tribes, under the leadership of Sofi Agha, Hazneder and Esehoğlu, had carried out several depredations and attacks on Armenian villages. As a result of these attacks, the Armenian peasants had abandoned their villages and lost their lands.[54] Several other examples can be added to the list of land disputes concerning Armenians before the 1870s, which contradicts Raffi's claim that such land disputes started in the 1870s, upon the initiative of the government to settle nomadic and semi-nomadic tribes in the region. Yet, these governmental initiatives did increase demand for land and contributed to an ongoing trend.

What was missing in the period before the 1870s was not land conflicts concerning Armenians themselves but communal attention to and recognition of land disputes concerning Armenians by the Armenian political and religious elite and their organisations. As will be analysed below, this absence of interest is explained by the fact that, until the 1870s, the dominant trend in Armenian nationalism was a cultural nationalism that lacked a territorial component.[55] It was with the development of the territorial aspect of Armenian nationalism that land became a fundamental component of Armenian public debate.

The Ottoman Government's Approach

The central government held three main concerns regarding land disputes in this period. First, the central government depended on local elites to establish and maintain the Tanzimat order in the region. Thus, not alienating the *agha*s, *bey*s and sheikhs who had gained a renewed influence constituted a primary concern of the central government. Furthermore, the Kurdish tribes maintained a significant military force along the strategic Ottoman-Persian border. As noted by the British Consul Taylor, the local governors feared that, if they oppressed these tribes, the tribes could easily cross the border and 'locate themselves in the rival territory of Persia'.[56] Thus, the central government 'was aware of the complexity of the local power relations in the region' and had to take the power of these local notables into consideration.[57] The third concern of the government was to increase its share of the agricultural surplus. These concerns shaped the Porte's approach to land disputes in the Ottoman East in general and land disputes concerning Armenians in particular.

In her study of the Ottoman land regime's transformation, Huri İslamoğlu has pointed out that, 'throughout the nineteenth century, the Ottoman central government was engaged in a continuous balancing act between the exigencies of a rule of justice (read absence of social strife) and a rule of property'.[58] The case of Vidin is a good example of such a balancing act on the part of the government. In Vidin, Christian cultivators working as share-croppers on the lands of Muslim landlords under harsh conditions protested the Muslim *agha*s and demanded the termination of *gospodarlık*, a form of land tenure that gave these *agha*s a position close to feudal lordship. These cultivators rebelled based on the claim that, since corvée labour had been abolished in the Ottoman Empire, the *agha*s had no right to demand forced labour from them. The central government became involved in the matter once the cultivators had started a rebellion. In the end, the government recognized the ownership rights of the *agha*s but also provided peasants with a chance to buy lands in the region – a solution that fell short of the demands of peasants. As noted by several researchers, the Ottoman authorities were aware of the political implications of this case and performed a balancing act to maintain the existing social hierarchy and public order, on the one hand, and prevent social strife, on the other.[59] Such a balancing act was also evident in the Porte's approach to land disputes in the Ottoman East in this period. The responses of the Sublime Porte to the memoranda of the Armenian Patriarchate indicate that the central government approached land disputes with caution.

Most of the memoranda presented by the Patriarchate remained unanswered. However, there existed cases in which the central government became involved. The case of Çarsancak, which evolved into a long-term legal and administrative battle between peasants and *agha*s, serves as one of the best examples of the Porte's balancing policy. In this case, the parties in dispute were directed towards administrative channels by the central government, which did not want to face the consequences of social strife. Correspondence between the Patriarchate and the agencies of the central government also indicates a serious degree of resistance on the part of the provincial authorities. In several cases, the orders of the Porte were not put into action. In some cases, the Porte decided to send commissions to the region to investigate the disputes. However, even when these commissions decided in favour of the peasants, the decisions were not carried out at the local level. In other cases, the Council of State did not take the reports of the commissions into consideration. Or local governments refused to apply them under the influence of local power dynamics. Thus, the outcomes of land disputes were determined through a series of negotiations at different levels of administration in this period.

Another point concerning the Porte's approach to land disputes involving Armenians before the Hamidian period is the absence of a demographic policy intended to decimate Armenians in the region. Correspondence among Armenian institutions and Ottoman authorities indicates that the Porte performed balancing acts between Armenian peasants and Muslim powerholders with regard to land disputes. These documents indicate that, whenever the Porte dismissed the claims of Armenian peasants, it did so on the grounds of maintaining the established social order and local power balance, rather than as part of a detailed demographic plan.

A final point to be mentioned is that the Sublime Porte showed a renewed interest in land disputes in the 1870s. In this period, the Porte faced increasing pressure from Armenian political and religious actors to resolve land disputes and other problems concerning Armenians in the Ottoman East, and it sent several orders to establish investigation commissions in different localities.

The Armenian Question as an International Issue

The Russo-Ottoman War of 1877–78 and the Treaty of Berlin

The most significant turning point regarding land disputes concerning Armenians in this period came with the internationalisation of the Armenian Question in the aftermath of the Balkan Crisis and the Russo-Ottoman War of 1877–78.[60] The Russo-Ottoman War broke out due to Russia's insistence on the implementation of reforms in Bulgaria, which it considered a zone of influence. While the Ottoman government tried to avoid implementing a regionally specific reform plan for Bulgaria, Russia insisted on specific reforms and declared war on the Ottoman Empire in 1877. As the eventual victor, Russia obliged the Ottoman Empire to sign a peace treaty with terms that considerably expanded Russian influence in the region.

According to the San Stefano Treaty, several provinces along the Ottoman-Russian border zone would be given to Russia, Bulgaria would become an autonomous principality, and the territories of Montenegro and Serbia would be extended. Moreover, Serbia, Montenegro and Romania would become independent.[61] The Treaty of San Stefano also included an article regarding reform in the eastern provinces, which were referred to as 'Armenia' in the text of the treaty.[62] According to the treaty, Russian troops would be removed from the occupied zones only if the Ottoman government carried out reforms. In the treaty, Russia was specified as the guarantor of these reforms.

Concerned about the expansion of Russian influence in the region, the Great Powers intervened in the matter and called for an international congress in Berlin. In the Treaty of Berlin signed at the end of this congress, the political gains of the Russian Empire were curbed considerably. While Romania, Serbia and Montenegro remained independent, the territorial gains of the Montenegrin, Serbian and Bulgarian autonomous regions were curtailed. The status of Bulgaria was modified, Bosnia-Herzegovina was given to Austria-Hungary, and Cyprus became a British dominion. The Treaty of Berlin also entailed a range of obligations and responsibilities for the Ottoman government with respect to reform in the eastern provinces. According to Article 69 of the Treaty of Berlin, the Sublime Porte was obliged 'to carry out without further delay the improvements and reforms demanded by local requirements in the provinces inhabited by Armenians, and to guarantee their security against the Circassians and Kurds'. Furthermore, the Ottoman government would 'periodically make known the steps taken to this effect to the powers, who will superintend their application'.[63]

Thus, while reform in the eastern provinces was included in the Treaty of Berlin, the realisation of reforms was not specified as a condition for the removal of Russian troops, and Russia was no longer specified as the sole guarantor of the reforms. There was also an Armenian delegation at the Congress of Berlin. This delegation, headed by the former patriarch Khrimian, proposed a plan that included the autonomy of Armenia with a detailed map and statistical information regarding the Armenian population, but this plan was not discussed in the Congress.[64] While the Treaty of Berlin included provisions regarding reform in the eastern provinces, it was seen as a setback by Armenian political actors.[65] As noted by Richard E. Antaramian, after Berlin, Armenians also found themselves facing a growing sense of isolation within the network and relations that formed imperial governance.[66]

The emergence of an 'Armenian Question' at the international level was accompanied by various debates in Armenian political circles and also constituted a turning point for Armenian nationalism. It should first be noted that disturbances on the Balkans, which preceded the Russo-Ottoman War, were carefully followed by Armenian politicians. As analysed by Etmekjian, the proceedings of the meetings of the ANA on 10–22 December 1876 provide important insights regarding the approach of the Armenian political elite to developments on the Balkans and their demands for reform regarding the Armenian population. Etmekjian has noted that some delegates feared that 'the Balkan people might obtain more through rebellion than the Armenians had through loyalty'.[67] While some delegates demanded that the National Assembly issue a statement to the Porte, informing it that 'the Armenians wished to enjoy whatever reforms were granted to the others' and that 'the Armenians deserved them more because they had never been disloyal, as others had', the assembly eventually agreed on a more conservative statement declaring that 'Armenians were "confident" that they would be given the same benefits accorded to the other subjects of the empire'.[68] After the outbreak of the war, Armenian politicians continued to underscore their loyalty – this time in the Ottoman Parliament, which had been established after the proclamation of the constitution. Several Armenian parliamentarians gave speeches condemning Russian intervention on behalf of Christian subjects of the Ottoman Empire and demanded that the Ottoman government take the necessary steps for the recruitment of Ottoman Christians into the Ottoman army.[69]

Following the disturbances on the Balkans, there occurred an interesting change in the way in which members of the ANA addressed the eastern provinces. Masayuki Ueno, who has presented an extensive analysis of Armenian political debates during the Tanzimat period based on Armenian and Ottoman sources, has pointed out that, prior to the disturbances on the Balkans in the mid-1870s, the delegates of the ANA referred to 'oppression in the provinces' when discussing attacks on Armenians in the Ottoman East. After the disturbances had begun, they started to use the phrase 'oppressions in Armenia (*Hayasdan*)'. Thus, Ueno has concluded that, as the Ottoman government was under pressure to implement reforms in specific provinces on the Balkans rather than across the entire empire, ANA members felt compelled to 'focus on their national fatherland when appealing to the government for the implementation of reforms in the Eastern provinces'.[70] This shift reflects a serious transformation in terms of Armenian nationalism and the territorialisation of the Armenian question.

As noted above, the internationalisation of the Armenian Question accompanied the transformation of Armenian nationalism, which gained a territorial aspect in this period. Razmik Panossian has underscored that Khrimian, who had served as Patriarch of Constantinople between 1869 and 1873, returned from the Congress of Berlin immensely frustrated, 'concluding that force was necessary in order to be listened to, even by the "Christian powers" of Europe'. Khrimian's message using the metaphor of an 'iron ladle' diminished the idea of Armenian victimhood, urged for a response and highlighted the situation in Armenia rather than concentrating on 'abstract constitutional issues'.[71] Together with Mgrdich Portukalian, an educator, writer and activist, Khrimian influenced the development of the territorial element of Armenian nationalism. Land was a fundamental component of the new nationalist approach that became dominant in the second half of the nineteenth century.[72]

Thus, the process by which the Armenian Question emerged as an international problem was accompanied by a turn in Armenian nationalism, which had gained a territorial dimension. In this period, the emphasis on 'love of nation' (*azgasirutyun*) was replaced by 'love of fatherland' (*hayrenasirutyun*).[73] For many years, Armenian nationalists had emphasised the importance of language and culture and worked for general reform in the Ottoman Empire. With the territorialisation of Armenian nationalism, they began to emphasise the need for reforms in the 'fatherland'. It should be noted that the Treaty of San Stefano or the Treaty of Berlin did not mark 'breaking points' in Armenian nationalism; Armenian nationalism had already been gaining a territorial aspect through the efforts of Armenian intellectuals in the second half of the nineteenth century. The Armenian fatherland, as a territorially bounded geographical space of an imagined Armenian community, was already being created through the efforts of intellectuals who, since the 1850s, had been calling on Armenians to settle in those provinces and become involved in agriculture and education.[74]

However, by demarcating the eastern provinces as 'Ottoman Armenia' or 'provinces inhabited by Armenians', the treaties of San Stefano and Berlin brought a new impetus to the territorialisation of Armenian nationalism. This transformation also underscored the significance of land itself because land was what tied the peasants to the 'fatherland'. Thus, the territorialisation of Armenian nationalism can be seen as one of the most critical factors that affected the approaches of the Armenian elite and Armenian institutions to land disputes concerning Armenians. As land began to be seen as a natural component of Armenian existence in the Ottoman East, possession of land by Armenians began to be seen as a national matter rather than an issue of property. In line with these developments, land disputes concerning Armenians began to be perceived as a national matter.

Early Reform Attempts and Change in the Government's Approach

Two simultaneous developments happened regarding state policies concerning Armenians in the post-Berlin period. First, the approach of the Ottoman government to the problems of Armenians and Armenian institutions changed. In this period, the government began to act with demographic concerns in mind, waged a battle against the symbols of the Armenian fatherland and the proponents of Armenian nationalism and attempted to strengthen the basis of its territorial sovereignty in the region. Second, the central government began to establish commissions in line with the stipulations of the Treaty of Berlin.

The political struggles of the 1870s had underscored the importance of demographics for substantiating territorial claims and claims to sovereignty. The Ottoman government conducted a new population census in the aftermath of the Berlin Congress. As noted by Fuat Dündar, the census of 1881–93, which included ethnic and religious categorisations, was carried out upon the order of the Minister of War, Rıza Pasha.[75] Aware of the importance of demographics for territorial claims, Abdülhamid II ordered the administrative redistricting of the eastern provinces 'to dilute the statistics reflecting the concentration of Armenians'.[76] In line with this attempt, Hakkari was integrated into Van Province.[77] As noted by Stephan Astourian, the government also intensified the targeted settlement of immigrants in the Armenian-inhabited areas to strengthen the majority of Muslims in this period.[78]

Another change in the approach of the central government was related to cultural nationalism. As noted by Libaridian, 'the Porte forbade the use of words it considered subversive, such as "Hayastan" (Armenia) in print or the printing, sale or ownership of pictures of King Leon V – very popular since he was the last of the Cilician, and as such of all Armenian kings – to be reproduced, circulated or owned'.[79] In 1885, the government exiled important political figures such as Portukalian and Khrimian from their centres of activity in the eastern provinces and closed several schools there. Another change in the approach of the central government concerned the Patriarchate and the ANA. In this period, the Sublime Porte tried to limit the authority of the Patriarchate and the ANA, informing them that the Ottoman government would no longer accept memoranda related to non-religious matters from these institutions.[80] It should be noted, however, that these institutions, in fact, continued to submit such memoranda to the Porte in the years that followed.

In this period, the Ottoman government also started sending special commissions to investigate the situation in the eastern provinces, in line with the obligations stipulated in the Treaty of Berlin.[81] Another development that triggered the formation of these commissions was the outbreak of the Zeytun rebellion in 1878, which was related to tax collection and the settlement of Circassian immigrants on Armenian lands.[82] As noted by Musa Şaşmaz, another development triggering the commissions consisted of the protest by the British consul that the Kurds were oppressing the Armenians after the withdrawal of Russian troops.[83] With these developments, the Sublime Porte decided to establish two commissions in February 1879. One commission, consisting of Yusuf Pasha and Sarkis Efendi, was responsible for the provinces of Erzurum and Van. The other commission, comprised of Abidin Pasha and Manas Efendi, was responsible for the Diyarbekir Province and its environs. On 6 April 1879, the Sublime Porte sent instructions (*talimatname*) to the commissioners. The instructions sent to the reform commission responsible for the Diyarbekir region stated that there were several complaints about Kurdish chiefs and tribes who had oppressed Christian communities, appropriated villages and imposed taxes on Christian cultivators in the districts of Cizre, Nusaybin, Silvan, Bitlis and Siird. The reform commission was authorised to investigate the situation and prevent oppression by Kurdish tribes and notables.[84]

Correspondence by the British consular staff provides important insights into the operation of these commissions. According to the British consul, 'the commissioners were at first disposed to execute the mission with energy and loyalty, the difficulties and obstructions which have been placed in their way, the opposition they received from local authorities, the want of support from Constantinople and the limited nature of their powers have ended by disheartening them'.[85] Yet, the early activities of the commissions substantially improved the situation, especially in the region of Diyarbekir. Commissioner Abidin Bey decided to exile notorious Kurdish chiefs responsible for the oppression of Armenians in the region. Abidin Bey first decided to exile more than a hundred beys to Albania, but later the *bey*s were settled in Aleppo. While the arrest of the Kurdish chiefs restored order in places such as Çapakçur, in other districts the situation became worse when the local population blamed the Armenians for the *bey*s' arrest. Abdülhamid II regretted the decision to allow Abidin Pasha to exile the *bey*s. A memorandum prepared on the orders of the sultan stated that 'Abidin Pasha caused the destruction of several influential Muslims' under the influence of the British consuls and the accusations of some Armenians.[86] In 1881, these Kurdish chiefs were allowed to return to their regions, and revenge attacks increased the pressure on the local Armenians.

The case of Kiğı, which was investigated by the reform commission, shows that the commissions were also interested in land disputes. The case of Kiğı illuminates the failure of the reform commissions in terms of solving land disputes among *agha*s, *bey*s and peasants. Several beys in Kiğı were under investigation by the commission for various crimes, including murder, extortion, plunder and seizure. One was İsmail Bey of Temran (Bağlarpınarı), accused of extortion, fraud and cruelty during his term of office as *kaimakam* (district governor) of Kiğı. He was dismissed from his post but maintained his influence in the region as a *bey*. The complaints of villagers included forced labour and the seizure of fields and pastures belonging to peasants.[87] Other *bey*s involved in such oppressive acts were Hacı Sadık Bey of Horhor (Gökçeli) and his brothers.[88] In a memorandum he wrote about the case, the British consul pointed out the role of the Land Code in aggravating tensions and increasing the power of local powerholders. In the memorandum, the consul stated that, …

> … remembering the ignorance, habits of neglect and corrupt practices of many of the officers sent to those out-of-the-way places, we can understand what difficulties arise. This reform has been a new source of trouble to the people and of profit to the beys and also to the officers, who are entrusted with discretionary power over the property of the poor villagers.[89]

The consul also underscored the importance of land ownership for local powerholders, stating that 'the beys in general being deprived of their old feudal rights and power of levying taxes etc. now feel the need of possessing property. They are therefore endeavouring to accumulate all kinds of standing property and this at any cost to the poor inhabitants of their districts'.[90] The evaluation of the consul supports the argument that land ownership gained a new character in the region in the late nineteenth century.

In the case of Kiği, the *bey*s used their knowledge of new procedures and formalities to acquire lands in dispute, by offering to help villagers complete the registration procedures. After collecting papers from the villagers, they registered the lands in their own names, dividing the property among themselves. Hacı Bey had collected money from peasants to register the lands in their names but had intentionally failed to do so. As a result of bargaining with local officials, Hacı Bey succeeded in becoming the legal owner of several fields belonging to Armenian peasants.

The preliminary investigations of the commission into the Kiği case convinced the commissioners 'that there was much to be said against the claims of proprietorship of the local chiefs'.[91] According to the British correspondence, the commissioners asked the Sublime Porte on three different occasions whether these land disputes should be seen before the sharia court or the local court; however, the question remained unanswered. After examining the case for four months, the commission concluded that, in many instances, *agha*s had used fraudulent means to obtain possession of lands to which they had no right. Regardless, the commission was not authorised to take these lands back from the *agha*s. Thus, the commission transferred complaints regarding the land disputes in Kiği to the court of first instance.[92]

The *agha*s and *bey*s were tried before the local court and received relatively light punishments for criminal cases. In September 1880, the *bey*s started to return to Kiği from Erzurum, and the oppression began anew. When İsmail Bey of Temran, İsmail Bey of Osnag, Hacı Bey of Horhor and Hasan Bey returned, they were welcomed by the local authorities. Acting British Vice-Consul Barnham noted that he had received letters from Kiği, one of which stated that, 'in all cases where land had been forcibly taken by the beys, it had been secured to them by a decision of the Erzurum government'.[93] Thus, British correspondence indicates that the *bey*s succeeded in maintaining their ownership rights to disputed lands after the investigation process in Kiği and that the reform commissions did not resolve the land disputes concerning Armenians.

Ottoman correspondence indicates that the commissioners found it difficult to improve the situation in the Ottoman East. According to the report of one commissioner, laws and regulations were not sufficient to improve the situation, as local officials were unable to follow through.[94] British Consul Sir A. H. Layard also warned that, 'unless the Porte takes care and acts with wisdom and foresight, it will someday have an Armenian Question in Asia, similar to the Bulgarian Question in Europe which led to the late war'.[95] The Porte itself was deeply concerned by this prospect. However, the lack of strong, persistent initiatives on the part of the central government indicates that the Porte did not see reform as the solution to the problems at hand. According to Garo Sasuni, concern that the Armenian Question could evolve into a quest for independence backed by the Great Powers drove the Porte to ally with Kurdish chiefs in the middle of the Russo-Ottoman War of 1877–78. He has argued that the Ottoman government had paid the price for not securing the support of Kurdish tribes in the Crimean War in which several Kurdish forces refused to fight alongside Ottoman troops. According to Sasuni, a new agreement between the Porte and Kurdish chiefs secured the involvement of Kurdish forces in the Russo-Ottoman War and emboldened the Kurdish chiefs who began attacking Armenians upon their return.[96] While evaluating the accuracy of these claims is beyond the scope of this study, the relations between the Porte and the Kurdish chiefs were radically reconfigured in the years following the Berlin Congress, which came as a turning point in terms of the internationalisation of the Armenian Question, the transformation of Armenian nationalism and the transformation of the Porte's approach to Armenians.

Conclusion

The centralisation efforts of the Ottoman government and the transformation of the land regime brought about the emergence of a series of land disputes in the Ottoman East. Similar to cultivators with other religious or ethnic backgrounds, Armenian cultivators also found themselves involved in land disputes after the adoption of the Land Code. Land disputes concerning Armenians in this period occurred almost exclusively between Armenian peasants and local powerholders. Due to their power and connections, the latter had the upper hand in these conflicts. However, the peasants did not quietly accept defeat. They developed strategies for registering lands in their names. Writing petitions, organising demonstrations and sending representatives to Istanbul to get the central authorities involved, they tried to stand against *agha*s, *bey*s, religious authorities and local officials. For their part, local powerholders were equally active agents, with broad repertoires of action that also included sending representatives to Istanbul to negotiate their cases before the Ottoman central authorities.

Moreover, this analysis of land disputes concerning Armenians before the 1880s shows that the Armenian Patriarchate played the role of an important institution in such matters. In several cases, the Patriarchate acted as an intermediary between the Armenian peasants and the Ottoman central government. The involvement of a religious institution in land disputes concerning Armenians to such an extent differentiates the land conflicts concerning Armenians from those concerning Ottoman subjects with other religious and ethnic backgrounds.

In the 1870s, Armenian institutions and the Armenian political elite began to see land disputes in a new light. Simultaneous with the territorialisation of Armenian nationalism, some Armenian intellectuals began to see land disputes as a national matter. There was also a change in the significance that the Patriarchate attached to the matter, which can be traced in the wording of the memoranda submitted to the Porte. The territorialisation of Armenian nationalism gained a new impetus in the late 1870s, especially after the treaties of San Stefano and Berlin. There was also a change in the Ottoman government's approach to the problems of Armenians in the 1870s. With the emergence of the Armenian Question at the level of international diplomacy, the Ottoman government became concerned with the demographics and distribution of the population in the eastern provinces and took measures to eliminate the symbols of Armenian territorial claims. After 1878, the Ottoman government also established reform commissions, although these commissions failed to change the situation at the local level. Their initiatives, such as the exile of local powerholders, were shelved within a couple of years. The operations of the reform commission in Kiği indicate that the commissions also tried to resolve some land disputes but lacked the necessary authority and did not have any effect on this matter.

As examined in this chapter, land disputes concerning Armenians in this period were mostly related to conflicts between Armenian cultivators and local powerholders. In this era, not a single Armenian large landowner claimed to be dispossessed. All claimants were small-scale peasants, village communities or communal organisations. And all Muslims claimed to have seized Armenian lands were people of power, such as *agha*s and *bey*s. Thus, in this period, class rather than ethnic or religious differences was the main factor that shaped these disputes over land.

In this period, the Ottoman government performed a balancing act about the demands of these groups, although there occurred cases in which the Ottoman authorities became directly involved, especially with regard to disputes arising from the settlement of immigrants. With the crystallisation of a new demographic policy after the consolidation of the Hamidian regime, the Ottoman government would become more involved in land disputes concerning Armenians. The next chapter will examine the process of property transfer from the Armenians, which acquired a new form and content in this later period, especially after the massacres of 1894–97.

Notes

1. *Reports on Provincial Oppressions*, 28.
2. Terzibaşoğlu, 'Eleni Hatun', 123–24.
3. Quataert, 'Age of Reforms'; Mundy and Smith, *Governing Property*; Gerber, *Social Origins*; Pamuk, *Osmanlı'dan Cumhuriyet'e Küreselleşme*.
4. On the Crimean war, see Candan Badem, *The Ottoman Crimean War (1853–1856)* (Leiden: Brill, 2010). For immigration and the settlement of immigrants following the war, see Mark Pinson, 'Russian Policy and the Emigration of the Crimean Tatars to the Ottoman Empire, 1854–1862', *Güney-Doğu Avrupa Araştırmaları Dergisi* 2–3 (1974): 101–14; Alan W. Fisher, 'Emigration of Muslims from the Russian Empire in the Years After the Crimean War', *Jahrbücher für Geschichte Osteuropas* 35, no. 3 (1987): 356–71; Musa Şaşmaz, 'Immigration and Settlement of Circassians in the Ottoman Empire on British Documents, 1857–1864', *OTAM* 9 (1998): 331–66.
5. Quataert, 'Age of Reforms', 875; Fuat Dündar, *Kahir Ekseriyet: Ermeni Nüfus Meselesi (1878–1923)* (Istanbul: Tarih Vakfı Yurt Yayınları, 2013), 44–45.
6. Bruinessen, *Agha, Shaikh and State*, 177–82. On the emirate system and its abolition, see also Wadie Jwaideh, *The Kurdish National Movement*, chap. 3; Hakan Özoğlu, *Kurdish Notables and the Ottoman State: Evolving Identities, Competing Loyalties, and Shifting Boundaries* (Albany: State University of New York Press, 2004); David McDowall, *A Modern History of the Kurds* (London: I. B. Tauris, 2004), chap. 3; Michael Eppel, 'The Demise of the Kurdish Emirates: The Impact of Ottoman Reforms and International Relations on Kurdistan during the First Half of the Nineteenth Century', *Middle Eastern Studies* 44, no. 2 (2008): 237–58.
7. Özok-Gündoğan, *Kurdish Nobilitiy*; Oya Gözel, 'The Implementation of the Ottoman Land Code of 1858 in Eastern Anatolia' (Master's thesis, Middle East Technical University, 2007).
8. For detailed information about this transformation, see Roderic H. Davison, *Reform in the Ottoman Empire, 1856–1876* (New York: Gordian Press, 1973); James Etmekjian, 'The Tanzimat Reforms and Their Effect on the Armenians in Turkey', *The Armenian Review* 25, no. 1 (1972): 10–23; Gerard Libaridian, 'The Ideology of Armenian Liberation: The Development of Armenian Political Thought before the Revolutionary Movement (1639–1885)' (PhD diss., University of California, 1987); Boğos Levon Zekiyan, *Ermeniler ve Modernite* (Istanbul: Aras, 2002); Ohannes Kılıçdağı, 'Ermeni Aydınlanması: Yeniden Doğuştan Yokoluşa', in *1915: Siyaset, Tehcir, Soykırım*, ed. Fikret Adanır and Oktay Özel (Istanbul: Tarih Vakfı Yurt Yayınları, 2015), 44–61; Antaramian, *Brokers of Faith*.

9. For detailed information on the Armenian Constitution, see Vartan Artinian, *The Armenian National Constitutional System in the Ottoman Empire, 1839–1863: A Study of Its Historical Development* (Istanbul: The Isis Press, 1988); Murat Bebiroğlu, *Tanzimat'tan II. Meşrutiyet'e Ermeni Nizamnameleri* (Istanbul: M. Bebiroğlu, 2003); Aylin Beşiryan, 'Hopes of Secularization in the Ottoman Empire: The Armenian National Constitution and the Armenian Newspaper *Masis*, 1856–1863' (Master's thesis, Boğaziçi University, 2007); Talin Suciyan, *Outcasting Armenians: Tanzimat of the Provinces* (Syracuse: Syracuse University Press, 2023), chap. 1. In this period, other Christian and Jewish communities also began to have constitutions (*nizamname*s) to regulate their internal and communal affairs. See Murat Bebiroğlu, *Osmanlı Devleti'nde Gayrimüslim Nizamnameleri*, ed. Cahit Külekçi (Istanbul: M. Bebiroğlu, 2008).
10. *Reports on Provincial Oppressions*. This report was first published in Armenian in 1876. See *Deghegakirk' Kawaṟagan Harsdaharut'eants'* (G. Bolis: Dbakrut'iwn Aramyan, 1876). For the first report, see also *Adenakrut'iwnk' Azkayin Ĕnthanur Zhoghov*, nist LA (session 31), 8/20 October 1871, 468–83.
11. Astourian, 'Silence of Land', 59.
12. Libaridian, 'Ideology of Armenian Liberation', 116. On the activities of Khrimian focusing on provincial issues, especially in Van, see Dzovinar Derderian, 'Nation-Making and the Language of Colonialism: Voices from Ottoman Van in Armenian Print Media and Handwritten Petitions (1820s to 1870s)' (PhD diss., University of Michigan, Ann Arbor, 2019). For an analysis of Khrimian and his activities in terms of Tanzimat reforms, see Antaramian, *Brokers of Faith*, chap. 4–5.
13. Ibid., 115–16. The commission that prepared the reports benefited from the petitions sent by provincial Armenians to the Patriarchate and the Sublime Porte. Petitions became important tools for raising complaints and grievances, not only but especially in the context of the Tanzimat. See Yuval Ben-Bassat, *Petitioning the Sultan: Protests and Justice in Late Ottoman Palestine* (London: I. B. Tauris, 2013), 62; Cengiz Kırlı, 'Tyranny Illustrated: From Petition to Rebellion in Ottoman Vranje', *New Perspectives on Turkey* 53 (2015): 32; Derderian, 'Nation-Making', 11–12.
14. Yaşar Tolga Cora, 'Osmanlı Taşrasındaki Ermeniler Üzerine Olan Tarihyazımında Sınıf Analizinin Eksikliği', *Praksis* 39 (2015): 26–27.
15. Odian, who served as the Undersecretary of Public Works, was one of the members of the drafting commission for the first Ottoman constitution. Robert Devereux, *The First Ottoman Constitutional Period: A Study of the Midhat Constitution and Parliament* (Baltimore: The Johns Hopkins Press, 1963), 259.
16. Lillian Etmekjian, 'The Armenian National Assembly of Turkey and Reform', *Armenian Review* 29, no. 1 (1976): 41.

17. 'First Report on Provincial Oppressions, Submitted to the Sublime Porte in the Name of the Armenian National Assembly', in *Reports on Provincial Oppressions*, 1–8.
18. Etmekjian, 'Armenian National Assembly', 43.
19. 'Second Report on the Oppression of the Armenians in Armenia and Other Provinces of Asiatic Turkey, Presented to the Armenian National Assembly, on the 17th September, 1876', in *Reports on Provincial Oppressions*, 8–57.
20. Astourian, 'Silence of Land', 59–60.
21. 'Second Report', 11–12. See also BOA: ŞD 2401/11, the Armenian Patriarchate to the Council of State, 11 Teşrin-i Sani 1288 (23 November 1872).
22. Ibid.
23. Ibid., 15–16. See also BOA: ŞD 2884/46, the order to the Sivas Province, 25 Zilhicce 1292 (22 January 1876).
24. BOA: DH.MKT 1310/82, the Ministry of the Interior to the Sivas Province, no date. It should be noted that the reports compiled by the Armenian Patriarchate claimed that the commission report suggested the removal of Circassian immigrants from those lands. See 'Second Report', 16.
25. Emphasis original. 'Second Report', 16.
26. Ibid., 16. As noted by Hamed-Troyansky, the land disputes between Armenians and Circassians in Yarhisar intensified during the massacres of 1894–97. The latter seized seven houses belonging to the former, which resulted in violent clashes between the two communities. The local government intervened in order to solve this dispute, relocating the Circassians from Yarhisar to Aziziye and giving Armenians loans through the Agricultural Bank in order to enable them to pay their debts. See Hamed-Troyansky, 'Imperial Refuge', 247–48.
27. 'Second Report', 27.
28. Karekin Vartabed Sırvantsdyants, 'Toros Ahpar Ermenistan Yolcusu', in *Palu-Harput 1878: Çarsancak, Çemişgezek, Çapakçur, Erzincan, Hizan ve Civar Bölgeler*, ed. Arsen Yarman, trans. Sirvart Malhasyan and Arsen Yarman (Istanbul: Derlem Yayınları, 2010), 470–87.
29. 'Second Report', 12.
30. BOA: MVL 638/29, 22 Ağustos 1278 (3 September 1862).
31. BOA: İ.MVL 569/25560, 4 Mart 1283 (16 March 1867); İ.MVL 571/25661, 26 Zilhicce 1283 (1 May 1867).
32. 'Second Report', 13.
33. Ibid., 13–14. See also BOA: ŞD 1454/4, a note (*müzekkere*), 23 Şaban 1289 (26 October 1872), and ŞD 2871/39, the petition sent by Karabet, representative of the Armenian community in Çarsancak, 12 Teşrin-i Evvel 1288 (24 October 1872).
34. Vahé Tachjian, 'Building the "Model Ottoman Citizen": Life and Death in the Region of Harput-Mamüretülaziz (1908–1915)', in *World War I and the End of the Ottomans: From the Balkan Wars to the Armenian Genocide*,

ed. Hans-Lukas Kieser, Kerem Öktem and Maurus Reinkowski (London: I. B. Tauris, 2015), 210–39; Kevork A. Yerevanian, *Badmutyun Charsanjaki Hayots* (Beyrut: Donigian, 1956), 411–40.
35. *Deghegakir Hoghayin Krawmants Hantsnazhoghovoy* [The Report of the Commission on Seizured Lands], vol. 4 (Istanbul: Doghramadjian Dbakragan, 1912), 12–13.
36. 'Second Report', 29. For the original of this document in the Ottoman archives, see BOA: ŞD 2408/27, copy of the memorandum of the Armenian Patriarchate, 24 Ağustos 1290 (5 September 1874).
37. 'Second Report', 29–30.
38. Ibid., 31.
39. Ibid., 32.
40. Ibid., 46–57.
41. BOA: ŞD 2418/17, Council of State to provinces of Erzurum, Diyarbekir, Ankara, Trabzon and Sivas, 17 Cemazeyilevvel 1292 (21 June 1875).
42. The articles of Raffi, written in 1877–80, were compiled as a book under the name *Tajkahayk*. There are three editions of this compilation (Tiflis, 1895; Vienna, 1895 and 1913). In this study, I have used the English translation of this compilation. Raffi, *Tajkahayk*, trans. Ara Stepan Melkonian (London: Taderon Press, 2008).
43. Ronald Grigor Suny, *'They Can Live in the Desert but Nowhere Else': A History of the Armenian Genocide* (Princeton: Princeton University Press, 2015), 75.
44. Raffi, 'Report', in *Tajkahayk*, 54. Raffi's analysis of the Patriarchate reports was first published in the newspaper *Mshak* in 1877.
45. Raffi, 'Report', 53.
46. Ibid., 55.
47. Ibid., 52–53.
48. According to David Gutman, migrants from Eastern provinces had for centuries flocked to Istanbul to find employment. These migrants, who were predominantly male, often worked as porters. Nearly 75,000 migrants from the region migrated to Istanbul in 1867. David Gutman, 'The Political Economy of Armenian Migration from the Harput Region to North America in the Hamidian Era, 1885–1908', in Cora, Derderian and Sipahi, *Ottoman East*, 46.
49. Consul Taylor to Earl Greanville, Erzurum, 4 July 1871, *Turkey*, no. 16 (1877), *Reports by Her Majesty's Diplomatic and Consular Agents in Turkey Respecting the Condition of the Christian Subjects of the Porte: 1868–75* (London: Harrison and Sons, 1877), 56–57.
50. Sinan Dinçer, '"Ya Sev Ya Terket"in Ermenicesi: Osmanlı Devletinde Tabiiyet ve Sınırdışı Uygulamalarından Bir Fasıl', in *Sınır ve Sınırdışı: Türkiye'de Yabancılar, Göç ve Devlete Disiplinlerarası Bakışlar*, ed. Didem Danış and İbrahim Soysüren (Istanbul: Notabene Publications, 2014); Christopher Clay, 'Labour Migration and Economic Conditions in Nineteenth-Century Anatolia', *Middle Eastern Studies* 34, no. 4 (1998): 4.

51. Raffi, 'Report', 51.
52. Talin Suciyan has also argued that, after the Crimean War (1853–56), there was a surge in petitions sent by Armenian peasants regarding land issues. See Suciyan, *Outcasting Armenians*, 63.
53. BOA: MVL 638/29, 22 Ağustos 1278 (3 September 1862).
54. Consul Taylor to the Earl of Clarendon, Erzurum, 19 March 1869, *Turkey*, no. 16 (1877), 26.
55. Sarkis Shmavonian, 'Mikayel Nalbandian and Non-Territorial Armenian Nationalism', *Armenian Review* 36, no. 3 (1983): 35–56.
56. Consul Taylor to Sir H. Elliot, Erzurum, 16 October 1871, *Turkey*, no. 16 (1877), 66.
57. Nilay Özok-Gündoğan, 'The Making of the Modern Ottoman State in the Kurdish Periphery: The Politics of Land and Taxation, 1840–1870' (PhD diss., Binghamton University, 2011), 160.
58. İslamoğlu, 'Property as a Contested Domain', 34. See also Yonca Köksal, '19. Yüzyılda Kuzeybatı Bulgaristan: Sessiz Toprak Reformu', *Toplumsal Tarih* 170 (February 2008): 24–30.
59. For detailed information, see İnalcık, *Tanzimat ve Bulgar Meselesi*; Halil İnalcık, 'Tanzimat'ın Uygulanması ve Sosyal Tepkileri', *Belleten* 27 (1964): 624–90; Pinson, 'Ottoman Bulgaria', 103–46; Huri İslamoğlu, 'Politics of Administering Property: Law and Statistics in the Nineteenth-Century Ottoman Empire', in *Constituting Modernity: Private Property in the East and West* (London: I. B. Tauris, 2004), 276–319. As noted by M. Safa Saraçoğlu, land ownership continued to be an important issue after the uprising and settlement of Caucasian immigrants in Vidin exacerbated the matter. See his *Nineteenth-Century Local Governance in Ottoman Bulgaria: Politics in Provincial Councils* (Edinburgh: Edinburgh University Press, 2018), 6–8.
60. Barbara Jelavich, *History of the Balkans: Eighteenth and Nineteenth Centuries*, vol. 1 (Cambridge: Cambridge University Press, 1983), chap. 7; F. A. K. Yasamee, *Ottoman Diplomacy: Abdülhamid II and the Great Powers, 1878–1888* (Istanbul: The Isis Press, 1996), 13–18; Hakan Yavuz and Peter Sluglett, eds, *The Political and Social Implications for the Ottoman Empire and Its Successor States of the Treaty of Berlin, 1878* (Salt Lake City: University of Utah Press, 2011).
61. Erik Jan Zürcher, *Turkey: A Modern History*, 4th edition (London: I. B. Tauris, 2017), 69–70.
62. 'The Preliminary Treaty of Peace, signed at San Stefano', http://pages.uoregon.edu/kimball/1878mr17.SanStef.trt.htm.
63. 'Treaty of Berlin', http://archive.thetablet.co.uk/article/20th-july-1878/11/the-treaty-of-berlin.
64. Arman J. Kirakossian, *British Diplomacy and the Armenian Question* (London: Gomidas Institute Books, 2003), 74; Fuat Dündar, *Crime of Numbers: The Role of Statistics in the Armenian Question (1878–1918)* (New Brunswick, NJ: Transaction Publishers, 2010), 12.

65. Libaridian, 'Ideology of Armenian Liberation', 168–71.
66. Antaramian, *Brokers of Faith*, 129–30.
67. Etmekjian, 'Armenian National Assembly', 46.
68. Ibid.
69. *Meclis-i Mebusan 1293=1877 Zabıt Ceridesi*, ed. Hakkı Tarık Us, vol. 2 (Istanbul: Vakit Gazetesi Matbaa Kütüphanesi, 1954).
70. Masayuki Ueno, '"For the Fatherland and the State"': Armenians Negotiate the Tanzimat Reforms', *International Journal of Middle East Studies* 45 (2013): 103.
71. Panossian, *Armenians*, 172–73.
72. Ibid., 175.
73. Libaridian, *Modern Armenia*, 66.
74. Dzovinar Derderian, 'Mapping the Fatherland: Artzvi Vaspurakan's Reforms through the Memory of the Past', *Houshamadyan* (16 December 2014), http://www.houshamadyan.org/en/mapottomanempire/vilayet-of-van/kaza-of-van/miscellaneous-scholarly-articles.html. See also Dzovinar Derderian, 'Shaping Subjectivities and Contesting Power through the Image of Kurds, 1860s', in Cora, Derderian and Sipahi, *Ottoman East*, 91–108.
75. Dündar, *Kahir Ekseriyet*, 35. For details on this population census, see Kemal Karpat, 'Ottoman Population Records and the Census of 1881/82–1893', *International Journal of Middle East Studies* 9, no. 3 (1978): 237–74.
76. Libaridian, 'Ideology of Armenian Liberation', 179.
77. François Georgeon, *Sultan Abdülhamid*, trans. Ali Berktay (Istanbul: Homer Kitabevi, 2006), 201–2.
78. Astourian, 'Silence of Land', 62. Hamed-Troyansky has also underscored that, after 1878, the Ottoman state had clear and refined ideas concerning the question of where the immigrants should be settled. See *Empire of Refugees*, 80–81.
79. Libaridian, 'Ideology of Armenian Liberation', 180.
80. Ibid, 180.
81. Antaramian, *Brokers of Faith*, 152–53.
82. Vahan M. Kurkjian, *A History of Armenia* (New York: Armenian General Benevolent Union, 1958), 290–91.
83. Musa Şaşmaz, *British Policy and the Application of Reforms for the Armenians in Eastern Anatolia* (Ankara: Turkish Historical Society Printing House, 2000), 35.
84. BOA: İ.DH 783/63676, Order issued to the commissioner responsible for the Diyarbekir region, 25 March 1295 (6 April 1879).
85. Sir A. H. Layard to the Marquis of Salisbury, 8 August 1879, *Turkey* no. 4 (1880), *Correspondence Respecting the Condition of the Populations in Asia Minor and Syria* (London: Harrison and Sons, 1880), 21.
86. Şaşmaz, *British Policy*, 58; BOA: Y.EE 4/36, a memorandum. There is no date on the document, but its date was catalogued as 29 Zilhicce 1313 (11 June 1896).

87. Pehlivan, 'Beyond the Desert', 98.
88. 'Memorandum', *Turkey*, no. 10 (1879), *Correspondence Respecting the Condition of the Populations in Asia Minor and Syria* (London: Harrison and Sons, 1879), 109–14.
89. Ibid., 112.
90. Ibid.
91. Major Trotter to the Marquis of Salisbury, 16 August 1879, *Turkey*, no. 4 (1880), 44.
92. Major Trotter to the Marquis of Salisbury, 3 October 1879, *Turkey*, no. 4 (1880), 87–88.
93. Acting Vice-Consul Barnham to Major Trotter, 12 September 1880, *Turkey*, no. 6 (1881), *Further Correspondence Respecting the Condition of the Populations in Asia Minor and Syria* (London: Harrison and Sons, 1881), 184.
94. BOA: Y.PRK.A 2/75, 11 February 1297 (23 February 1882).
95. Sir A. H. Layard to the Marquis of Salisbury, 12 June 1879, *Turkey*, no. 10 (1879), 93.
96. Etmekjian, 'Armenian National Assembly', 48. See also Garo Sasuni, *Kürt Ulusal Hareketleri ve 15. yy'dan Günümüze Ermeni Kürt İlişkileri*, trans. Bedros Zartaryan and Memo Yetkin (Istanbul: Med Yayınları, 1992), 150–51.

Chapter 3

Mass Violence and Mass Seizures (1880–1908)

In the last decades of the nineteenth century, vast changes affected the population, politics and socio-economic life in the eastern provinces. The rise of Armenian political parties, the transformation of the relationship between Kurdish tribes and the central government through the formation of the Hamidian Regiments and, most importantly, a series of massacres targeting Armenians led to drastic changes. In this chapter, I will examine how these events affected land disputes, explore the effects of massacres that led to the death, uprooting and migration of hundreds of thousands on landholding patterns and agrarian disputes, and reveal the extent to which mass violence was intertwined with mass dispossession and property transfer.

While it is known that a large number of Armenian properties changed hands in the Hamidian period, the geographical distribution of these transfers has not yet been analysed. These property transfers have either been studied on a local scale or conflated to represent the six eastern provinces as a whole. In this chapter, I will fill this gap in the literature with an extensive analysis. I will discuss the seizure of Armenian properties during and after the massacres of 1894–97, with a particular focus on their geographical pattern and regional differences. Based on correspondence among Ottoman officials, the reports of the Armenian Patriarchate and British consular reports, I will map out the geographical distribution of seizures and the actors involved in them.

This analysis reveals three points about the characteristics of land disputes concerning Armenians in the Hamidian period. First, it shows that there was a significant change in the characteristics and extent of land disputes at that time. As examined in the previous chapter, land disputes concerning Armenians before this period were confined to disputes between local powerholders and Armenian peasants and villagers.

In some of these conflicts, the disputed lands consisted of the common property of village communities – such as pastures and places of harvest. In other conflicts, disputed lands were owned by individual peasants. Yet, land disputes in the Hamidian era also involved Armenians who held vast tracts of land. The seizure of large-scale lands was a significant phenomenon in this period. While most properties seized were agricultural lands, factories, shops and plots in city centres also figured among the properties seized. Another important change is related to the involvement of ordinary Muslim subjects in the seizure of Armenian properties. Thus, the basis of land disputes concerning Armenians shifted from class to ethno-religious differences.

A second important point revealed by this research is the following: while property transfers in the Hamidian era were generally concentrated in the eastern provinces, there also existed several cases outside of these provinces. As will be examined in detail, a significant number of seizures occurred in the Cilicia region, especially in Maraş. Studies regarding the seizure of Armenian properties at that time mostly focus on the eastern provinces and emphasise the role of the Hamidian Regiments in the processes of property transfer. The findings of this study suggest that, while the transfer of Armenian properties was concentrated there, the phenomenon was not exclusive to these provinces and that a variety of actors – including tribal chiefs, local notables, immigrants, religious authorities and ordinary subjects – were involved.

Thirdly, important regional differences existed among the eastern provinces in terms of the transfer of Armenian properties during the Hamidian period. While small-scale land transfers and seizures affecting village communities accompanied the seizure of large plots of land in Muş, property transfers from Armenians to Muslims in Diyarbekir mostly concerned large plots. Thus, even the eastern provinces themselves exhibited significant variation and cannot be lumped together.

The Historical Context

The last decade of the nineteenth century saw radical changes in intercommunal relations and state-society relations in the Ottoman Empire. As noted in Chapter 2, the emergence of the Armenian Question as a question of international diplomacy contributed to the territorialisation of Armenian nationalism at that time. One of the most important developments of this period was the establishment of Armenian political organisations. While they professed different goals and political agendas, all these organisations had a territorial understanding of Armenian nationalism and underscored the link between the population and the land. The first of these organisations, the Armenakan Party, had been established in Van by the disciples of Mgrdich Portukalian, an important figure in the development of the idea of an Armenian fatherland. The Armenakan Party aimed to 'win for the Armenian the right to rule over themselves through revolution'.[1] Another important organisation was the Hunchakian Revolutionary Party, established in Geneva in 1887.[2] As noted by Gerard J. Libaridian, 'territoriality was integral for the success of the Hunchak program of change'.[3] At the time of the party's establishment, the Hunchaks had two main objectives: to promote socialism and an independent Armenia in the eastern provinces. In 1909, after its sixth congress, the party abandoned its claim to an independent Armenia. Another important Armenian political organisation of this period, the Armenian Revolutionary Federation (ARF), was founded in Tiflis in 1890. As noted by Ronald G. Suny, the ARF proposed a programme of autonomy within the Russian and Ottoman empires.[4] As analysed by Libaridian, the Tashnags were more moderate than the Huncaks with respect to the Ottoman East, and independence did not officially become an issue for the Tashnags until 1919. In the ARF's political discourse, freedom was a 'less clearly defined' goal and meant 'liberation from the oppressive political system and an end to Ottoman policies that led to the disintegration of the Armenian economic base'.[5] Thus, from the beginning, land disputes in particular and agrarian problems in general played an important role in the Tashnags' political debates. The rise of these organisations also contributed to the revitalisation of reform debates and the radicalisation of the Armenian Question in the 1890s.

Another novelty in this period was the emergence of a new approach on the part of the Ottoman government. Following the Balkan Crisis and the Treaty of Berlin, through which the Armenian Question emerged as an international matter, the Ottoman government's approach to matters of population and the eastern provinces changed. As noted by Selim Deringil, Ottoman officials and the political elite began to differentiate between 'us' (Muslims) and 'them' (Christians).[6] After 1878, Abdülhamid II sought to establish a direct tie with the country's Muslim population, by reformulating the basis of his legitimacy to rule. He even used his own private properties to strengthen his rule and the territorial sovereignty of the Ottoman state, purchasing state lands in critical locations.[7]

The Ottoman government also attempted to carry out a social engineering project regarding the Kurdish population in the Ottoman East.[8] The most important elements of this initiative, which was directly tied to the sultan, consisted of the establishment of Hamidian Regiments and the Tribal School.[9] In an attempt to re-organise local tribes around a model derived from the Russian Cossacks, Abdülhamid II formed the Hamidian Regiments, which were recruited from among Kurdish tribes, along with other groups such as the Karapapaks under the command of Zeki Pasha.[10] Thousands of Kurdish tribesmen were armed in line with this initiative, and Deringil has noted that this constituted part of a social engineering plan to transform the Kurdish population, on the one hand, and prevent the realisation of the territorial claims of Armenian political organisations, on the other.[11] A couple of years following the establishment of the Hamidian Regiments, the Great Powers issued a memorandum to the Ottoman Empire to implement reforms, and the Armenian Question once more became an international matter.[12] This development coincided with the outbreak of a series of massacres in which thousands of Armenians were killed.[13] The massacres of 1894–97 led to the dispossession and uprooting of thousands of Armenians and affected the demographics in the Ottoman East.[14] The following pages will examine the processes of property transfer that accompanied this wave of mass violence.

Finally, ecological events and their consequences on humans and animals in the region also affected the escalation of tension between different communities. As Zozan Pehlivan has shown, from the mid-nineteenth century to the 1890s, the cycles of a climate pattern called El Niño Southern Oscillations severely impacted the eastern provinces, destroying pastoral lands, increasing animal mortality and causing internal migration.[15] Moreover, severe droughts led to poor harvests, and, starting in the 1870s, occasional famines struck, causing desperate peasants to eat their livestock and, in some cases, migrate to other villages.[16] As Pehlivan and Matthew Ghazarian have noted, ecological events also affected the context of the massacres.[17]

Mass Seizures and the Transformation of the Land Question

Reports prepared by the Armenian Patriarchate serve as an important source for understanding the geographical distribution of property transfers and the ways in which they took place. 'The Commission on Seized Lands',[18] established on the order of the Civil Assembly (*Meclis-i Cismani*, or *K'aghak'agan Zhoghov*) on 29 November 1908 to inquire into the seizures and usurpations of private and communal properties, submitted a four-volume report to the Patriarchate on 7 April 1909. These volumes were published separately between 1910 and 1912.[19] The commission reviewed the documents and lists provided by the Patriarchate and held several meetings. The documents reviewed included notices of seizure and usurpation sent to the Patriarchate from different localities during the Hamidian period.

The first volume of these reports lists the churches, monasteries, cemeteries and church properties seized at that time. The second volume consists of a list of significant lands belonging to Armenian individuals, which had been seized. The usurped lands listed in the second volume were either larger than 100 *dönüm*s (10 hectares) or worth more than 100 liras. The third volume lists seizures that affected more than three Armenian individuals and also includes data regarding the seizures of entire villages. The fourth and last volume of the reports presents a list of properties seized due to various forms of debt, as well as seizures carried out before the Hamidian period.

It should be noted that, while they provide rich information on more than 7,000 cases, the reports do not exhaustively list all Armenian properties that were forcefully seized in this period. For example, cases in which properties measured less than 100 *dönüm*s or valuated at less than 100 liras were excluded, unless they were owned by religious institutions or a group of Armenians. As will be seen in Chapter 5, this omission was criticised by some Armenian intellectuals who accused the Patriarchate of reducing the scope of the land question by excluding numerous small-scale cases from its reports. Moreover, the reports list cases that had not been resolved at the time the reports were prepared. Thus, they do not contain data regarding seizures that had been resolved by 1908.

The reports do not provide uniform data regarding the size or value of seized properties. The acreage of land was variously specified in *dönüm*, *arşın*, or *çap*. In some cases, the reports only provide information regarding the value of lands. In others, the reports' authors used vague statements, claiming that the 'lands of all villagers' or the 'lands of most villagers' had been seized, but without specifying the number of claimants. Thus, the most uniform data concerned the number of units, and I used these data to prepare the maps included here.

Finally, the facts presented in the reports are open to debate. From the Ottoman correspondence, it is understood that in several places the authorities did not carry out a title deed registration process.[20] The reports state that in some of these places Armenians held title deeds or possessed edicts (*ferman*) or official documents of sale (*hüccet*). I was unable to determine whether these documents were title deeds (*tapu*) or deeds of possession (*tasarruf senedi*). Despite these shortcomings, the reports constitute an important source for understanding the geographical distribution of seizures, the actors involved in property transfers and the effects of the local power structure on the ways in which Armenian properties were seized.

These reports have been briefly mentioned in several studies on agrarian relations in the Ottoman East and the land question;[21] however, their data have remained under-examined since no studies analyse the details of the cases in these reports. The following section will offer a detailed examination of this important source.

THE SCOPE AND GEOGRAPHICAL DISTRIBUTION OF PROPERTY TRANSFERS

In his study of agrarian relations in the Ottoman Empire and the Armenian Question, Stephan Astourian has pointed out the rural character of property seizures and noted that seizures concerning Armenians mostly involved agricultural lands.[22] The findings of this research support the argument that the transfer of properties from Armenians in the Hamidian period was predominantly a rural matter. Among all the cases documented in the Patriarchate reports, only one factory was seized in the Hamidian period. This was a flour factory in Kızılağaç, Sivas, belonging to Mgrdich Chilian. The factory was valued at 1,200 liras, and it was seized by an accountant employed in the Ottoman administration, Hamdi Bey, as recompense for Chilian's debt of 300 liras.[23] Twenty-six shops were listed among the seized properties in the reports, six of which were located in Çüngüş (Diyarbekir), five in Palu, five in Gürün (Sivas) and nine in Osmaniye (Adana). Furthermore, an indeterminate number of shops belonging to seventeen Armenians in Behesni (Besni, Adıyaman) had been seized, along with agricultural lands, houses and gardens belonging to the same persons.[24] No artisan workshop figured among the seized properties listed in the reports. Except for the factory, shops, houses and a small number of plots in city or town centres, all the listed properties were related to agricultural production and animal husbandry. They included agricultural lands, pastures, olive gardens, olive mills, vineyards, fruit and vegetable gardens, sheep pens, alfalfa fields (*yoncalık*), haystacks, water sources and flour mills.[25]

Figure 3.1 shows the distribution of seized lands that were either larger than 100 *dönüm*s or worth more than 100 liras. As the report does not provide uniform data regarding all the cases, it is not possible to draw a comparison based on the size or aggregate value of seized properties. Thus, Figure 3.1 was prepared based on the number of seized units.

As illustrated here, a large proportion – 92 per cent – of these lands were agricultural fields. Yet, there were also several seized pastures located in Muş, Erzurum and Sivas. The number of seized pastures in these centres amounted to seventy-four, fifty and twenty-two, respectively.

Armenians and Land Disputes in the Ottoman Empire

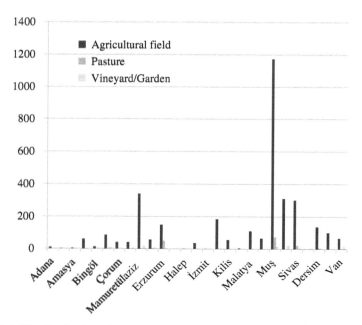

Figure 3.1 The distribution of seized agricultural lands larger than 100 *dönüm*s (10 hectares) or worth more than 100 liras. Source: *Deghegakir*, vol. 2.

Raising livestock was an important economic activity in these provinces; as pointed out by Şevket Pamuk, important regional differences existed among the eastern provinces in terms of their socio-economic activities.[26] The distribution of the types of land seized in the post-1890 period reflects these differences.

The Patriarchate reports also claimed farms to have been among the seized properties. Farms consisted of large plots of land generally used for market-oriented production.[27] The seizure of this type of property belonging to Armenians was a novelty of the Hamidian period, because it differed from the processes of property transfer that took place before the period (see Chapter 2). The seizures and land disputes concerning Armenians in the Tanzimat period concerned properties owned by the small-scale peasantry, religious institutions and village communities. Conversely, a total of sixteen farms were seized in the Hamidian period, distributed among the provinces as follows: Kastamonu (1), Bursa (1), İzmid (1), Amasya (1), Sivas (3), Adana (2), Maraş (1), Haleb (1), Erzurum (1), Van (2) and Bitlis (2). One seized farm in Van was located in Erciş and belonged to the Mendzop Monastery. Other farms were either owned by individuals or by village communities.[28] The size of these farms varied between 600 and 6,050 *dönüm*s.

Map 3.1 illustrates the geographical distribution of forcefully seized lands larger than 100 *dönüm*s or worth more than 100 liras. Due to a lack of comparable data regarding the size of all the lands mentioned in the reports, the quantification is based on the number of seized units. This map elucidates the forceful seizure of all kinds of rural lands belonging to Armenian individuals, including gardens, pastures, vineyards, farms and agricultural fields.

The forced transfer of property in the Hamidian period has often been discussed as an exclusively eastern phenomenon confined to the six provinces.[29] Although the data presented in the Patriarchate's reports show that the transfer of Armenian properties at that time was concentrated in the eastern provinces, the seizure of Armenian properties was not confined to this region. As seen in Map 3.1, the extent of forceful seizures of significant lands – that is, seizures concerning lands larger than 100 *dönüm*s or worth more than 100 liras – was even greater in Maraş than in central Diyarbekir. This indicates that the Cilicia region was also affected by forced property transfers during the Hamidian era.

The confiscation of the Telan farm belonging to the Armenian Catholicosate of Sis in the district of Kozan in northeast Adana serves as another example in this regard. The farm consisted of 10,000 *dönüm*s of land, half of which was used agriculturally to provide the needs of the monastery; it was confiscated by the state. The farmland was designated as empty; later on, Muslim refugees were settled there. The Catholicos and the Armenian Patriarchate pushed for the removal of the settlers from the land and its return to the monastery. Eventually, the Sublime Porte accepted the petition and ordered its return, but the local government refused to implement this decision.[30] As historian Bedross Der Matossian has noted, after the 1908 revolution, the Telan Farm conflict caused friction between Muslims and Armenians, leading to a violent clash that resulted in the killing of a few of the former.[31] Thus, the Cilicia region was not immune to the land conflict either.

In several cases of seizure in the eastern provinces, the land disputes were related to the resettlement of Muslim immigrants fleeing territories lost by the Ottoman Empire, as well as direct seizures carried out by such immigrants. Immigrants from the Balkans were involved in a number of seizures in Western Anatolia and the Cilicia region. In some cases, the transfer of Armenian properties to Muslim immigrants was carried out via state institutions. For instance, in Erzurum's Xozlu village (Alınteri), 4,000 *dönüm*s of agricultural land and pastures belonging to Armenian peasants were seized by the government and redistributed to Muslim immigrants.[32] In other cases, local notables or religious authorities acted

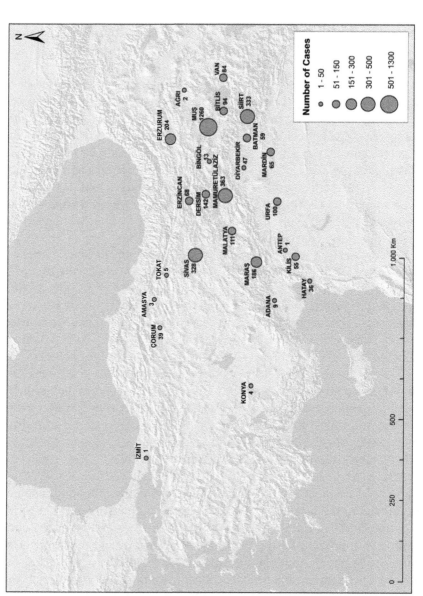

Map 3.1 Geographical distribution of forcefully seized lands larger than 100 *dönüms* or worth more than 100 liras.

as intermediaries in the transfer of properties to immigrants. For example, a chestnut grove in Gemgem-Bursa (the city centre neighbourhood of Işıklar today) belonging to Hripsime Melkonian was forcefully seized by Sheikh Sabit[33] and given to immigrants.[34] There also existed cases in which the immigrants themselves directly seized lands. In Kastamonu, Ereğli, Abhaz/Georgian immigrants forcefully seized a farm of 3,000 *dönüm*s, three houses, three haylofts and one bakery belonging to Kevork Enfiejian. While Enfiejian held a title deed and managed to obtain a court order for the return of these properties, the order was not implemented.[35]

Sometimes, the purpose of the lands in question changed in the course of the transfer. For example, the agricultural lands of the Armenian peasants in the village of Nacarlı Nalvirani (Dörtyol-Hatay) in Adana were occupied by immigrants from Rumelia in 1901. The reports state that the immigrants destroyed the harvested crops on the ground and overnight built seventy wooden houses there. The immigrants expanded the lands which they occupied in the years that followed, and while an investigation commission was formed in 1905, the case remained unresolved until the 1910s.[36]

Usurpers in Central Anatolia were Karapapak and Circassian immigrants from the Caucasus, along with local Kurds and Turks. Considering the seizures in Central Anatolia listed in the Patriarchate reports, it can be said that the Karapapak Major Hüseyin Pasha of the Hamidian Regiments played an important role in the property transfers in this region. Employing physical violence, he and his men in 1891 had begun seizing lands, houses and pastures belonging to sixty-two Armenians in Mancılık, Üçtepe and Kargakale in Sivas.[37] Hüseyin Pasha and his brother-in-law were also involved in the seizure of lands and pastures belonging to the Surp Toros Monastery in Mancılık.[38] He also seized the Canlıveran farm belonging to the Karamanugian family of Mancılık. This farm contained 167 plots of agricultural fields, twenty-one houses, pastures and hayfields, amounting to 1830 *dönüm*s and worth 3,000 liras in 1895. At that time, there were 1,850 sheep, 146 cattle and 345 *kile*s of wheat on the farm. This seizure was carried out under threat of violence, but Hüseyin Pasha also paid 13,000 piasters to complete the sales procedure (*ferâğ*).[39]

In addition to seizing several properties in line with his individual interests, Hüseyin Pasha played a crucial role in the resettlement of immigrants in Sivas. Even in cases in which he was not the direct usurper of the lands in dispute, he was party to the legal proceedings. For example, lands in the village of Kızıldikme were claimed by the government and used for the resettlement of immigrants. The case was taken to the civil court of Sivas, and although the lands had been taken by the government, Hüseyin

Pasha legally represented the resettled immigrants.[40] Apart from these immigrants and Hüseyin Pasha – whose activities were concentrated in a particular part of Sivas Province – several ordinary subjects, local notables and local officials were involved in property transfers in Central Anatolia.

As noted above, a great portion of the seizures listed in the reports of the Patriarchate focused on the eastern provinces. A detailed examination of these cases indicates that local powerholders were influential in these property transfers. In Van, several local powerholders played key roles; the seizures of Emin Pasha and Hüseyin Pasha from the Haydaranlı tribe and Sheikh Hamid Pasa from Arvas exemplify this. While Emin and Hüseyin Pashas owed their influence to their positions in the Hamidian Regiments and the men under their control, the local power of Sheikh Hamid Pasha was mostly the result of his status as a *seyyid* (descendant of the Prophet) and his religious authority. While the usurpers in Van were not confined to these three men, they were the ones to take the lion's share of the properties transferred from Armenians in Van and its environs.

Emin and Hüseyin Pashas both acquired enormous swaths of land after the massacres. According to the Patriarchate reports, Emin Pasha and his immediate family acquired vast tracts around Erciş in Van.[41] His sons, his brothers and his wife Cevher Hanım were also involved in the process. Cevher Hanım was among the few women[42] appearing in the reports, who were specifically mentioned as direct usurpers. She was noted to have destroyed the church in Amizon (Karlıyayla) in the district of Erciş, and to have forcefully seized five pastures (700 *çap*s) and several agricultural fields (4,000 *çap*s) on her own.[43]

The Armenian Patriarchate also submitted several memoranda (*takrir*s) to the Sublime Porte about seizures carried out by Emin Pasha. One of these reports, submitted on 11 September 1899, claimed that Emin Pasha had seized lands and agricultural fields belonging to peasants by 'exploiting the situation of people who were in desperate circumstances' because of the massacres.[44] According to this memorandum, Emin Pasha had appropriated vast lands in Erçiş, pushed peasants into forced labour and had not seen any reaction or intervention from the local government. Following this memorandum, the Inspection Commission (*Tesrî'-i Muamelât Komisyonu*), which had been established in 1894 to manage the reform process, sent an order to the local government, instructing them to investigate the situation and find a just solution to the problem.[45] According to two other memoranda submitted in June 1907, Emin Pasha forcibly settled his men in the village of Asraf (Bayramlı) in the district of Erciş, seizing a church, houses, lands and pastures belonging to the villagers. The Armenian Patriarchate submitted another memorandum in September, informing the Porte that seized properties had not been returned to their owners, despite an order by the governor of Van. The last memorandum also stated that Emin Pasha had increased his oppression of the Armenian population because he was angered by the Armenians' attempts to take back their lands.[46]

His actions show that the seizure of Armenian properties in the Hamidian period was not confined to the transfer of properties from Armenians to local powerholders during the massacres. Emin Pasha was involved in several seizures carried out after the Porte had established special commissions for the investigation of land disputes after the Treaty of Berlin and in the aftermath of the massacres. In other words, the cases in which he was involved demonstrate that property transfers from Armenians to local powerholders were not confined to the time of the massacres but extended across the entire Hamidian period. Another important point regarding the case of Emin Pasha is that the governor of Van had made the decision to return the lands to the Armenians, but this was not put into action.[47] This highlights the fact that in some regions the local authorities lacked the capacity to enforce the return of seized properties to their original owners. As will be examined in the next chapter, what hindered the return of these properties was the direct intervention of Zeki Pasha and the sultan.

Another leading figure in Van was Haydaranlı Hüseyin Pasha.[48] The properties which he seized were concentrated around Adilcevaz, but he was equally involved in cases in southern Erzurum and eastern Bitlis.[49] Agricultural fields, olive oil presses, pastures and hayfields counted among the properties he seized. He also destroyed the church in the village of Grakom of Erciş (today Eskikonak in the Patnos district of Ağrı) and transformed it into his palace.[50] Moreover, he used the stones of a church in the Patnos district for the construction of a mansion. Faced with Hüseyin Pasha's oppression, the local Armenians began to emigrate to Russia. The grand vizier sent an order to the governor of Van to prevent this exodus.[51] According to another memorandum of the Patriarchate dated June 1907, Hüseyin Pasha also used the lands and houses which he had seized to settle the members of his tribe.[52] A further important figure in the seizure of Armenian properties in Van was Sheikh Hamid Pasha of Arvasi,[53] who seized large plots of agricultural land, pastures and gardens in the vicinity of Başkale. While most of these seizures were carried out through coercion, some among the cases in which he was involved were also due to small debts. His case exemplifies forced property transfers by religious authorities in the region.[54]

Map 3.2 shows the geographical distribution of land seizures with communal effects, as listed in the third volume of the Patriarchate reports.

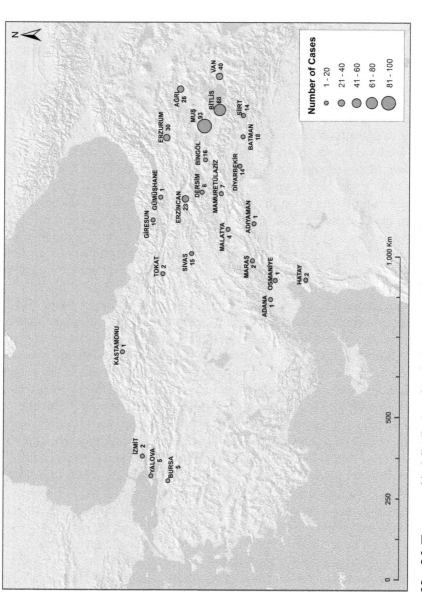

Map 3.2 The geographical distribution of land seizure cases with communal effects.

The reports' authors used the term 'communal seizures' to describe cases that concerned the seizure of properties belonging to more than three individuals.[55] As will be analysed in Chapters 5 and 6, the disruption of the demographics in the Ottoman East became a serious concern for Armenian political organisations in the years following the massacres. While the loss of properties larger than 100 *dönüm*s or worth more than 100 liras entailed loss of wealth and dispossession, the uprooting of the peasantry also brought with it the risk of the erosion of the Armenian population in the 'Armenian fatherland'. As examined in Chapter 2, this concern began to be raised by Armenian intellectuals such as Raffi in the 1870s and in subsequent years became increasingly important for Armenian political and religious institutions. Thus, seizures that affected groups of individuals (and, in some cases, entire villages) were separated from the others, and the Armenian political and religious elite placed special significance on them.

As seen in Map 3.2, land seizure cases with communal effects were primarily concentrated in Muş and Bitlis. There were also a significant number of seizures with communal effects in Van, Erzurum, Ağrı and Erzincan. The inconsistent nature of the data provided in the report makes it impossible to draw a comparison based on the number of persons affected. Indeed, in many cases, the number of individuals whose properties were seized was not specified, and they simply were referred to as 'villagers', 'half of the villagers' or 'all villagers'. According to the report, in forty-three cases, the properties of 'almost all' or 'all lands of the villagers' had been seized. Three of these cases occurred in Erzurum,[56] and one in Van.[57] The remaining thirty-nine cases had happened in different parts of Bitlis. It is not possible to determine whether entire village communities were directly affected in those cases where the claimants were merely defined as Armenians or villagers. Nonetheless, the available data indicate that this was a widespread occurrence in Bitlis Province. In Bitlis and its environs, the actors involved in seizures during which whole Armenian villages were dispossessed included the Balaklı Kurds, who acquired dozens of villages, especially in 1908; Sheikh Seyyid Ali of Hizan; Kurds from the Dermakan, Zilan[58] and Reşkotan tribes;[59] Hüseyin Pasha from the Haydaranlı tribe; Mehmed Said,[60] Beşar[61] and Rıza Bey[62] from the Hasenanlı tribe; Menteşezade Yusuf Ağa;[63] and various individuals from Musa Bey's family in Mutki, including Kasım, Cezayir and Fethullah Beys.[64] All in all, Circassians, the above-mentioned Kurdish tribes, urban notables and religious authorities were all involved in the process of property transfer in Bitlis province.

The properties seized in the Hamidian period also consisted of agricultural lands, pastures, mills and cemeteries belonging to churches and monasteries. Map 3.3 shows the geographical distribution of such church and monastery properties seized or destroyed. Buildings not burned or torn down were often used for non-commercial purposes such as mansions or mosques. As these properties belonged to the Armenian community rather than to individuals, the Patriarchate placed special importance on their seizure and submitted the report on these cases to the Porte earlier than on the others.

The findings of my research indicate crucial differences within the eastern provinces in terms of the processes of property transfer during the Hamidian period. As a comparison of Maps 3.1 and 3.2 demonstrates, while the seizure of large-scale agricultural properties constituted an important phenomenon in the provinces of Mamuretülaziz and Sivas, this was not the case for seizures with communal effects – in other words, those that directly led to the dispossession of small-scale peasants. The situation differed in Muş, where the seizure of large plots of land was accompanied by numerous seizures with communal effects.

Data derived from the Patriarchate reports regarding Diyarbekir Province reveal a strikingly low number of seizures in comparison with the number of the province's Armenian population. Another important point regarding Diyarbekir is that a significant number of the lands were large-scale properties. Almost half of all seized properties larger than 100 *dönüm*s or worth more than 100 liras in Diyarbekir were located in Palu.[65] A significant example in Diyarbekir is the seizure of the properties of the Sherigjian family, which shows that in localities such as these, large landowners also lost extensive amounts of land: in 1895, Faki Hasan forcefully seized thirty-five agricultural fields comprising 2,800 *dönüm*s and belonging to the Sherigjian family in Beşiri. Milli İbrahim Pasha seized 100 plots of the Sherigjians' agricultural fields in Salmeköy, Siverek, in 1895. Milli İbrahim Pasha had also seized sixty-five plots of agricultural lands comprised of 10,000 *dönüm*s belonging to the same family in Siverek, Deşiköy.[66] These findings show that there were significant regional differences among the eastern provinces in terms of the processes of property transfer during the Hamidian period.

The Means of Property Transfer in the Hamidian Period

On 29 March 1896, Rauf Bey, the governor of Erzurum Province, informed the Sublime Porte about complaints regarding seizures carried out by Hasenanlı tribesmen and Emin, Hüseyin and Hacı Timur Pashas from the Haydaranlı tribe. This telegram stated that reports had been received regarding the forceful transfer of lands by Kurdish tribesmen

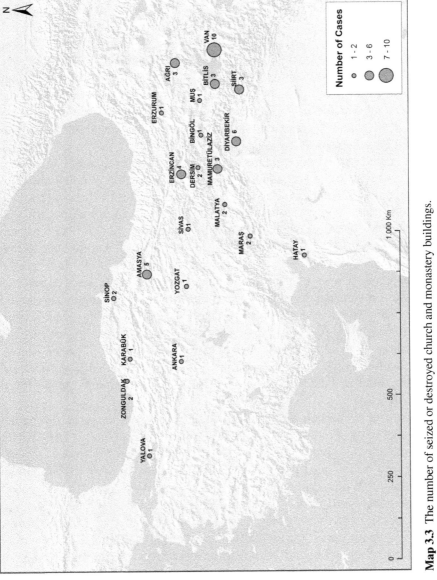

Map 3.3 The number of seized or destroyed church and monastery buildings.

who in return promised protection to the Armenians. Rauf Bey warned that such complaints would attract the attention of the European press and show the Ottoman Empire in a negative light.[67] Consequently, several title deeds acquired by Hasenanlı tribesmen were returned to their owners.[68] Regarding the issue, the Commander in Chief (*Serasker*) cautioned that, if the government was to appoint a commission for the resolution of such disputes in the future, a military official needed to be on the commission. In their report, the members of an investigation commission led by Şefik Bey concluded that the title deeds would only be returned to the claimants if they could prove that they had been taken by trickery. If the timing and manner by which the title deeds had changed hands could not be determined, or if the illegitimacy of the transaction was debatable, the cases would be delegated to the local courts.[69]

As noted by several scholars, property transfer via threat or use of force was common in the Hamidian period.[70] According to the calculations of Kegham Der Garabedian, the distribution of the sizes of forcefully seized lands by province was as follows: 100,000 acres in Erzurum, 200,000 in Harput, 80,000 in Sivas, 200,000 in Diyarbekir, 100,000 in Van and 350,000 in Bitlis – 1,030,000 acres in total.[71] Several examples show that such seizures did not begin with the massacres of 1894–97 but became widespread as a wave of mass violence emerged. Brute force alone was not the only means by which Armenian properties changed hands and by which Armenian peasants were dispossessed in the Hamidian period. Some properties were seized to collect debts, and other properties the peasants had to sell because of the desperation caused by the massacres. Especially in such transfers, a series of developments, such as the commodification of land and the monetisation of the economy, also played important roles.

Another phenomenon that contributed to the dispossession of Armenian peasants in the Hamidian era was cattle rustling. As noted by Janet Klein, among others, some Kurdish tribes in the Ottoman East were historically known for raids carried out against settled Kurdish and Armenian peasants.[72] While raids themselves were not new, their intensity and number increased during the Hamidian period. This situation prevented peasants from cultivating their fields and pushed them out of their villages. Oxen were important for agricultural production in Anatolia. As noted by Çağlar Keyder and Şevket Pamuk, peasants in Anatolia depended on oxen for agricultural production, especially for ploughing, which into the twentieth century was still carried out mostly by ancient methods.[73] The seizure of oxen in various localities prevented cultivation by small-scale peasants. In some cases, the oxen were found and returned; however, the theft of oxen was so widespread that British consular staff came to question the value of providing oxen as relief for Armenian peasants. Francis E. Crow, vice-consul in Bitlis, noted that the oxen which they had provided were periodically stolen. Thus, according to Crow, such relief activity was neither sustainable nor meaningful.[74] This example shows that, even if not directly forced into handing over the documents showing their usufruct rights or ownership, cultivation became impossible for many Armenian peasants in the eastern provinces following the massacres. This situation contributed to the escalation of migration and emigration.

A careful examination of the cases listed in the reports of the Patriarchate reveals that threat or use of force and raids constituted not the only means of property transfer in the Hamidian period. Map 3.4 shows the geographical distribution of Armenian properties seized for debts. In some cases, properties were seized by using a combination of methods. In other words, in several cases use of force and debt relations were both in effect during the transfer of property. The rise of land disputes stemming from debt relations was a phenomenon directly related to the commodification of land in the late-nineteenth-century Ottoman Empire. The classical regime of land tenure, which remained in effect until the nineteenth century, did not allow for the mortgaging of land. Thus, land could not be seized as repayment for debts. As will be examined below, the transformation of the regime of land tenure affected the processes of property transfer in the Hamidian era, and numerous lands began to be seized due to debt.[75]

As seen in Map 3.4, seizures for debt were far more significant in Muş than in any other district or province. Almost all property transfers due to debt in Muş were related to the practice of *selef/selem* – that is, a specific debt relation. Kegham Der Garabedian has stated that *selef* was an illegal practice and a type of usury. He has defined *selef* as a credit of 25 piasters, obliging the borrower to provide one sheep or one *kile* (bushel) of wheat after seven or eight months. He has noted that, on average, the worth of one sheep or one *kile* of wheat amounted to 45 piasters. This value could reach up to 100–150 piasters, depending on the harvest and annual economic trends. If this sum was not given to the creditor on time, the amount to be paid by the borrower doubled each year. Interestingly, *selef* had almost been forgotten by the 1890s. While acknowledging that this particular form of credit had historically been used in the region, Garabedian has underscored that the use of the *selef* boomed with the introduction of new tax collectors.[76] According to Safrastian, the dragoman in charge of the vice-consulate of Britain in Bitlis, *selef* had been introduced to the Muş region by Circassian immigrants and was soon taken up by local Kurds. Safrastian has also highlighted that the collection

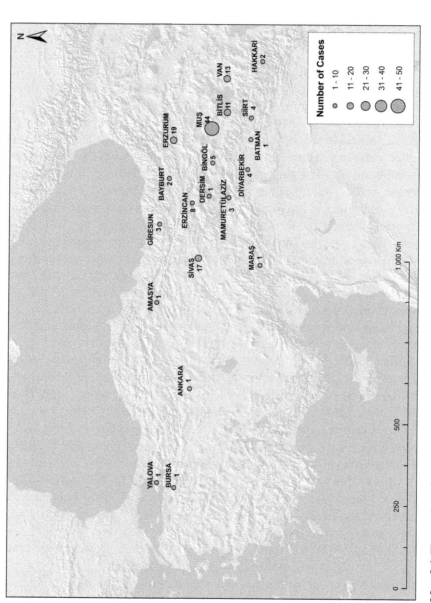

Map 3.4 The number of properties seized for debt.

of monetary taxes pushed peasants into taking credit by means of *selef*.[77] Thus, the expansion of this practice was related to the monetisation of the economy in the region and the transformation of the tax collection regime.

No properties in the reports of the Patriarchate were seized for *selef* debt, except in Bitlis.[78] This supports the argument that there existed important local differences among the eastern provinces in terms of property transfer from Armenians in the Hamidian period.

Another form of property transfer was seizures related to credit from the Agricultural Bank (*Ziraat Bank*).[79] The reports mention a few examples of this kind of property transfer. One case was related to the three agricultural fields of one Avedis Avedisian in Kiği – consisting of 200 *dönüm*s and valued at 800 kuruş – that were confiscated by the bank in 1906. Another case cited in the reports concerned Garabed Vartanian's 300 *dönüm*s of agricultural fields worth 200 liras in Hınıs, Erzurum, appropriated by the bank in exchange for his debt of 30 liras.[80] The memorandum that the Armenian Patriarchate submitted to the Sublime Porte on 9 August 1901 indicates that in some cases the directors of the local branches of the Agricultural Bank participated in these property transfers. It states that the Kurdish tribes who wanted to settle in Armenian villages bought the lands of Armenian peasants who were in debt to the bank at low prices. In one such transaction, the relations between Kurdish tribesmen and Hilmi Efendi, the director of the local branch of the Agricultural Bank, played an important role. Takurlu Osman bought several plots in the village of Azare for 18 liras and settled eighteen families and 14,000 sheep in the village. The Armenian Patriarchate demanded a resolution to this dispute, stating that the peasants would perish and be scattered if their lands were seized in such a way.[81] In this case, the Inspection Commission sent an order for the governor of Van to investigate.[82]

Problems regarding tax collection had figured among the issues raised by the Patriarchate and the Armenian political elite since the Tanzimat period. A note sent by the British consul in Van in 1907 indicates that problems regarding tax collection contributed to the impoverishment of Armenian peasants and the process of property transfer in the region after the massacres of 1894–97. The consul noted that …

> … the new vali has been collecting arrears of taxes among the villages in this vilayet with great severity and in a quite illegal manner. These arrears were nearly all incurred in the years immediately succeeding the massacres when the villagers were penniless and in many cases were not even in the country, at that time the government did not collect these taxes and in many cases it was believed that they had been remitted, now, these arrears are being collected and in cases where the money is not produced at once the collectors seize any

articles they find and sell them at low prices to various Kurds and moneylenders who accompany them, in many cases illegal articles have been thus sold i. e. oxen for ploughing, seed corn, beds[,] cooking utensils etc. and in villages where the people are dependent on fruit farming, the fruit trees have been ruthlessly cut down and sold for absurd prices as firewood.[83]

As this example suggests, it was not just mass violence and raids that made rural life hard for Armenian peasants in the Ottoman East during the Hamidian period. Problems related to the collection of taxes amplified the pressure that they felt and contributed to property transfer.[84]

Another important practice related to property transfer in this period consisted of *miribalık/marabalık*, of which there existed two forms. First, the term was used to define a share-cropping relation in which the proprietors of land had tenants cultivate their land in exchange for a certain percentage of the production. The costs of agricultural tools, animals and seeds used in the cultivation were deducted from the share of the *maraba*.[85] After losing their lands, many Armenian peasants in the eastern provinces found themselves in this situation. For example, according to the reports of the Patriarchate, an Armenian named Parsamian – whose lands (50 *dönüm*s) and pastures (30 *dönüm*s) in Khaçköy (Başbudak) in the district of Tercan, worth 200 liras, had been forcefully seized by Ali Haydar, Rüsdem and Yusuf Beys – found himself labouring as a *maraba* in Pasin (Pasinler, Erzurum).[86] The other form of *marabalık* was to lend money to peasants who possessed small-scale plots of land. In Armenian political debates and analyses, the term *marabalık* was usually employed to denote this second form. Garabedian has explained *marabalık* as the mortgaging of agricultural tools or animals belonging to a landowning borrower in exchange for a particular sum of cash, giving the lender the right to half of the harvest. Garabedian has noted that, in the past, lenders in this form of *marabalık* had not attempted to take control of debtors' lands. He has argued that lenders began to demand the mortgaging of lands over the century's last decades, highlighting the transformation of this form of *marabalık* at the end of the nineteenth century.[87] Indeed, the nature of *marabalık* agreements began to change with the commodification of land in the Ottoman Empire, and this transformation contributed to the processes of property transfer.

During the massacres of 1894–97, thousands of Armenians fled their villages to save their lives. In some cases, the local populations, especially Kurdish tribes, compelled the Armenians to abandon their houses and lands and appropriated them. In other cases, they also forcibly prevented the return of Armenians. For instance, in 1896, in the aftermath of an outbreak of violence against Armenians in Maraş, several Armenians returned to their villages. But Turkish peasants forcibly prevented their stay by blaming them for setting two Turkish houses on fire. According to the British consul, 'the whole affair was plotted by the Turks in order by terrifying the Armenians to prevent their being reinstated to compel them to abandon their properties and lands to the profit of the former'.[88]

The impact of the massacres on the seizure of lands was evident in the case of Tadem, a village in the Mamuretülaziz province. In 1895, Hacı Bey and his family played an active role in organising the massacre of 270 Armenians in the village.[89] During the massacres, Hacı Bey's son Ahmed and his brother Hafız seized numerous Armenian properties in the region.[90] In some instances, the houses and shops belonging to Armenians were burned and destroyed during the massacres, and this situation compelled them to flee to other provinces or abroad. German missionary and intellectual Johannes Lepsius stated that 2,493 towns and villages were plundered during the massacres of 1894–97.[91] In the province of Erzurum, including Erzincan and Bayburt, 11,173 houses and shops were looted during the unrest in the months of October and November 1895. In Harput, thousands were killed and 8,000 houses and shops were plundered and burned.[92] In Aintab, almost all Armenian-owned businesses were looted, and the houses of Armenians were also pillaged during the massacres.[93] In parts of the province of Diyarbekir, Armenians' houses were set on fire, and local Kurds forced Armenians to 'make over their lands to them on condition of rebuilding their houses for them'.[94] According to Jelle Verheij, more than 900 workshops and shops were burned to the ground.[95]

The Armenian Patriarchate applied to the Sublime Porte concerning the lands of Armenian peasants from the Boğazkesen and Çakmak villages of Van Province, who had to flee from their villages after the massacres. The peasants had begun returning to their villages, but their lands had been seized by Kurds from neighbouring villages. The Patriarchate asked for the return of these lands to the peasants, stating that they would otherwise die of starvation. Following this memorandum, the Inspection Commission sent an order to the provinces of Erzurum, Bitlis, Mamuretülaziz, Sivas and Diyarbekir to ensure the right to life and property of all Ottoman subjects and to prevent such attacks.[96] One year later, the Armenian Patriarchate sent another memorandum regarding this matter, noting that the Armenian peasants of Boğazkesen and Çakmak, along with many others in the province of Van, had not received back their lands and that their previous appeals had remained unsuccessful. Responding to this issue, the governor of Van claimed that security had been established in the villages of Boğazkesen and Çakmak and that measures for the resettlement of the villagers had been taken. However, the governor also informed the Minister of the Interior that he had contacted the Hamidian Regiments to remove Nimet Agha and his men who had settled in the village of Hezare.[97] However, the governor's telegram did not clarify whether the land and fields had been returned to their owners. Moreover, seizures of Armenian properties continued in the years following the massacres. For example, in 1901 Hamidian Haydar and his Cibranlı tribesmen appropriated 156 agricultural fields (2,100 *dönüm*s) and forty-seven buildings belonging to the peasants of the village of Akrag (Demirkapı) in Bulanık, who had fled four years earlier.[98]

Two articles of the Land Code complicated the issue of return for Armenians who had been scattered after the massacres. As discussed in Chapter 1, according to Article 68 of the Land Code, the title deeds of *miri* lands not cultivated for three consecutive years became invalid, except for cases in which the lands could not be cultivated for unusual reasons, such as floods. Another exceptional reason was non-cultivation due to being a prisoner of war. Another article of the Land Code that complicated the situation of Armenians dispersed around the region after the massacres consisted of Article 78, which recognized the prescriptive rights of those who cultivated state or *mevkufe* lands for ten years without dispute. In such cases, occupiers who based their claims on prescriptive rights were able to register themselves as the owners of these lands.[99] These two articles contributed to the rise of land disputes concerning Armenians in the Hamidian period. In the absence of their Armenian cultivators, the lands were either not cultivated or were invaded by neighbours who managed to acquire prescriptive rights to the disputed lands.

Apart from these two articles, an imperial order was also adopted in 1901, addressing the issue of tax arrears on lands allocated to immigrants.[100] Ellinor Morack has highlighted that this order introduced the term '*emval-i metruke*' (abandoned properties), which indicated that the land was still 'owned by those who left it'.[101] The order waived the tax arrears of the owners of *mahlul* land, which had been distributed for free to immigrants. Morack has argued that this order might be linked to the massacres of 1894–97, as 'land of people killed in those years must have become mahlul from 1898 onwards'.[102] As will be discussed in Chapter 5, following the 1908 revolution, Armenians began to return to their hometowns and to reclaim their lands, while the Patriarchate started to challenge the claim that these lands were *mahlul*, underlining that these people had fled because of violence and had not left their lands voluntarily.

Conclusion

Following the consolidation of the Hamidian regime, there occurred important changes in the extent and character of land disputes concerning Armenians. As examined in the previous chapter, the Tanzimat period witnessed several land disputes concerning Armenian peasants and village communities. The Hamidian period then saw a significant increase in the number of seizures and transfers concerning such properties. With the massacres and uprooting of various Armenian communities in the Ottoman East, the scale of the problem expanded enormously.

A second important difference concerns the characteristics of these disputes. The disputes of the previous era had mostly been between Armenian cultivators and local powerholders. In other words, class rather than ethnic or religious differences marked the divide among the parties to these earlier disputes. In the Hamidian period, local powerholders such as tribal chiefs, local notables, sheikhs and local notables continued to take part in these seizures. However, in this period, the group who forcefully seized Armenian properties expanded beyond such people of power and started to include ordinary people – that is, members of Kurdish tribes, peasants and immigrants. The group of dispossessed Armenians also changed in this period, because during and after the massacres many Armenian large landowners equally lost their lands. This also differed from developments in the Tanzimat period, when dispossessed Armenians were exclusively people of limited means. Thus, it can be said that mass violence and the mass uprooting that accompanied it radically changed the characteristics of the Armenian land question. With these developments, the basis of the problem shifted from class to ethno-religious differences.

While ethno-religious differences rather than socio-economic means began to mark the dividing line between the parties to these seizures, political economic processes – including the commodification of land, the monetisation of the economy and the transformation of the tax collection regime – continued to play a significant role in shaping these conflicts as well as the means and options of the persons involved. Thousands of plots were seized by force. But there also existed thousands of others that changed hands due to legal or illegal debt relations, arising from a combination of factors including the deterioration of the socio-economic conditions of peasants and the growing need for cash. Thus, despite the rising significance of land as a factor of politics and the shift of the basis of the problem to ethno-religious differences, socio-economic processes and policies continued to affect land disputes concerning Armenians in the Hamidian era.

Armenians and Land Disputes in the Ottoman Empire

The massacres changed many things in the eastern provinces. Thousands were killed or fled the region. There was enormous destruction and disruption. As this chapter has shown, the massacres also changed the scale and characteristics of land disputes, paving the way for the eruption of a massive social problem with crucial political and economic implications.

Notes

1. Louise Nalbandian, *The Armenian Revolutionary Movement: The Development of Armenian Political Parties through the Nineteenth Century* (Berkeley: University of California Press, 1967), 97. For detailed information about Armenian political organisations, see also Anaide Ter Minassian, *Ermeni Devrimci Hareketi'nde Milliyetçilik ve Sosyalizm (1887–1912)*, trans. Mete Tunçay (Istanbul: İletişim, 2012); Houri Berberian, *Roving Revolutionaries: Armenians and the Connected Revolutions in the Russian, Iranian, and Ottoman Worlds* (Oakland: University of California Press, 2019).
2. The name of the party was changed to Hunchakian Social Democrat Party in 1905 and then to Social Democrat Hunchakian Party in 1909. See Nalbandian, *Armenian Revolutionary*, 207. On the Hunchaks, see also the latest volume edited by Bedross Der Matossian, *The Armenian Social Democrat Hnchakian Party: Politics, Ideology and Transnational History* (London: I. B. Tauris, 2023).
3. Gerard J. Libaridian, 'What was Revolutionary about Armenian Revolutionary Parties in the Ottoman Empire', in *A Question of Genocide: Armenians and Turks at the End of the Ottoman Empire*, ed. Ronald Grigor Suny, Fatma Müge Göçek and Norman M. Naimark (Oxford: Oxford University Press, 2011), 98.
4. Ronald Grigor Suny, *Looking toward Ararat: Armenia in Modern History* (Bloomington: Indiana University Press, 1993), 100.
5. Libaridian, 'What was Revolutionary', 91.
6. Selim Deringil, '"The Armenian Question is Finally Closed": Mass Conversions of Armenians in Anatolia during the Hamidian Massacres of 1895–1897', *Comparative Studies in Society and History* 51, no. 2 (2009): 346.
7. Naz Yücel, 'On Ottoman, British, and Belgian Monarchs' Ownership of Private Property in the Late Nineteenth Century', *Comparative Studies of South Asia, Africa and the Middle East* 43, no. 2 (August 2023): 217.
8. Deringil, 'From Ottoman to Turk', 170–75.
9. Alişan Akpınar and Eugene L. Rogan, *Aşiret, Mektep, Devlet: Osmanlı Devleti'nde Aşiret Mektebi* (Istanbul: Aram, 2001).
10. Stephen Duguid, 'The Politics of Unity: Hamidian Policy in Eastern Anatolia', *Middle Eastern Studies* 9, no. 2 (1973): 139–55; Klein, *Margins*

of Empire; Edip Gölbaşı, 'Hamidiye Alayları: Bir Değerlendirme', in Adanır and Özel, *1915*, 164–75.
11. Deringil, 'From Ottoman to Turk', 175.
12. Donald Bloxham, *The Great Game of Genocide: Imperialism, Nationalism, and the Destruction of the Ottoman Armenians* (Oxford: Oxford University Press, 2005), 52.
13. For detailed information about the massacres of 1894–97, see Christopher J. Walker, *Armenia: The Survival of a Nation*, rev. 2nd ed. (London: Routledge Publication, 1991), chap. 5; Yves Ternon, *Ermeni Tabusu*, trans. Emirhan Oğuz (Istanbul: Belge Yayınları, 1993); Vahakn N. Dadrian, *The History of the Armenian Genocide: Ethnic Conflict from the Balkans to Anatolia to the Caucasus* (Providence: Berghahn, 1995), chap. 8; Stephen Duguid, 'Centralization and Localism, Aspects of Ottoman Policy in Eastern Anatolia 1878–1908' (Master's thesis, Simon Fraser University, 1970), chap. 8; Selim Deringil, *Conversion and Apostasy in the Late Ottoman Empire* (Cambridge: Cambridge University Press, 2012); Hans-Lukas Kieser, *Iskalanmış Barış: Doğu Vilayetleri'nde Misyonerlik, Etnik Kimlik ve Devlet, 1839–1938*, trans. Atilla Dirim (Istanbul: İletişim, 2005), part 2; Jelle Verheij, 'Diyarbekir and the Armenian Crisis of 1895', in *Social Relations in Ottoman Diyarbekir, 1870–1915*, ed. Jelle Verheij and Joost Jongerden (Leiden: Brill, 2012), 85–146; Edhem Eldem, '26 Ağustos 1896 "Banka Vakası" ve 1896 "Ermeni Olayları"', *Tarih ve Toplum Yeni Yaklaşımlar* 5 (2007): 113–46; Mehmet Polatel, 'The Complete Ruin of a District: The Sasun Massacre of 1894', in Cora, Derderian and Sipahi, *Ottoman East*, 179–98; Mehmet Polatel, 'The Armenian Massacre of 1895 in Bitlis Town', *Kurdish Studies* 9, no. 1 (9 May 2021): 59–76; Edip Gölbaşı, '1895–1896 Katliamları: Doğu Vilayetlerinde Cemaatler Arası "Şiddet İklimi" ve Ermeni Karşıtı Ayaklanmalar', in Adanır and Özel, *1915*, 140–63; Ümit Kurt, 'Reform and Violence in the Hamidian Era: The Political Context of the 1895 Armenian Massacres in Aintab', *Journal of Holocaust and Genocide Studies* 32, no. 3 (2018), 404–23; Bedross Der Matossian, 'The Ottoman Massacres of Armenians, 1894–1896 and 1909', in *Cambridge World History of Genocide*, vol. II, ed. Ned Backhawk et al. (Cambridge: Cambridge University Press, 2023), 609–33; Edip Gölbaşı, 'The Anti-Armenian Riots of 1895–1897: The "Climate of Violence" and Intercommunal Conflict in Istanbul and the Eastern Anatolian Provinces of the Ottoman Empire' (PhD diss., Simon Fraser University, 2018). See also Ronald Grigor Suny, guest ed., 'The Sassoun massacres', *Armenian Review* 47 (Summer 2001), Nos. 1–2; and two special issues of *Études arméniennes contemporaines* on the Hamidian massacres: 'Les massacres de l'époque hamidienne (I): Récits globaux, approches locales', *Études arméniennes contemporaines* 10 (2018); and 'Les massacres de l'époque hamidienne (II): Représentations et perspectives', *Études arméniennes contemporaines* 11 (2018). Stephan H. Astourian has underlined that a number

of factors, including competition over land and land disputes, shaped the outbreak of massacres in the Hamidian period. See 'On the Genealogy of the Armenian-Turkish Conflict, Sultan Abdülhamid and the Armenian Massacres', in *Collective and State Violence in Turkey: The Construction of a National Identity from Empire to Nation-State*, ed. Stephan H. Astourian and Raymond H. Kévorkian (New York: Berghahn, 2020), 13–55.

14. Astourian, 'Silence of Land'; Klein, *Margins of Empire*; Raymond H. Kévorkian, 'The Property Law and the Spoliation of Ottoman Armenians', in *Documenting the Armenian Genocide: Essays in Honor of Taner Akçam*, ed. Thomas Kühne, Mary Jane Rein and Marc A. Mamigonian (Cham: Palgrave Macmillan, 2024), 165–66.
15. Pehlivan, 'Beyond the Desert', 47.
16. Pehlivan, 'Abandoned Villages in Diyarbekir Province at the End of the "Little Ice Age", 1800–50', in Cora, Derderian and Sipahi, *Ottoman East*, 223–46. On famines, see also Özge Ertem, 'British Views on the Indian and Ottoman Famines: Politics, Culture, and Morality', *RCC Perspectives* 2 (2015): 17–27; Özge Ertem, 'Sick Men of Asia Minor in an Ailing Empire: Famine, Villagers and Government in Missionary Accounts (1873–75)', *International Review of Turkish Studies* 2, no. 2 (2012): 72–94; Semih Çelik, 'Scarcity and Misery at the Time of "Abundance beyond Imagination": Climate Change, Famines and Empire-Building in Ottoman Anatolia (c. 1800–1850)' (PhD diss., European University Institute, 2017).
17. Pehlivan, 'Beyond the Desert', 233–34; Matthew Ghazarian, 'Ghost Rations: Empire, Ecology, and Community in the Ottoman East, 1839–94' (PhD diss., Columbia University, 2020), 202–3.
18. The members of this commission were Dr Nazaret Daghavarian, Ghazaros H. Bezazian, Rupen Papazian, Aram Halacian and Kegham Der Garabedian.
19. *Deghegakir Hoghayin Krawmants Hantsnazhoghovoy* [The Report of the Commission on Seized Lands], vol. 1 (Istanbul: Doghramadjian Dbakragan, 1910; vol. 2, 1911; vol. 3, 1912; vol. 4, 1912). The first volume was also published in Ottoman Turkish: *Anadolu'nun Muhtelifesinde Emlak ve Arazi-i Magsube Hakkında Ermeni Patrikhanesince Teşkil Eden Komisyon-u Mahsusa Tarafından Tanzim Olunan Raporların Suret-i Mütercimesi* (Dersaadet: Doğramacıyan Matbaası, 1327/1911).
20. For example, the governor of Van and the office of the director of the financial administration of the province (*defterdar*) stated that the registers of the tax office and title deeds were not regularly registered and included conflicting entries. They were also not sufficient to prove ownership of the properties. BOA: DH.SYS 67/1-5, the province of Van and *defterdarlık* to Ministry of Finance, 13 Haziran 1326 (26 June 1910). For a detailed analysis of the cadastre process focusing on Istanbul, see Alp Yücel Kaya and Yücel Terzibaşoğlu, 'Tahrir'den Kadastro'ya: 1874 Istanbul Emlak Tahriri ve Vergisi: "Kadastro tabir olunur tahrir-i emlak"', *Tarih ve Toplum Yeni Yaklaşımlar* 9 (2009): 9–58.

Mass Violence and Mass Seizures

21. Astourian, 'Silence of Land', 65; Yaşar Tolga Cora, 'Doğu'da Kürt-Ermeni Çatışmasının Sosyoekonomik Arkaplanı', in Adanır and Özel, *1915*, 136–38; Ohannes Kılıçdağı, 'Socio-Political Reflections and Expectations of the Ottoman Armenians after the 1908 Revolution: Between Hope and Despair' (PhD diss., Boğaziçi University, 2014), 136–39; Kévorkian, 'Property Law', 168.
22. Astourian, 'Silence of Land', 59.
23. *Deghegakir*, vol. 4, 7.
24. *Deghegakir*, vol. 3, 3–4.
25. Patriarchate reports show that there had been seized olive groves in Kilis, Antep, Muş, Van and Beyazıd. Except for four in Antep, all other olive groves were small in scale. There were three olive oil mills listed in the Patriarchate reports. Two of these were located in the Ağpak (today Başkale) district of Van. These mills, along with a flourmill, seventeen houses, land and trees, were forcefully bought by Hamid Pasha in 1901, in exchange for 15 liras. Their total worth was estimated to be around 500 liras (*Deghegakir*, vol. 2, 7). The other olive mill, located in Patnos, Ağrı, was forcefully seized by Haydaranlı Hüseyin Pasha, along with agricultural lands and pastures (*Deghegakir*, vol. 2, 8).
26. Pamuk, *Türkiye'nin 200 Yıllık İktisadi Tarihi*, 135. See also Zozan Pehlivan, 'El Niño and the Nomads: Global Climate, Local Environment, and the Crisis of Pastoralism in Late Ottoman Kurdistan', *Journal of the Economic and Social History of the Orient* 63 (2020): 316–56.
27. The definition of the term farm (*çiftlik*) has been debated in the literature for years. For an overview of these debates, see Gilles Veinstein, 'On the Çiftlik Debate', in Keyder and Tabak, *Landholding*, 35–56. In the reports examined here, the term 'farm' was used to refer to large landholdings. However, not all large landholdings mentioned in the reports were referred to as farms. In the case of farms, the reports list the number of animals, houses, pastures, fields, stables and other buildings within the scope of the properties defined as farms. This indicates that the authors of the reports employed this category to refer to a specific mode of the spatial organisation of agricultural production.
28. *Deghegakir*, vol. 1, 9.
29. Astourian, 'Silence of Land', 56. As shown by Astourian, Armenians continued to buy lands in the region of Adana. Yet, there are also cases showing the dispossession of Armenians in this region. Thus, dispossession of and property acquisition by Armenians were not mutually exclusive phenomena.
30. Bedross Der Matossian, *The Horrors of Adana: Revolution and Violence in the Early Twentieth Century* (Palo Alto: Stanford University Press, 2022), 63–65.
31. Ibid., 65, 89–92. See also Gratien, *Unsettled Plain*, 131–32.
32. *Deghegakir*, vol. 3, 12.

33. Şeyh Sabit was an important Bektaşi religious authority in Bursa. For more information, see Salih Çift, 'Bursa'da Bir Mısrî Dergâhı ve Son Postnişîni: Seyyid Baba Tekkesi ve Şeyh Sâbit Efendi', *Uludağ Üniversitesi İlahiyat Fakültesi* 13, no. 2 (2004): 197–214.
34. *Deghegakir*, vol. 2, 1.
35. Ibid., vol. 2, 1.
36. *Deghegakir*, vol. 3, 5–6.
37. *Deghegakir*, vol. 3, 2.
38. *Deghegakir*, vol. 1, 10.
39. *Deghegakir*, vol. 2, 1.
40. *Deghegakir*, vol. 3, 2.
41. The reports state that Emin Pasha forcefully seized thirty-five houses, several agricultural fields and pastures (750 *çap*s), a watermill and thirty gardens in Paninköy (Taşlıçay), Erciş, in 1890 (*Deghegakir*, vol. 3, 6); a monastery in the same village in 1896 (*Deghegakir*, vol. 1, 6); another monastery along with three water mills, two vineyards, three pastures and agricultural lands which amounted to 1,500 dönüms in total in Kineper in Van, in 1896 (*Deghegakir*, vol. 1, 6); twenty vineyards, fifteen gardens, agricultural fields (200 *çap*s) and three pastures (350 *çap*s) in the village of Tilan, Erciş, in 1896 (*Deghegakir*, vol. 3, 6–7); two pastures (150 *çap*s) of the Armenian villagers of Murzavank, Erciş, in 1895; and two pastures (150 *çap*s), another pasture (the size of which was not specified) and an agricultural field (1500 *çap*s) in the above-mentioned village, at an unspecified time (*Deghegakir*, vol. 3, 6). In Azoraf, Van, he tore down a church and built a dairy farm in its place (*Deghegakir*, vol. 1, 6). His family was also extensively involved in land seizure. The church in the village of Kantsag (Kırkdeğirmen) was destroyed by his son, Ahmed Bey, also accused of forcefully seizing twenty-five vineyards, ten orchards with a total of 2,000 trees, six water mills, thirty hayfields and thirty houses belonging to Armenians in the same village (*Deghegakir*, vol. 3, 7). His other son, Ebubekir, forcefully seized three water mills, six vineyards, twenty-five gardens, twenty-five hayfields, two pastures and several agricultural fields (2500 *çap*s) belonging to the Armenians of the village of Cüdgear (Karatavuk), who held title deeds (*Deghegakir*, vol. 3, 6). His third son, Hüseyin Bey, seized the church in Küpkıran, Beyazıt (*Deghegakir*, vol. 1, 6). His brother Abdullah seized two olive mills, two water mills, ten vineyards, fifteen gardens, twenty hayfields (200 *çap*s), three pastures (200 *çap*s), a haystack, a large pasture worth 200 liras (300 *çap*s) and other lands in the village of Dzadzgag (Akçayuva), Erçiş (*Deghegakir*, vol. 3, 6).
42. In another case, a woman named Hatice, daughter of Ali, seized land belonging to an Armenian named Minasian in Kemah, Balaban, in 1895, by use of force (*Deghegakir*, vol. 4, 12).
43. *Deghegakir*, vol. 1, 6 and vol. 3, 7.
44. 'BOA: DH.TMIK.M 61/38, the Armenian Patriarchate to the Ministry of the Interior, 30 Ağustos 1315 (11 September 1899).

45. BOA: DH.TMIK.M 61/38, the Inspection Commission to the province of Van, 12 Teşrin-i Sani 1315 (24 November 1899).
46. BOA: BEO 3152/236389, the Armenian Patriarchate to the Sublime Porte, 25 Haziran 1323 (8 July 1907), and 3 Eylül 1323 (16 September 1907).
47. BOA: BEO 3152/236389, the Armenian Patriarchate to the Sublime Porte, 3 Eylül 1323 (16 September 1907).
48. For detailed information on the Haydaranlı Tribe and Hüseyin Pasha, see Klein, *Margins of Empire*; Erdal Çiftçi, 'Fragile Alliances in the Ottoman East: The Heyderan Tribe and the Empire, 1820–1929' (PhD diss., Bilkent University, 2018).
49. He and his servants forcefully seized large swaths of lands belonging to Mgrdich Avedisian in Adilcevaz in 1896 (*Deghegakir*, vol. 2, 4); an olive oil mill, a water mill and a pasture in Grakom (Eskikonak), Erciş (*Deghegakir*, vol. 3, 7); the pastures of the Armenian peasants in Güzelköy, Adilcevaz, in 1906; the houses of the Armenians in Ayketsor (Gümüşdöven), Adilcevaz; lands of the Armenians in Norşin (Heybeli), Adilcevaz; the properties of the Armenians of the village of Çırakköy, Adilcevaz, which included agricultural fields (100 *çap*s), several pastures, hayfields, houses and lands; the pastures of the Armenians in the village of Kocirin (Erikbağı) in Adilcevaz (from which villagers procured a yearly income of 600 liras); and the lands of the villagers of Keyaçukh, Adilcevaz (*Deghegakir*, vol. 3, 7). He forcefully seized all lands belonging to the villagers of Marmus in Malazgirt, Bitlis (today Koçaklar in Patnos, Ağrı) in 1900 (*Deghegakir*, vol. 3, 22). He also seized the properties of the Armenians of Poti (Tutak) (*Deghegakir*, vol. 3, 10) and the olive oil mill, pastures (6,000 *otluk*) and wheat field (1,000 *kile*s and fourteen dönüms) belonging to Garabed Parseghian in Patnos, Beyazıd (*Deghegakir*, vol. 2, 8).
50. *Deghegakir*, vol. 1, 6.
51. BOA: Y.A.HUS 286/58, the Grand Vizier to the Yıldız Palace, 5 Kanun-ı Evvel 1309 (17 December 1893).
52. BOA: BEO 3152/236389, the Armenian Patriarchate to the Sublime Porte, 25 Haziran 1323 (8 July 1907).
53. Sheikh Hamid Pasha was neither a tribal chief nor even connected to a tribe. He was a member of the prestigious Arvasi family whose religious influence in the region came from the fact that they traced their bloodline to the Prophet Muhammed. Several members of this family held privileged offices and served as muftis, preachers or district governors. Sheikh Taha Arvasi became a member of the Ottoman parliament after 1908. The family had branches in Müküs, Doğubeyazıt, Başkale and Hizan. Many of the most famous sheikhs in the region – such as Sheikh Seyyid Sıbgatullah (known as Gavs), Sheikh Sahabettin, Sheikh Seyyid Ali, Sheikh Celalüddin, Sheikh Emin and Sheikh Hazret (Allame) – hailed from this family. See İsmail Kıran, 'Aristokrat Kürt Aileler: Arvasiler', *Kurdiyat* 3 (2021): 119–44. İbrahim Arvas wrote in his memoirs about how Bekir Sami Bey,

the governor of Van appointed in 1909, visited his father Sheikh Hamid in Başkale. During this visit, the governor stated that he could not even drink the coffee that they offered until they returned the lands of the Armenians. In response, Sheikh Hamid argued that the land issue was a nuisance; what Armenians really wanted was not land but independence. See İbrahim Arvas, *Tarihi Hakikatler* (Ankara: Resimli Posta Matbaası, 1964), 5–6.

54. Hamid Pasha and his followers were listed as the perpetrators of seizures concerning the trees and stones of the Surp Asdvadzadzin Monastery in Başkale (*Deghegakir*, vol. 1, 9). He forcefully seized all the properties, agricultural fields (900 *çap*s), pastures and gardens belonging to Apkar Krikorian and his seven brothers, as well as the lands (210 *çap*s), pastures and four gardens belonging to Sulto Kalusdian in the village of Avak (probably Erek), Başkale. In the same village, he acquired a water mill, two olive oil mills, seventeen houses, agricultural fields and trees which belonged to Nerses Bedrosian and were worth 500 liras in total, in exchange for 15 liras in 1901 (*Deghegakir*, vol. 2, 4–5). In the same village, he also forcefully seized the agricultural lands (1,000 *çap*s) of several Armenian peasants who then emigrated from the region as a result. He forcefully took the properties and lands of eleven villagers in Pağ, Van. Armenians in this village also fled to Iran. He seized the agricultural fields, gardens, pastures, threshing ground and water mill belonging to twenty-nine Armenians in different locales of Başkale in 1893, together with Said Bey, Sadık Hacı Ali's son Badho and Muzaffer Mahmud Perin (*Deghegakir*, vol. 3, 8). While Başkaleli Osman forcefully seized lands, agricultural fields and a water mill in the village of Hasbadan (probably Atlılar), belonging to Vosgi Saisian and worth 200 liras in total, Hamid Pasha took an agricultural field (150 *çap*s) belonging to the same person. In 1902, he seized twelve properties, one garden, one plot, six mills, one bakery and one farm belonging to Aslan Der Hovhannesian in Başkale, together with Derviş, the son of Komodir (*Deghegakir*, vol. 2, 5). He was involved in a number of cases in which Armenian properties were taken due to small debts. Such cases include the lands, agricultural fields, pastures and other properties of five peasants in Pağ; the properties, agricultural fields, pastures and other properties of seven villagers in Başkale (which his son Emin took together with Pira Agha, Musaffer, Uso, Osman Beşir and others); the agricultural fields, pastures, houses and other properties of eight peasants in the village of Soran (Barışköy), Başkale, due to debt (taken by Telo Saro, Hamid's son Osman, Hacı Ömer and others); and the agricultural lands and pastures of four villagers in the village of Hasbısdan (Atlılar), Başkale. He seized the agricultural fields (300 dönüms) of Hovhannes Panosian in the village of Arag (Erek), Başkale, in 1902, due to the latter's debt, along with the agricultural fields and water mills of Krikor Muradian and Nerso Bedrosian as well as the agricultural lands of two other Armenian peasants from the same village (*Deghegakir*, vol. 4, 4).

Mass Violence and Mass Seizures

55. This report was titled '*Hay-Hasaragut'ean Verapereal Kraweal Galvadzner*' [Seized Properties Concerning the Armenian Community].
56. One of these was the village of Simo in Hınıs (probably Kurganlı, in Bulanık, Bitlis), which the government seized in its entirety and allocated to immigrants. The other case in Erzurum was related to the village of Lak-Budak in Hınıs, which included thirty households. The village was forcefully seized by Circassians, and the owners of the lands became vagabonds. The third case in Erzurum concerned the seizure of all properties of Armenian peasants in the village of Küpkıran, Beyazıt, by Hüseyin Bey, son of Zilanlı Eyüp Pasha (*Deghegakir*, vol. 3, 10–12).
57. This case was related to lands in the village of Pis (Yurttepe), in Başkale. According to the Patriarchate, all lands were forcefully seized in 1896 by the sons of Molla Muhammed, Emin and Hasan, who later prepared false title deeds. The dispossessed villagers held the actual title deeds (*Deghegakir*, vol. 3, 8). They also seized the monastery, its lands and the cemetery of the same village (*Deghegakir*, vol. 1, 5, 7).
58. The reports stated that the Sheikh of Zilan, Resul Bey and his men were involved in several seizures carried out by force in the area between Siirt and today's Batman. For instance, in 1893, the Sheikh seized sixty dönüms of agricultural lands belonging to Armenian peasants in the Daranca village of Siirt. He also seized the lands of the villages of Caldakan, Gago and Tapi (Alıçlı) in Batman (*Deghegakir*, vol. 3, 16).
59. For example, Hacı Razık, Resul and Alo Lare from the Reşkotan tribe seized 3,000 dönüms of agricultural lands belonging to Armenian peasants in the village of Avink Hacre in the Mutki region in 1901 (*Deghegakir*, vol. 3, 15).
60. Mehmed Said Bey was especially influential in the Muş region and was noted to have been the usurper of plots of land belonging to Armenians in this region. One case in which he was involved concerned the lands of thirteen Armenian families in the village of Kharapa (Örenkent) in Bulanık, Muş. These 160 tracts of land altogether totalled more than 1,500 dönüms in total (*Deghegakir*, vol. 3, 18).
61. Beşar Bey and Fehim Bey seized agricultural lands belonging to several Armenian peasants in the village of Kostanlı in Malazgirt (Kotanlı, in Bulanık), Muş, in 1895. These lands were estimated to be worth more than 100 liras (*Deghegakir*, vol. 2, 15).
62. In addition to many other lands, Rıza Bey, who served as major in the Hamidian Regiments, seized all lands of the village of Gasımi (Arslankaya) in Malazgirt, Muş. He also appropriated several houses in this village. These seizures were carried out by use of force in 1895 (*Deghegakir*, vol. 3, 22).
63. Menteşezade Yusuf Agha seized thirteen agricultural tracts of land, a house and a forest belonging to Aliksan Aprahamian in the village of Khımbılçur in Siirt. He also seized all lands belonging to Sarkis Simonian by use of force and *selef* (*Deghegakir*, vol. 2, 12).

64. The reports mention dozens of cases regarding seizures by members of this family. These cases, some of which concerned vast tracts of agricultural land, concentrated around the Muş district. Some of these seizures led to the dispossession of large groups of Armenians. For example, thirty-three Armenian families in Kızılağaç lost their lands due to seizures carried out by Cezayir Agha (*Deghegakir*, vol. 4, 9). Musa Bey himself seized several plots of land and pastures in this region. In one of these cases, he seized lands and pastures larger than 400 dönüms, belonging to Armenian peasants in the village of Avzud (Büvetli) in the Hasköy region, Muş, in 1890 (*Deghegakir*, vol. 3, 17).
65. On Palu, see Özok-Gündoğan, *Kurdish Nobilitiy*.
66. *Deghegakir*, vol. 2, 5–6.
67. BOA: A.MKT.MHM 620/15, Rauf Bey, governor of Erzurum to the Sublime Porte, 17 Mart 1312 (29 March 1896); BOA: Y.PRK.BŞK 45/75, Rauf Bey, governor of Erzurum to the Yıldız Palace, 17 Mart 1312 (29 March 1896).
68. BOA: A.MKT.MHM 620/15, Ömer Sabri, governor of Bitlis to the Sublime Porte, 22 Nisan 1312 (4 May 1896).
69. BOA: A.MKT.MHM 620/15, decision of the investigation commission, 15 Mayıs 1312 (27 May 1896).
70. See Astourian, 'Silence of Land'; Klein, *Margins of Empire*.
71. Kegham Der Garabedian, *Hoghayin Harts'ĕ Hayap'nag Nahankneru Meç* (G. Bolis: H. Y. Taşnagtsutyan, Hradaragutyun, 1911), 43–44. See also A. S. Hamparyan, *Akrarayin Haraperut'yunnerĕ Arevm'dyan Hayasdanum* (Yerewan: Haygagan Soṛ Kidut'yunneri Agatemiayi Hradaragch'ut'yun, 1965), 207.
72. Klein, *Margins of Empire*, chap. 4.
73. Çağlar Keyder and Şevket Pamuk, '1945 Çiftçiyi Topraklandırma Kanunu Üzerine Tezler', *Yapıt* 8 (December/January 1984–85): 61.
74. The National Archives of the UK (TNA): FO 195/1981, Mr. Crow to Sir P. Currie, 'Visit to the Cazas of Akhlat, Boulanyk, and Malasgird, August 1897', 10 October 1897.
75. There were various examples listed in the report: in Ankara, Circassian Beyzade Hanik seized the agricultural land and the vineyard of Sahag Ghazarian due to the latter's debt; in Maraş, Hasan Fehmi Efendi took Hagop Mtenian's land worth 150 gold pieces, due to the latter's debt of ten gold pieces; in the Khoşmat (Çakırkaş) village of Palu, Mamuretülaziz, Hacı Şerifzade Mehmed acquired the land (20 dönüms) and the garden (18,000 kuruş) belonging to Nazaret Arpajian due to a debt of 300 kuruş; in the Hıntsan (Üzümlü) village of Tatvan, Bitlis, properties such as the agricultural fields, vineyards and a forest belonging to fourteen Armenian villagers were seized by usurpers, including Farhad Agha, due to debt; Hacı, son of Zıki Agha, seized a house, a store and a garden which belonged to Tomvas Boghosian and was worth 150 liras in total in the Piran (Atalar)

village of Çüngüş, Diyarbekir, in exchange for a debt of 200 kuruş; and in Bayburt, the seven agricultural fields (worth 250 liras) of Arshag Sarkisian were seized by Pato for the former's debt of 47 liras (*Deghegakir*, vol. 4, 4–8).
76. Garabedian, *Hoghayin*, 28–29.
77. TNA: FO 195/2283, A. Safrastian to H. S. Shipley, 8 February 1908. Veli Yadırgı has argued that the *selef* became a significant tool for Kurdish notables to enrich themselves by buying Armenian lands at lower prices. See *The Political Economy*, 119–20.
78. Based on the Russian archives, the historian M. S. Lazarev has also given an example of *selef*, stating that 208 fields, twenty-four houses and six mills belonging to Armenian peasants were taken by local Kurdish *selefdar*s in the village of Hasköy in Bitlis province. See Charles Issawi, ed. *The Economic History of Turkey, 1800–1914* (Chicago: University of Chicago Press, 1980), 66.
79. Matthew Ghazarian has demonstrated that, during the famine years of the 1890s, the state implemented a programme which forced the peasants to register their land, receive title deeds and use them as collateral to obtain credit from the Agricultural Bank. These loans helped the peasants deal with the immediate impact of the famines, but in the long term the peasants faced the risk of losing their land due to debt. See Ghazarian, 'Ghost Rations', 190–98.
80. *Deghegakir*, vol. 4, 3.
81. BOA: DH.TMIK.M 111/41, the Armenian Patriarchate to the Sublime Porte, 27 Temmuz 1317 (9 August 1901).
82. BOA: DH.TMIK.M 111/41, the Inspection Commission to the province of Van, 24 Eylül 1317 (7 October 1901).
83. TNA: FO 195/2250, Captain B. Dickson to Sir N. O'Conor, 28 April 1907.
84. For an elaboration of taxation policies, practices and their effects in the region, see Nadir Özbek, 'The Politics of Taxation and the "Armenian Question" during the Late Ottoman Empire, 1876–1908', *Comparative Studies in Society and History* 54, no. 4 (2012), 770–97.
85. 'Report by Consul Palgrave respecting Land Tenure in Eastern Turkey', in *Reports from Her Majesty's Representatives Respecting the Tenure of Land in the Several Countries of Europe: 1869–70* (London: Harrison and Sons, 1870), 279–80.
86. *Deghegakir*, vol. 2, 8.
87. Garabedian, *Hoghayin*, 29–30.
88. TNA: FO 195/1932, Acting Consul Alatoni to M. H. Herbert, 10 June 1896.
89. TNA: FO 424/187, Vice-Consul Fontana to Sir P. Currie, 2 May 1896; Robert Aram Kaloosdian, *Tadem, My Father's Village: Extinguished during the 1915 Armenian Genocide* (Portsmouth: Peter E. Randall, 2015), 17–25.
90. USC Shoah Foundation VHA, Hovannisian Oral History Collection, Boghos Kaloosdian interviewed on 23 April 1983, no. 56602.

91. Richard G. Hovannisian, 'The Armenian Question in the Ottoman Empire, 1876–1914', in *The Armenian People from Ancient to Modern Times, vol. II: Foreign Dominion to Statehood: The Fifteenth Century to the Twentieth Century* (New York: St Martin's Press, 2004), 224.
92. TNA: FO 195/1941, to Sir Philip Currie, 7 January 1896 and 8 January 1896. Regarding the massacres in Harput, see Kieser, *Iskalanmış Barış*, 284–91; Ali Sipahi, 'At Arm's Length: Historical Ethnography of Proximity in Harput' (PhD diss., University of Michigan, 2015), chap. 10.
93. Ümit Kurt, *The Armenians of Aintab: The Economics of Genocide in an Ottoman Province* (Cambridge, MA: Harvard University Press, 2021), 48.
94. TNA: FO 195/1930, Mr. Hallward to Sir Philip Currie, 26 May 1896.
95. Jelle Verheij and Joost Jongerden (eds.), *Social Relations in Ottoman Diyarbekir, 1870–1915*. Leiden: Brill, 2012), 106.
96. BOA: DH.TMIK.M 58/64, the Armenian Patriarchate to the Sublime Porte, 18 Temmuz 1314 (30 July 1898); the Inspection Commission to the provinces of Erzurum, Bitlis, Mamuretülaziz, Sivas and Diyarbekir, 16 Ağustos 1314 (28 August 1898).
97. BOA: DH.TMIK.M 71/33, the Armenian Patriarchate to the Sublime Porte, 12 Mayıs 1315 (24 May 1899); the Inspection Commission to the province of Van, 27 Mayıs 1315 (8 June 1899); the Governor of Van to the Minister of the Interior, 19 Haziran 1315 (1 July 1899).
98. BOA: DH.TMIK.M 111/54, petition to the Sublime Porte, 29 Ağustos 1317 (11 September 1901).
99. Fisher, *Ottoman Land Laws*, 24–26.
100. 'Bilâ bedel muhacirine terk ve tahsis edilip sahibi evvellerinin emval-i metrukesi olmayan arazi-i mahlûle müterakim vergilerinin terkin-i kaydı hakkında irade, 9 Nisan 1317 [22 April 1901]', *Düstur*, vol. 1, no. 7 (Dersaadet: Matbaa-i Amire, 1289), 672.
101. Morack, *Dowry of the State*, 66.
102. Ibid.

Chapter 4

Controlling Outcomes: The Hamidian Government and Land Disputes

As examined in the previous chapter, the Hamidian era witnessed significant changes in the scale and characteristics of land disputes. Especially during and after the massacres, the basis of land disputes shifted from class to ethno-religious difference, and there was a massive wave of dispossession, migration and uprooting. In this chapter, I will discuss how the state affected this process and shaped the consequences of these massacres in terms of the population's demographic characteristics and land ownership patterns, scrutinising the ways in which Ottoman state actors approached the issue of Armenian land disputes. To do so, Chapter 4 will examine the correspondence among different agencies, as well as the orders, laws and agreements issued by the Ottoman authorities.

In the literature on the Armenian land question during the Hamidian period, the role of the central government has not been discussed in detail, and correspondence, negotiations and conflicts among the different agents operating in the Ottoman state with regard to this matter remain under-utilised.[1] This study, the first to examine Ottoman documents on this matter in detail, suggests that these processes cannot be understood without taking the role of the central government into consideration. The findings of this research indicate that, instead of merely reacting to events, the central government actively shaped the outcomes of mass violence and the processes of property transfer.

The correspondence among Ottoman officials, the regulations and laws issued by the Sublime Porte, as well as the reports of British consular staff scrutinised in this chapter show that the Ottoman government tried to control the outcomes of the massacres and property transfer with a demographic approach that was intended to weaken the Armenian population and increase Muslim domination in the Ottoman East. The attempt to control the outcomes of the massacres and the property transfer that accompanied them can be traced in several policy areas. The first of these consists of the ineffectiveness of the commissions established by the central government when it came to resolving land disputes. Nationality and emigration regulations constitute other areas shaped by the concerns of the central government with respect to demographics. A third policy area is to be found in the resettlement of Muslim immigrants. The demographic objective also entailed the introduction of administrative barriers to Armenians' entry into the land market in the Ottoman East, the implementation of which caused confusion and debate among the Ottoman authorities.

The Activities of the Reform Commissions

Before going into detail about the central government's approach to land disputes concerning Armenians, it should be noted that reform in the six provinces once again became an international political matter in the mid-1890s. Following the massacres in the district of Sasun, the pressure for reforms that would improve the conditions of Armenians in the six provinces increased.[2] The problem of seizure of land belonging to Armenians was also discussed during attempts at reform in the 1890s.

On 11 May 1895, Britain, France and Russia gave the Ottoman government a memorandum, including a draft reform scheme, to be implemented in the Ottoman East.[3] According to Article 26 of the proposed scheme, a special commission consisting of one president and four members (two Muslims and two Christians) would be established for the revision of title deeds.[4] In its reply to this reform plan on 3 June, the government revised this article, suggesting that the title deed administration send a permanent inspector to investigate property issues.[5] The Sublime Porte gave another detailed response to the reform plan on 2 August 1895. In this response, after summarising the established principles regarding property rights and the registration attempts by the government, the Porte claimed that an investigation by a special commission would not be sufficient to solve the problems; these could only be solved by the title deed offices and archives. The Porte also emphasised that, even if such a commission were to be established, provincial administrative councils had to approve their decisions and the parties could take the decisions to court.[6]

After lengthy negotiations between the three Powers and the Ottoman government, the latter approved the final reform scheme and published it on 20 October 1895. This scheme included a chapter concerning land disputes. According to Article 29 of the reform scheme, commissions would be established for the revision of title deeds. These commissions would consist of four members (two Muslim and two non-Muslim) under the chairmanship of the director of archives or the superintendent of real estate. The decisions of the commissions would be submitted to the administrative councils. Moreover, four delegates would be sent from Istanbul to the provinces on an annual basis, to inquire into any irregularities regarding land ownership.[7]

The commissions and delegates were responsible for investigating the records of the title deeds offices and the revenues from title deeds, organising the sale of vacant lands, examining individual complaints and property disputes, and inspecting the conduct of the officials of the title deeds offices. There exist few documents about the activities and investigations of these commissions in the Ottoman and British archives. As can be gleaned from these documents, the commissions were first established in late 1896. Although the regulation concerning the duties of the four delegates was drafted in August 1896, it was not ratified until the end of that year. On 27 October 1896, the Minister of Property Registration suggested sending the four delegates immediately, without waiting for ratification because of the significance of the matter.[8] According to this regulation, the operations and duties of the delegates would be published in local newspapers, and they would work exclusively on the basis of complaints. Thus, the delegates were not authorised to investigate land disputes or misconduct, unless a formal application had been submitted to them. Another regulation concerning the duties of the commissions established under the supervision of officials of the title deeds offices was prepared as well. According to its instructions, like the duties of the delegates, the commissions would also work based on applications by complainants; their examinations would not surpass court decisions, and their decisions would be submitted to the administrative councils for approval.[9] These two regulations were finally ratified at the end of 1896.[10]

In 1899, Commissioner Şakir Pasha asked the governors of the six provinces for information about the activities of these commissions. In response, the governor of Bitlis stated that, while the commissions had been founded in the districts of the province and numerous announcements had been made, there were few petitioners due to the lack of awareness (*gaflet*) among the people. The applications submitted to the commissions concerned notices regarding vacant (*mahlul*) lands. The governor stated that there existed no title deeds in Genç, as the title deed office in this district had been established only two years prior. He also noted that no applications had been submitted to the commissions in the districts of Genç, Muş and Siirt.[11] The governor of Bitlis sent an additional telegram to Yıldız Palace about the commissions, stating that Şakir Pasha had only inspected the records and revenues of the title deeds and organised the sale of *mahlul* lands. According to the governor, most of the land in Bitlis belonged to Muslims who had failed to register their lands for a number of reasons, including poor judgment and ignorance. The governor stated that Armenian tenants and share-croppers who were paying the land tax were claiming ownership, and only this group of people had applied to the commission.[12] The governor noted that, after examining their cases, the commission did not find their claims admissible. The governor of Mamuretülaziz informed the Ministry of the Interior that only a handful of applications had reached the commissions.[13] He noted that the commissions carried out investigations based on complaints and that people may not be aware of the procedure, which had only been announced in the local newspaper. The governor suggested the preparation and distribution of pamphlets written in such a way that common people would understand.[14]

In sum, even though property commissions had been established in a number of districts in the eastern provinces, they failed to resolve land disputes concerning Armenians in the late 1890s. The limited archival sources on the operation of these commissions indicate that few applications were lodged with them. The difference in the tone of the evaluations by the prospective governors of Mamuretülaziz and Bitlis indicates that local governors approached the issue quite differently from each other. While some of them, such as the governor of Mamuretülaziz, seemed to be eager to solve the disputes with the help of these newly introduced mechanisms, others, such as the governor of Bitlis, underplayed the problem and did not seem very enthusiastic.

Emigration Policies and Regulations

Mass violence in the 1890s led to internal migration movements and accelerated the emigration of Armenians from the eastern provinces. The primary destinations of Armenian emigrants were Russia, Persia and the United States. The central government tried to control the demographic outcomes of these emigration movements with a number of regulations and initiatives.[15] The government had two objectives concerning the issue of Armenian emigration: one was to prevent the diffusion of the perception that Armenians were forced to emigrate, whereas the other was to secure the permanence of these migratory movements and decrease the Armenian population in the Ottoman East.

The escalation of the Armenians' emigration abroad negatively impacted the image of the Ottoman government in the international arena. Upon protests by foreign powers, the Ottoman authorities took steps to prevent the emigration of Armenians to foreign countries. For example, on 8 December 1899, an order from Yıldız Palace was sent to the governors of Bitlis, Van, Mamuretülaziz and Trabzon. This order stated that the Russian consul had protested that local authorities coerced the Armenians to emigrate, and Russian-Armenian traders holding valid passports and visas were not being permitted into the Ottoman provinces. The order noted that 'this was very inappropriate and could lead to several problems'.[16] The local authorities were ordered to inform the palace whether such practices had indeed been carried out. In response, all the governors denied the allegations. The governor of Van stated that those who were trying to emigrate without permits were captured at the border and returned to their place of origin.[17]

Correspondence between the embassy in Washington and the central government indicates that some Ottoman officials saw the emigration of Armenians to other countries as a favourable trend that would strengthen the Muslim element in the eastern provinces in the long run. A telegram by the Ottoman Ambassador in Washington, Mavroyani Bey, clearly shows this demographic approach:

> As the number of our enemies and the number of those who are used by our enemies decrease, our strength and power will increase. I know that the return of expatriate Armenians to their hometowns is a matter of concern for the government [...] However, every political matter and everything that happens has good and bad sides. This emigration decreases the strength of Armenians and proportionally increases the strength of other nations in the Royal Domains. This emigration can be the introduction to a gradual solution of the matter that is called the Armenian Question in the Royal Domains.[18]

As outlined in this telegram, the Ottoman ambassador in Washington saw the emigration of Armenians, which was causing diplomatic problems due to accusations of forced emigration, as a positive development. There was a clear distinction in the assessment of the ambassador between 'us' and 'our enemies and those used by enemies'. Moreover, based on population, there existed a negative correlation between the powers of these groups in the eyes of the ambassador. Although it caused diplomatic problems, the emigration of Armenians would decrease the Armenian population in the Ottoman Empire and weaken the territorial claims of Armenians. It would also increase the strength of other nations in the region. This, according to the ambassador, was a step towards the end of the Armenian Question.[19] As noted by Sinan Dinçer, the extant correspondence does not indicate whether the ambassador's suggestions were taken into consideration. Still, the government policies in the period that followed were in line with them.[20]

The Ottoman government tried to control the population movements caused by the massacres with policies and regulations shaped by demographic concerns. Two articles of the Nationality Law regulated the issues of expatriation and change of nationality.[21] According to Article 5 of this law, those who acquired foreign nationality with the permission of the government would be treated as foreigners. However, Ottoman nationals who changed their nationality and acquired foreign citizenship without an imperial decree permitting them to do so would not be considered foreign nationals. Such people would continue to be treated as Ottoman subjects. Their foreign citizenship would not be recognized by the Ottoman authorities. According to Article 6 of the Ottoman Nationality Law, Ottoman subjects who became foreign nationals without the permission of the Ottoman government and those who served in the militaries of foreign countries could be expatriated. The return of expatriates to the territories of the Ottoman Empire would not be permitted.[22] Dinçer has noted that the expatriation of Ottoman nationals who changed their nationalities was a rarely used practice. However, after the US-Ottoman agreement of 1893, Article 6 was used exclusively for Armenians who had become United States nationals. In the case of immigrants of other ethnicities, Ottoman authorities applied Article 5.[23]

The immigration policies of the United States provided immigrants with the opportunity to naturalise after five years. The Ottoman government attempted to restrict the return of these immigrants to Ottoman lands. The arrest of such returnees by the Ottoman authorities created a diplomatic crisis between the two countries in the early 1890s. While the US consulate intervened for their release and claimed that they were under the protection of the US government, the Ottoman authorities resisted, countering that they would be treated as Ottoman nationals in the absence of permits issued by the Ottoman government, acknowledging their change of nationality. After long negotiations, the two states signed an agreement in 1893.[24] According to this agreement, Armenians who became US nationals would be expatriated from the Ottoman Empire in accordance with Article 6 of the Ottoman Nationality Law. Following this agreement, Armenian immigrants in the United States began losing their property and inheritance rights in the Ottoman Empire.[25]

The exclusive application of Article 6 of the Nationality Law to Armenians who had immigrated to the United States and their expatriation in line with this article held great significance in terms of property transfers. On 5 March 1893, the Ottoman government adopted a specific law for matters of inheritance and property ownership of Ottoman nationals who had been expatriated. According to Article 2 of this law, those who became foreign nationals without the permission of the government and were expatriated would lose their rights to property and inheritance in the Ottoman Empire. Procedures regarding the properties of such expatriates were specified in Article 3. *Mülk* and moveable properties belonging to such persons would be distributed among their heirs, while *miri* and *waqf* lands would be considered *mahlul* based on Articles 110 and 111 of the Land Code of 1858.[26] Article 111 stipulated that the lands of those who abandoned Ottoman nationality would not be transferred to their children, fathers or mothers through inheritance, regardless of the nationality of the heir. Such lands would be considered abandoned and would be put up for auction.

A case from Kutlig, Bitlis, shows the implications of the implementation of Article 6 of the Nationality Law. In a memorandum submitted to the Sublime Porte, the Armenian Patriarchate stated that the lands of Armenian peasants who had immigrated to foreign countries were tilled by families and relatives. These lands were then declared *mahlul* by the local government and sold at auction.[27] Following this memorandum, the acting governor of Van forwarded a note written by the directorate of title deeds. In this note, the directorate emphasised that the lands of those expatriated were considered *mahlul* in line with existing legislation. On this basis, the acting governor underscored that the sale of these lands was entirely legal.[28]

After the outbreak of violence in Istanbul in October 1896, an imperial order concerning the emigration of Armenians was issued.[29] This order, published on 9 October 1896, stipulated that all Armenians in foreign countries would be subject to Article 6 of the Ottoman Nationality Law. Thus, all would be expatriated. This order also introduced a new rule in terms of emigration procedure: all Armenians who planned to leave the Ottoman Empire would sign a document guaranteeing that they would not return. This document would then be confirmed by the Patriarchate and submitted to the Ottoman authorities before emigration. Moreover, the passports to be issued to such persons would state that they would not set foot on Ottoman territory again. The order also stipulated that those Armenians who had emigrated in the previous twenty years and those who were agitators would not be permitted to return. Those who had left the empire without the permission of the Ottoman authorities were given two months to return.[30] Following this order, the central government began to implement new security measures along the borders and at harbours to prevent the return of emigrants.[31] According to the British consul in Erzurum, this order put an end to emigration, 'the impression being general among the people that the terms of the circular cover an intention on the part of the government to confiscate the property of all Armenians who have left or may leave the country and who will now lose their rights as Ottoman subjects'.[32]

As mentioned above, the Ottoman government implemented different policies with respect to Armenian immigrants, depending on the country to which they emigrated. The Russian Empire received the bulk of the Armenians who fled from the massacres. Ottoman correspondence regarding the Armenian emigrants to Russia indicates that they were not expatriated, despite the order of October 1896 stipulating the expatriation of all Armenians in foreign countries. According to the Ministry of the Interior, Armenians in Russia were considered Ottoman nationals by the government, and Article 6 of the Nationality Law did not apply to them.[33]

According to an estimate by the Russian consulate in Istanbul, there were 30,000 Armenian immigrants in Russia by 1899. According to Zeki Pasha, the number of Armenian immigrants in Russia totalled between 20,000 and 25,000. In 1901, this number increased to 40,000.[34] This massive movement of people led to a diplomatic crisis between Russia and the Ottoman Empire when in 1899 Russia decided to return 10,000 Armenians to the Ottoman Empire. The Ottoman Empire strongly opposed this decision and attempted to dissuade the Russian government. Yıldız Palace claimed that these Armenians either had been expatriated or were persons who had stayed in Russian-occupied territories by choice and that, 'even if they were honourable and honest people, their arrival to the Royal Domains would pave the way for the establishment of an Armenian majority in some locations and bring harm to the Ottoman Empire in the future'.[35] This statement alone shows that the Ottoman government approached the issue of returning Armenian refugees from an ethno-demographic standpoint and tried to control the implications of the massacres by utilising this demographic approach. The problem for Yıldız Palace was beyond the potential rebelliousness of returnees; the problem was their Armenian-ness and the fact that their return would increase the Armenian population in the region.

The Ottoman government tried to prevent the prospect of the return of these Armenians by offering Russia a population exchange.[36] According to this plan, Russia would send Muslims, such as Tatars and Circassians, to the Ottoman Empire but settle Armenians on their lands.[37] Moreover, the Ottoman government would give 100,000 liras to Russia for resettlement expenses.[38] The Russian authorities rejected this offer and stated that the Armenians in question were agriculturalists who did not pose a threat to the Ottoman Empire.[39] After long negotiations between the two countries, the Russian government stepped back from its decision to send the

Armenians back to the Ottoman Empire, in exchange for the privilege of building a railway along the coast of the Black Sea.[40] Following this agreement between the two countries, Russia no longer permitted Armenian immigrants to return to the Ottoman Empire. Those who managed to return would be sent back to Russia by the Ottoman authorities.

These regulations and policies that controlled the demographic outcomes of population movements were carefully planned by the central government, but their application at the local level was much more complicated. Correspondence between the local authorities and the central government indicates that the land and houses belonging to Armenian emigrants were often occupied by relatives or the local population and that much land remained uncultivated. In 1895, the governor of Erzurum informed the Sublime Porte that the lands of the 889 Armenians who had emigrated to Russia from Beyazıd within the last four years had not been put up for auction by the local government, with the exception of one house. The governor noted that some parts of these properties were occupied by the emigrants' relatives and neighbours, while others were occupied by Kurdish tribes. In the Pasinler district, several properties belonging to 913 Armenian emigrants were occupied by Kurdish tribes. In the Tortum district, the properties of three households were given to Muslim immigrants.[41] Agricultural fields, meadows and houses worth 514,605 kuruş which belonged to Armenians who had fled to foreign countries were appropriated by Karapapaks, and some properties belonging to emigrants from several villages of Erzurum Province had been seized by Muslim immigrants.[42] The governor of Van informed the Porte that the lands of the Armenians who had emigrated from Hakkari to Russia and Persia had not been allocated by the local government and remained uncultivated.[43] These telegrams indicate that, in Erzurum and in the Hakkari district of Van, the government as of 1898 had neither put the properties of Armenian emigrants up for auction nor officially re-allocated them to Muslim immigrants.

Correspondence between the Sublime Porte and the local governments also reveals that some local authorities were unfamiliar with the procedures and rules that should be applied to the estates and properties of Armenian emigrants. The governor of Diyarbekir, Mehmed Nazim Bey, asked the Ministry of the Interior to provide information about the rights of the heirs to the lands and properties of emigrants who had been expatriated.[44] Following this telegram, the central government demanded information from local governors regarding the number of Armenians who had emigrated, their country of destination and their properties. According to the governor of Mamuretülaziz, the number of Armenians who had fled to the United States from Mamuretülaziz Province without the necessary permits amounted to around 15,000.[45] The Erzurum governor informed the Ministry of the Interior that the numbers and destinations of emigrants were not certain. He stated that some properties were rented out in return for the tax debts of their owners, while the majority were seized by third parties.[46] Proving expatriation was also a challenge for the local governments. In Bitlis Province, thirty-one plots of land belonging to Vartan Chukajian, who had been in Russia for ten years, were demanded by his brother, who claimed ownership rights to them based on inheritance. The Bitlis governor stated that there was no record of Vartan's expatriation; hence, the administrative council (*meclis-i idare*) did not know whether the lands should be given to his brother.[47] Following this correspondence, which clearly showed the confusion among the local officials about the ways in which they should deal with the properties of expatriated Armenians, the Inspection Commission sent a detailed note to the grand vizierate. This note stated that the order published on 9 October 1896 had included no instructions on the real estate and land belonging to the Armenians who had emigrated without permits. Therefore, each case was being examined individually, but applications and demands for instruction continued to be sent to the commission. As the authorities did not provide the instructions demanded by the Inspection Commission, the commission insisted on their provision, emphasising that ownership rights should not be left in question for such an extensive period.[48]

In sum, the Ottoman government started to develop new emigration policies based on ethno-demographic concerns in this period. The prohibition of the return of Armenian emigrants and the application of Article 6 of the Nationality Law specifically to Armenians were practices connected to these policies. Considering the number of emigrants – 40,000 to Russia and more than 10,000 to the United States – controlling the transfer of the properties of these emigrants constituted an important issue for the central government. As shown in several examples, the central government issued numerous regulations and laws to manage the outcomes of this process. Yet, the implementation and the actual consequences of these regulations and laws depended on local dynamics.

The Ban on the Sale of Immovable Property to Armenians

At the end of the nineteenth century and in the early twentieth century, discussions over property ownership took a new turn in the Ottoman East. The question of who could own land or who should own the land in the region became contested within the Ottoman bureaucracy. One of the most significant developments concerning the land policies of the central government in this period was the administrative prohibition of property and land sales to Armenians.

On 5 July 1899, an urgent cipher telegram was sent from Yıldız Palace to the governors of Erzurum, Sivas, Trabzon, Bitlis, Van, Diyarbekir and Mamüretülaziz.[49] With this imperial order, the governors were informed that the palace had received intelligence indicating that the Armenian Patriarchate was involved in international monetary transactions. It was reasoned that Armenians would try to buy properties to secure the return of those who were not permitted to return to the Ottoman Empire. The governors were ordered to 'immediately and urgently' report 'whether Armenians were directly or with a proxy trying to buy properties and lands' and whether the governors had had any correspondence with Şakir Pasha regarding the matter. Moreover, if Armenians were, in fact, attempting to buy land or properties, the governors should suspend the transfer procedures until a second order was issued.[50] Thus, this order de facto prohibited Armenians from directly or indirectly acquiring property or land in the Ottoman provinces of Erzurum, Sivas, Trabzon, Bitlis, Van, Diyarbekir and Mamüretülaziz.

The telegram sent by Hasan Hilmi, the governor of Sivas, to Yıldız Palace on 2 August 1899 provides important information regarding the implementation of this order. The governor reported that, since the local authorities had received the order, they had suspended transfer procedures concerning sales of properties and lands to Armenians. Still, 'applications to the authorities in the region indicated that the continuation of this situation would be a headache'.[51] The governor noted that an additional directive ordered the local authorities to suspend the transfer procedures with respect to the sale of valuable properties and lands such as farms, shops, *hans*, *hamams*, factories, forests and winter pastures to Armenians in or outside of the Ottoman Empire. They were also ordered to investigate the secret aims of Armenian buyers. The governor indicated that clarification was needed with regard to the appropriate approach to the sale of properties and lands that were not as valuable as those encompassed by the second directive.[52]

Correspondence between the acting governor of Bitlis and the Inspection Commission in 1900 reveals that the orders sent from Yıldız Palace caused confusion and debate at different levels of the administration. In Bitlis, the order to suspend property sales to Armenians had been issued to the Court of First Instance by the governor. On 23 December 1899, the court applied to the governorate of Bitlis, demanding clarification. The court noted that some Armenians residing in the region were attempting to buy the properties of other Armenians, which the treasury had confiscated due to debt. On 2 January 1900, the acting governor of Bitlis sent a telegram to the Inspection Commission. After summarising the contents of the order sent from the palace, the governor asked for orders regarding the appropriate course of action to be taken regarding Armenians' attempts to buy properties put up for auction by the Debt Collection Office (*İcra Dairesi*) in Bitlis.[53]

In its reply dated 26 February 1900, the Inspection Commission gave the acting governor the following orders: if those who wanted to buy the properties in question were Armenians residing in the region, he should separate their cases. However, if those applying to buy the properties were not native (*yerli*), then the transfer procedures regarding the sales should be delayed (*mu'âmele-yi ferâğiyesinin te'hîr-i icrâ'sı*).[54] In his response, the acting governor informed the commission that the Armenians seeking to buy these properties were, in fact, residents of the province.[55] Following this correspondence, the Inspection Commission sent a telegram to the grand vizier, stating that 'the prohibition of land and property acquisition to native Armenians was not appropriate' and requesting that the grand vizier inform the Yıldız Palace about the situation.[56]

These documents show that Sultan Abdülhamid II had previously sent an order to suspend procedures related to the sales of property and land to Armenians in the Ottoman East. While underscoring concern for preventing the return of Armenians abroad, Yıldız Palace in this order did not make a distinction between Armenians residing in the Ottoman Empire and those residing elsewhere. The order stipulated that all property sales to all Armenians were to be suspended in the provinces of Erzurum, Sivas, Trabzon, Bitlis, Van, Diyarbekir and Mamüretülaziz. From the text of this order, it is also clear that Armenians were to be prohibited from acquiring property indirectly. The telegram of the Sivas governor indicates that Yıldız Palace had sent a second order to some provinces, specifying the types of properties covered by this ban. The governor's telegram also demonstrates that the text of the second order did not distinguish between Armenians inside and outside the empire. From the correspondence between the acting governor of Bitlis and the Inspection Commission, it is understood that the commission introduced a distinction limiting the scope of this administrative ban.

These documents show that the issues of property transfer from Armenians and changes in land ownership patterns in the eastern provinces in this period cannot be understood, if the involvement and agency of the central authorities are not taken into consideration. In this case, the sultan introduced an administrative barrier to the Armenians' entry into the land market in the above-mentioned provinces. The concern of the sultan, as also underscored by the Inspection Commission, was to prevent the return of Armenians abroad, because such Armenian refugees could strengthen the basis of their right to return by using property ownership in the Ottoman Empire as a justification.

Armenians could buy land in any province of the empire to substantiate a claim to return, but the sultan chose these specific provinces to introduce an administrative barrier to Armenians' entry into the land market. Clearly, what worried the Porte was the Ottoman East, where Armenians had a substantial population and political claims to land. From the government's point of view, the return of the Armenians and their purchase of land in the six provinces could strengthen these claims. Another point illuminated by the documents is that the Inspection Commission introduced a distinction between native and other Armenians, stating that it would be inappropriate to prohibit native Armenians from acquiring property and land. This shows that Ottoman agencies such as the Inspection Commission were actively shaping the implementation of the orders coming out of Yıldız Palace. As underlined by Christine M. Philliou, it is difficult to see the Ottoman state as an 'it' because, at certain moments, it was more like a total of 'constituent institutions and competing factions'.[57] This ban and the resulting debates can be seen as one of these moments where differences of opinion within the state were revealed.

It should be noted that there existed no legal obstacles for Armenians residing abroad to buy land in the empire directly or with the help of a proxy. As discussed in Chapter 1, the changes in the land law and the adoption of a law allowing foreigners to buy property in the empire eased this process. Thus, the distinction made by the Inspection Commission between native Armenians and foreign nationals, accepting that the latter be prevented from acquiring land, was also problematic in terms of Ottoman law.

These documents illuminate one further point: some Armenians were active in the land market after the massacres of 1894–97 and sought to buy properties in Sivas and Bitlis. The properties that local Armenians wanted to buy in Bitlis included agricultural fields, houses with gardens and haylofts that had been confiscated by the Ottoman authorities due to the debts of their Armenian owners.[58] Correspondence between the Sivas governor and the central government does not provide details regarding the quality of the properties that the local Armenians wanted to buy. Yet, the Sivas governor noted that small-scale properties were in question. These correspondences indicate that property acquisition by Armenians and the dispossession of Armenians were not mutually exclusive phenomena.

Armenians and Land Disputes in the Ottoman Empire

Still, available documents do not provide the data to conclude that the participation of Armenians in the property market was not affected by the waves of mass violence against Armenians.

These findings lead one to conclude that the central government worked as an active agent in shaping the processes of property transfer from and the dispossession of Armenians in the Hamidian period. By introducing an administrative ban on property sales to Armenians, the central government changed the basic rules of the property market in general and the land market in particular. This study also indicates that differences in niche overlap in Cilicia and the eastern provinces examined by Astourian were directly influenced by the acts and policies of the central government. In his study, Astourian has noted that Armenians continued to acquire property in the Cilicia region, even while there was a massive property transfer from Armenians in the eastern provinces. The findings of this study show that the policies of the central government might have contributed to the difference between these regions.

A series of correspondence from the early 1900s reveals the hypocritical nature of the Yıldız Palace's approach to the property rights of Ottoman subjects and the ways in which the centre used its power to ensure Muslim dominance in terms of land ownership. This series of correspondence started with a telegram from the Fourth Army Commander Zeki Pasha on 16 October 1900, which seemingly shocked the Palace. In this missive, Zeki Pasha claimed that 'the tribesmen were banned from acquiring lands in Armenian villages', and because wealthy Muslims of Bitlis, Van and Erzurum were tribesmen, the lands that were confiscated for debt and put on auction were bought by Armenians or left vacant. 'If this continued', so claimed Zeki Pasha, 'the lands of the Muslim population would be slowly transferred to Armenians' and the state treasury would suffer losses.[59] In a highly alarming tone, he wrote that, 'if this ban was not lifted, the land of the region would be taken over by Armenians within thirty-forty years'.

After receiving this telegram, the Commander in Chief directed it to the Palace, stating that the Zeki Pasha's warning should be taken serious, because the issue of population and land statistics was of rising importance.[60] Apparently, the claim that tribal leaders were prevented from entering the land market made the Palace and the sultan furious. The Palace sent a very harsh order regarding this matter:

> It is not reasonable or legitimate to prevent the Muslim people from possession in imperial dominions, and it is contrary to safety and patriotism to opt for such a practice, which would cause the gradual transfer of the land belonging to the Muslim people to the Armenians. Is there no Islam left that the Islamic law and

the interests of Muslims are being betrayed and not protected? Which apostate dares to do this? These parts are not understood. Since our benefactor who does not scold one, our Master, our caliph, His Excellency, will also treat those who dare to do this in accordance with the requirements of the sharia, with the discussion of the matter by the Council of Ministers, the current practice which prevents Muslim people's acquisition of land should be entirely and absolutely prohibited, and the means of restoring and returning the Islamic lands that have been possessed by the Armenians again to the Muslims should be found.[61]

Thus, the idea of the transfer of Muslim lands to Armenians and the possibility of the exclusion of some Muslims from the land market infuriated the sultan. The sultan's anger was reflected in the order. He went as far as calling the responsible officials 'apostates' and threatening to punish them in line with the sharia, which prescribed capital punishment for apostasy.

Following the order of the sultan, the Council of Ministers evaluated the situation and noted that there existed no decision regarding the exclusion of tribal leaders from the land market. They stated that this issue might be related to a misinterpretation of the order regarding the exclusion of tribesmen from tithe-farming in Christian villages. As 'within the scope of the law, no one should be prevented from possessing real estate and land', and if this type of practice existed in the region, it had to be abandoned.[62] At that moment, the sultan had already introduced the de facto ban on the Armenians' entry to the land market in the Ottoman East. In other words, some Ottomans had already been prevented from buying real estate and land. Thus, this concern for property rights was rather hypocritical.

After the decision of the Council of Ministers, the Grand Vizier sent an order to the Ministry of the Interior, requesting that it inform the local authorities that, according to Ottoman law, no one could be banned from acquiring property or land; that the local authorities were responsible for preventing such practices; and that those acting contrary to these principles would be absolutely and severely punished.[63] The ministry asked for information about this matter from the provinces of Van, Bitlis, Diyarbekir, Erzurum, Sivas and Ankara.[64] The governors of Van and Diyarbekir responded that not a single person had been denied the right to purchase real estate and land.[65] A few days after this information request, Zeki Pasha sent another telegram, claiming that the transfer procedure of the lands bought by some tribal *agha*s from Armenians in Erzurum, Van and Bitlis had not been completed because of the complaints of Armenians, and those *agha*s were now forcibly removed from the land. He also noted that, just a few days ago, some leaders and members of the Haydaranlı Tribe had been forcibly evacuated from the villages that they inhabited.[66]

Thus, Zeki Pasha was not able to substantiate his claim that tribesmen were excluded from the land market. In fact, at the basis of this crisis which he had provoked rested the initiatives of local governors wishing to protect the property rights of Armenians to some extent and the evacuation of tribesmen from the villages that they had seized. Covertly accusing the local officials of serving Armenian interests, alluding to the ethno-demographic significance of land ownership and using the fears of the sultan, the Pasha managed to have the local officials scolded and disciplined with the harshest threats imaginable. In this period, the pleas of Armenians for the protection of their property rights and for the return of their properties would remain unheard. This crisis provoked by Zeki Pasha and the sultan's harsh involvement in this affair suggest that this lack of response was shaped by the priorities of state officials and the balance of power among them.[67]

The Settlement of Muslim Immigrants

Another policy area in which the central government's demographic concerns can be seen concerns the settlement of Muslim immigrants in the eastern provinces.[68] The central government tried to increase the Muslim population in the region by settling Muslim immigrants fleeing Russia following the Crimean War and the 1877–78 Ottoman Russian War. As Donald Bloxham has put it, immigrant settlement in the eastern provinces aimed to consolidate central control 'over lands whose future disposition had been threatened in 1877–8'.[69] Vladimir Hamed-Troyansky has explained the rationale of the Ottoman government behind the settlement of immigrants by highlighting three issues – namely, demographic engineering, security and economic concerns.[70] Especially after the Treaty of Berlin, the government's concern in the Ottoman East was demographic and security-related.[71]

On 28 January 1888, Yıldız Palace sent an imperial order asking for information on the amount of vacant lands (*arazi-i hâliye*) in Erzurum and other Armenian-inhabited provinces.[72] The grand vizier informed the Palace that the total amount of vacant lands in the provinces of Van, Adana, Sivas, Bitlis, Mamuretülaziz, Aleppo, Diyarbekir and Erzurum was 1,523,013 *dönüm*s.[73] Then, the Sublime Porte issued another order on 29 April 1889, asking for the resettlement of immigrants from the Caucasus on vacant lands in Erzurum, Van and Hakkari. Five years after this initial order, the grand vizier stated that, despite the order, which had aimed 'at increasing the Muslim population in some provinces of Anatolia', the local authorities had failed to take the necessary measures.

Controlling Outcomes

The grand vizier ordered the settlement of immigrants in designated areas on 1 December 1894.[74]

Examining the role of the central government in the massacres of 1894–97 is beyond the scope of this study. However, these orders, which reflect a clear concern for strengthening the Muslim element in some regions of the Ottoman East, indicate that the Ottoman government had adopted a particular demographic policy to weaken the demographic basis of the Armenian political organisations' territorial claims in the region in the late 1880s. Thus, one may deduce that the Ottoman government did not start developing such a demographic policy after the massacres; rather, it had already commenced formulating a demographic policy to change the population balance in the region before the massacres occurred and even before the official establishment of the Hamidian Regiments. However, the massacres gave the state an opportunity to reach its ethno-demographic goals quickly and definitively. In the words of a governor who evaluated the results of the massacres of 1894–97 in terms of demographic policy, 'now, thanks to the wise steps taken by Your Majesty, the majority [of the population] everywhere is secured for the Muslims'.[75]

After the massacres, the central government demanded information regarding the acreage of land in regions populated by Armenians and the acreage of the land that could be used for the settlement of immigrants.[76] Upon this, a table was prepared. The sections of this table pertaining to Diyarbekir and Erzurum note that the central government on two occasions had demanded information regarding the acreage of land that could be used for the settlement of immigrants in places inhabited by Armenians.[77]

According to the table, there existed 907 plots of land (8,007 *dönüm*s) in Beyazıd, Erzurum, which had been abandoned by Armenians who had fled to Russia and not returned within the legally regulated period that would allow them to claim the properties. In the Hınıs district, there were 23,300 *dönüm*s in Armenian-populated villages that were available for the settlement of immigrants, and an additional 18,400 *dönüm*s were available in mixed villages. In Pasinler, 1,500 *dönüm*s were reported to be available in Armenian and mixed villages. The table also included information regarding the amounts of land in the provinces of Bitlis, Sivas, Van and Baghdad, but these sections were not as detailed as those for Diyarbekir and Erzurum, and it is not possible to determine whether the acreage of land specified in the table refers to lands in the regions inhabited by Armenians in particular or vacant land in general. These documents indicate that the central government took into consideration the demographic structure of the locations where Muslim immigrants would be settled and collected detailed information regarding the abandoned lands of Armenians who had fled the country.

The settlement of Muslim immigrants on lands belonging to Armenians became an issue of international public debate when European newspapers published news of the settlement of Circassian immigrants on lands belonging to Armenians in the districts of Bulanık, Ahlat, Çukur and Muş. When these incidents received international attention, the governor of Bitlis, Hüsni Bey, reported that immigrants were not settled in Ahlat and Çukur and that Circassians in Muş were settled on *mahlul* lands or lands that could legally be sold to third parties.[78] Thus, he assured the central government that the settlement procedure was carried out in line with the Ottoman legislation.[79]

In the 1900s, the settlement of immigrants in the eastern provinces and the operations of local governments with regard to the land question were followed closely by foreign consuls in the region. In 1907, the British vice-consul in Van reported that there were four important developments in the region concerning this issue. The first of these was the illegal manner of the collection of tax arrears. The second development noted by the vice-consul consisted of the new orders and regulations regarding the emigration of Armenians, which had accelerated with the collection of taxes. The vice-consul reported that the governor had informed him of orders received from the Sublime Porte that all Armenians who had left the country without permission in the previous ten years would be considered revolutionaries, and their property could be confiscated, while they would be exiled to Russia.[80] The third development was related to the lands belonging to those Armenians who had fled the country. According to the vice-consul, the governor had 'asked what he should do with these, and the Porte informed him that Mussalmen emigrants will be sent to occupy them'. Fourth, the vice-consul noted that the governor was refusing to grant permission to many Armenians who asked to leave the imperial territory. According to the vice-consul, these developments indicated a new approach on the part of the Ottoman administration. He claimed: 'Putting these four facts together, it seems to me that the policy is that as massacring Armenians is no longer fashionable, he [the governor] wishes to get them to leave the country without permission, thus outlawing them and place Mussulman colonists on their land'.[81]

Conclusion

In the Hamidian period, there happened drastic changes in the scale and characteristics of land disputes involving Armenians, as well as in the

Ottoman government's approach to these disputes. In the Tanzimat period, the Ottoman state had performed balancing acts between the demands of the Armenian cultivators and those of local powerholders. In the Hamidian period, the state was not concerned with balance and did not perform such balancing acts trying to keep a distance between itself and the parties. In this period, the state was operating based on a new conception of territoriality and demographic politics and started to develop specific measures targeting Armenians.

As examined in the previous chapter, the massacres of the 1890s were major events affecting the course of these disputes. The role of the government in the organisation of these massacres has been debated in the literature. However, the present chapter makes it clear that the state tried to control the social, political, demographic and economic outcomes of these massacres. The central government developed several policies and measures to ensure the decimation and weakening of the Armenian population and the socio-economic and demographic dominance of Muslims. In addition to leaving the perpetrators and organisers of mass violence unpunished, the state implemented specific immigration, settlement and property policies and regulations, which ensured that the massacres would cause a mass uprooting and weaken the Armenian population. Thus, while thousands were killed or forced to flee from their hometowns, thousands became serfs or *maraba*s working the lands that they once had owned.

One of the most striking among these policies is the Armenian land ban, which was introduced specifically for the Ottoman East. During the massacres, many Armenians were left destitute. The ruin caused by the massacres, as well as the growing need for cash resulting from the tax collection system, led to a miserable situation, prompting many to sell their lands or incur massive debts, often with illegal return demands. The ban ensured that these impoverished Armenian peasants could not sell their lands to other Armenians. Moreover, as it outlawed all property transfers to Armenians, Armenians who had immigrated or fled to another town or country would also be unable to transfer their lands to relatives or buyers. In sum, this ban ensured that Muslims would be on the receiving end of all property transfers concerning Armenian lands and introduced a distinct land regime for Armenians in the Ottoman East.

The land ban stood not only in conflict with the liberal legal framework introduced during the Tanzimat, but it also created tension within the Ottoman bureaucracy. It was Sultan Abdülhamid II who introduced this measure and insisted on its implementation. However, this openly discriminatory and illiberal measure created discontent among the high-level

Ottoman bureaucrats in Istanbul. These disagreements and tensions highlight the fact that the Ottoman state was not a unitary mechanism.

The exclusion of Armenian buyers from the land market and the restriction of their property rights certainly contradicted the Tanzimat and the liberalisation of the land regime. However, it was in line with the nationalisation trend linked to the rise of a new conception of territoriality. It is important to note that Prussia's policies targeting Poles and Russia's policies targeting Jews also took a similar turn in the same period. Thus, the transformation of the Armenian land question in this period was not only linked to domestic developments but also to the new territorial turn that transformed the relations between land, people and political power.

Notes

1. Astourian, *Silence of Land*, 55–81; Klein, *Margins of Empire*, chap. 4.
2. Taner Akçam, *A Shameful Act: The Armenian Genocide and the Question of Turkish Responsibility*, trans. Paul Bessemer (New York: Holt Paperback, Metropolitan Books, 2007), 41–42. For the massacre in Sasun, see Owen Miller, 'Sasun 1894: Mountains, Missionaries and Massacres at the End of the Ottoman Empire' (PhD diss. Columbia University, 2015); Polatel, 'Complete Ruin', 179–98.
3. For the reform negotiations, see Şaşmaz, *British Policy*, chap. 4.
4. TNA: FO 424/182, no. 182, Sir P. Currie to the Early of Kimberley, 11 May 1895.
5. TNA: FO 424/182, no. 356, Sir P. Currie to the Early of Kimberley, 4 June 1895.
6. TNA: FO 424/183, 'Observations on the Draft of Reforms presented by the ambassadors of the three Powers for certain Vilayets in Anatolia', enclosed in no. 153, Sir P. Currie to the Marques of Salisbury, 3 August 1895.
7. Sir P. Currie to the Marques of Salisbury, 'Scheme of Reforms', 22 October 1895, in *Turkey*, no. 1 (1896), *Correspondence Respecting the Introduction of Reforms in the Armenian Provinces of Asiatic Turkey* (London: Harrison and Sons, 1896), 168.
8. BOA: DH.TMIK.S 1/84, draft regulation, 14 Teşrin-i Evvel 1312 (26 October 1896); from the Minister of the Property Registration to the Ministry of the Interior, 15 Teşrin-i Evvel 1312 (27 October 1896); BOA: A.DVNS. NZAM.d 7, regulation on the duties of the four delegates by the Council of State, 3 Kanun-ı Evvel 1312 (15 December 1896), 249–54.
9. BOA: A.DVNS.NZAM.d 7, regulation on the duties of the commissions by the Council of State, 3 Kanun-ı Evvel 1312 (15 December 1896), 247–49.
10. BOA: A.DVNS.NZAM.d 7, the imperial order, 19 Kanun-ı Evvel 1312 (31 December 1896), 254.

11. BOA: DH.TMIK.S 23/21, the Governor of Bitlis to the Ministry of the Interior, 17 Kanun-ı Sani 1314 (29 January 1899).
12. BOA: Y.PRK.UM 46/17, the Governor of Bitlis to the Yıldız Palace, 5 Mayıs 1315 (17 May 1899).
13. BOA: DH.TMIK.S 23/78, the Governor of Mamuretülaziz to the Ministry of the Interior, 21 Şubat 1314 (5 March 1899).
14. BOA: DH.TMIK.S 23/62, the Governor of Mamuretülaziz to the Ministry of Property Records, 14 Şubat 1314 (26 February 1899).
15. David Gutman, *The Politics of Armenian Migration to North America, 1885–1915: Migrants, Smugglers and Dubious Citizens* (Edinburgh: Edinburgh University Press, 2019); Dinçer, 'Ya Sev Ya Terket', 322–54; Sipahi, 'At Arm's Length', 276–84.
16. BOA: Y.PRK.UM 49/6, the Yıldız Palace to the provinces of Bitlis, Diyarbekir, Van, Mamuretülaziz and Trabzon, 26 Teşrin-i Sani 1315 (8 December 1899).
17. BOA: Y.PRK.UM 49/6, the Governor of Van to the Yıldız Palace, 27 Teşrin-i Sani 1315 (9 December 1899).
18. BOA: HR.SYS, 2851/29, translation of tahrirat dated 22 June 1893 of Washington Embassy to the Ministry of Foreign Affairs, 30 Haziran 1309 (12 July 1893).
19. Sinan Dinçer has also underscored that this suggestion was based on an ethno-religious classification of the nationality regime. See Sinan Dinçer, 'Osmanlı'dan Dışarıya Ermeni Göçü ve Tabiiyyet Politikaları', in Adanır and Özel, *1915*, 210–28.
20. Ibid., 218.
21. 'Tâbiiyet-i Osmaniye Kanunnamesidir', *Düstur*, vol. 1, no. 1 (Dersaadet: Matbaa-i Amire, 1289), 16–18.
22. Ibid.
23. Dinçer, 'Ya Sev Ya Terket', 322–54. For further information regarding the Ottoman nationality law, see Will Hanley, 'What Ottoman Nationality Was and Was Not', in *The Subjects of Ottoman International Law*, ed. Lâle Can, Michael Christopher Low, Kent F. Schull and Robert Zens (Bloomington: Indiana University Press, 2020), 55–75; Tuğrul Arat, 'Türk Vatandaşlığından İskat Edilen Kişilerin Mülkiyet ve Miras Hakları', *Ankara Üniversitesi Hukuk Fakültesi Dergisi* 31, no. 2 (1974): 279–360; İlhan Unat, *Türk Vatandaşlık Kanunu* (Ankara: Ankara Üniversitesi Siyasal Bilgiler Fakültesi, 1966).
24. Gutman, *Politics of Armenian Migration*, 102–3.
25. Dinçer, 'Ya Sev Ya Terket', 322–54.
26. 'Ecânibin hakkı istimlâki kânununun birinci maddesinde istisnâ' olunan eşhâsın emlâk ve arâzisine mahsûs kânundur', *Düstur*, vol. 1, no. 3 (zeyl) (Dersaadet: Matbaa-i Amire, 1300), 96.
27. BOA: BEO 3317/248766, the Armenian Patriarchate to the Sublime Porte, 5 Mayıs 1324 (18 May 1908).

28. BOA: BEO 3317/248766, the Acting-Governor of Van to the Sublime Porte, 29 Haziran 1324 (12 July 1908) and derkenar of the Title Deeds Office, 19 Haziran 1324 (2 July 1908).
29. On the outbreak of violence in Istanbul, see Eldem, '26 Ağustos 1896', 113–46; Florian Riedler, 'The City as a Stage for a Violent Spectacle: The Massacres of Armenians in Istanbul in 1895–96', in *Urban Violence in the Middle East: Changing Cityscapes in the Transformation from Empire to Nation State*, ed. Ulrike Freitag, Nora Lafi and Claudia Ghrawi (New York: Berghahn Books, 2015), 164–78.
30. United States Department of State, *Papers Relating to the Foreign Relations of the United States, with the Annual Message of the President Transmitted to Congress December 7, 1896, and the Annual Report of the Secretary of State* (Washington DC: U. S. Government Printing Office, 1896), 937–38; 'tebligat-ı resmîye', *Tercüman-ı Hakikat*, no. 340, 27 Eylül 1312 (9 October 1896); BOA: DH.TMIK.M 18/38, 29 Eylül 1312 (11 October 1896). Those Armenians who wanted to emigrate were also obligated to submit photographs of themselves. See Hazal Özdemir, 'Osmanlı Ermenilerinin Göçünün Fotoğrafını Çekmek: Terk-i Tâbiiyet ve Pasaport Politikaları', *Toplumsal Tarih* 304 (April 2019): 82–90; Zeynep Devrim Gürsel, 'Looking Together as Method: Encounters with Ottoman Armenian Expatriation Photographs', *Visual Anthropology Review* 39, no. 1 (March 2023): 200–29.
31. İlkay Yılmaz, 'Governing the Armenian Question through Passports in the Late Ottoman Empire (1876–1908)', *Journal of Historical Sociology* 32, no. 4 (December 2019): 388–403. For a more comprehensive analysis on travel regulations and mobility in the late Ottoman Empire, see İlkay Yılmaz, *Ottoman Passports: Security and Geographic Mobility, 1876–1908* (Syracuse: Syracuse University Press, 2023).
32. TNA: FO 195/1941, Graves to Sir P. Currie, 16 October 1896.
33. BOA: A.MKT.MHM 549/10, Minister of the Interior to the Sublime Porte, 28 Kanun-ı Evvel 1320 (10 January 1905). The Inspection Commission also stated that the Armenians who had emigrated to Russia continued keeping their Ottoman nationality, and as some of them applied for returning to the country, the commission asked for instructions about how to manage their properties. See BOA: DH.THMIK.M 143/15, the Inspection Commission to the Grand Vizierate, 13 Kanun-ı Sani 1320 (26 January 1905).
34. BOA: HR.SYS, 2840/22, translation of the memorandum dated 14 March 1899 of the Russian Embassy to the Ministry of Foreign Affairs, 16 March 1899; BOA: Y.PRK.ASK, 151/15, cipher telegram from Fourth Army Commander Zeki to the Yıldız Palace, 5 Mayıs 1315 (17 May 1899); BOA: HR.SYS, 2840/37, translation of tahrirat dated 23 December 1901 of Tiflis Consulate to the Ministry of Foreign Affairs, 15 January 1902.
35. BOA: Y.PRK.EŞA 33/81, 24 Temmuz 1315 (5 August 1899), in *Osmanlı Belgelerinde Ermeni-Rus İlişkileri (1899–1906)*, vol. 2 (Ankara: Başbakanlık Devlet Arşivleri Genel Müdürlüğü, 2006), 25–26.

36. Yılmaz, 'Governing the Armenian Question', 396–97. On the earlier population movements between Russia and the Ottoman Empire, see Karpat, *Ottoman Population*, 68; Hamed-Troyansky, 'Imperial Refugee', 271–87.
37. BOA: Y.PRK.BŞK, 58/104, Yıldız to the Russian Embassy, 6 Mart 1315 (18 March 1899).
38. BOA: Y.PRK.HR, 27/38, Ministry of Foreign Affairs to the Petersburg Embassy, 15 May 1899.
39. BOA: HR.SYS, 2840/22, translation of the memorandum dated 14 March 1899 of the Russian Embassy to the Ministry of Foreign Affairs, 16 March 1899.
40. BOA: Y.PRK.HR, 28/63, Ministry of Foreign Affairs to the Sublime Porte, 1 Nisan 1316 (14 April 1900). The agreement between Russia and the Ottoman Empire regarding the railway in the Black Sea region was signed on 4 April 1900. See Murat Özyüksel, *The Berlin-Baghdad Railway and the Ottoman Empire: Industrialization, Imperial Germany and the Middle East* (London: I. B. Tauris, 2016).
41. BOA: A.MKT.MHM 534/4, the Governor of Erzurum to the Sublime Porte, 22 Şubat 1310 (6 March 1896).
42. BOA: DH.MKT 2140/16, the Ministry of the Interior to the province of Erzurum, 14 Teşrin-i Sani 1314 (26 November 1898).
43. BOA: A.MKT.MHM 534/4, the Governor of Van to the Sublime Porte, 9 Şubat 1310 (21 February 1896).
44. BOA: DH.THMIK.M 143/15, the Governor of Diyarbekir to the Ministry of the Interior, 2 Şubat 1319 (15 February 1904).
45. BOA: DH.THMIK.M 143/15, the Governor of Mamuretülaziz to the Ministry of the Interior, 18 Nisan 1320 (1 May 1904).
46. BOA: DH.THMIK.M 143/15, the Governor of Erzurum to the Ministry of the Interior, 1 Mayıs 1320 (14 May 1904).
47. BOA: DH.THMIK.M 143/15, the Governor of Bitlis to the Ministry of the Interior, 16 Mart 1322 (29 March 1904).
48. BOA: DH.THMIK.M 143/15, the Inspection Commission to the Grand Vizierate, 13 Kanun-ı Sani 1320 (26 January 1905).
49. BOA: Y.PRK.BŞK 59/114, cipher telegram from Yıldız Palace to the provinces of Erzurum, Sivas, Trabzon, Bitlis, Van, Diyarbekir, and Mamuretülaziz, 23 Haziran 1315 (5 July 1899).
50. Ibid.
51. BOA: Y.PRK.UM 47/55, the Governor of Sivas to the Yıldız Palace, 21 Temmuz 1315 (2 August 1899).
52. Ibid.
53. BOA: DH.TMIK.M 81/47, the Acting-Governor of Bitlis to the Inspection Commission, 21 Kanun-ı Evvel 1315 (2 January 1900).
54. BOA: DH.TMIK.M 81/47, the Inspection Commission to the province of Bitlis, 14 Şubat 1315 (26 February 1900).
55. BOA: DH.TMIK.M 81/47, the Acting-Governor of Bitlis to the Inspection Commission, 27 Şubat 1315 (11 March 1900).

56. BOA: DH.TMIK.M 81/47, the Inspection Commission to the Sublime Porte, 8 Mart 1316 (21 March 1900).
57. Christine M. Philliou, *Biography of an Empire: Governing Ottomans in an Age of Revolution* (Berkeley: University of California Press, 2011), xviii.
58. BOA: DH.TMIK.M 81/47, a memorandum, 11 Kanun-ı Evvel 1315 (23 December 1899).
59. Ibid.
60. BOA: Y.PRK.ASK 164/99, Commander in Chief to the Yıldız Palace, 15 Teşrin-i Evvel 1316 (28 October 1900).
61. BOA: İ.HUS 85/36, imperial order, 7 Receb 1318 (31 October 1900).
62. BOA: İ.DH 1378/49, the decision of the Council of Ministers, 19 Teşrin-i Evvel 1316 (1 November 1900). As noted by Nadir Özbek, upon receiving various complaints regarding oppression by tribes in the Hamidian Regiments in the process of collecting tithes, the Sublime Porte issued an order in 1898, limiting the tithe-farming granted to tribes in the Hamidian Regiments to villages inhabited by Muslims in 1898. Özbek, *İmparatorluğun Bedeli*, 206.
63. BOA: DH.TMIK.M 96/66, the Grand Vizier to the Ministry of the Interior, 23 Teşrin-i Evvel 1316 (5 November 1900).
64. BOA: DH.TMIK.M 96/66, the cipher telegram from the Ministry of the Interior to the provinces of Van, Bitlis, Diyarbekir, Erzurum, Sivas and Ankara, 26 Teşrin-i Evvel 1316 (8 November 1900).
65. BOA: DH.TMIK.M 96/66, the province of Diyarbekir to the Ministry of the Interior, 29 Teşrin-i Evvel 1316 (11 November 1900), and the province of Van to the Ministry of the Interior, 30 Teşrin-i Evvel 1316 (12 November 1900).
66. BOA: Y.PRK.ASK 165/39, a cipher from the Fourth Army Commander Zeki Pasha, 28 Teşrin-i Evvel 1316 (10 November 1900).
67. On the discrepancy between Zeki Pasha and other local Ottoman officials, see Gölbaşı, 'Anti-Armenian Riots', 70–71.
68. For the demographic policies of the Ottoman government, see Dündar, *Crime of Numbers*.
69. Bloxham, *Great Game of Genocide*, 48.
70. Hamed-Troyansky, *Empire of Refugees*, 75–85.
71. Ella Fratantuono, 'Producing Ottomans: Internal Colonization and Social Engineering in Ottoman Immigrant Settlement', *Journal of Genocide Research* 21, no. 1 (2 January 2019): 18.
72. BOA: İ.DH 1067/83643, the imperial order, 16 Kanun-ı Sani 1303 (28 January 1888).
73. BOA: Y.A.HUS 211/60, the Grand Vizier to the Ministry of the Interior, 18 Kanun-ı Sani 1303 (30 January 1888); The Ministry of the Interior to the Grand Vizier, 16 Şubat 1303 (28 February 1888); the Grand Vizier to the Yıldız Palace, 20 Şubat 1303 (3 March 1888).
74. BOA: Y.A.HUS 314/14, the Grand Vizier to the Yıldız Palace, 19 Teşrin-i Sani 1310 (1 December 1894).

Controlling Outcomes

75. Astourian, 'Silence of Land', 65–6.
76. BOA: Y.PRK.DH 12/41, no date. A document from the Ottoman Archives Yıldız Catalogue indicates that this information was compiled together with the central authorities. This document includes an untitled table. It is not possible to determine the exact date of the document, but its date was catalogued as 29 March 1903.
77. Ibid.
78. BOA: DH.MKT 683/41, the Governor of Bitlis to the Ministry of the Interior, 3 Nisan 1319 (16 April 1903).
79. It should also be noted that the settlement of Circassian immigrants in 'the east of a line extending from Erzincan in Eastern Anatolia, through Tokat and Amasya, to Samsun on the Black Sea' was restricted due to the Russian pressure in 1867. However, after the 1877–78 war, some new refugees started to be settled in this area. See Georgi Chochiev and Bekir Koç, 'Migrants from the North Caucasus in Eastern Anatolia: Some Notes on Their Settlement and Adaptation (Second Half of the 19th Century-Beginning of the 20th Century)', *Journal of Asian History* 40, no. 1 (2006): 86; Morack, *Dowry of the State*, 58, 61.
80. TNA: FO 195/2250, Vice-Consul Captain Dickson to Sir N. O'Conor, 28 April 1907.
81. Ibid.

Chapter 5

Revolution, Resolution and Resistance (1908–12): The Land Question under the Young Turks

Following the re-establishment of the constitutional regime in 1908, a new chapter, which promised equality and legal protection for all Ottoman subjects, opened up in Ottoman history.[1] The return of the Armenian properties that had been seized in the Hamidian period emerged as a pressing matter for the new regime. After 1908, thousands of Armenians began to demand the return of the properties seized during the Hamidian period. Armenians lodged hundreds of protests against usurpers, with the aim of getting their seized lands back.[2]

According to İsmail Hakkı Bey, the governor of Bitlis, there were three distinct groups of claimants.[3] First were the refugees who had left their hometown following the Hamidian massacres. These refugees, numbering more than 50,000, demanded permission to return to the Ottoman Empire and the return of their properties. Some of these properties had been seized, others had been distributed to immigrants, and yet others had been considered *mahlul* (vacant) and sold by the government. The second group of claimants consisted of those persons who had been scattered around the Ottoman East following the 'disturbances'. These people had left their homes for other Ottoman localities and began to return after the proclamation of the constitution. They, too, demanded the return of their lands. According to İsmail Hakkı Bey, this group of people which consisted of 'helpless peasants [and] poor commoners [...] had not dared to pursue' their claims during the Hamidian period.[4] After the proclamation of the constitution, 'they had realised that they too were the members and sons of this country' and began to apply to the authorities for a resolution.[5] The third group of claimants were widows and orphans who had not demanded their rightful inheritance until the post-1908 period. The governor stated that, 'with the feeling that the cadres and pressures of the ancient regime had been extinguished', they began to feel 'empowered' and to pursue their rights.[6] Although the governor did not use the word 'Armenian' to refer to these three groups of claimants, Armenians clearly counted among the groups specified by the governor. In some cases, Armenians submitted collective petitions, presenting their cases to the authorities in lists. For example, the Armenians from twenty villages of Adilcevaz presented a detailed list to the local governor, demanding restitution for stolen items and resolution of land disputes between them and the Kurdish chiefs, especially Hüseyin Pasha.

In this chapter, I will discuss the responses to these demands and explore how the premises of justice and equality transformed the debates and contestations over seized lands. Examining the impact that the revolution had on the transformation of the Armenian land question, this chapter will analyse the policies of the central government regarding the issue of land disputes, the reactions of the Armenian political and religious elite and the Kurdish powerholders to these policies, as well as the interplay between central policies and local dynamics.

The Constitutional Regime and Early Regulations

Following the proclamation of the constitution, Armenian individuals and groups began to apply to the Ottoman authorities to claim their land, and they were directed to the courts for resolution. However, several Armenian bodies – from the clergy over the Hunchaks to the ARF – were against such recourses for the resolution of land disputes and instead insisted on arbitration procedures to be carried out through administrative bodies such as local councils. The importance that several Armenian groups attached to the establishment of arbitration procedures was linked to the fact that the courts rarely resolved land disputes concerning Armenians in a satisfying manner. The vulnerability of local courts to the pressures exerted by powerholders such as chiefs and notables was one factor that produced such outcomes. The scarcity of title deeds in the eastern provinces, which were prioritised in the administrative and judicial decision-making processes, constituted another factor that hindered the resolution of land conflicts in local courts. Furthermore, the judicial infrastructure of the region was weak, and in several districts no courts existed. This situation also made resolution through the courts difficult.

Moreover, recourse to judicial procedures was practically closed to those Armenians who had fled during the massacres of 1894–97. As they had left the lands in dispute unattended for a long period of time, those who cultivated these lands after their flight could claim possession on the basis of prescriptive rights. In such cases, the government could also consider the lands as *mahlul* and sell them at auction. The Armenian political and religious elite underscored exceptions in several articles of the Land Code that suspended the application of principles such as the prescriptive rights or sale of *mahlul* lands by the government. They especially highlighted Articles 68 and 72 of the Land Code. According to Article 68, if landholders left lands uncultivated for more than three years without a valid excuse, the title deed of the lands would be invalidated, and the lands would require new title deeds (*müstahakk-ı tapu*). Valid excuses specified in the article included the necessity of leaving flooded land fallow until the water receded and being a prisoner of war. Article 72 of the Land Code stipulated that, if all or a portion of the inhabitants of a village or town left their country for a legitimate reason, their title deeds would not be invalidated (*müstahakk-ı tapu*) and their lands would not need to be registered again. In this case, immigrants had to return within a period of three years following the day when the legitimate reason for their flight ceased. If they had left without a legitimate reason or if they failed to return within three years, their title deeds would be considered invalid.[7]

The Armenian political and religious elite stressed that the oppression of Armenians in the Hamidian period was a legitimate reason that had driven thousands of people from their homes and argued that their lands could not be considered as *müstahakk-ı tapu* based on the Land Code. However, the Ottoman courts declined to implement these articles in the cases of the returning Armenians. Another important aspect of the Armenian political and religious elite's demands regarding the land question's resolution was that they did not accept monetary compensation and insisted on the return of the seized properties. As examined in the previous chapters, the preservation of the Armenian population in the Armenian fatherland formed an important concern for these actors. Thus, they tried to reverse the Hamidian policies' effects by securing the Armenians' return to their original localities.

By the end of 1909, the local courts began to hand down decisions regarding land disputes brought before them following the constitutional revolution. The results were disappointing for the Armenian public. This disappointment was reflected in the Tashnag newspaper *Azadamart*, which on 7 October 1909 published the details of nine land disputes in Muş that had been taken to court.[8] In some of these cases, men who had died long before the sales had been recorded as parties to transfer contracts. In all nine cases published in the newspaper, the Armenians who had demanded the return of their lands had failed to achieve that outcome in court. According to the paper, the first reason was that the usurpers had produced false witnesses. The second factor highlighted by *Azadamart* consisted of the influence of a certain Reşid Efendi who had served as an official in the Hamidian period. Reşid Efendi, who was accused of forging papers during his term as inspection officer (*yoklama memuru*), represented the Kurds who were claimed to have unlawfully seized the properties of the Armenian individuals. *Azadamart* claimed that Reşid Efendi had gained considerable influence due to his role in establishing the local branch of the CUP and that, thus, no one dared challenge him.

On 4 February 1910, *Azadamart* reported that the local court of Muş had finalised thirty to thirty-five land disputes concerning Armenians. In all these decisions – even in those cases in which the local administrative council had ruled in favour of Armenians– the Armenians' demands had been overruled. The newspaper claimed that, 'if the local court in Muş continues as it is, it will only serve to provide legal cover to illegal and unjust seizures in the period of oppression in the favour of a bunch of Muslim bullies while denying lawful claims and taking away people's subsistence'.[9]

Immediately after the beginning of the constitutional period, the ARF and the CUP began to negotiate a resolution to the Armenian Question. These negotiations concluded with an agreement that included the return of seized Armenian properties.[10] During the negotiations, the ARF demanded the establishment of arbitration procedures to diminish the need for judicial action for the return of disputed properties. According to the agreement between the ARF and the CUP, the Armenian land question would be resolved with the introduction of arbitration procedures, to be implemented by committees of inquiry. The usurpers would also be compensated.[11]

The Armenian Patriarchate also pushed for the resolution of land disputes after 1908. As early as on 3 November 1908, the Armenian Patriarchate sent a memorandum to the government, stating its disappointment regarding the lack of resolutions to land disputes and the lack of punishment for crimes against Armenians. The tone of this memorandum was harsh and reflected the frustration of the Patriarchate:

> Doubtful of the seriousness of our felicitous revolution, oppressors did not return the seized lands and even attempted to get back that tiny per cent of properties [that had been restored to their owners]. Those who were detained for a while were released and returned to their localities. Yet, as the constitutional government passes the time with correspondence and information-gathering instead of making [the oppressors] feel its existence and the seriousness of public order through its actions, and as it overlooks – for some reason without care – the misery and desolation of Ottoman returnees that has arisen from their inability to settle in their own homes and on their own land, the fact that these

acts are severely contrary to the new regime and that the dangers of this situation extended the threatening of Ottomans seeking the help of the Constitution with massacres are undeniable, despite the refutations of the Ministry of the Interior.[12]

The Patriarchate raised several demands for the improvement of this situation. First, it demanded the assignment of high-ranking officials without ties to the Hamidian government to the commissions that were rumoured to have been established to inquire into and solve these problems. Another demand consisted of the arrest of those who had been convicted of murder just after the constitutional revolution. These arrestees had been released in the days that followed, and the Patriarchate demanded that they be tried before the courts in Istanbul rather than in their hometowns. Thirdly, the Patriarchate demanded the return of the seized properties, as well as that the government consider Armenian returnees without land as immigrants and resettle them accordingly. Finally, the Patriarchate requested punishment for those who had collected illegal taxes or coerced Armenians into forced labour, in line with the criminal code.[13]

Another institution concerned with the issue of the return of seized Armenian properties in this period was the Society for Kurdish Mutual Aid and Progress (*Kürt Teavün ve Terakki Cemiyeti*, hereafter SKMAP).[14] In a memorandum presented to the government, the SKMAP underscored the urgency of a resolution to the land disputes and warned that, if not resolved, the situation would be exploited by domestic and foreign agitators. The memorandum demanded the resolution of conflicts between Armenians and Kurds. The second demand was a peaceful resolution to land disputes between Armenians, Kurds and others, on just, legal grounds. It also requested the resolution of disputes that might arise between landowners and cultivators. Finally, the memorandum authors pointed to the need to eliminate conflict among Kurdish tribes and chiefs. According to the SKMAP, it was necessary to form an advisory committee (*nasihat heyeti*) comprised of members including civil and military officials, as well as Kurdish and Armenian notables, to investigate these problems in depth.[15]

THE GOVERNMENT'S REACTIONS TO THE RESOLUTION OF THE LAND QUESTION

On 3 December 1908, the Council of Ministers evaluated the Patriarchate's and SKMAP's memoranda together. In its decision on the matter, the council stated that the contents of these memoranda were worthy of notice and that it was already designating an investigation and reform committee to improve the situation in Anatolia, punish those responsible for the situation and establish order and stability.[16] The members of the committee had already been selected by the Council of Ministers, but their responsibilities were left unspecified.[17] The matter was thus transferred to the Ministry of the Interior.

The CUP took the initiative to establish a committee of inquiry regarding the seized Armenian properties to the cabinet in the first months of 1909. In his memoirs, Cemal Pasha, one of the two designated members of this committee, pointed out that the CUP suggested this plan to the cabinet.[18] When the cabinet opened the issue for discussion in parliament, the deputies of the eastern provinces harshly objected. Mehmet Efendi, the deputy of Genç, argued that the re-instatement of the constitution marked the beginning of a new era for many people in the region who had 'kissed and made up' after 1908; the establishment of such a committee 'would not only impair the treasury but would also drive people to revolt against each other'.[19] Elaborating on this initiative in the Armenian National Assembly (ANA) in November 1911, Krikor Zohrab argued that this initiative had been taken by the government in response to the pressure of Armenian politicians and was opposed from all sides in parliament. According to Zohrab, the reactions of the parliamentarians had convinced the Armenian political elite that the parliament was 'less friendly' than the government with respect to the Armenians' problems and that 'raising Armenian matters in the parliament would do more harm than good'.[20]

The 31 March counterrevolution attempt[21] and the Adana Massacre of 1909 that followed disrupted the attempts to resolve the land question. While the former raised serious doubts about the future of the constitutional regime, the latter cast doubts on whether it could guarantee the lives of Armenians. The Adana Massacre resulted in the deaths of about 20,000 Armenians, and rumours that the local branch of the CUP was complicit in the bloodshed strained relations between the CUP and Armenian political organisations.[22] The Adana Massacre also triggered disputes among Armenian political organisations. While the ARF continued to officially cooperate with the CUP, the role of the CUP in the Adana Massacre and its subsequent approach to massacres became significant matters of debate in the congresses of both the Tashnagists and Hunchakists.[23]

On 7 August 1909, a few months after the Adana Massacre, an imperial order regarding the resolution of land disputes was issued.[24] This was not a specific order for the resolution of land disputes concerning Armenians, but a general order to apply to all land disputes. According to this order, land disputes would be resolved by administrative councils because prolonged cases were causing detriment to the parties in dispute and to the treasury. If both parties in dispute had deeds of possession (*tasarruf senedi*) and if the more recent deed did not state that the disputed land had been transferred to the new owner through official sale or transfer procedures (*satış ya da ferâğ*), then the lands would be returned to the holder of the older deed. If the more recent deed stated that the disputed land had been transferred to the current occupier through sale or transfer, then the land would stay in the possession of the party with the more recent deed. If only one of the parties in dispute held a deed of possession, then the disputed land would be given to the holder of the official deed. If either of the parties in dispute had a deed of possession, then the disputed land would be given to the party who was paying the land tax. In all cases, those parties discontent with the decision made by the administrative council could apply to court.

THE ADMINISTRATIVE RESOLUTION AND LOCAL RESISTANCE

The decision to apply an administrative resolution to the land disputes affected the course of events at the local level. In November 1909, a series of meetings was held in Van, with the participation of thirty-three Kurdish chiefs and twelve local Armenian leaders, including the bishop.[25] These meetings were called by Sheikh Abdulkadir, a founding member of the SKMAP; according to the British Consul Marling, it was the governor of Van himself who had induced Sheikh Abdulkadir to take such action.[26] The only notable absences from these meetings were Haydaranlı Hüseyin Pasha of Patnos and Şakir Agha of Şatak.

In the final meeting held under the chairmanship of the governor, all the Kurdish chiefs present signed a formal document specifying the resolutions accepted in the course of the meetings. These resolutions included 'a promise on part of the Kurds to live in friendship with their Armenian brothers, to work for the union of all elements and to help the government to punish wrong-doers' and to 'establish and further industries in the province and to spread education by opening schools in various villages'.[27] This final document also included a stipulation regarding land disputes by which Kurdish chiefs promised to hand over disputed lands in their possession for which Armenians possessed title deeds, by the spring of 1910. Disputes in which Armenians did not possess title deeds would be settled by the local government.[28] While this can be seen as an important local step toward the resolution of land disputes, the Armenians seriously objected to these meetings. As pointed out by James Morgan, British vice-consul in Van, ...

> ... the Armenians were opposed from the beginning to the convocation of the chiefs, saying that there was no necessity for it, and the fact that the government

officials had seen fit to recognize the chiefs' authority by summoning them to deliberate with them on matters which it was the Government's province to settle alone, and given a new life to their power over the tribesmen, a power which had always been harmful to the tribesmen and to the country, which was unnecessary under a constitutional regime, and which had shown signs of diminishing since the proclamation of the Constitution.[29]

As noted by Morgan, these meetings were seen as an initiative to strengthen the position of those Kurdish chiefs whose powers had been curbed by the proclamation of the constitution. Another point raised by the Armenians opposing these meetings was that the chiefs were already obliged to return the lands for which Armenians held title deeds, provided that the local councils made decisions in line with the order of 7 August.

Correspondence among Ottoman authorities shows that between August 1909 and April 1910 several properties were returned to Armenians, based on administrative resolutions. According to the acting governor (*vali vekili*) of Bitlis, Selim Bey, the province's administrative council returned to their owners 730 properties worth more than 5,000 liras in total. Selim Bey noted that the number returned to the owners by administrative action in the Muş district were excluded from this number.[30] In another telegram, dated 26 February 1910, Selim Bey reported that a total of 235 cases had been submitted to sharia and civil courts in the city, and 134 of these had been dismissed. He also noted that most cases concerned disputes among parties of the same ethnicity, and only a few concerned disputes between Armenians and Kurds. In this telegram, Selim Bey also informed the central government about the number of properties returned through administrative action in the Muş district. Some 538 properties had been returned in this manner, and one of these was very valuable, worth alone more than 168,000 *kuruş*.[31]

In several cases, the administrative actions concerning the return of seized properties carried out by the local authorities failed to produce results. Governors trying to implement the order of 7 August 1909 faced resistance from local officials under their supervision. For example, in Mendan (Yatıksırt), a village of Archag (Erçek) in the province of Van, the Kurdish chief Said Bey possessed lands that had belonged to Armenian villagers. The governor ordered the director (*müdir*) of Archag to remove the Kurds settled on the disputed lands. While it was reported that the orders had been carried out, it was later discovered that the officials at the district level had done nothing of the sort. The governor dismissed the director due to this inaction, and Said Bey was ordered to be imprisoned. Two days after his capture, Said Bey suspiciously managed to escape.

According to James Morgan, the attitude of the governor of Van in this case created hostility against him at the local level.[32]

Cases in Huyt (Kavakbaşı) and Taghavank (Uran) in Bitlis also indicate the extent of local resistance. In Huyt, the lands of the Armenians who held title deeds were occupied by local Kurds. Upon the complaints of the Armenians to Selim Bey, the acting governor of Bitlis, gendarmerie officers were ordered to conduct an inquiry in the village and to prepare a report. While the governor threatened to dismiss the gendarmerie officers, who were natives of the region, for failing to comply with his orders, the officers raised several objections to leave the matter hanging.[33] A similar case concerned the Armenians of Taghavank, Bitlis, who applied to the administrative council for the return of their lands that had been seized by Kurds. In this case, the governor informed the administrative council that the claimants possessed title deeds and that the lands should be restored to them, in line with the orders of the Ministry of the Interior. However, this initiative was strongly opposed by the qadi, the mufti and a Kurdish member of the administrative council. The case was delegated to the court despite the governor's efforts to restore the lands to the Armenians through arbitration.[34] These examples indicate that there existed a serious degree of resistance by government officials at the local level, as well as by local powerholders who hindered the use of arbitration procedures for the resolution of land disputes.

Land disputes in Çukur, Bitlis, illuminate the local notables' resistance to the prospect of returning the properties which they had seized in the Hamidian period. On 2 April 1910, Selim Bey reported that the Muslim and Armenian farmers of several villages had attempted to retake from the city's notables the lands that they had disposed of fifteen or twenty years ago. According to the deputy governor, who asked permission to arrest those who pioneered this movement, the situation was grave; 'almost an idea of socialism had erupted in the region'.[35] In the petition sent to the Sublime Porte, Armenians and Muslims from thirty-three villages in the region accused one of the members of the administrative council, Necmeddin Efendi, his son Şemseddin Efendi, the head of the administrative council by the name of İbrahim Efendi and their men of having usurped their lands through coercion and fraud during the Hamidian period. They claimed that these notables and their men had threatened Muslims by accusing them of being deserters and by accusing Armenians of being guerrilla fighters (*feda'is*). For them, an administrative resolution was not an option due to the position that the usurpers held in the ranks of the administrative council, and they demanded the formation of a commission for the resolution of their problems. In their terms, it was a matter of life and death, and if no solution was forthcoming, they would be 'buried alive'.[36]

On 26 April 1910, the people of Çukur sent another petition to the Sublime Porte, complaining about the local authorities' inaction. The peasants claimed that the armed men of Hacı Necmeddin prevented them from cultivating their lands and that thousands of people would perish if the case remained unresolved.[37] The new governor of Bitlis, İsmail Hakkı Bey, was of the opinion that the peasants' claims against the notables were just since the latter had used their influence over local officials to register lands in dispute in their names. He suggested that, rather than the thousands of peasants who could not afford to pay for court expenses, the notables should be directed to the courts.[38]

In his visit to Çukur, İsmail Hakkı Bey delivered a fierce speech reassuring the peasants. In this speech he purportedly said that 'he would sacrifice himself as a "feda'i" in defence of the rights of the peasantry, and that he would blow up usurpers and oppressors', such as Hacı Necmeddin Efendi of Bitlis, 'with dynamite'.[39] Despite numerous petitions by Kurdish and Armenian peasants and the reassurances of the governor, the people of Çukur did not manage to achieve any results. As noted by the British Vice-Consul Safrastian, the case involved several Bitlis notables who had extraordinarily enriched themselves in the Hamidian period. If the problem was handled with equity, 'many notables [would be] unmasked and their fiendish wickedness [would be] brought to light'.[40] It was probably this factor that hindered the resolution of land disputes in Çukur, disputes that affected the lives of thousands of Muslims and Armenians.

While some properties were indeed returned in this period, Kurdish chiefs began to object to the procedures introduced by the central government. Kurdish chiefs started developing strategies to maintain their position, along with the properties which they had seized. Said Bey, who was forced to return the properties he had seized in Van's village of Mendan, started a personal rebellion against the government. This extraordinary brigand confined himself to attacking government officials, amassed around seventy followers and was never captured by government forces, despite several expeditions in the ensuing years.[41]

The chiefs from prominent tribes affiliated with the Hamidian Regiments also protested the local authorities' attempts to resolve land disputes. In a joint telegram sent from Malazgirt to Mahmud Şevket Pasha on 8 September 1909, district governor (*aşiret kaymakamı*) Halid Bey of the 26th regiment, district governor Fethullah Bey of the 27th regiment, district governor Mehmed Emin Bey of the 28th regiment, Major Mustafa Bey of the 29th regiment, Major Hüseyin Bey of the 28th regiment and Major

Süleyman Bey of the 27th regiment claimed that the acts of local officials were driving people to react against each other. According to these chiefs, authorising local officials and administrative councils to resolve land disputes (instead of the courts) was a breach of law that would bring harm to the people. Legal principles such as prescriptive rights and statutes of limitations, so they claimed, were not respected by the local authorities.[42]

Mehmed Sıddık Agha of Abagha (Çaldıran), Van, took another path of protest in the winter of 1909. When the governor ordered him to pay his tax debts and to return the Armenian lands he had seized, he fled with his family to Persia. In the waning days of 1909, many Kurdish chiefs, including Haydaranlı Hüseyin Pasha, joined those who fled with their sheep and men.[43] Some, like Ali Bey, the brother of Haydaranlı Emin Pasha of Erciş, Van, attacked Armenians on their way to Persia.[44] During his flight, Hüseyin Pasha had word spread around that he was leaving the Ottoman Empire because the local authorities had pushed him into returning the Armenian properties that he had seized. This claim was denounced by the governor of Erzurum, who stated that, 'during his nine-month term (as governor), not even an inch from the lands seized by tribal chiefs have been returned to the Armenians by administrative means'.[45] This document indicates that the introduction of the administrative resolution did not bring about the return of seized Armenian lands in Erzurum. Hüseyin Pasha's claims, however, reflect the extent to which the issue of land disputes was strategic manoeuvring on the part of those Kurdish chiefs who fled to Persia. The flight of Kurdish chiefs was a clear stance against the Ottoman government and the policies of restitution. Kurdish chiefs were clearly aware of the geo-political fragility of the border region.[46] As their men constituted an important part of Ottoman military power in the region, their flight raised serious concerns about security in the Ottoman East.

The Changes in the Government's Approach

In 1910, there occurred a change in the central government's approach to the issue of the land question. This change can be traced in three areas. First, in a cabinet decision on 31 March 1910 the Ottoman government introduced a limitation on the use of administrative resolution procedures. Another indicator of this shift was that Ottoman authorities began to settle immigrants in the eastern provinces. This practice was new to the constitutional regime; in the first two years following 1908, the Ottoman authorities had not settled any immigrants there. Then there was the rapprochement between the Ottoman authorities and the Kurdish chiefs who had fled to Persia. These chiefs were invited back and officially welcomed by the Ottoman authorities.

THE ORDER OF 31 MARCH 1910 AND LIMITS TO THE ADMINISTRATIVE RESOLUTION

The order of 7 August 1909 was amended by a cabinet decision on 31 March 1910, in which the government introduced a limitation on the use of the arbitration procedures that the administrative councils could employ in the resolution of land disputes.[47] This cabinet decision was made after a recommendation by the Council of State.[48] The cabinet decision of 31 March stipulated that the administrative councils could arbitrate only on conflicts that emerged within a year, while all other disputes would be directed to courts. Thus, the decision limited the use of arbitration to recent seizures. According to this decision, the seizures that had taken place in the Hamidian era would not be resolved by administrative councils. The documents in the Ottoman archives also show that this decision was the outcome of extensive correspondence and planning by the Ottoman authorities.

This cabinet decision, which introduced a limitation on the use of arbitration procedures, took place after several complaints by local officials and governors from different parts of the empire, including Edirne, İzmir, Diyarbekir, Erzurum and Bitlis.[49] The Bitlis governor reported that the priority given to title deed holders in administrative councils afforded them an unjust advantage over those who had tilled the lands for many years and thus should have acquired prescriptive rights. The governor of Erzurum informed the Ministry of the Interior regarding the case of immigrants settled on lands belonging to an Armenian named Boghos in the Pasinler district, noting that the administrative council had decided to return the lands to Boghos and to evacuate the settlers by force if necessary. The governor of Edirne warned that 'the country is populated by ignorant peasants who will resort to their guns, if the lands they hold as dear as their lives are interfered with', and he demanded the establishment of a special commission and the introduction of extraordinary measures – such as those taken for the suppression of brigands in Rumelia – for the resolution of land disputes.[50] Another complaint was raised by the General Assembly (*meclis-i umumi*) of Diyarbekir, which underscored that the administrative councils lacked the authority to enforce their decisions and could not compel usurpers to give back the lands that they had decided to return to their original owners. Members of the assembly argued that the central government should either establish mobile courts (*seyyar mahkemeler*) for the resolution of land conflicts, which they estimated to comprise 60 per cent of all disputes in the province, or to improve the conditions of the local courts in the centre.[51] Such criticisms regarding the use of administrative resolutions indicate that the local authorities played a role in shaping the policies of the central government regarding land disputes in this period.

The Ministry of the Interior directed the complaints of the local authorities to the grand vizier and the Council of State and stated that several problems arose from the current regulations.[52] According to the ministry, the first problem concerned the exclusion of claims based on prescriptive rights from the proceedings of administrative councils. The second complication underscored by the ministry was the fact that those who had tilled the land in different parts of Anatolia had not received proper title deeds; many only had simple contracts (*sened-i 'âdî*) rather than title deeds. They were said to have been deprived of their legal rights by the excessive authority allocated to the administrative councils. Third, the ministry argued that even those who had disposed of their lands on their own volition by issuing sales documents (*beyn senedi*) to those who had bought their lands were securing their return due to title deeds they had hidden for many years. The fourth problem underscored by the ministry was the fact that administrative councils lacked the authority to determine the borders of the disputed lands.

The ministry was of the opinion that, however just the decisions reached by administrative councils might be, they would always be open to question by the parties involved in the dispute, because they were administrative rather than judicial decisions. The Ministry of the Interior demanded the introduction of a limitation on the use of administrative resolutions, the introduction of a special regulation concerning refugees settled on disputed lands and the formation of temporary courts in Rumelia, Anatolia and Arabia for the resolution of land conflicts.[53] It was following these developments that the cabinet introduced a limitation on the use of arbitration procedures. According to the same cabinet decision, those whose lands were considered *mahlul* and sold in their absence would be given the sum for which their lands were sold at auction, and those whose lands were used for the establishment of new villages and settlements would either be monetarily compensated or given other land from the treasury.[54]

The cabinet decision of 31 March closed the door on the councils' resolution of disputes related to seizures that had taken place before 1908. This posed a major setback for the restitution of Armenian properties and hence created significant resentment among the Armenian political and religious elite and population. According to Sir G. Lowther, who prepared the annual consular report on Turkey for the British Foreign Office, the government's actions indicated that the promise of the CUP to return Armenian lands had 'now resolved itself into the sentiment that it would be wrong to dispossess the Kurdish usurpers'.[55]

Another development to be mentioned here is in the change of the political understanding of the CUP after the party congress held in Salonika in October-November 1910 under the leadership of Halil Bey.[56] Following the congress, the proceedings were published, and the published decisions mostly contained responses to criticism regarding the simultaneous existence of a party and a committee within the CUP organisation. Correspondence among the British consular staff shows that debates and decisions in this congress extended beyond political debates regarding the structure and operations of the CUP. According to British consular staff, the CUP members made several other decisions in secret meetings during the congress. Vice-Consul Geary, who was in Monastir at the time, reported that he had obtained the actual details of the proceedings of the congress 'from a confidential source, on which perfect reliance can be placed' and that the information given to the press had little connection 'with the subjects which actually occupied the attention of the assembly'.[57]

According to the account, members of the CUP had made it clear in the deliberations that they distinguished first between Muslims and Christians and second between Turks and other Muslims. They referred to Christians as 'unreliable elements'. In this account, the CUP leaders were claimed to have reached a number of secret resolutions regarding several matters, from boycotts to the establishment of new parties. One of these secret resolutions concerned the settlement of immigrants. Vice-Consul Geary summarised this resolution as follows:

> Mahommedan immigrants must be planted on the Greek and Bulgarian frontiers to prevent the incursion of bands. For this purpose, 20,000 immigrants were necessary, involving an additional expenditure of £ T. 220,000. At Erzeroum also a commission should be created for the settlement of immigrants from the Caucasus and Turkestan. Land must be found and with this view old chiftlik system must be abandoned, and Christians prevented from purchasing property.[58]

According to this account, the CUP changed its approach to the matter of land ownership as a result of the Salonika congress and began to see land as a means of ethno-religious domination. Since these were secret resolutions, it is not possible to know the exact content of the deliberations and resolutions. Yet, several other documents indicate that the CUP and some Ottoman officials more generally began to see land as a means of ethno-religious dominance after 1910 and actively worked to settle immigrants in zones prone to territorial disputes, such as Macedonia and the eastern provinces.[59]

While examining land disputes and ethno-politics in Western Anatolia, Yücel Terzibaşoğlu has pointed to an interesting document dated 1911, which reflects the rise of ethno-nationalist concerns on the part of the Ottoman authorities with respect to land.[60] This document was attached to the draft law on immovable properties, the details of which have been examined in relation to the development of individual and exclusionary ownership rights to land in Chapter 1. As noted by Terzibaşoğlu, the unnamed author of this report put great political emphasis on land ownership:

> At a time when many precedents are conceded for the spreading of the objective of forming states based on the principle of nationality, and when there are many obvious indications of stoking up the objectives of separatism and independence in some places, the issues of the sale of land and land in general, as proposed in this draft law, attain an urgent importance.[61]

The author of the report emphasised that Bulgarians, Greeks and Serbians had managed to gain control of large tracts of land and to use them in a correct, productive way in line with their national interests. According to the author, the success of these Balkan nations was related to ...

> ... the distribution of the land acquired according to capacity and need; the administration of the issues regarding land by cadres who were cognizant that ownership of land is the basis of the transformation from a captive to a sovereign nation; the availability of cheap credit facilities for land transactions; and the carrying out of these measures with courage and perseverance.[62]

After underscoring the importance of land and presenting an evaluation of the success of Balkan nations in terms of their land policies, the author presented warnings regarding the disposal of lands by Muslims to non-Muslims. According to the author, it was necessary ...

> ... to explain in plain language to all the Muslims the danger and damage that disposing of land will cause them. This advice, however, should not be made in a manner so as to create animosity among the Muslims against the Christians, otherwise it could be counter-productive. The question of land should be delegated to capable cadres who understand how critical it is for the Muslims to remain in ownership of the land if they are to remain in the ruling *millet* (community). For this, loans with low interest should be extended to Muslims for the purchase of land.[63]

This report, attached to the draft law on immovable properties, indicates that ethno-nationalist concerns were shaping the approach of some

Ottoman officials to the matter of land ownership after 1910. The approach of Ottoman officials in Istanbul, CUP members and local officials to land disputes, as well as the actions and inactions of the central government regarding the land question, should be considered in this light.

THE ARMENIANS' REACTIONS TO THE CHANGE IN THE GOVERNMENT'S POLICY

The cabinet decision of 31 March 1910, which introduced a limitation on the use of arbitration procedures, was countered with protests and complaints from Armenians. On 20 April 1910, the governor of Erzurum sent a telegram indicating the extent to which the cabinet decision had created disturbances at the local level. He reported that the Armenian bishop in Erzurum objected to the decision, claiming that 'the decision would force the people into mutual killing'.[64] In the same telegram, the governor noted that land disputes constituted the majority of applications to the local government and that approximately 80 per cent of all applications were related to such conflicts. Moreover, most crimes and murders in the province were related to land disputes. According to him, if land disputes were to be directed to the courts, their judicial procedures and capacity had to be improved first.[65] Thus, he suggested the abolition of court expenses, which hindered the application of people to the courts, as well as the appointment of new judges to improve judicial capacity.

The introduction of a limitation on the use of arbitration procedures had broad repercussions in the Armenian press. On 30 April 1910, *Azadamart* published an editorial titled 'The Vicious Circle: The Unresolved Land Question'.[66] This article noted that the promises concerning the establishment of a commission and the resolution of the land question had remained unrealised since the proclamation of the constitution and that the land question had become a vicious circle in the constitutional period. The article underscored that the problem was more than an Armenian issue; the problem was 'the bullying of some *bey*s, sheikhs and *agha*s and the harm done to Armenian, Kurdish and Turkish peasants – to those without power'.[67] The article stated that 'interest-seekers from several nationalities had deprived Armenian peasants and Kurdish cultivators of their lands through force and fraud and seized not only properties belonging to private persons but also lands and pastures belonging to communities'.[68] Thus, the author of this article not only objected to forceful seizures but also to the liberalisation of the land regime and the privatisation of communal properties such as pastures. In this article, Armenian parliamentarians and the Patriarchate were also called to action.

Azadamart went a step further and openly accused the government of conspiring against Armenians, in another editorial titled 'The Real Intention of the Government: A New Disposition, A New Blow', published on 15 June 1910. In this article, the introduction of a limitation on the use of arbitration procedures was defined as a 'governmental blow to Armenian peasants'.[69] It argued that this new regulation would only serve to give legal protection to oppressors, promote brigandage and annihilate the Armenian peasantry. The author stated that neither the Patriarchate nor the Armenian political parties and parliamentarians could comply with or remain silent regarding their demands and concerns related to this matter. The final part of the article was just as assertive:

> The Armenian people have decided to defend their rights regarding the land question on absolute and final terms. We know no words or resolutions other than this. The government will either rely on rights and justice or proclaim itself as the bearer of oppressive, anti-constitutional and Hamidian rationality.[70]

As seen in these examples, the Armenian press closely followed the policies of the central government regarding the land question. The introduction of a limitation on the use of administrative resolution procedure was interpreted as a blow to the Armenian peasantry by *Azadamart*, which called Armenian political and religious actors to action. The articles published in *Azadamart* also show that, in the ARF circles of this period, class-related concerns were raised side-by-side with nationalist concerns.

THE RAPPROCHEMENT BETWEEN THE GOVERNMENT AND KURDISH TRIBES AND THE OUTBREAK OF A NEW WAVE OF VIOLENCE

The emergence of a new rapprochement between Kurdish chiefs and the central government by the spring of 1910, together with the marginalisation of the arbitration procedures by the limitation of its use to disputes that had occurred in the year following the proclamation of the constitution, marked the beginning of a new era for land disputes and for the living conditions of Armenian peasants in the Ottoman East. As noted above, the second action of the Ottoman government indicating a serious change in the approach to the issue of land disputes was the invitation of Bekir Sami Bey, governor of Van, to the Kurdish chiefs who had fled to Persia to return to the country in the first months of 1910. In April, the chiefs were informed that their ranks would be abolished and that their properties would be taken over by the state if they did not come back within a reasonable period of time. If they returned, they would maintain their privileges, together with the properties they had seized. They took up the offer and received an official welcome upon their return to Van.[71]

On 13 February 1911, the Ministry of the Interior sent an order to the governors of Bitlis, Van, Mamuretülaziz and Erzurum, stating that the Ottoman diplomats in Tiflis were warning the central government to take action against the Russian attempts to sway Kurdish chiefs to the Russian side. The Ministry of the Interior, upon the request of the Ministry of War, ordered the local governors to act to prevent such an outcome. The Ministry of the Interior stated that …

> … while it is necessary to protect the Armenian element from the oppression that prevailed in the previous period, it is also necessary to flatter and praise the Kurdish element, and, if needed, this should be carried out through rewarding chiefs through effective instruments such as allocating money and giving honours to secure their loyalty to the sovereign government.[72]

A new wave of violence, unprecedented in the constitutional period, erupted after this change in the state's approach. Attacks on Armenians with respect to land disputes intensified, and even in cases where Armenians had secured the return of their properties, they were hindered in their efforts to cultivate the returned lands. According to the acting vice-consul of Britain in Bitlis, around forty Armenians had been killed in the province over a period of two months (April-June 1910), and in several cases the murders were related to land disputes.[73]

After 1910, Huyt became one of the most problematic regions in the Ottoman East. As mentioned above, there existed many disputed lands in this district. Some properties were returned to the Armenians; however, during almost every harvest season, the crops and the livestock of the Armenian villagers were taken away by Kurdish tribesmen under the leadership of Musa Bey and his brothers.[74] The Kurds also prevented the Armenians from ploughing the lands recently restored to them. Between March and July 1911, around a dozen Armenians were killed on separate occasions in this district.[75] All these murders were related to land disputes. Due to the significant resistance of local Kurds, murderers were not effectively prosecuted.[76] As the disorder escalated, some seventy Kurds were arrested following a military expedition, but those directly accused of instigating the violence, such as Musa Bey, were not captured. After a few months, all those detained were released.

Recognizing that the local government lacked either the capacity or the will to enforce the rule of law, several new seizures were carried out with the use of force after 1910. In February 1911, a Kurd named Mervan killed five Armenians over a land dispute in Hizan. Following this, the local Kurds united to guarantee his freedom by providing false witnesses to say that he was a minor. In the end, Mervan was not taken to court for his crimes. The procedural impunity evident in such cases alarmed the local Armenians. In the spring of 1911, tensions escalated as the Sheikh of Hizan began to pressure Armenian peasants to transfer their lands to him. In order to secure this transfer, the servants of the sheikh prevented the Armenian villagers from ploughing their fields and from taking their animals to pasture or water.[77] In some cases, the targets were specifically chosen. The only murder of an Armenian in Hizan in the summer of 1911 was of an Armenian notable named Kantcho, who 'had fought for years against the sheikh for defending the lands of his fellow-villagers'.[78]

Apart from the resurrection of violence, old practices such as levying illegal protection tax (*hafir*) resurfaced. For example, in the autumn of 1911, the Kurdish chiefs in Modki (Mutki), including Hacı Musa Bey and Hacı Reshid Agha, sent word to twenty Armenian villages to prepare to repay their *hafir* debts for the previous three years. Upon the insistence of the Armenians that they were only obliged to pay taxes to the government under the new regime, the men under the leadership of Hacı Musa and Hacı Reshid began to take their 'share' by robbing the villages of their sheep. During these raids to collect *hafir*, several women were raped, and one Armenian named Avag Muradian was murdered by the men of Musa Bey.[79]

Another change with regard to land disputes after 1910 was related to the distribution of Armenian properties to immigrants. In the Hamidian period, immigrants from the Caucasus and Balkans had been settled on lands belonging to Armenians. These properties used for resettlement mostly belonged to the Armenians who had fled the country. After the establishment of the constitutional regime in 1908, thousands of Armenians returned to their lands, and serious conflicts between the settlers and returnees arose. These kinds of dispute remained unresolved for the most part. In the autumn of 1910, the government began anew to grant land belonging to Armenians to immigrants. In the Yoncalı village of Bitlis, the Armenians had successfully reclaimed their rights to the disputed lands in court, and in the autumn of 1910 the Circassian immigrants were evacuated from the village. However, in the spring of 1911 the same immigrants were settled on other Armenian lands near the village. In the villages of Dermend (Tirmit/Alazlı) and Vartenis (Altınova) of Bitlis, land disputes between Armenian villagers and Circassian immigrants who had been settled there around 1904 were taken to court. As the court proceedings continued, twenty-one new parcels of land belonging to the same Armenians were given to the immigrants in the spring of 1911.[80]

According to Consul McGregor, in this period the Circassian immigrants also started to be settled on Kurdish peasants' properties.[81]

In addition to the settlement of Circassian immigrants on Armenian lands and the allocation of new Armenian lands to immigrants beginning in 1911, the Ottoman government began to use disputed Armenian lands to settle the nomadic Sheikhbezemli Kurds in Lusonk (today the village of Yaylapınar in Bayburt) in the province of Erzurum.[82] The government initiative to resume the distribution of Armenian lands to immigrants was interpreted by the British Consul McGregor as indication of a change in government policy. He noted that, 'in thus reverting to the time-honoured policy of stiffening the reliable element on their frontiers by the importation of Muhajirs, the government appears to be carrying out the programme generally supposed to have been decreed by the CUP and similar developments may be looked for in other frontier districts'.[83]

The dispute between the Kurdish peasants from the Zomik village of Tutak and Haydaranlı Hüseyin Pasha reveals the extent to which Kurdish chiefs were able to exploit their newly recognized significance among the Ottoman authorities to secure the ownership of the lands that they had seized.[84] During the Hamidian regime, the Kurds of Zomik, who were also members of the Haydaranlı tribe, had requested the help of Hüseyin Pasha in the face of pressure from the Sipkanlı (Sipki) tribe. In this period, the villagers had given Hüseyin Pasha some land in return for his protection. During his term as director of Patnos, Hüseyin Pasha registered many parcels in the village in his name;[85] in the meantime, he began to act as the owner of the entire village and to banish those who challenged him, settling others from among his tribe in their places.

Upon the proclamation of the constitution, the Kurdish peasants whom Hüseyin Pasha had banished from the village began to return. Upon this challenge, Hüseyin Pasha took the matter to the administrative council, claiming that the returning peasants were interfering with his use of the properties that belonged to him. According to a later evaluation by the Erzurum administrative council, the administrative council of the time had been under the influence of the Beyazıt deputy, Süleyman Sudi Bey, and had decided to evict eleven returning families from the village, on account of the deputy's influence.[86]

Upon the complaints of these peasants, an investigation commission was sent to the village. This commission – comprised of the director of education, Şükrü Bey, and the head of the registry office, Mahmud Bey – found that the village had more than a thousand plots of land amounting to more than 25,000 *dönüm*s. The title deeds held by Hüseyin Pasha concerned only four plots of agricultural land, fifteen pastures and a winter quarter. Thus, his claims to the ownership of the entire village were groundless. The commission noted that Hüseyin Pasha had been protected by the government, at the expense of the poor peasants who had been brought to ruin; not only the villagers of Zomik but also those of Patnos and Van were raising complaints against Hüseyin Pasha. According to Şükrü Bey and Mahmud Bey, an inspection to determine the borders would reveal the exact size of the parcels of land belonging to Hüseyin Pasha and resolve the case. On 20 June 1911, the Erzurum administrative council evaluated the issue and decided on a resolution to the problem. This decision noted that 'the usurpations and crimes of the Haydaranlı chief Hüseyin Pasha are well-known, and there is not a single village in the Beyazıd district which was not harmed by him through pillage, looting and expulsion during the previous regime'.[87] The administrative council demanded a resolution to the land conflicts, which they claimed hindered people's inclination towards the new regime and provided a receptive ground for harmful political activities.

In the meantime, Hüseyin Pasha decided to use all his leverage to affect the outcome of this process. He wrote several petitions to the grand vizier and the Ministry of War, demanding their intervention to secure his rights to the disputed lands. In the petition sent to the Ministry of War, Hüseyin Pasha claimed that he had been a faithful servant of the Ottoman Empire for many years and sought refuge in Persia due to the pressures of the governor of Erzurum, whom he accused of paving the way for the 'looting of his property' during his absence. On 20 June 1911, the Ministry of War sent a note to the Ministry of the Interior, stating that the ministry had received complaints from Hüseyin Pasha that the local authorities had not prevented the interference of third parties on his lands – instead, they protected those who interfered.[88] Hüseyin Pasha also began to throw around threats that he would once again flee to Persia if the lands in dispute were taken from his possession.[89] He also contacted Ömer Naci Bey and Cavid Bey, leading CUP members who were visiting the region, and openly declared that he was himself a Unionist.

While the governor of Van argued that Hüseyin Pasha was conspiring to start an uprising in collaboration with Abdürrezzak Bedirxan and demanded the deployment of troops to the region to secure public order, he was unable to obtain the assistance of the army.[90] In the governor's own terms, he was of late 'unable to get any help from the army for any sort of matter' and his orders were not followed.[91] The governor's demands that the army be deployed to the region were dismissed by the grand vizier on 18 September 1911.[92] A couple of days later, the governor stepped back and suggested that the case be suspended; he had come to conclude that

Hüseyin Pasha's possible 'flight to Persia was not in line with the interests of the state for the time being'.[93] The governor informed the Ministry of the Interior that he would orally explain the details of the case when he arrived in Istanbul, en route to his new office in Edirne. The Ministry of the Interior accepted the suspension of the case and informed the grand vizier of the situation.[94]

According to a telegram sent by the new governor of Erzurum, Mehmed Emin, the resolution of the case was once more transferred to the administrative council, and both Hüseyin Pasha and the villagers received warnings not to violate each other's property until the case was resolved.[95] Ali, the headman of the village, complained to the Ministry of the Interior that the villagers continued to be banned from agricultural activities and that their animals were dying because of the conflict. The ministry ordered that the issue be resolved based on previous orders and 'with due care for the protection of the people's rights'.[96] The last document that I found in the Ottoman archives regarding this case is dated 5 May 1912. According to this document, the issue would be taken care of when Hüseyin Pasha came to Erzurum within a few days.[97]

The Local Ottoman Officials' Approach to Land Disputes

As illuminated in the case of Zomik, the local officials of the Ottoman Empire found themselves in a difficult situation in these years. On the one hand, they received numerous applications from Armenians and Kurds who claimed that their constitutional rights were overridden by those who had gained influence and power in the Hamidian period.[98] As representatives of the new regime, they were compelled to respond. On the other hand, the governors had to manage the notables and chiefs whose cooperation with the new regime the central government saw as fundamental, especially the military authorities. Correspondence between the central government and the local governors also reveals that the latter often disagreed with the former when it came to land disputes and the appropriate course of action to be taken with respect to Kurdish chiefs and notables.

On 8 November 1910, the governor of Bitlis, İsmail Hakkı Bey, sent a long report to the Ministry of the Interior, regarding the issue of land disputes in the province.[99] In this report, sent at the height of the Çukur case, İsmail Hakkı Bey noted that the situation had nothing to do with socialism, as the previous governor had claimed. He provided an extensive list of properties seized by the local notables Hacı Necmeddin Efendi, Şemseddin Efendi and İbrahim Efendi, underscoring that none of the disputed villages were inherited by these notables who had no sources of income other than their salaries. According to İsmail Hakkı Bey, these facts alone were enough to prove that these notables had unjustly usurped the lands and properties in question. The governor also noted that the acts of these notables had damaged the treasury; after usurping these properties, the notables reduced the tax burden on these lands by using their influence over local officials. According to İsmail Hakkı Bey, it was impossible to solve these disputes through administrative action because these usurpers held important positions on the administrative council. He demanded the establishment of either a special commission or temporary courts.

Another point which he raised with respect to land disputes concerned prescriptive rights and statutes of limitations. According to the governor, anyone who knew the social structure of the province and the practices of the previous regime would acknowledge that the dispossessed peasants could not dare to raise objections or claims during the Hamidian period. The governor argued that 'the fact that the properties belonging to the treasury or third parties were held by a bunch of interest-seeking usurpers and notables for ten or more years due to the practices of the ancient regime cannot be seen as a fact that gives these men a legitimate right in this regard'.[100] Thus, according to the governor, prescriptive rights should not be recognized in land conflicts in the region.

Another matter of dispute between the central government and local governors was related to the appropriate course of action to be taken towards Kurdish chiefs and notables. As noted above, the Ministry of the Interior had sent an order to the provincial governors, ordering them to flatter and praise Kurdish chiefs by allocating them money and honours. In his reply, İsmail Hakkı Bey suggested that it was exactly this policy of flattering and praising the chiefs that had ruined the country in the Hamidian period.[101] While emphasising that it was beyond his 'authority to determine the appropriateness of resurrecting the evils of the governmental approach of the ancient regime', the governor presented a detailed evaluation regarding the Hamidian policy and its effects on the Ottoman East:

> As a political consequence of this sort of governmental approach, this region has long become a site of pillage and murder: the number of undesirable events, murders and lootings increased; everyone lost their sense of security with respect to property and life; the influence and power of the government diminished; and every chief began to act autonomously and felt free to act in line with his own desires and ends in accordance with the honours and privileges he had been granted. As an unfortunate result of this situation, these regions suffered a lack of government and security for a long time. Is providing the opportunity to scratch this wound that has been slowly healing – reopening

this door which seemed to be closed by resurrecting this sort of governmental approach just as the situation calmed after the dawn of the sun of freedom, when everyone started to breathe, open their eyes, live in a relative degree of security with regard to their properties and lives, when public security and order have begun to increase day by day due to the approach and objective conduct of the government, when the people's sense of security and trust has begun to flourish – suitable for the well-being of the country, for the prosperity of the people and the state? I do not know!![102]

This telegram also noted that the Kurdish peasants were suffering under the pressure of chiefs and notables and that their misery was comparable to that of the Armenians. According to the governor, the state had to take steps to eliminate the conditions that hindered strong commitment to the new regime among the various Ottoman elements – not only Kurdish chiefs – and to work to reform the administrative and judicial structure in the region, in line with the needs of the people.

İsmail Hakkı Bey was not alone in raising objections about the new policy of the central government to praise and flatter the chiefs. Responding to the same order, Celal Bey, the governor of Erzurum, noted that the Kurdish chiefs were spreading rumours to maintain their power and influence. According to Celal Bey, the fact that Haydaranlı Hüseyin Pasha had failed to secure the commitment of a large group of followers to flee to Persia, despite the deliberations he had carried out, was an indicator of the extent to which the power and influence of the chiefs had been curbed in the aftermath of the constitutional revolution.[103]

Celal Bey argued that Kurdish commoners were content with the new regime and that many had started to cultivate and rear livestock, secure from the raids and pillage that had prevailed during the Hamidian period. He noted that the area under cultivation was increasing year by year throughout the region and that the tribes whose only source of living was livestock were taking up agricultural activity due to the security provided by the new regime. Celal Bey suggested that, if some Kurdish chiefs decided to flee, then honours and money would not be enough to change their minds. According to the governor, instead of flattering and praising the chiefs, it would be more beneficial and effective to undertake reforms to improve the conditions of the general population and the governmental infrastructure. The governor also proposed the implementation of a land reform project to curb the power of the chiefs over the poor Kurds and to strengthen the loyalty of the Kurdish people to the regime. The governor stated that …

> … making the poor people under the domination of a certain tribal chief land owners – attaching them to land and eliminating the influence of the chiefs in this

way – is a more rational measure than attempting to secure the commitment of a tribal chief through titles, honours, money, [or] rank [...] The people are compelled to work for their bare subsistence on lands that were usurped from their fathers, grandfathers or even from themselves by *bey*s, *agha*s and rich people. The recovery and prosperity of Kurdistan can be achieved if a land survey is carried out [using a fund that will be established] by adding some money to the sum planned to be given to the chiefs and if lands determined to be vacant [in this survey] are distributed to the poor [...] In my opinion, increasing the number of gendarmes, establishing gendarmerie posts at necessary points, and opening schools would be more effective than giving titles and honours to some chiefs.[104]

Thus, according to Celal Bey, the state could solve the problems in the region and establish public order by increasing the number of gendarmes, opening schools and making Kurdish commoners landholders. Celal Bey not only proposed measures that would be more influential than flattering the chiefs, but also underscored the dangers of such a policy:

Flattering the chiefs – giving them titles and money – will spoil them and corrupt their morals. Moreover, a tribal chief who becomes accustomed to receiving money will demand money as frequently as he needs it. God forbid, if they sense that the government is attempting to obviate them through promotion and flattery in response to its anxiety about their actions, they will dare to violate public order and peace by devising several appropriate and inappropriate demands. Promoting them and giving them honours will have an adverse effect on poor Kurds. Thinking that the old days of the chief's glory and grandeur have returned, they will conclude that they have no choice but to obey every order [of the chiefs]. Thus, the chiefs will see no obstacles to hinder them from taking up the acts they were carrying out until three years ago. The effects of this situation on the Armenians need not be stated or expressed. And as chiefs will be flattered and their power will be amplified, the trust of the Armenians in the government will diminish. It will be impossible to convince any Armenian notable or intellectual that this course of action was taken as a precaution against the attempts and intrusions of the Russian state. Because the Tashnagts'ut'iwn and Hunchakian committees, which have extended their network down to the villages, have the capacity to start an uprising in the country in a couple of days if they wish to do so, God forbid, causing them to have such suspicions may invite tremendous evil.[105]

The telegram sent by the district governor of Tercan to the Ministry of the Interior illuminates the difficulties faced by the local authorities with regard to land disputes. According to the district governor, there were several types of complaints regarding the use and ownership rights to lands in the province, and the government was paralysed. He noted that order and security in the district was compromised and that local officials found themselves in a difficult position, due to the ineffectiveness of the courts and the lack of authority on the part of the civil administration.[106] The district governor demanded immediate measures for the resolution of land disputes and the expansion of the civil administration's authority until the implementation of those new measures.

In order to investigate land disputes in the Ottoman East, the central government commissioned Ali Seydi Bey and Staff Major Mustafa Bey as inspectors in 1910. During their mission, the inspectors visited Erzurum, Bitlis, Diyarbekir and Aleppo and questioned the local officials. It should be noted that they interviewed only the local officials, but not those affected by the disputes. This was criticised by the local Armenians and seen as an indication that the central government lacked the will to thoroughly investigate the land disputes.[107] In their report, Ali Seydi Bey and Mustafa Bey underscored the widespread nature of the problem, noting that the number of applications submitted to them in the three days after their arrival in Erzurum reached ninety and that land disputes were not confined to conflicts between Armenians and Kurdish chiefs but also included disputes among Muslims. The inspectors pointed out that the judicial infrastructure in the region was weak and that courts existed in only two districts in the province. According to the inspectors, it was beyond hope that those who were directed to the courts due to the limitation on the use of administrative resolution procedures could take their lands back through judicial channels. The inspectors argued that the problem could only be solved if the central government took action; the central government should carry out a land survey and distribute vacant and *miri* lands to rightful claimants and landless peasants. According to them, land conflicts were 'the source of all kinds of social conflicts and disputes' and 'hindered the unity of [different Ottoman] elements and the provision of order and peace'.[108]

This examination of the approach of the Ottoman officials to the matter of land disputes and the appropriate policy to be adopted towards Kurdish powerholders indicates that there existed differences of opinion between the central government and some local governors. The early governors of the constitutional regime criticised the central government's initiatives that attempted to secure the loyalty of chiefs and insisted on allying with the Kurdish people rather than with the Kurdish powerholders.

The Armenian Political and Religious Elite's Initiatives for the Resolution of the Land Question

The lingering land disputes and the emergence of an appeasement policy towards Kurdish chiefs led to concern in several Armenian circles after

1910. As noted above, the Patriarchate, the Armenian deputies, politicians and national assembly were frequently called to action by the Armenian press. After 1910, all of them began to take a more active role when it came to this issue. The traces of this increased activity on the part of the Armenian political and religious elite and their institutions can be found in publications, memoranda and other initiatives, such as the commissioning of lawyers to provide legal support for Armenian claimants in land disputes.

After 1910, Armenian institutions and the political elite prepared several publications regarding the land question. The reports of the Armenian Patriarchate, the first of which was published in 1910, are among the most significant of these. As examined in detail in Chapter 3, these reports, published in four volumes, contain significant details, including the names of the usurpers and original owners, as well as the processes by which the lands in question changed hands.[109] Another important publication of this period can be found in the book *The Land Question in the Provinces Inhabited by Armenians* by Kegham Der Garabedian. Criticising the Patriarchate reports for narrowing the scope of the issue by excluding seizure of lands under a certain value (100 liras), Garabedian pointed out that the problem was far greater than portrayed by the Patriarchate commission.[110]

Another significant book published in this period was authored by the Armenian politician Harutiun Shahrikian who used the pen-name Adom. In his *State Reform and the Land Question*, Adom noted that a feudal social structure was incompatible with the governmental structure of the period.[111] If the new regime wanted to abolish oppression, it had to end feudalism. According to Adom, this was not only necessary to solve the problems of the peasants and the land question, but also to create a new Turkey, reform the state and establish a constitutional environment. Adom stated that Tanzimat reforms had failed to eliminate certain feudal elements, the existence and structure of which were maintained. What is more, new feudal elements such as notables and elites were added to the picture. After the Tanzimat, these elements were promoted, and such promotions peaked during the Hamidian period. According to Adom, 'feudalism – [the elements of which were] *agha*s and *torun*s, *bey*s and notables' posed an 'eternal threat' to the regime, public order and the constitution. He argued that, 'for the Ottoman state, which adopted the constitution after [a period of] authoritarianism, advocated democracy and promoted the idea of self-regeneration and resurrection, abolishing that class that was representative of nothing but oppression and self-interest was an obligation that could not be postponed or avoided'.[112] Adom noted that the existence of feudal elements was also an impediment to the economic development of the Muslim people.

In the second part of this book, Adom evaluated the Land Code and land disputes in detail. He stated that neither the officials nor the implementers understood the spirit and objectives of the Land Code. In reference to Articles 8, 45 and 46, he stated that the Land Code sought to eliminate large land ownership and promote the expansion of a landed peasantry in lieu of large landholders. He also expressed that the principle of prescriptive rights (*hakk-ı karar*) could not be applied to those properties the abandonment (*mahluliyet*) of which was disputed on legal grounds.[113]

Another Armenian intellectual who published extensively regarding the land question in this period was Hovhannes Der-Mardirossian. Der-Mardirossian wrote using the penname A-Tō. In his book titled *The Provinces of Van, Bitlis and Erzurum: A Study of the Country's Geographical, Statistical, Legal and Economic State*, A-Tō presented his evaluations and ethnographic observations which were based on his personal visits to the region.[114] While the book is not exclusively on the land question, it includes important details regarding the conditions of the peasants and the practices of share-cropping. In this book, A-Tō also listed the usurped properties in Tercan and Adilcevaz.[115] Most of the disputed properties in Adilcevaz in A-Tō's list were related to land seizures perpetrated by Haydaranlı Hüseyin Pasha.

In May 1910, the ANA discussed the issue of land disputes in the Ottoman East.[116] In his speech, Kegham Der Garabedian noted that the problem was grave in Bitlis, Bulanık, Van, Diyarbekir, Tercan, Muş and Palu and that Armenian peasants from all over the region were coming to Istanbul to seek a resolution. Garabedian noted that, even though their claims were justified, the peasants lost their cases due to their lack of knowledge and their inability to present their cases before the courts in an appropriate manner. Garabedian suggested that the ANA commission should include three lawyers to follow the cases concerning land disputes in Van, Muş and Bitlis.[117] Despite criticism that the matter could only be solved by the government and that sending three lawyers would not change the course of events, Garabedian's suggestion was approved.[118]

THE MEMORANDA OF THE ARMENIAN PATRIARCHATE AND THE DEPUTIES

On 20 July 1911, the Armenian Patriarchate submitted an extensive memorandum to the grand vizier, the Ministry of the Interior and the Ministry of Justice regarding the land question.[119] In this memorandum, the Patriarchate accused the chiefs and notables of taking action to destroy the Armenians and hinder the implementation of reforms that would curtail their power. According to the Patriarchate, the chiefs and notables had provoked ordinary, simple-hearted people by spreading false rumours regarding the intentions of Armenians, declaring that the Armenians were deprived of all kinds of protection granted by the sharia and civil law, and that their honours, lives and properties were beyond the protection of law (*helal*). The massacres of the Hamidian period were claimed to have resulted from such actions of the chiefs and notables.

In this memorandum, the Patriarchate underscored the economic aspect of the massacres, making a distinction between physical and economic violence. Upon receiving a strong reaction from the Ottoman and European publics, the rulers of the authoritarian regime had abandoned the policy of massacre by the sword (*katliam-ı seyfi*) and adopted a policy of administrative and economic massacre (*katl-i idari ve iktisadi*) instead.[120] The memorandum stated that government officials, notables and common people had taken advantage of the calamities experienced by the Armenians, by usurping their lands in various ways, including coercion and fraud. The memorandum also summarised the findings of the commission established by the Patriarchate to investigate the land disputes. The Patriarchate pointed out that those Armenians who had left the empire during the Hamidian period were forced to sign documents stating that they would not return to the Ottoman Empire and that the central government had even granted railway privileges to Russia to ensure that they would not return.[121]

In this memorandum, the Patriarchate underscored five specific points with regard to land disputes. The first point concerned the return of Armenians who had fled to other countries and their property rights. The Patriarchate underscored that the Armenians had left the country under extreme duress and that the property rights of all Armenian citizens, regardless of whether they had left the country with or without official permission, should be protected. The second point had to do with the principle of *hakk-ı karar*. The Patriarchate suggested that cases involving Armenians whose properties were usurped by third parties in their absence should not be subject to the statute of limitations as outlined in Article 20 of the Land Code. The Patriarchate stated that the Armenians were unable to apply to the authorities within the legally prescribed period, due to their flight as result of oppression. According to the Patriarchate, the statute of limitations also should not apply to properties allocated to and tilled by Muslim immigrants. The Armenians had justified reasons for not being able to raise their claims on time.

The third point raised by the Patriarchate was related to the properties the title deeds of which were considered invalid because the land had not been cultivated for more than three years (*müstahakk-ı tapu*). Regarding these lands, the Patriarchate underscored the fact that the Armenians had not left their lands uncultivated by their own will, but that they had fled to save their lives and their honour. According to the Patriarchate, such cases should be considered within the scope of Article 68. Fourth, the Patriarchate claimed that there existed only one exceptional condition that should prevent the return of disputed properties to Armenians. This condition, as specified in Article 35, was related to those properties upon which buildings were erected or trees planted. If a dispute emerged between those who held valid title deeds and third parties, if the value of the buildings or trees was assessed to be more than the value of the land, and if the claimant proved their right to the land, then only the value of the land would be given to the claimant. The Patriarchate argued that, other than in this specific situation, all disputed lands should be returned to the Armenians.

Finally, the Patriarchate underscored that the right to property was a foundational principle of social peace and public order, and it demanded that the state take precautions to guarantee the Armenians' right to property. The Patriarchate noted that the imperial decree that land disputes be resolved through the arbitration of civil authorities had been restricted by a cabinet decision which introduced limitations. This had no legal basis because the annulment or amendment of an imperial decree by a cabinet decision was not in line with the Ottoman legislative process.[122]

The shift in government policy, the resurrection of a new wave of violence and further land seizures pushed the Armenian deputies to take action in the last months of 1911. Istanbul deputy Krikor Zohrab, Erzurum deputy Vartkes Serengülian, Van deputy Vahan Papazian, Sivas deputy Dr Nazareth Daghavarian, Muş deputy Kegham Der Garabedian, Kozan deputy Hampartsum Boyadjian, Tekfurdağı deputy Agob Boyadjian, Istanbul deputy Bedros Haladjian, Aleppo deputy Artin Boshgezenian and Erzurum deputy Karekin Pastermadjian in December 1911 presented a joint memorandum, emphasising the need for reform in the eastern provinces.[123] The joint memorandum underscored the Armenians' optimism at the beginning of the constitutional period and listed several criticisms with regard to the lack of order and security. Comparing the Hamidian and constitutional periods, the deputies stated that the new regime had failed to improve the rule of law in the region.

The joint memorandum also included a series of demands including the dismissal of corrupt officials, the empowerment of governors and military forces to establish order in the region, the just punishment of those who had committed crimes against Armenians and the resolution of land disputes. In the joint memorandum, the land question was defined as a problem of 'vital importance' (*ehemmiyet-i hayatiyeye haiz*), and it was emphasised that there had been no significant improvement regarding the resolution of land disputes since the beginning of the constitutional period. The cabinet decision of 31 March 1910 was interpreted as an initiative by the government to annul the imperial order of 7 August 1909. The deputies demanded that the limitation introduced in the decision of 31 March be rescinded. The deputies' demands in the joint memorandum were confined to the swift implementation of court decisions and the withdrawal of the limitation on the use of arbitration procedure.

In addition to signing the joint memorandum of the Armenian deputies, Istanbul deputy Krikor Zohrab presented another, personal memorandum.[124] According to Zohrab, 'the policy of ruining Armenians in economic terms' had been revealed in several of the actions of the government.[125] According to Zohrab, in order to resolve the land question in the eastern provinces the government needed to send a commission of inquiry to the region, employ Armenian officials in land registry offices to prevent abuse, recognize that those who pay the taxes for a particular piece of land are the de facto owners, return the lands of those who had fled in the previous era, pay compensation or provide other land to the current occupiers of such lands, return communal properties that had been seized and implement the settlement regulations issued for Muslim immigrants to settle landless Armenian returnees.[126]

In this period, representatives of the Armenian community at the local level also took an active role in raising the land question. In November 1911, thirty-two bishops (*murahhasa*) gathered to discuss the problems of the Armenian community in the region. The points that they raised – including the misery of the Armenian peasantry which they associated with the oppression by the notables, *agha*s and *bey*s – were published in the Armenian newspaper *Harach* on 2 November 1912. As *Harach* was associated with the ARF, the congregation of *murahhasa*s was interpreted as a Tashnagist congress by Ottoman authorities, who were alarmed by the prospect of an Armenian uprising rumoured to be carried out if the land question was not resolved by spring 1912.[127]

The non-resolution of the land question, the shift in the policy of the central government in favour of Kurdish chiefs and the rise of a new wave of violence against Armenians in the eastern provinces also strained relations between the CUP and the ARF. According to the Armenian deputy Vahan Papazian, the sixth ARF congress was a turning point in this regard. This congress was held in Istanbul in August 1911.[128] On this occasion, the ARF declared that 'the Union encouraged medieval landlords who were the remnants of the feudal system by pursuing a policy of appeasement instead of eliminating this strata', and that 'the Union had stepped back from democratic principles over time'.[129] Another important claim raised at that time was that the CUP promoted 'oppressors, looters and fraudsters to continue pillage, massacres and seizures by leaving them unpunished'.[130] The ARF decided to send a memorandum to the CUP and to sever all ties if it failed to provide guarantees to take active steps to solve the problems addressed by the congress. According to Papazian, the relations between the two organisations soured after this point, and members of the ARF began to be pressured and persecuted in various regions of the empire. Relations between the CUP and the ARF were officially terminated in the autumn of 1911,[131] but it should be noted that the two organisations continued to cooperate behind closed doors, especially during the elections of 1912.[132]

The programme of the ARF, as published in the *Harach* newspaper in the first months of 1912, provides important insights into its approach to the land question and to the agrarian question – a larger question that also included labour relations.[133] This programme, prepared for the ensuing parliamentary term, shows the importance that the ARF attached to these matters. In the section titled 'The Elimination of the Remnants of Feudalism', the ARF raised four demands. First, the ARF argued that the state should take systematic, effective measures against the usurpers who constituted remnants of feudalism. The second point was that serfdom and slavery needed to be abolished by law and that those who violated these laws should be severely punished. The ARF proposed an amendment to the criminal code to this end. The third demand was the severe punishment of those who levied illegal taxes or demanded corvée labour, as well as of *agha*s and tribal leaders who were subject to special treatment. The fourth demand raised in this section of the form consisted of the exclusion of tribal leaders and those under their influence from public service in districts in which they lived or over which they had influence. The ARF requested the re-assignment of such state officials to other districts. The programme also included a section titled 'Administrative Demands for the Armenian Regions'. In this section, the ARF raised demands regarding the resolution of the land disputes, in addition to several other requests regarding the administration. This section of the programme included the following demands related to the land disputes and the agrarian question:

5. the return of the lands, water sources and other immovable properties that were seized from labourers by force, fraud, coercion or other means, to their

Armenians and Land Disputes in the Ottoman Empire

original owners, and the resolution of disputes arising [from this problem] through *administrative* resolution in line with existing regulations and instructions which will be prepared in accordance with the spirit of the law,

6. the return of the lands that were confiscated for being *mahlul* or *müstehak-ı tapu*, which were given to the immigrants, and which were illegally sold by the Agricultural Bank, to their former owners by the state, the allocation of vacant lands belonging to the state to *miriba*s and Muslim immigrants who were dispossessed due to these land disputes,
7. in addition to [the return of] the lands, recognition of all rights given to [Muslim] immigrants for those who had fled due to the oppression by the ancient regime but have today returned, or reduction of the tax payments of villagers or villages that emigrated in the same way.[134]

As indicated in this programme, the land question and agrarian problems held an important place in the ARF's political programme. The programme also shows that the ARF saw the land question as a problem between 'labourers' from all ethnic and religious backgrounds and the 'remnants of feudalism'. Yet, it should be noted that the emphasis on class was placed side by side with references to nationality, which referred to the eastern provinces as Armenian regions.

THE GOVERNMENT RESPONSE

The government discussed the joint memorandum of the Armenian deputies and Krikor Zohrab's memorandum in a cabinet meeting.[135] The suggestions related to the land disputes presented in the joint memorandum were found admissible. The cabinet in this meeting also decided to send a notification to the Ministry of Justice for the faster implementation of court orders related to land conflicts and to abolish the limitation on the use of arbitration procedures. Regarding Krikor Zohrab's individual memorandum, the cabinet stated that a regulation concerning the land disputes of Armenian immigrants who had fled during the Hamidian period was being prepared. Claims regarding escheated communal properties would be investigated, and the Minister of Pious Foundations would be consulted on the matter. Zohrab's other suggestions were disregarded. With the memoranda presented by the Armenian deputies, the establishment of a special commission re-entered the agenda of the Ottoman government, and public debate on the issue gained momentum.

In the spring of 1912, a commission formed by the Council of State prepared a detailed draft bill for regulating the nationality, property and lands of those who had emigrated to foreign countries before 23 July 1908.[136] Although the title of the bill does not mention land disputes concerning claimants other than emigrants, the text of the bill included articles concerning the resolution of land disputes more generally. The bill was later examined and amended by the Ministry of the Interior, which gave the draft its final form. This draft bill was never enacted into a regulation or law. It seems that it was either shelved by the Ministry of the Interior or dismissed by the Council of Ministers. Either way, it can be seen as a failed initiative. Still, the draft bill is extraordinary because it was the most detailed plan for the resolution of land disputes to have been prepared by the Ottoman authorities. Thus, it is necessary to examine its provisions in detail.

The first part of this draft bill was related to the nationality problems of emigrants. The emigrants' return to Ottoman nationality would have been facilitated by the regulations. The second part was related to property problems and land disputes. It stipulated that, if lands belonging to emigrants[137] were claimed by others who had managed to obtain deeds based on prescriptive rights, then the lands in dispute would be returned to their original owners (Article 7). If the intervening party had made improvements to the lands and properties, then the value of these additions would be taken into consideration when compensation was calculated. If the value of the additions was less than the value of the property, the value of the additions would be paid by the government to the occupier, on the condition that the original owner would later pay this sum to the government. If the value of the additions was more than the value of the property, then the government would pay to the original owner the value of the property – estimated on the basis of its value at the time of acquisition – on the condition that the occupier would pay this sum to the government in the future. In the latter case, the property would be granted to the occupier. If lands belonging to emigrants were transferred to others in return for title deed payments without being put up at auction, either a sum equal to the value of the land or land belonging to the treasury would be given to the occupier. The property would be returned to the original owner (Article 8).

However, if properties belonging to emigrants were considered *mahlul* by the government and had been sold at auction, then the property would stay in the possession of the buyer, and the government would give the sum of the auction sale to the original owner (Article 9). If lands belonging to emigrants were given to immigrants (*muhacir*), then these immigrants would be resettled in other localities, and the lands would be restored to their original owners, regardless of the length of the period of time that the immigrants had been in possession of the properties (Article 10). If the emigrants had sold the disputed properties by means of unofficial sales documents (*sened-i 'âdî*), then the value of the properties and the sales price indicated in the unofficial sales documents would be compared. If there was a significant difference (*gabn-i fâhiş*) between the estimated value of the property and the value as stated in the unofficial sales document, the sale would be considered null and void, and the sum paid by the occupiers would be repaid to them by the government, on the condition that the original owners would pay this sum back to the government in the future. The property in dispute would be given to the original owners. If there was no significant difference between the value of the property and the price paid, the sales document would be considered valid, and the occupier would be given a title deed (Article 11). In the case that property or land belonging to an emigrant was under the illegitimate occupation (*fuzûlen tasarruf edilen*) of a third party who had no claim to it based on prescriptive rights, transfer by *müstahakk-ı tapu*, transfer through auction, or an unofficial sales document, then the property or land would be taken from the occupier and returned to the original owner (Article 11).

If emigrants had no title deeds or registration documents, then the properties in dispute would be granted to the occupiers and the emigrants would be directed to the courts (Article 13). The draft bill also recognized one of the most widely articulated demands of the Armenian political and religious elites: it stipulated that the statutes of limitations would not apply for the period when the emigrants were abroad – even for those who did not have official permits to leave the country (Article 14). Finally, the draft bill stipulated the establishment of mobile courts (Article 15) and that the decisions of the courts of the first and second instance could not be appealed (Article 17).

As mentioned above, the draft bill included regulations regarding land disputes concerning claimants who were not emigrants. This issue was addressed in the last two articles. Article 18 of the draft bill indicates that the law was to be implemented in a specific region:

> If a person from any social group who is an inhabitant of the regions in which this law will be implemented claims and proves that [their] lands were forcefully seized within the period beginning fifteen years before the proclamation of the constitution, deeds of possession with respect to the land in question will be considered null and void, and the land would be returned to the previous owner.[138]

Article 19 of the draft bill stipulates that ...

> ... regardless of whether it is proven that the disputed lands were forcibly seized or not, if it is understood that the occupier is in possession of more land than what is described in the deed and upon examination the excess reaches up to five times what is written in the title deed – for example, if the deed concerns

eight *dönüm*s and examination shows that the occupier is in possession of forty *dönüm*s – [then the land] will be given to the original owner; and if [the land in possession of the occupier] is more than fivefold [of what is written in the deed], then the excess will be claimed by the government and sold to anyone who demands it, and the deeds will be revised as required by the circumstances.[139]

Thus, the draft bill stipulated two conditions under which land would be returned to claimants who were not emigrants but other inhabitants of the regions, conditions under which the law would be implemented. The first of these conditions was related to forcible seizures. In these cases, the claimants would have to prove that their lands had been forcibly seized. However, the last article also stipulated the return of land to claimants if it was found that the current occupier was in possession of vastly more land than indicated in the title deeds. In such cases of large land seizure, the lands could be returned even if claims of forcible seizure were not proved. As mentioned above, this comprehensive draft bill was shelved and not enacted into regulation or law in the ensuing years.

As noted at the beginning of this section, the establishment of a commission became an important part of public debate in first months of 1912. British consular correspondence indicates that the reform commission was expected to arrive in the eastern provinces as early as in March 1912. It was rumoured that the commission had already left Istanbul.[140] Delays in the establishment of the commission were met with suspicion at the local level, especially among the Armenian population which began to see it as an electioneering device. According to the Armenian bishop in Erzurum, this initiative was ill-conceived; the resolution of so many disputes over such a vast geography by a single commission given the authority to spend 100,000 liras for compensation payments was not possible. The governor of Erzurum was also opposed to this initiative and claimed that 'the money to be spent on the mission might as well be thrown into the sea and the final result would merely be to make matters worse than they were already'.[141] Finally, on 15 May 1912, the government officially adopted the decision to create a reform commission for the eastern provinces. In the draft bill prepared in line with this decision, the commission was authorised primarily to investigate land conflicts. The reform commission would be allocated 100,000 liras for compensation payments. The commission would finalise all disputes in absolute terms and could suspend or dismiss local officials.[142]

In an article series titled 'Reflections' and published in *Ḥarach* in June 1912, Adom evaluated the decision of the Council of State that re-introduced the arbitration procedures by administrative councils as well as the decision to establish an investigation commission.[143] His evaluation indicates that the Armenian intellectuals found the central government's actions to be inadequate; they were disappointed with the developments following the constitutional revolution. In this evaluation, Adom claimed that these initiatives of the central government were aimed at creating illusions and spreading false hopes. He noted that the investigation commission was not authorised to decide, regulate or implement any measures, and that the authority to make decisions lay with the administrative councils.[144] In addition to raising doubts about the legal basis of the Council of State's decision, he stated that the decision would not suffice to solve the land question.

Adom noted that, according to the decision of the Council of State, administrative councils would give disputed lands to the holders of the most recent title deeds and that dissatisfied parties would be directed to the courts. According to Adom, such a decision would not suffice to solve the land question, for three reasons. First, there were no title deeds for seized lands in most cases. Second, existing title deeds and registers of most seized lands had been falsified. Finally, most of the seized lands were either illegally sold or declared *müstahakk-ı tapu* and registered in the names of third parties. Adom underscored that these seizures were carried out *'by the government, with its knowledge, and with its cooperation'*.[145] Adom harshly criticised the priority given to the most recent title deeds in administrative resolution procedures, as well as the fact that administrative councils were given the authority to make decisions in land disputes:

> In [disputes concerning] such title deeds, who will be given priority?
> Will the priority be given to the most recent title deeds? All title deeds issued by fraud and illegal means have recent dates.
> Thus, will legal cover be given to all frauds and illegalities? Those claimants, who naturally have older title deeds, will be dissatisfied. Will they be directed to the courts?
> Is this what is expected? Is this the solution to our land question?
> What if a land registry has not been carried out? What if there are no title deeds? And what will happen to the seized lands of those who have ancient rights transmitted through inheritance for centuries? There are no instructions in the decision of the Council of State regarding these.
> The real owners have title deeds and are registered [as owners] in only a tiny proportion of [cases related to] seized lands.
> Who will check all these and who will decide?
> Administrative councils...

> Who are the members of these administrative councils? The same fraudsters, oppressors and state officials who helped the usurpers – the representatives of the same feudal usurpers.
> Are these the men who will investigate, provide and implement just decisions in opposition to themselves or contrary to their self-interest and influence?
> What a great naïveté this is.
> If only I was wrong.[146]

Adom also criticised the Armenian press which was complaining about the delay in the establishment of the investigation commission. According to Adom, since it lacked the authority to decide, regulate and implement decisions, the investigation commission was nothing but an imaginary initiative. The delay in the establishment of the commission should not be a matter of complaint but an opportunity to criticise such imaginary initiatives. The evaluation presented by Adom shows that Armenian intellectuals were dissatisfied with the re-introduction of the procedures of arbitration and the recent initiatives of the central government.

In June, the Ottoman Empire's ambassador in London, Tevfik Pasha, sent a warning to Istanbul regarding the delay in forming the reform commission. In his telegram, Tevfik Pasha noted that, 'if claims that the establishment of the reform commission for Anatolia is retracted is true, this would have a harmful impact and lead to misinterpretations'. Pointing out that the situation in the eastern provinces would probably become more threatening in the near future, he argued that the failure to establish the commission would eventually lead 'to the escalation of current troubles – born out of developments in Rumelia – into violence', in a way that would invite foreign intervention.[147] The Ministry of Foreign Affairs replied to Tevfik Pasha with a note refuting the claims that the decision to establish a commission had been withdrawn. The ministry stated that the commission had not been established because of the health issues of the Minister of Pious Foundations, Hayri Bey, who was supposed to supervise it.[148] Despite these attempts, the land question remained unresolved for the most part, and the commission was never established. The detailed draft bill for the return of properties was shelved. Moreover, there arrived an increasing number of reports about attacks against Armenians and additional seizures of properties.

On 24 August 1912, the ANA discussed the steps to be taken for the resolution of security problems and the land question.[149] In this session, Rupen Zartanian and Vartkes Serengülian brought a proposal to the assembly, stating that the problems could only be solved if a series of effective measures were taken. According to Zartanian and Serengülian, the first of these would be the adoption of a punitive approach by the Ottoman government and the punishment of criminals who oppressed Kurds and Armenians, especially in districts such as Şatak, Huyt, Mutki, Hizan and Çarsancak, where the situation was dire. Second, they suggested increasing the number of gendarmes in the region and arming peasants. The third suggested measure consisted of the abolishment of irregular troops to which Kurdish tribesmen were recruited. The fourth of the measures that the deputies demanded was the resolution of the land question through substantial and effective measures.[150] With regard to these suggestions, Hampartsum Boyadjian noted that the only alternative for the Armenian people would be self-defence and self-armament if the problems were not solved.[151]

Traces of the escalating tensions in Armenian circles on the brink of the Balkan Wars can also be seen in the actions and discourse of the Patriarchate. The Armenian Patriarchate presented another memorandum on 9 September 1912, the tone of which clearly reflects its frustration. It accused the constitutional regime of utter indifference to the problems of the Armenian population. In this memorandum, the Patriarchate claimed that 'the government has done nothing in the last four years' to improve the conditions of Armenians and that the situation had become unbearable for Armenians in the Ottoman East. The Patriarchate stated that none of its complaints and petitions had received serious and effective responses from authorities.[152] Simultaneous with the submission of this memorandum, the Armenian Patriarch resigned.

The relations between the ARF and the CUP, which were officially terminated but continued behind closed doors, became even more strained after the summer of 1912. According to Sir Gerard Lowther, who prepared the annual report for the British consulate in 1912, there was 'a general increase in the unpopularity of the government and even the Tashnakists' had 'turned against the CUP'.[153] According to British consular reports, tensions were also mounting between CUP and ARF members at the local level in Diyarbekir and Bitlis. On 4 September 1912, Mr Marling informed the consulate that 'the local Tashnakists were reported to have quarreled with the Union and Progress party in regard to the non-settlement of the land question'.[154]

Conclusion

Following the proclamation of the constitution, the return of seized properties and the resolution of the land question became important topics in public debate in the Ottoman Empire. In these years, several Armenian actors – including the Patriarchate, ANA, ARF and the Armenian political elite – took an active role in raising the issue. In line with their demands, the central government in 1909 issued an order for the administrative resolution of land disputes by means of administrative councils. The decision to resolve land disputes through administrative councils and to return some Armenian properties upon the orders of the local authorities was met with a strong reaction from Kurdish powerholders, including notables and tribal leaders. Some of these powerholders were also nervous about the prospect of losing possession of lands that they had seized from fellow Kurdish tribesmen and peasants. Some powerholders from Van Province fled to Persia, protesting the prospect of having to return the properties that they had seized and the collection of tax arrears.

As examined in this chapter, there happened a significant shift in the central government's approach to land disputes concerning Armenians after 1910. The traces of this shift are visible in the legislative changes that introduced a limitation on the use of the administrative resolution procedures, in resuming the policy of settling immigrants in the eastern provinces, and in the rapprochement between Kurdish powerholders and the central government, the first sign of which was the invitation of those tribal leaders who had fled to Persia to return to the Ottoman Empire. The central government also sent orders to the local governors to praise and flatter Kurdish chiefs so as to secure their loyalty to the state. This initiative was met with strong opposition from the governors of Bitlis and Erzurum. Changes in the ethno-national politics of the CUP and concerns about security, which necessitated the co-optation of Kurdish powerholders, both played a role in the Ottoman government's shifting approach to the land question after 1910.

This examination of the Ottoman correspondence regarding land disputes and the appropriate course of action with respect to the Kurdish chiefs demonstrates that several governors opposed the central government's orders to secure the loyalty of the chiefs and took the initiative to resolve land disputes concerning powerholders and Armenian and Kurdish peasants. These findings suggest that the Ottoman administration in this period was not a uniform mechanism operated by men with identical approaches and ideological inclinations with respect to the Ottoman people's problems.

The lingering land disputes and the emergence of a rapprochement between the Ottoman government and the Kurdish chiefs led to the escalation of tensions in Armenian circles. While reactions and protests to the situation brought about the termination of official relations between the CUP and the ARF, the Patriarchate and the Armenian deputies presented to the government extensive memoranda concerning the resolution of the Armenians' problems, including the land question. Following these memoranda, the Ottoman government abolished the limitation on the use of administrative resolution procedures and declared that a reform commission would be established to resolve land disputes. In fact, the government failed to carry out this plan to establish a reform commission. As tensions in the Balkans rose rapidly, tensions in Armenian circles also began to escalate. In the next chapter, I will examine the developments after the outbreak of the Balkan Wars and the internationalisation of the question of reform in the eastern provinces.

Notes

1. On the ideology of the Young Turks and the reestablishment of the constitutional regime in 1908, see Eric Jan Zürcher, *Unionist Factor: The Role of the Committee of Union and Progress in the Turkish National Movement, 1905–1926* (Leiden: Brill, 1984); M. Şükrü Hanioğlu, *Preparation for a Revolution: The Young Turks, 1902–1908* (Oxford: Oxford University Press, 2001; M. Şükrü Hanioğlu, *The Young Turks in Opposition* (Oxford: Oxford University Press, 1995); Tarık Zafer Tunaya, *Türkiye'de Siyasal Partiler, cilt 3: İttihat ve Terakki, Bir Çağın, Bir Kuşağın, Bir Partinin Tarihi*, 3rd edition (Istanbul: İletişim, 2007); Şerif Mardin, *Jön Türklerin Siyasi Fikirleri, 1895–1908*, 15th edition (Istanbul: İletişim Yayınları); Feroz Ahmad, *The Young Turks: The Committee of Union and Progress in Turkish Politics, 1908–1914* (London: Hurst, 2010); Aykut Kansu, *1908 Devrimi* (Istanbul: İletişim, 1995). For an analysis of the effects of the re-establishment of the constitutional regime on the various regions of the Ottoman Empire and the reactions of different communities to this development, see Bedross Der Matossian, *Shattered Dreams of Revolution: From Liberty to Violence in the Late Ottoman Empire* (Palo Alto: Stanford University Press, 2014); Hasan Kayalı, *Arabs and Young Turks: Ottomanism, Arabism, and Islamism in the Ottoman Empire, 1908–1918* (Berkeley: California University Press, 1997); Naci Kutlay, *İttihat Terakki ve Kürtler* (Ankara: Beybun Yayınları, 1992); Michelle Campos, *Ottoman Brothers: Muslims, Christians, and Jews in Early Twentieth-Century Palestine* (Palo Alto: Stanford University Press, 2011); Yuval Ben-Bassat and Eyal Ginio, eds, *Late Ottoman Palestine: The Period of Young Turk Rule* (London: I. B. Tauris, 2011).
2. TNA: FO 424/218, Sir G. Lowther to Sir E. Grey, Constantinople, 31 December 1908.
3. BOA: DH.SYS 23/1, report of Ismail Hakkı Bey, Governor of Bitlis, 26 Teşrin-i Evvel 1326 (8 November 1910).
4. Ibid.
5. Ibid.
6. Ibid.

7. Çeker, *Arazi Kanunnamesi*, 44–50.
8. 'Hoghayin Harts', *Azadamart*, 21 October 1909.
9. 'Mushi Kavarĕ: Tadaranagan Goghm'nagtsutiwn/Hayots Hoghayin Kh'ntirnerun Tēm', *Azadamart*, 4 February 1910.
10. Dikran M. Kaligian, 'Agrarian Land Reform and the Armenians in the Ottoman Empire', *Armenian Review* 48, no. 3–4 (2003): 22–45. On the relations between the CUP and Armenian political organisations, see Arsen Avagyan and Gaidz F. Minassian, *Ermeniler ve İttihat Terakki: İşbirliğinden Çatışmaya* (Istanbul: Aras Yayınları, 2005); Dikran Kaligian, *Armenian Organization and Ideology under Ottoman Rule, 1908–1914* (London: Transaction, 2009); Yektan Türkyılmaz, 'Devrim İçinde Devrim: Ermeni Örgütleri ve İttihat-Terakki İlişkileri, 1908–1915', in Adanır and Özel, *1915*, 324–53; Raymond Kévorkian, *The Armenian Genocide: A Complete History* (London: I. B. Tauris, 2011), part 2.
11. Kaligian, *Armenian Organization*, 49–50.
12. BOA: BEO 3454/258998, memorandum of the Armenian Patriarchate, 21 Teşrin-i Evvel 1324 (3 November 1908).
13. Ibid.
14. The SKMAP was established in Istanbul on 2 October 1908. The organisation can be seen as an initiative of some Kurdish elites to affiliate themselves with the new regime. The improvement of education in the eastern provinces was one of the primary aims of this organisation. For more information, see Gülseren Duman, 'The Formations of the Kurdish Movement(s), 1908–1914: Exploring the Footprints of Kurdish Nationalism' (Master's thesis, Boğaziçi University, 2010); Ayhan Işık, 'Kurdish and Armenian Relations in the Ottoman-Kurdish Press' (Master's thesis, Bilgi University, 2014); Janet Klein, 'Kurdish Nationalists and Non-nationalist Kurds: Rethinking Minority Nationalism and the Dissolution of the Ottoman Empire, 1908–1909', *Nations and Nationalism* 13, no. 1 (January 2007): 135–53.
15. BOA: BEO 3454/258998, memorandum of the Society for Kurdish Mutual Aid and Progress, 8 Teşrin-i Evvel 1324 (21 October 1908).
16. BOA: MV 123/13, decision of the Council of Ministers, 9 Zilkade 1326 (3 December 1908).
17. At this stage, Daniş Bey, governor of Salonika, would lead the planned committee. Other designated members were Süleyman Nazif Bey, chief secretary of Konya; Diran Efendi, member of the Beyoğlu Court of First Instance; Major Vehib Bey from the General Staff and Adjutant Major Fahreddin Efendi from the Fourth Army.
18. Cemal Paşa, *Hatıralar* (Istanbul: Türkiye İş Bankası Kültür Yayınları, 2012), 377.
19. *Meclis-i Mebusan Zabıt Ceridesi*, period 1, vol. 1, session 1 (26 Kânun-ı sâni 1324/8 February 1909), 494–508. '... bir taraftan hazîneyi ızrâr, diğer taraftan ahâlîyi yekdiğeri 'aleyhine kıyâm edeceğinden...' Ibid., 504–5.

For discussions in the parliament about this bill, see Matossian, *Shattered Dreams*, 136–40.

20. *Adenakrut'iwnk' Azkayin Ênthanur Zhoghov* (National General Assembly), nist K (session 11), 25 November 1911, 442.
21. Sina Akşin, *31 Mart Olayı* (Ankara: Ankara Üniversitesi Siyasal Bilgiler Fakültesi, 1970); David Farhi, 'The Şeriat as a Political Slogan: Or the "Incident of the 31st Mart"', *Middle Eastern Studies* 7, no. 3 (1971): 275–99; Nader Sohrabi, *Revolution and Constitutionalism in the Ottoman Empire and Iran* (Cambridge: Cambridge University Press, 2011), chap. 5; Matossian, *Shattered Dreams*, chap. 6.
22. Meltem Toksöz, 'Adana Ermenileri ve 1909 "İğtişaşatı"', *Tarih ve Toplum Yeni Yaklaşımlar* 5 (2007): 147–57; Matossian, *The Horrors of Adana*.
23. Avagyan and Minassian, *Ermeniler ve İttihat Terakki*, 75; Kévorkian, *Armenian Genocide*, 114–17.
24. BOA: MV 130/20, the decision of the cabinet regarding the land disputes, 11 Receb 1327 (29 July 1909); 'Emvali gayr-i menkûleye vukû' bulan tecâvüzâtın idâreten sûret-i men'iyle ol babdaki ihtilâfât-ı mütehaddisenin mecâlis-i idârece halli hakkında irâde-i seniye', 25 Temmuz 1325 (7 August 1909), *Düstur*, vol. 2, no. 1 (Dersaadet: Matbaa-i Osmaniye, 1329), 428–33.
25. TNA: FO 424/250, Sir Gerard Lowther to Sir Edward Grey, *Annual Report on Turkey for the Year 1909*, 31 January 1910, 42.
26. TNA: FO 424/221, Mr Marling to Sir Edward Grey, Constantinople, 16 November 1909.
27. TNA: FO 195/2318, James Morgan to Sir Gerard Lowther, Van, 17 November 1909.
28. Ibid.
29. Ibid.
30. BOA: DH.SYS 67/1-2, cipher telegram from the province of Bitlis to the Ministry of the Interior, 19 Kanun-ı Sani 1325 (1 February 1910).
31. BOA: DH.SYS 67/1-2, the Acting-Governor of Bitlis to the Ministry of the Interior, 13 Şubat 1315 (26 February 1910).
32. TNA: FO 195/2318, James Morgan to Sir Gerard Lowther, Van, 2 October 1909.
33. TNA: FO 195/2318, Mr Safrastian to Sir Gerard Lowther, Bitlis, 28 September 1909.
34. Ibid.
35. BOA: DH.SYS 67/1-2, cipher telegram from the province of Bitlis to the Ministry of the Interior, 20 Mart 1326 (2 April 1910).
36. BOA: DH.SYS 67/1-2, petition from the inhabitants of thirty-three villages to the Sublime Porte, 10 Mart 1326 (23 March 1910).
37. BOA: DH.SYS 67/1-2, petition to the Sublime Porte, 13 Nisan 1326 (26 April 1910).
38. BOA: DH.SYS 67/1-2, the Governor of Bitlis to the Ministry of the Interior, 27 Teşrin-i Sani 1326 (8 December 1910).

39. TNA: FO 424/225, Acting Vice-Consul Safrastian to Consul McGregor, Bitlis, 19 November 1910.
40. TNA: FO 195/2347, Acting Vice-Consul Safrastian to Consul McGregor, Bitlis, 6 April 1910.
41. TNA: FO 424/225, Vice-Consul Mollyneux-Seel to Sir G. Lowther, Van, 30 September 1910; TNA: FO 424/229, Vice-Consul Molyneux-Seel to Sir G. Lowther, Van, 3 October 1911; TNA: FO 371/1484, Sir G. Lowther to Sir Edward Grey, Pera, 15 October 1912; TNA: FO 371/1486, Vice-consul Molyneux-Seel to Sir G. Lowther, Van, 10 July 1912.
42. BOA: DH.MUİ 6-2/19, 26 Ağustos 325 (8 September 1909). In his evaluation regarding this telegram of protest, Galip Bey, the governor of Diyarbekir, reported that the activities of these tribal chiefs were not suspected to turn into an uprising against the government. Yet, immediate actions should be taken to settle land disputes. The governor demanded the establishment of mobile courts with absolute authority to resolve such problems. BOA: DH.MUİ 6-2/19, cipher telegram from the Governor of Diyarbekir to the Ministry of the Interior, 2 Eylül 1325 (15 September 1909).
43. TNA: FO 195/2347, James Morgan to Sir Gerard Lowther, Van, 3 January 1910.
44. Ibid.
45. BOA: DH.MUİ 6-3/23, Celal Bey, governor of Erzurum to the Ministry of the Interior, 28 Mart 1326 (10 April 1910).
46. Tibet Abak, 'Kürt Politikasında Hamidiye Siyasetine Dönüş ve Kör Hüseyin Paşa Olayı, 1910–1911', in Adanır and Özel, *1915*, 277–92.
47. BOA: MV 138/50, decision of the Council of Ministers, 18 Mart 1326 (31 March 1910).
48. BOA: ŞD 27/29, the Ministry of the Interior to the Grand Vizirate, 23 Kanun-ı Sani 1325 (5 Şubat 1910), and the report of the Council of State, 17 Şubat 1325 (2 March 1910).
49. BOA: DH.MUİ 6-3/6, the Ministry of the Interior to the Sublime Porte, 23 Kanun-ı Sani 1325 (5 February 1910); the Ministry of the Interior to the Council of State, 20 Şubat 1325 (5 March 1910); BOA: DH.MUİ 6-1/1, district governor of İzmir to the Ministry of the Interior, 17 Kanun-ı Sani 1325 (30 January 1910), and the Ministry of the Interior to the Sublime Porte, 23 Kanun-ı Sani 1325 (5 February 1910); BOA: DH.MUİ 6-3/16, the General Assembly of Diyarbekir to the Ministry of the Interior, 10 Şubat 1325 (23 February 1910).
50. BOA: DH.MUİ 6-3/6, the Ministry of the Interior to the Sublime Porte, 23 Kanun-ı Sani 1325 (5 February 1910).
51. BOA: DH.MUİ 6-3/16, the General Assembly of Diyarbekir to the Ministry of the Interior, 10 Şubat 1325 (23 February 1910).
52. BOA: DH.MUİ 6-3/6, the Ministry of the Interior to the Council of State, 20 Şubat 325 (5 March 1910).
53. Ibid.

54. This cabinet decision was published as an imperial order (*irade*) on 13 September 1911. 'Emval-i gayr-ı menkulenin tasarrufundan mütehaddis ihtilafatın suret-i halline mütedair 20 Receb 1327 tarihli kararın senesi içinde zuhura gelen tecavüzata hasrı ve teferruatı hakkında irade-i seniye', *Düstur*, vol. 2, no. 3 (Dersaadet: Matbaa-i Osmaniye, 1330), 738–39.
55. TNA: FO 424/250, Sir Gerard Lowther to Sir Edward Grey, *Annual Report on Turkey for the Year 1910*, 31 January 1911, 38–39.
56. On the CUP congresses, see Tarık Zafer Tunaya, *Türkiye'de Siyasi Partiler, cilt I: İkinci Meşrutiyet Dönemi* (Istanbul: Hürriyet Vakfı Yayınları, 1988), 28–31.
57. TNA: FO 371/1017, Vice-Consul Geary to Mr Marling, Monastir, 3 December 1910.
58. Ibid. Vahakn N. Dadrian has seen the deliberations about Turkification during the congress as a plan for the elimination of Armenians; see *Warrant for Genocide: Key Elements of Turko-Armenian Conflict* (New Brunswick, NJ: Transaction, 2006), 96–99. On the CUP congresses, see also Kévorkian, *Armenian Genocide*, chap. 4; for a new article discussing the timing of the decision for the Armenian Genocide, see Taner Akçam, 'When Was the Decision to Annihilate the Armenians Taken?' *Journal of Genocide Research* 21, no. 4 (2 October 2019): 457–80.
59. Dündar, *Kahir Ekseriyet*, 57–59.
60. Terzibaşoğlu, 'Land Disputes', 171. For the document, see BOA: DH.İD 135/3.
61. Terzibaşoğlu, 'Land Disputes', 172.
62. Ibid.
63. Ibid.
64. BOA: DH.MUİ 6-3/25, the Governor of Erzurum to the Ministry of the Interior, 7 Nisan 1326 (20 April 1910).
65. Ibid.
66. 'Hoṙi Sh'rchan: Hoghayin Anludzeli Khntirĕ', *Azadamart*, 30 April 1910.
67. Ibid.
68. Ibid.
69. 'Gaṙavarut'ian Pun Nbadagĕ: Nor Dnōrinut'iwn, Nor Harowadz', *Azadamart*, 15 June 1910.
70. Ibid.
71. Klein, *Margins of Empire*, 159–60.
72. BOA: DH.SYS 23/1, the Ministry of the Interior to the provinces of Erzurum, Van, Bitlis and Mamuretülaziz, 31 Kanun-ı Sani 1326 (13 February 1911).
73. TNA: FO 424/224, Acting Vice-Consul Safrastian to Consul McGregor, Bitlis, 18 July 1910.
74. TNA: FO 424/225, Acting Vice-Consul Safrastian to Consul McGregor, Bitlis, 24 October 1910.
75. TNA: FO 424/228, Acting Bishop of Mush to Consul McGregor, Mush, 5 June 1911; TNA: FO 424/228, Mr Marling to Sir Edward Grey, Constantinople, 4 July 1911.

76. TNA: FO 424/228, Acting Vice-Consul Safrastian to Consul McGregor, Bitlis, 9 July 1911.
77. Ibid.
78. TNA: FO 424/228, Acting Vice-Consul Safrastian to Consul McGregor, Bitlis, 18 August 1911.
79. TNA: FO 424/229, Acting Vice-Consul Safrastian to Consul McGregor, Bitlis, 13 November 1911.
80. TNA: FO 424/228, Acting Vice-Consul Safrastian to Consul McGregor, Bitlis, 18 June 1911.
81. TNA: FO 424/228, Consul McGregor to Sir G. Lowther, Erzurum, 27 June 1911.
82. TNA: FO 424/228, Consul McGregor to Mr Marling, Erzurum, 7 July 1911. I thank Chen Gong for sharing the current name of the village with me.
83. TNA: FO 424/228, Consul McGregor to Sir G. Lowther, Erzurum, 27 June 1911.
84. For the case of Zomik, see also Çiftçi, 'Fragile Alliances', 290–92; Mehmet Polatel, 'Köylüler "Senyör"e Karşı: Zomik Köyü Ahalisi ile Haydaranlı Hüseyin Paşa'nın Arazi Davası', *Kürt Tarihi Dergisi* 47 (April 2022): 22–27.
85. BOA: DH.H 74/3, report by Erzurum director of education Şükrü Bey and head of the registry office Mahmud Bey, 4 Haziran 1327 (17 June 1911).
86. BOA: DH.H 74/3, decision of Administrative Council of Erzurum, 7 Haziran 1327 (20 June 1911).
87. Ibid.
88. BOA: DH.H 74/3, the Minister of War to the Ministry of the Interior, 7 Haziran 1327 (20 June 1911).
89. BOA: DH.H 74/6, the Governor of Erzurum to the Ministry of the Interior, 25 Temmuz 1327 (7 August 1911).
90. BOA: DH.H 74/6, the Governor of Erzurum to the Ministry of the Interior, 23 Temmuz 1327 (5 August 1911).
91. Ibid.
92. BOA: DH.H 74/6, the Grand Vizier to the Ministry of the Interior, 5 Eylül 1327 (18 September 1911).
93. BOA: DH.H 74/6, the Governor of Erzurum to the Ministry of the Interior, 25 Temmuz 1327 (7 August 1911).
94. BOA: DH.H 74/6, the Ministry of the Interior to the Grand Vizier, 30 Temmuz 1327 (12 August 1911).
95. BOA: DH.H 74/7, the Governor of Erzurum to the Ministry of the Interior, 25 Şubat 1327 (9 March 1912).
96. BOA, DH.H 74/7, the Ministry of the Interior to the Governor of Erzurum, 24 Mart 1328 (6 April 1912).
97. BOA, DH.H 74/7, the Governor of Erzurum to the Ministry of the Interior, 22 Nisan 1328 (5 May 1912).

98. For a detailed examination of petitions written by Kurdish peasants, requesting the return of lands seized by powerholders in the Hamidian period, see Özok-Gündoğan, 'A Peripheral Approach'.
99. BOA: DH.SYS 23/1, report of İsmail Hakkı Bey, governor of Bitlis, 26 Teşrin-i Evvel 1326 (8 November 1910). He compiled his reports as a book. See İsmail Hakkı Bey, *Raporlarım* (Adana: Osmanlı Matbaası, 1328/1912).
100. BOA: DH.SYS 23/1, report of İsmail Hakkı Bey.
101. As noted by Edip Gölbaşı, during the Hamidian period the strategy of flattering the chiefs and ensuring their support and loyalty was promoted by Zeki Pasha. See '1895–1896 Katliamları', in Özel and Adanır, *1915*, 146.
102. BOA: DH.SYS 23/1, the Governor of Bitlis to the Ministry of the Interior, 5 Mart 1327 (18 March 1911).
103. BOA: DH.SYS 23/1, the Governor of Erzurum to the Ministry of the Interior, 16 Şubat 1326 (1 March 1911).
104. Ibid.
105. Ibid.
106. BOA: DH.SYS 67/1-6, the district governor of Tercan to the province of Erzurum, 15 Temmuz 1326 (28 July 1910).
107. TNA: FO 424/225, Vice-Consul Matthews to Sir G. Lowther, Diarbekir, 19 October 1910.
108. BOA: DH.MUİ 102-2/14, cipher telegram from inspector Ali Seyidi and staff major Mustafa Bey to the Ministry of the Interior, 25 Mayıs 1326 (7 June 1910). The year on the document was mistakenly written as 1325.
109. *Deghegakir Hoghayin Krawmants Hantsnazhoghovoy*.
110. Garabedyan, *Hoghayin*.
111. Adom, *Bedagan Veranorokut'iwnn u Hoghayin Harts'ĕ* (G. Bolis: Dbaran A. Shahēn, 1910).
112. Ibid., 33.
113. Ibid., 43–50.
114. A-Tō, *Vani, Pit'lisi ew Ērzrumi vilayēt'nerĕ: Usumnasirut'yan mi p'orts ayt yergri ashkharhakragan, vijagakragan, irawagan ew d'ndesagan trut'yan* (Yerewan: Dbaran Guldura, 1912).
115. Ibid., 390–99.
116. *Adenakrut'iwnk' Azkayin Ēnthanur Zhoghov*, nist Zhe (session 15), 28 May 1910, 259–64.
117. Ibid., 260.
118. Ibid., 264.
119. *Anadolu Vilayat-ı Osmaniyesindeki Arazi Meselesine Dair Ermeni Patrikhanesinden 7 Temmuz 327 Tarihiyle Makam-ı Sami-i Sadâret-i Uzmâ ile Dâhiliye ve Adliye ve Mezahib Nezaret-i Celilelerine Arz ve Takdim Kılınan Takririn Suretidir* (Dersaadet: Dikran Doğramacıyan Matbaası, 1328).
120. Ibid., 2–3.
121. Ibid., 4.

122. Ibid., 6–10.
123. BOA: BEO 3997/299747, Anadolunun Vilayât-ı Şarkîyesinde Te'min-i Asayiş ve Adalet Vesaitine Dair Muhtıra, 26 Teşrin-i Sani 1327 (9 December 1911).
124. BOA: BEO 3997/299747, Krikor Zohrab to the Sublime Porte, 28 Teşrin-i Sani 1327 (11 December 1911).
125. Ibid.
126. Ibid.
127. In line with this intelligence, the 11th Army Corps in Van warned the governors of Van and Erzurum to take necessary precautions. BOA: DH.SYS 67/1-4, cipher telegram from the governor of Erzurum with the copy of cipher telegram of the 11th Army Corps in Van, 16 Kanun-ı Sani 1327 (29 January 1912).
128. Kaligian, *Armenian Organization*, 85.
129. Vahan Papazian, *Im Husherĕ*, vol. 2 (Beyrut: Hamazkayin Dbaran, 1952), 159.
130. Ibid., 160.
131. Ibid., 163.
132. Kévorkian, *Armenian Genocide*, 132. On 18 July 1912, the ARF published a declaration announcing that it had ended its relations with the CUP (Ibid., 134). See also Gaidz F. Minassian, 'Birinci Dünya Savaşı Öncesinde İttihat ve Terakki Cemiyeti ile Ermeni Devrimci Federasyonu Arasındaki İlişkiler', in Avagyan and Minassian, *Ermeniler ve İttihat Terakki*, 183–89.
133. 'H. H. Tashnagts'ut'ean Bahanchnerĕ: Kordznēut'ean Dzrakir mĕ', *Ḥarach*, 1 March 1912.
134. Emphasis in the original. Ibid.
135. BOA: BEO 3997/299747, copy of the decision of the Council of Ministers, Kanun-ı Evvel 1327 (December 1911).
136. BOA: DH.SYS 67/1-6, 'Teba'a-yı Devlet-i Âlîyeden Olub 10 Temmuz 324 tarihinden mukaddem Memâlik-i Ecnebîyye'ye giderek bu kere 'avdet etmek isteyenlerin tâbi'iyyetleri ile emlâk ve arâzileri hakkında olunacak mu'âmeleye dâ'ir (mukaddema şûrâ-yı devlette müteşekkil komisyon tarafından tanzîm edilen kânun lâyihası ta'dîlen bu kere dâhiliye nezâretince kaleme alınan lâyihayı kânuniye) kânun lâyihasıdır', 8 May 1912 (?).
137. In this draft law, a distinction is drawn between emigrants (those who left the empire with official permits) and deserters (those who left the empire without official permits and the necessary documents). This distinction concerned only nationality regulations; the procedures to be applied to deserters and emigrants in the second part of the law vis-à-vis land disputes were identical; therefore, I prefer to refer to these two groups as one, using the term 'emigrants'.
138. Ibid.
139. Ibid.
140. TNA: FO 424/230, Consul McGregor to Sir G. Lowther, Erzurum, 5 March 1912.

141. Ibid.
142. BOA: MV 164/72, decision of the cabinet, 2 Mayıs 1328 (15 May 1912).
143. Adom, 'Antratartsumner-1', *Ḥarach*, 16 June 1912; Adom, 'Antratartsumner-2', *Ḥarach*, 19 June 1912.
144. Adom, 'Antratartsumner-1'.
145. Emphasis in the original. Adom, 'Antratartsumner-2'.
146. Adom, 'Antratartsumner-2'.
147. BOA: HR.SYS 2818/1, Ottoman Embassy in London to the Ministry of Foreign Affairs, 11 May 1912.
148. BOA: HR.SYS 2818/1, the Ministry of Foreign Affairs to the Grand Vizier's Office, 20 June 1912.
149. *Adenakrut'iwnk' Azkayin Ēnthanur Zhoghov*, nist T' (session 9), 24 August 1912, 109–18.
150. Ibid., 114–15.
151. Ibid., 117–18.
152. BOA: BEO 4088/306557, the Armenian Patriarchate to the Ministry of Justice, 27 Ağustos 1328 (9 September 1912). In response to the claim of the Patriarchate that nothing had been done, the Ministry of Justice pointed out that several steps had been taken to improve the situation. BOA: BEO 4088/306557, 29 Ağustos 1328 (11 September 1912).
153. TNA: FO 371/1812, Sir G. Lowther to Sir Edward Grey, Constantinople, 17 April 1913, *Annual Report on Turkey for the Year 1912*, 52.
154. TNA: FO 371/1484, Mr. Marling to Sir Edward Grey, Constantinople, 4 September 1912.

Chapter 6

The Reforms and the Land Question after the Outbreak of the Balkan Wars

In the fall of 1912, Montenegro, a small Balkan state which had recently become independent, declared war on the Ottoman Empire. Soon, it was joined by Bulgaria, Greece and Serbia. The Balkan Wars constituted one of the most impactful events of the late Ottoman era. Leading to the loss of the bulk of the remaining Ottoman territories in Europe, as well as the displacement and refuge of thousands of Muslims from the Balkans, the wars caused a humanitarian catastrophe and a political crisis.[1]

The Balkan Wars stood as a major turning point for the empire. The influx of Muslim immigrants, many of whom fled from violence or were forced into migration, created a refugee settlement problem, increased the pressure on land and changed the population demographics. The loss of the majority of Ottoman European territories heightened fears of territorial shrinkage and increased the political importance of Anatolia.[2] The Balkan Wars also intensified the debates about the future of the empire, contributing to the escalation of disputes among the Great Powers. Moreover, this course of events led to the rise of more nationalist approaches among the Ottoman bureaucracy and political elite, undermining the idea of Ottoman brotherhood.[3]

In this chapter, I will examine the impact of the Balkan Wars and its consequences on the issue of reforms concerning Armenians and the Armenian land question. I will show that, with the outbreak of the war in 1912, Istanbul's policy towards 'Armenian' lands changed once again. Ottoman vulnerability during a succession of military losses encouraged the Armenians to raise their grievances and make calls for broad reforms to the agendas of the Great Powers and international diplomacy. This chapter will discuss the implications of these efforts, the reform negotiations and the ways in which Ottoman officials and CUP members tried to domesticate and tame the prospect of reforms.

The Historical Context

Before delving into the details of the internationalisation of reform debates and developments regarding the land question after the Balkan Wars, it is necessary to examine two important points surrounding the historical context. The first point to be examined here is the rivalry between the Great Powers and the conflict of German and Russian interests with regard to the Ottoman Empire.[4] The second development consists of the rise of a national economy (*millî iktisat*) perspective among the ranks of the CUP.

The outbreak of the Balkan Wars affected reform debates in the eastern provinces in a significant way.[5] The wars made it clear that the Ottoman Empire's power to control developments on its periphery was in decline. This was particularly alarming for the Great Powers. The main international actors in the reform debates were Russia and Germany, which had competing interests. While Russia was anxious that German influence would expand with the decline of the Ottoman Empire, Germany was trying to hinder the expansion of Russian influence in the eastern provinces and to prevent the secession of these provinces from the empire. Reform debates, which after the Balkan Wars had become a matter of international concern, were primarily shaped by discussions among these actors in the post-1912 period.[6]

The Russian approach to the Armenian Question had begun to change by 1905, because the Russian Empire began to see its own Armenian population as an asset rather than a threat and to develop a conciliatory policy towards their demands, rather than trying to control them through oppression.[7] It was in this context that the confiscated Armenian communal properties in the Caucasus were restored to the Armenian community, on the initiative of the government. Besides domestic reforms, Russia equally supported reform in the eastern provinces of the Ottoman Empire. The Russian foreign office also continued its efforts to develop relations with the Kurdish chiefs in the Ottoman East. Thus, Russia played a double game in the Ottoman East after 1905; while promoting reform in the eastern provinces and the improvement of the living conditions of Armenians, it also supported Kurdish political and religious leaders such as Abdürrezzak Bedirxan and Sheikh Selim, who objected to the same reforms.[8] An important concern for Russia, as highlighted by the Balkan Wars, can be found in the possible expansion of German influence in the region. The fall of the Ottoman Empire would create a power vacuum that Germany would be enthusiastic to fill.[9] Moreover, an Armenian revolt in the Ottoman East could disturb the fragile order in the Caucasus region.[10]

The Land Question after the Outbreak of the Balkan Wars

Another Great Power that played an important role in the reform debates following 1912 was Germany. Germany's influence in the Ottoman Empire began to increase in the Hamidian period, and there existed significant trade relations between the two countries. Germany also had undertaken the construction of the Baghdad Railway. As underscored by Roderic H. Davison, the main objective of Germany in diplomatic negotiations concerning the Ottoman Empire was to prevent the partitioning of Ottoman lands. German support for the territorial integrity of the Ottoman Empire was related to the geographically scattered nature of German investments in Ottoman lands.[11] Austria and Italy also sided with Germany and provided support for the protection of the territorial integrity of the Ottoman Empire.

Britain was yet another imperial power with political and economic interests in the region. As will be examined in detail in this chapter, the Ottoman government tried to secure a reform agreement to be carried out with the assistance of Germany and Britain and without Russian interference; however, Britain, not wishing to antagonise Russia, refrained from committing to such a reform plan. As discussed in the following pages, British authorities also refused an Ottoman proposal to assign British inspectors to the whole Ottoman Empire, underscoring that this would deepen conflicts of interest among the Great Powers. This brief investigation into the Great Powers' positions will illuminate the increasing polarisation among them in this period.

Another significant historical development was the rise of Turkish nationalism and a national economy approach among the ranks of the CUP. As noted by Zafer Toprak, a liberal approach to the economy, which until 1913 had dominated the socio-economic understanding and policies of the CUP, was replaced by a national economy approach in this period.[12] This new approach rested on the model of national economy proposed by Friedrich List. In List's approach, any country except for Britain – which was the motherland of the Industrial Revolution – would fail to keep up with the success of Britain if it followed liberal economic policies.

Another important figure in the development of this approach in the Ottoman Empire was Israel Lazarevich Helphand, known as Parvus,[13] whose thinking was shaped by a Marxist reading of history and economics. When Parvus moved to Istanbul in 1910, he engaged in speculative international trade transactions. In Istanbul, Parvus developed close ties with leading members of the CUP. According to Parvus, the solution to the Ottoman Empire's socio-economic problems depended on the implementation of three measures. The empire should abandon economic liberalism, create a strong national economy and take steps towards rapid industrialisation. Another important matter was the improvement of the conditions of the peasantry. Parvus argued that ignoring the peasantry not only brought socio-economic harm but hindered the development of Turkish nationalism. According to Parvus, mass support for the nationalist cause and especially the support to the peasantry was crucial for strengthening the nation-state.[14]

The ideology of a national economy merged with the ideology of Turkish nationalism in the discourse of the Young Turks' political ideologues – such as Ziya Gökalp, Yusuf Akçura and Moise Cohen, who later changed his name to Munis Tekinalp. Apart from these conceptual and discursive changes, in this period the Muslim masses began to be mobilised in line with the political aims of the ruling elite, through boycotts. In his detailed study of boycotts in the constitutional period, Doğan Çetinkaya has underscored the social aspect of nationalism and the role of boycotts in the rise of Turkish nationalism.[15] Çetinkaya has argued that boycotts, which were first instigated in 1908 against foreign countries (namely, Bulgaria and Austria-Hungary), subsequently played an important role in the deterioration of relations between Muslims and Christians after 1909, at which time a boycott against the Greeks was instigated.[16] The boycotts gained a new significance after the Balkan Wars, and the Greeks remained the primary targets of boycotts until 1914.[17] After the Russo-Ottoman Accord for reform in the eastern provinces, the boycotts turned towards the Armenians, and the Patriarchate demanded that the government take the necessary measures with regard to pressure being put on Armenian shopkeepers.[18]

After the Balkan Wars, the CUP also developed a new approach to the Greek population, adopting new and more radical policies aimed at decimating them in the Western parts of the country. Attacks on Greek communities and the forced displacement of Greeks from the Aegean coast caused the uprooting of thousands.[19] Thus, with the Balkan Wars, there occurred a radicalisation in the ethno-demographic approach of the CUP elite and in the policies adopted by the state.

Ottoman Attempts at Reform after the Outbreak of the Balkan Wars

When the tension in Rumelia escalated into war in the fall of 1912, the issue of reform in the eastern provinces re-entered the purview of the Ottoman government. As examined in the previous chapter, the establishment of a reform commission had already been on the government's agenda for almost a year, but the commission had not yet been established. The Ottoman government attempted to prevent the internationalisation of the issue of reform. In a telegram sent to the grand vizier's office on 18 December 1912, Rıfat Pasha, the Minister of Foreign Affairs, noted that it was 'urgently necessary to recognize the rightful and legitimate claims of Armenians in collaboration with the Patriarchate in a way that will prevent the intervention of the Great Powers'.[20] When Rıfat Pasha sent this telegram, the Ottoman government had already requested the assignment of British inspectors for a reform programme to be carried out in the eastern provinces.[21] Reacting positively to this request, British diplomats asserted that the Ottoman government must finalise the necessary legal arrangements for the reform scheme before British inspectors could be appointed.[22] In line with these developments, the government prepared a draft bill for the assignment of British inspectors as advisors in November 1912.[23]

By 18 December 1912, the Ottoman authorities had drafted a reform plan for the provinces of Van, Bitlis, Diyarbekir and Mamüretülaziz.[24] This reform plan stipulated the appointment of a general inspector and the assignment of a foreign person as advisor to the general inspector, as well as the establishment of a special commission. According to the reform plan of 18 December 1912, the general inspector, foreign advisor and special commission were given the responsibility to establish order in the region. All public officials would be obliged to follow the orders of the general inspector. The plan also stipulated the establishment of a special commission made up of six members. Three Muslims, two Armenians and one Chaldean would serve in this commission, which would be responsible for a number of duties including resolving land disputes between Armenians and Kurds, eliminating the problems between these communities, taking measures for the provision of security and public order, ensuring legal equality, bringing the police and gendarmerie forces in these provinces into order and working for the development of transportation facilities, agriculture, livestock and manufacture.[25]

In this plan, the land question was specified as a problem between Armenians and Kurds, and the special commission was authorised to solve such disputes in absolute terms. This issue was specified in the plan's first article, which stated that the special commission was responsible for 'solving the land question that is related to disputes between Kurdish and Armenian elements in line with the laws and regulations of the state[,] necessary justice and equity and in a way that will eliminate complaints of both parties in absolute terms'.[26] Thus, according to this plan, arbitration would be carried out by a special commission rather than by administrative councils. Furthermore, the decisions of the special commission would have to satisfy both parties.

As comprehensive as it was, the reform plan for Van, Bitlis, Diyarbekir and Mamüretülaziz came to be shelved after the CUP coup d'état (*Bâb-ı Âlî Baskını*) at the beginning of 1913. However, in the spring of 1913, the Ottoman government would resort to the same diplomatic strategy upon which the reform plan of 18 December rested, once again applying to Britain for assistance in an attempt to minimise Russian interference.

The Armenians' Demand for Reform and the Internationalisation of Reform Debates

The attempts of the Ottoman government to institute reform were also followed by the Armenian political elite who were raising concerns regarding the reliability of the Ottoman government. These concerns were reflected in *Harach*, which published news and articles regarding the recent initiatives of the central government to implement a reform plan. On 4 December 1912, the newspaper announced that the Ministry of the Interior had sent orders to local governors in the eastern provinces regarding the improvement of security and a resolution to the land disputes.[27] According to the newspaper, these orders included the allocation of 20,000 liras to each province for the resolution of land disputes and the establishment of local commissions, to be led by local governors and to include a mufti, a *murahhasa* and two reliable Kurds and Armenians as members. These local commissions were to hand down just decisions that would satisfy both parties and give compensation or land to those who failed to prove their claims in the proceedings. It was claimed that the order of the Ministry of the Interior also included instructions to the local governors to bring the Kurdish tribes in the tribal regiments (*aşiret alayları*) under control. An editorial article published in *Harach* on 6 December 1912 reflects the frustration of the Armenian political elite about the prospect of domestic reform. This editorial stated that ...

> ... two or three years ago, when we still had hopes for a true renaissance – a real constitution – we used to welcome such decisions with pure and untainted trust; but now, in the fifth year of the constitutional period, such correspondence does not excite us any more... We have seen many plans like this, we have read many [such plans], but [they] stayed on paper.[28]

The outbreak of the Balkan Wars and the shift in the international context triggered a significant mobilisation of the Armenian political elite. This change of context brought about changes in terms of domestic and local politics. In this period, disparate Armenian political parties for the first time began to act in accord for the adoption of a reform programme.[29]

The Land Question after the Outbreak of the Balkan Wars

One example of such cooperation at the local level consists of the telegram sent to the grand vizier and the Armenian Patriarchate by three Armenian political parties in Van – the ARF, the Hunchakian Revolutionary Party and the Armenian Democratic Liberal Party (*Ramgavar*). In this joint telegram, political activists demanded 'reform guarantees for the honour, lives and property of the Armenian population against the small number of Dere-Bey [*feudal*] Kurds who were the blood-suckers also of the Kurdish population, and against the incapable and corrupt officials who protected and encouraged them'.[30] These kinds of telegrams, emphasising the need for reform, were also sent from Armenian political parties and organisations in Cairo, Tehran, Izmir and Istanbul.[31]

ATTEMPTS AT THE INTERNATIONALISATION OF THE REFORM QUESTION

A significant development regarding the pressure of the Armenian political elite for reforms was the ANA's decision to internationalise the reform question. On 21 December 1912, the assembly held an extraordinary meeting. During the proceedings, the president of the assembly stated that numerous strategies had been tried to solve the problems, and since all these strategies had failed, it was time for the internationalisation of the issue. The ANA expressed support for this suggestion and extended authority to the presidency. Following this meeting, the Patriarchate established a political mission authorised to follow the Armenian Question, carry out international deliberations, prepare a reform plan and advance efforts for the implementation of reforms.[32]

Weeks before the ANA made the decision to internationalise the reform question, the Etchmiadzin Catholicosate had applied to Illarion Vorontsov-Dashkov, the Russian viceroy in the Caucasus, demanding Russian assistance for the internationalisation of the issue. Following this, a commission under the presidency of Boghos Nubar Pasha[33] was sent to Europe to lobby on behalf of reform.[34] Thus, the Armenian political and religious elite outside the Ottoman Empire had already taken action to internationalise the reform question before the Armenian political elite and Armenian institutions in the Ottoman Empire. The Ottoman Armenians, including the Patriarchate, were not even informed of these initiatives.[35] Following negotiations among the Ottoman Armenians, the Etchmiadzin Catholicosate and Boghos Nubar Pasha, it was decided that the Etchmiadzin Catholicosate would take the lead and act as representative of all Armenians. However, the Catholicosate would act in line with the Ottoman Armenians' decisions, instead of pursuing an independent agenda. Before his mission received authorisation from the security council formed by the Patriarchate, Boghos Nubar Pasha was also ordered to inform and consult with the Patriarchate at every step.

Publications

Apart from the political mission, the Patriarchate also established a security council during this process. This council began to communicate with bishops at the local level and requested from them reports regarding illegalities, looting and usurpation in the country. The security council collected these reports, translated them into French and every two weeks distributed them in booklets to European governments, consulates, parliaments and public figures. Furthermore, the council started to publish books on a wide range of topics, including the history, politics and culture of Armenia and the Armenian nation – starting with a French translation of the report on the Adana massacres, which had been prepared by Hagob Babigian.[36]

Several books were published in this period, in line with the propaganda efforts. Krikor Zohrab, under the pseudonym of Marcel Léart, wrote a book about the history of the Armenian Question and the need for reform in order to improve the conditions of the Armenians in the Ottoman Empire.[37] In his book, Zohrab also provided statistical and empirical information on and evaluations of demography, trade, industry and education concerning the Armenian population.[38] Zohrab specified three principles that should guide reform attempts. The first of these was the assignment of European governors with broad operational authority. According to Zohrab, this governor should be assigned in consultation with the Great Powers. The second principle consisted of the participation of a fair ratio of Armenians in public service. The third principle of reform should be administrative decentralisation.[39] Zohrab stated that a reform programme that included these three principles would also improve the living conditions of Kurds and Turks in the eastern provinces. Zohrab underscored that the Balkan Wars had triggered anti-Christian feelings among the population, and this could result in violence if the government failed to take precautionary measures. The only way to prevent this outcome was the appointment of European governors to the provinces inhabited by Armenians:

> The loss of Rumelia and the atrocities against the Muslim population [on the Balkans] has created a desire for revenge against Christians among the Muslim population which is quite understandable, and only the Armenians will suffer the terrible outbursts of this feeling [...] Only a European governor can prevent such a movement. The assignment of European governors to a couple of Ottoman provinces does not mean 'separation', 'autonomy' or a 'special regime'.[40]

The Land Question after the Outbreak of the Balkan Wars

In this period, the Patriarchate prepared pamphlets in French so as to reflect the grievances of the Armenian population and propagate the need for reforms. The Patriarchate prepared nine pamphlets that were later printed in book format and sent to consulates. The first of these pamphlets covered the issue of the land question and included information regarding the number and characteristics of properties that had been seized in the Hamidian period. The second pamphlet contained the memoranda (*takrir*s) of the Patriarchate about cases of depredation, rape, violence and injustice against Armenians. The third pamphlet consisted of Babigian's report on the Adana massacre. Other pamphlets presented injustices, misdeeds, murder and pillage in the eastern provinces.[41]

THE ARMENIAN REFORM PLAN

While the Armenian political elite and religious and administrative institutions were engaged in numerous publications and propaganda activities, there also happened deliberations within the Armenian community regarding the appropriate content and extent of a reform programme. Boghos Nubar Pasha prepared a plan based on the 1895 reform scheme, but the Armenian political elite in the Ottoman Empire found this plan insufficient to meet the needs of the Ottoman Armenians. The main concern of the Armenian Patriarchate's political mission was the exclusion of any signal of autonomy or secession from the reform plan, as these could lead to the termination of relations with the Unionists and would risk the support of foreign governments. After several meetings and negotiations among Armenian actors, the final draft of the reform plan prepared by Armenians was submitted to the Russian consulate in Istanbul at the beginning of April 1913, by a delegation headed by the Armenian Patriarch. Sdepan Karayan and Zohrab served as the other two members of this delegation. This draft was later revised by André Mandelstam who submitted it as a Russian proposal at the Yeniköy Conference.[42]

The Ottoman Government's Attempts to Domesticate the Prospects of Reform

Faced with the attempt of Armenian actors to internationalise the reform issue, the Ottoman government began to take precautions to prevent such an outcome. The CUP held two concerns regarding the internationalisation of the reform scheme. First, the adoption of an international reform plan and international guarantees for the implementation of reforms would mean the direct intervention of the Great Powers in the Ottoman Empire, leading to a serious breach of Ottoman sovereignty. Second, the CUP was concerned with preserving the territorial integrity of the empire – that a territorial reform plan backed by the Great Powers could lead down a path to the establishment of an independent Armenia.

It can be argued that the Ottoman government adopted two strategies to deal with the reform issue after the Balkan Wars. The CUP tried to convince the Armenian political elite that a domestic reform plan would be carried out by the Ottoman Empire and that there was no need for an international reform plan or international guarantees for the implementation of reforms. In line with this strategy, the Ottoman government began to adopt measures to solve some of the problems raised by the Armenian political and religious elite since the proclamation of the constitution in 1908. At the same time, the government, CUP members and the newspaper *Tanin* began to make declarations regarding domestic reform and measures being taken by the government. Yet, the Ottoman government refrained from officially committing itself to solving major problems such as the land question. In fact, in the spring of 1913, the CUP government again blocked the use of arbitration procedures. The second strategy adopted by the government was to play the Great Powers off one another.

Telegrams sent by Ottoman ambassadors show that the Armenian reform efforts in Europe were closely followed by Ottoman diplomats. On 8 February 1913, the Ottoman ambassador to Vienna, Hüseyin Hilmi Pasha, sent a telegram to the Ministry of Foreign Affairs, noting that Boghos Nubar Pasha had established a committee in Paris, aiming to secure foreign states' support for reforms in the Ottoman East. The ambassador reported that these activities were being published in European newspapers, and that the Armenian delegation had contacted Sir Edward Grey to raise the issue at the London Conference, where the political and territorial outcomes of the First Balkan War would be decided. The ambassador suggested that the government take immediate measures to foster the welfare of the Armenian and Kurdish people in the eastern provinces, as well as to implement security measures and economic reforms to eliminate the threat of foreign intervention.[43] Nabi Bey, the Ottoman ambassador to Rome, reported that Italy, Germany and Austria were trying to prevent Russia from raising the issue of Armenia. He urged the government to take measures to appease the people in the eastern provinces. Turhan Pasha, the Ottoman ambassador in St Petersburg, offered similar warnings. After receiving such warnings, the Sublime Porte sent an order to the consulates to contact the foreign ministers of the countries to which they had been assigned, to inquire about the protection of the Ottoman Empire's territorial integrity.[44]

The Land Question after the Outbreak of the Balkan Wars

Based on these warnings from ambassadors and the correspondence among the Ottoman authorities, one may argue that the Ottoman authorities were seriously concerned with the possibility of a clash between Armenians and Kurds (or massacres of Armenians), a development that might pave the way for Russian intervention in the Ottoman East. A telegram sent by the Ministry of Foreign Affairs to the Ministry of the Interior on 4 February 1913 illuminates this concern. This telegram noted that Armenians on Russian territory had established brigands who were ready to cross the border. At the same time, the Russian Minister of Foreign Affairs, Sergei D. Sazonov, declared that the Kurds might attack the Armenians in the region. The Ottoman Ministry of Foreign Affairs stated that the timing of Sazonov's declaration was alarming and requested that the Ministry of the Interior send orders to the local governors to take precautions so as to prevent breaches of public order between Armenians and Kurds, breaches that would invite Russian intervention.[45] Beginning in 1913, the Ottoman government began to undertake several measures to maintain security and public order in the region. For example, the number of gendarmes in the eastern provinces was increased.[46] Moreover, gendarmerie inspectors were sent to visit the provinces under the leadership of Bauman Pasha.[47]

Domestic Reform Initiatives

In the first months of 1913, the Ottoman government adopted several decisions and decree-laws (*muvakkat kanun*) in line with domestic reform initiatives. On 26 March 1913, the government adopted 'The Decree-Law on the General Administration of Provinces', which extended the powers of the governors and provincial councils. The law also specified the duties of the local officials and provincial councils.[48] On 1 March 1913, another decree-law was adopted. This was the decree-law on the use of immovable properties by legal persons. With this decree-law, legal persons were allowed to register their properties under their own name in the title deeds.[49] This decision was important for non-Muslim charitable foundations, including churches, schools and monasteries, because it enabled them to register their properties in the names of their foundations for the first time. This was a significant issue for the foundations, which had demanded such a regulation since 1908. Before this decree-law, charitable foundations had had to register their properties under the names of trustees. In several cases, when a trustee had died, properties registered in their name were considered *mahlul* and sold by the government. On 24 April 1913, the decree-law on peace court judges (*sulh hâkimleri kânunu*) was adopted.[50]

The government also made the decision to facilitate peasants' access to loans in order to improve agriculture.[51]

PUBLIC DEBATES REGARDING THE PROSPECTS OF DOMESTIC REFORMS

In May 1912, the newspaper *Tanin*, the CUP organ, claimed that the Council of Ministers was planning to establish a reform commission under the presidency of the former Minister of Pious Foundations, Hayri Bey, to solve the problems in the eastern provinces. According to the article, this reform commission would be authorised to solve the land question and to take steps to improve security in these provinces.[52] It was also rumoured that the commission would be given 100,000 liras to resolve land disputes and that additional funds would be provided for other matters related to reform.[53] However, the commission would not be established in the ensuing months.

The newspaper *La Turquie* interviewed the Armenian Patriarch, Hovhannes Arsharuni Efendi, about the reform commission designated by the Ottoman government. This interview was also published in *Tanin*. The Patriarch said that the bishops in the eastern provinces were continuously sending information about Kurdish depredations and the oppression of Armenians, and that the bishops complained about the indifference of the local officials who took no measures to stop this oppression. According to the Patriarch, to solve these problems, the gendarmerie should be reformed under the supervision of the European powers, schools should be opened for both Armenians and Kurds, and the government should improve these provinces' transportation by building roads and railways. But most importantly, all those who had committed crimes should be prosecuted and punished. The Patriarch denied the claim that the Armenians demanded autonomy. He said that the Armenian people were carrying out their duties and responsibilities as Ottoman subjects and that the government was obliged to protect them. As to the plans of the Council of Ministers to establish a reform commission, the Patriarch noted that the Patriarchate had not been officially informed of this initiative and that he did not know whether any measures were being taken to implement the reforms. The Patriarch's comments regarding the plans to establish a reform commission reflect the frustration of the Armenian elite with the Ottoman government's approach in trying to solve problems with commissions: 'So far, we have seen several commissions, but none of them produced results. If this commission takes two or three legions of soldiers with it to implement its orders, only then may we have hope regarding this [initiative]'.[54] With respect to the land question, the Patriarch stated that he had heard that the government was planning to allocate a sum of 100,000 liras to compensate the parties involved in land conflicts and that the Patriarchate preferred an administrative rather than a judicial solution to the problem.[55]

İsmail Hakkı Babanzade, a former deputy and CUP member, wrote an article reflecting on the interview conducted with the Armenian Patriarch. He stated that the government intended to implement reforms to improve conditions in the eastern provinces but failed to take serious steps to realise this aim. He noted that 'even a serious start to reforms has not yet been carried out, let alone reforms'.[56] İsmail Hakkı summarised the situation by noting that 'decisions were made, orders were sent, commissions were established [and] funds were allocated, but each time a domestic or foreign obstacle obstructed the implementation of these initiatives'.[57] According to İsmail Hakkı, the land question, which he believed to be a temporary matter, could be easily resolved by a just commission, an appropriate programme and adequate funds.[58]

While rumours about the establishment of a reform commission circulated, a final decision in this regard was not immediately taken. This situation caused much public debate. Hacı Adil Bey, the Minister of the Interior, declared that the Council of Ministers had discussed the issue and that persons familiar with conditions in the region would be appointed as members of the designated commission.[59] In the meantime, *La Turquie* published a news piece claiming that the government would not send a reform commission to the eastern provinces but instead establish local committees to investigate and solve problems. The Minister of the Interior denied this claim and said that the government was still working on the matter.[60]

On 27 May 1913, the Council of Ministers made several decisions regarding reform in the eastern provinces.[61] Specifying land disputes and several other problems related to the lack of security and equality, the Council decided to notify the relevant ministries to implement the existing legislation and principles.[62] The decisions of the Council of Ministers show that the Ottoman authorities were still discussing plans regarding the establishment of an investigation commission[63] and a special commission. The special commission would consist of one president and six members, and its members would be dispatched to different localities. If possible, the special commission would solve land disputes through arbitration; if not, the cases would be sent to administrative commissions to be established by the commission. If the administrative commissions also failed to arbitrate the cases, the parties would be directed to the courts. Apart from this special commission procedure, the reform commission would also have the authority to investigate land disputes. It should be noted that the Council of Ministers did not establish a special commission or investigation commission on 27 May 1913. The decision only shows that the Ottoman authorities were discussing the matter.

The CUP Leaders and Reforms

While not officially adopting a reform plan or establishing a reform, investigation or special commission, CUP leaders were trying to keep the matter in the public eye and to convince the Ottoman public that the government was spending effort on reforms. Talat Pasha gave an interview to *Tanin* on 7 July 1913, at the height of international reform debates. In this interview, Talat Pasha repeated the problems specified by the Council of Ministers and underscored that the government was committed to solving these problems. He said that the government intended to provide security and public order in the eastern provinces; the government had taken several measures to achieve this goal, including increasing the number of gendarmes in the region, dispatching gendarme officers from Rumelia to the East and assigning a foreign major and a civil inspector to each legion. With regard to the land conflicts, Talat Pasha stated that the government was considering establishing a special commission and an investigation commission, but he believed that, unless land registry procedures were carried out, it would be impossible to solve the problem.[64]

Cavid Bey also gave an interview about the prospects of domestic reform to an Armenian newspaper, *Azadamart*. Thus, his declarations were intended to appeal to the Armenian public. Cavid Bey's statements regarding the necessity of reforms reflect the desire to convince the Armenian public that the CUP was cognizant of the importance of and need for reforms.[65] In this interview, Cavid Bey stated that ...

> ... demands regarding reform in the eastern [provinces] will certainly be recognized. Presently, no one should doubt that. Do you know why? Because the meaning of this matter – the degree of its importance – changed after the last war. Now, the Armenian Question is one of the most important issues of the Ottoman Empire [...] We have come to the conclusion that, from now on, a disturbance that may happen in the eastern provinces will have adverse effects on the whole state.[66]

According to Cavid Bey, the government was committed to the implementation of reforms. Regarding the reform plan of the government, he stated that ...

> ... the land question will resolve on its own after the reformation of the administrative structure. Competent governors and an authorised general inspector, who will supervise them, will be assigned. In addition to this, financial

inspectors and gendarme commanders will be assigned, and they will be under the command of foreign commanders [...] The solution to the land question in the desired manner is no great deal. If necessary, the government can buy the disputed lands and return [them] to their original owners, and this is what it will do. The interests of the state require this anyway.[67]

It should be noted that, as these leading CUP members were declaring the government's plans to solve the land question, the Ottoman government blocked the use of arbitration procedures by administrative councils once again. Thus, one may say that the Ottoman government employed the administrative resolution as political leverage in this period.

NEGOTIATIONS BETWEEN THE CUP AND THE ARMENIAN ELITE

In addition to giving interviews about the willingness of the Ottoman government to enact reforms, CUP leaders also communicated with the Armenian religious and political elite to persuade them to give up their insistence on an international reform scheme and on international guarantees for reform. At the beginning of July, Talat Pasha, the Minister of the Interior, visited the Armenian Patriarch to discuss the issue of reform. Talat Pasha said that brigands in the eastern region were being chased and prosecuted and that 'the government was determined to save the country from brigands' and 'to implement reforms in the eastern provinces of Anatolia'.[68] The Patriarch raised concerns, stating that, 'if this reform would be carried out with a centralised approach, nothing would be achieved'.[69] Talat Pasha responded:

> No, sir, the reform will be implemented using a decentralised approach. I request your assistance [in this matter]. We shall do this in such a way that European states do not intervene. Apart from several European officials, we will even assign general inspectors to oversee the implementation of reforms in every single province.[70]

One of the most important meetings between the Unionists and the Armenian political elite occurred between leading CUP and ARF members. When this meeting was held, relations between the CUP and ARF had already been officially terminated. According to Papazian, reports of Armenian negotiations with the Russian consulate drove the Unionists to demand such a meeting. The meeting was held in the house of Bedros Halladjian and was attended by Talat, Menteşe deputy Halil and Mithat Şükrü from the CUP, as well as Agnuni, Vartkes and Garo from the ARF. According to Papazian, during this meeting, the Unionists gave assurances that they would carry out radical reforms, as in Eastern

Rumelia in the 1880s. They wanted Armenian politicians to trust them about the scope of the reform programme and the implementation of reforms instead of seeking the support of foreign powers.[71] The meetings between the Unionists and Tashnagists yielded no positive outcome. As Rober Koptaş has highlighted, both parties blamed each other for the failure of these negotiations. While the Armenian political elite pointed to the fact that the Unionists gave many promises but failed to realise them, the Unionists accused Armenian politicians of relying on foreign intervention.[72] Ultimately, what led to the failure of these negotiations was the lack of trust between the parties.

Reform Questions at the International Level

The second strategy of the Ottoman government and the CUP in dealing with the reform issue was to create division among the Great Powers and to play them against each other. In line with this framework, the Ottoman government sought Britain's help to implement a domestic reform programme. Beyond this, the Ottoman government tried to expand the geographical scope of the reform plan and to generalise the reforms by carrying out an empire-wide reform scheme. The government hoped to prevent the territorialisation of the reform scheme, as this could result in the separation of the eastern provinces from the Ottoman Empire under the rubric of Armenia. This was a great concern for the government, and it was aggravated by the experiences in Rumelia and Lebanon.

THE OTTOMAN REQUEST FOR BRITISH ASSISTANCE

Halil (Menteşe) Bey's memoirs shed light on the Ottoman government's approach to the issue of reform. He recounts warning Grand Vizier Mahmud Şevket Pasha about the Armenian efforts in Europe to internationalise the reform issue and urging him to seek Britain's assistance by requesting British consultants for the implementation of reforms. This request would be based on the Cyprus Convention, which stipulated British support for the Ottoman Empire against potential Russian aggression. Halil Bey proposed that the Ottoman government request a British general inspector be assigned to the Ministry of the Interior. Mahmud Şevket Pasha and Talat Pasha accepted this approach, and the government instructed Tevfik Pasha, the Ottoman ambassador in London, to make the necessary arrangements.[73]

On 15 April 1913, the Council of Ministers made an official decision regarding the appointment of the British inspectors.[74] The Ottoman

The Land Question after the Outbreak of the Balkan Wars

ambassadors in London, Tevfik Pasha and Hakkı Pasha, were authorised to conduct negotiations with the British authorities for Britain's involvement in the reform scheme. Since it was unclear whether the British government would be willing to undertake this role, Italy, Germany and Austria were to be consulted as well. The designated reforms were to be carried out in the empire as a whole, but in the initial stage they would be implemented in Eastern and Northern Anatolia. The eastern section included Van, Bitlis, Mamuretülaziz and Diyarbekir, whereas the northern section included Erzurum, Sivas and Trabzon. The government planned to assign British majors to gendarme legions in these sections. A general inspector would be assigned to each section, and general inspectors would be assisted by inspectors of gendarmes, justice, agriculture and public works. Furthermore, two British officials would be employed in the central administration. One of them would be assigned as a consultant to the Ministry of the Interior, and the other British official to the general inspectorate of the Ministry of the Interior.[75]

On 24 April 1913, Tevfik Pasha officially applied to the British government regarding the assignment of these British officials.[76] The initial reaction of the British government was positive, but the British officials responded to the Ottoman diplomats with caution since the British government did not want to antagonise Russia. Thus, they demanded that the Russian authorities be informed of the request being made by the Ottoman government. The British authorities also rejected the request of the Ottoman Empire for advisers in its Ministry of the Interior, stating that this might 'create embarrassments with other Powers'.[77] Britain reformulated the Ottoman proposal and agreed to assign British officials to the gendarmes.[78] After Britain had informed the Russian authorities of the request by the Ottoman government, Sazonov, the Russian Minister of Foreign Affairs, said that the issue of gendarmes could not be separated from the question of reform in the Ottoman Empire. He suggested that the matter be discussed by the British, French and Russian ambassadors in Istanbul.[79]

Tevfik Pasha once more applied to the British authorities on 21 May 1913. In this second application, the Ottoman government requested that additional British officials be assigned to the southern and western provinces. The Foreign Ministry of Britain sent a response to Tevfik Pasha, noting that they wanted 'to limit their assistance to the provision of inspectors and officers of gendarmerie in the two sectors'.[80] The British government did not want to expand the scope of the reform scheme in which it would be involved, because other powers had interests in various parts of the Ottoman Empire. Such an expansion in the geographical scope of

British involvement could trigger conflicts of interest between the Great Powers. According to Davison, Germany also agreed with the Ottoman plan and sought Anglo-German cooperation to protect the territorial integrity of the Ottoman Empire.[81]

Disagreements among the Great Powers

The British authorities faced strong protest from Russia after informing the Russian authorities that they had accepted the Ottoman government's request to assign British officials as inspectors of the gendarmes. In his evaluation of this development, the Russian Minister of Foreign Affairs, Sazonov, stated that some time ago representatives of the Armenians had 'approached the Russian Government with a request for the annexation of Turkish Armenia to Russia'. According to Sazonov, the Russian authorities had denied this request but promised to secure the implementation of effective reforms in the region. Sazonov stated that this promise 'put Russia under peculiar obligations to the Armenians', and that Russia 'could not play second violin in this matter'.[82] Sazonov also added that the Russian government would not remain passive and would intervene in the case of massacres of Armenians, such as those carried out in the 1890s.[83] France and Britain tried to convince Russia that, if the Ottoman proposal were to be rejected, the Ottoman authorities would turn to Germany and give them a leading role in carrying out the reforms. But they were unable to convince the Russian authorities.[84] In the end, Britain postponed its response to the Ottoman Empire until after the Ambassadors' Conference that was to be held in Istanbul that July.

The diplomatic initiatives and tensions among these powers escalated in the first weeks of June. Germany began to assume a more active role, and the German ambassador in London stated that, 'if other powers made claims, Germany would have to put in her own claim'.[85] Moreover, Germany and Austria demanded that representatives of the Ottoman Empire be included in the Conference of Ambassadors.[86] Yet, British diplomats were concerned about the prospects of reform, noting that the Armenians were of the opinion that effective reform could only be carried out under the auspices of Russia. Referring to the failure of reform plans in 1895, they also underscored that conflict between Russia and Britain might hinder the implementation of reforms. The British consul in Istanbul reported that the CUP government hoped to secure an Anglo-German reform scheme that would exclude Russia. The consul noted that 'the opinion of Armenians and other competent observers that any projects of reform of an anti-Russian tendency in the provinces inhabited by the

The Land Question after the Outbreak of the Balkan Wars

Armenians are almost certain to be fraught with disastrous instead of beneficial results to the latter'.[87] In the meantime, Sazonov suggested that the Great Powers take the reform project of 1895 as a starting point for the meeting of ambassadors in Istanbul.

THE MANDELSTAM PLAN

After the Great Powers decided to hold an ambassadors' meeting in July, Russia prepared a reform scheme, which it submitted to the French and British authorities. The French and British diplomats did not grant approval to this plan and declared that they would consider it as Russian proposal for reform.[88] The Russian plan was prepared by André Mandelstam, the dragoman of the Russian embassy in Istanbul, and it reflected the demands of the Armenians.[89] According to the Mandelstam plan, the six provinces would be united as one, the 'Armenian Province', and an Ottoman Christian – or preferably European – would be assigned as the governor-general for a term of five years. The governor-general would have extensive powers, including the authority to appoint and dismiss any officials (including judges). Gendarmes and police forces in the province would also be under the command of the governor-general. The province would have a provincial assembly in which Muslims and Christians would be represented equally. The number of Muslims and Christians employed as officials, judges, gendarmes and police in the province would be equal. According to the Mandelstam plan, the Hamidian Regiments would be abolished. All laws and decrees would be published in three languages (Turkish, Kurdish and Armenian). The Great Powers would ensure the implementation of these provisions.[90]

Two articles of the Mandelstam Plan (Articles XVII and XIX) were related to the land question. According to these articles, land disputes concerning Armenians would be resolved by a special commission operating under the supervision of the general inspector. This commission would also be given the authority to 'determine the circumstances under which seized lands of Armenians would be returned'. The special commission could compensate claimants with land or cash.[91] The Mandelstam Plan also stipulated that Muslim immigrants would not be settled in the region.

The Mandelstam plan was strongly opposed by the German authorities.[92] According to the German ambassador in Istanbul, ...

> ... Russian proposals about Armenia went too far. They went, indeed, beyond even what existed for the Lebanon. They would create a complete autonomy, and separate Armenia entirely from the rest of Asiatic Turkey. This would be a

bad precedent, and would make for the break-up and not for the consolidation of the Turkish Dominions.[93]

Sazonov rejected this claim and warned that, 'if the Mandelstam plan were not adopted, the Armenians would revolt, Russian military intervention would be forced, and partition would then ensue'.[94] As underscored by Davison, Germany and Russia presented opposing approaches to the matter. While Germany thought that the Mandelstam plan would lead to the partitioning of the Ottoman Empire, Russia thought that its partitioning would be inevitable without this plan.[95]

THE OTTOMAN PLAN FOR REFORM

In the last week of June, the Ottoman government prepared its own reform plan and sent it to the Great Powers. On 25 June 1913, Said Halim Pasha, the grand vizier of the Ottoman Empire, sent a telegram to the Ottoman ambassadors to London, Paris, Berlin, Vienna, St Petersburg and Rome, about the reform measures that had been carried out by the Ottoman government in the previous six months.[96] Said Halim Pasha also informed the ambassadors of an amendment to the decree-law on the general administration of provinces. According to this amendment, the general inspector would be appointed by the Council of Ministers for a term of five years, and the number of local and foreign officials working under the auspices of the general inspector would be determined by the Council of Ministers.[97] The duties of the general inspector were also specified in the Ottoman reform plan,[98] according to which they would supervise the implementation of all legislation. The general inspector would carry out reforms pertaining to the gendarmes, police, justice, the tax system, agriculture, forestry and mines, in consultation with the central government.

Despite the declarations of the CUP leaders that the land question would be resolved within the framework of the Ottoman reform plan, the text of the official Ottoman plan included no provisions regarding land disputes,[99] nor did it specify the region in which reforms would be implemented. In other words, the plan was designed for empire-wide implementation, not solely for the provinces inhabited by Armenians. According to the British consul in Istanbul, the Ottoman plan was guided by the German ambassador, who declared that he would oppose 'any proposal which [would] create a special privileged position for Armenian provinces, and therefore [insisted] on taking the Turkish scheme providing reforms for whole Empire'.[100]

The Land Question after the Outbreak of the Balkan Wars

Just before the conference, the Sublime Porte sent another written note to the Great Powers, specifying the geographical regions to which the two general inspectors would be assigned. According to this note, the northern and eastern parts of the empire were designated as sections three and five. The provinces of Erzurum, Sivas, Trabzon and Canik were grouped into the northern section, and Bitlis, Van, Diyarbekir and Mamuretülaziz were grouped together in the eastern section.[101] This note indicates that the Ottoman government did not give up on generalising the reform scheme, even as it demarcated specific regions in which initial reforms would be carried out.

The Yeniköy Conference and Negotiations between Germany and Russia

Two different proposals for reform and division among the six powers framed the discussions in the Ambassadors' Conference. The eight sessions of the conference were held in Austria's summer embassy at Yeniköy, between 3 and 24 July 1913.[102] Although the Ottoman Empire was not represented in the conference, the German and Austrian ambassadors, who opposed the Mandelstam plan, brought the Ottoman reform plan to the table. The Yeniköy Conference ended without an agreement, due to the depth of the disagreements among the Great Powers, especially between Germany and Russia. In spite of the failure to solve the question of reform, the conference provided a forum for discussion among the Great Powers and for the clarification of their interests. Davison has summarised:

> The British had early said the obvious, which needed saying: that the Russian plan was of no use because it led only to disagreement, that any effective action had to be united, and any effective reform had to be accepted voluntarily by the Porte. The French, at the end of the conference, sought a basis to conciliate the Turk and Russian plans. The Italians, starting to delimit a sphere in Adalia and to negotiate a railway concession with Turkey, wanted peace and quiet. The Austrians were even less prepared for an explosion or partition of Turkey.[103]

After the Yeniköy Conference, Russia and Germany negotiated the course of future discussions and agreed that the issue of reform should be negotiated between Russia and the Ottoman Empire. In the middle of September, Russian Ambassador Giers and German Ambassador Wangenheim prepared a new plan in line with the Ottoman proposal. According to the plan accepted by Giers and Wangenheim, two inspectors to be recommended by the Great Powers would be assigned to carry out the reforms in the Ottoman East. The inspectors would have extensive control over the reforms' administration.[104] Other powers also accepted this plan, but the Ottoman government initially did not. Davison has claimed that the Ottoman government was aware of the divisions among the powers, and the Ottoman officials had thought that the Great Powers would fail to reach an agreement.[105] The Ottoman government insisted on its own reform plan. In line with this approach, the Ottoman government once again applied to Britain, requesting the appointment of two general inspectors for a term of five years. The British authorities rejected this request, noting that all the powers had already discussed the Armenian reform issue.[106]

The Last Attempt at a Domestic Reform Scheme

After Britain's rejection of the Ottoman diplomats' request for British inspectors to oversee the implementation of an Ottoman reform scheme, the CUP tried to reach an agreement with the Armenians to prevent the intervention of foreign powers. In December 1913, Halil Bey visited Krikor Zohrab to discuss the reform issue. In this meeting, he told Zohrab that 'the Unionists would accept all conditions that were demanded by the Armenians, on one condition: Armenians would declare that they give up [on demanding] foreign intervention'.[107] Zohrab explained that, for the reform issue, foreign intervention did not mean the establishment of foreign control but was rather a measure of guarantee for the implementation of reforms. According to Zohrab, Halil Bey said that the reform scheme would include measures for the equal employment of Muslims and Christians in public office, a re-organisation of the education tax and a resolution to the land question. Halil Bey assured Zohrab that the CUP would agree to a negotiation process that would involve the Great Powers and the assignment of a European general inspector, but that it would oppose international guarantees for the implementation of reforms. Halil Bey noted that the CUP demanded a limit to the intervention of foreign powers. He argued that the Sublime Porte should receive oral approval from foreign countries with regard to the assignment of the general inspector.

Agreeing with Halil Bey, Krikor Zohrab brought this 'domesticated' plan before the representatives of the Patriarchate, the ARF and the Hunchaks.[108] About the meeting in which this plan was discussed among several Armenian actors, Zohrab noted that no one listened to him and that he was opposed without any counter-arguments.[109] As underscored by Koptaş, the Armenian actors and institutions' distrust of the CUP, based on the CUP's failure to carry out promises made over previous years, constituted the main reason for the rejection of this proposal to domesticate the issue of reform. Thus, the Ottoman government's strategies to prevent the intervention of the Great Powers, especially that of Russia, by limiting reform to a British-supervised scheme or by reaching an agreement with the Armenians failed.

THE RUSSO-OTTOMAN AGREEMENT OF FEBRUARY 1914

After the CUP had failed to persuade Britain to accept a reform plan that would be supervised by Britain and after it had failed to persuade the Armenian political elite of a domestic reform scheme, the path was paved for the adoption of the Giers-Wangenheim plan. Negotiations between Russia, Germany and the Ottoman Empire were concluded within six months, and Russia and the Ottoman Empire signed an accord on 8 February 1914.[110] According to this agreement, the Great Powers would verbally recommend two general inspectors to the Porte, and these general inspectors would hold extensive control. The two foreign general inspectors would be assigned to the Ottoman East, to be divided into sections. Erzurum, Trabzon and Sivas were grouped into one section, and Van, Bitlis, Mamuretülaziz and Diyarbekir into the other. The general inspectors would have control over administration, justice, police and the gendarmes. Laws, regulations and official announcements would be published in the local languages. The Ministry of Education would take the necessary steps to allocate the funds of the ministry fairly with respect to the ratio of education taxes collected from different groups in each province. Tribal regiments would be transformed into reserve cavalry.[111]

The religious, national and linguistic characteristics of the region's population would be determined by a census, to be carried out within a year. Until the census data were collected, Muslims and non-Muslims would be represented equally in the general assemblies (*meclis-i umumi*) and committees (*encümen*) in Van, Bitlis and Erzurum. In Sivas, Mamuretülaziz and Diyarbekir, religious groups would be represented in general assemblies and committees in proportion to their populations. In these provinces, the population distribution would be assessed based on election data for Muslims, while population data for non-Muslims would be provided by community representatives. Muslims and Christians would continue to be equally represented in administrative councils. According to this final accord, land disputes would be 'resolved under the direct supervision of general inspectorates'.[112] It should be noted that the land clause of the Russo-Ottoman Agreement was vague when compared to that of the Mandelstam plan.

Conclusion

The Balkan Wars constituted one of the most impactful events of the late Ottoman period. The ripple effects that they generated were felt far and wide. As examined in this chapter, the outbreak of the war also changed the course of developments concerning the Armenian land question, because it highlighted the need for reforms and led to the internationalisation of reform debates and negotiations.

In this round of international reform debates, there emerged a situation concerning the international powers that was quite different from the situation in the 1880s. In the 1910s, Germany was one of the main actors involved in the negotiations, and it worked for the adoption of a reform scheme closer to the demands of the Ottoman bureaucrats. Moreover, Russia, which had improved her relations with the Armenians in the Caucasus in the early 1900s, insisted more strongly on the adoption of an extensive reform scheme. The Reform Accord of 1914 was drafted and signed under the impact of deliberations between these two international players.

After the outbreak of the war in the Balkans, the Ottoman government, which had supressed demands for reform and delayed the resolution of problems such as the land question, declared that it intended to carry out reforms and tried to convince its public as well as the Great Powers that it would stand behind its promises. However, due to its record of unkept promises, this was not found convincing. After long negotiations and various drafts, an international reform plan that also included a clause about the resolution of land disputes was adopted and put into action. As the next chapter will examine, these negotiations and the adoption of the reform plan would have drastic repercussions in the Ottoman East, causing good cheer and joy, as well as disgust, anxiety and rebellion.

Notes

1. Zürcher, *Turkey*, 102–7.
2. Dündar, *İttihat ve Terakki*, 32–38.
3. M. Şükrü Hanioğlu, *A Brief History of the Late Ottoman Empire* (Princeton: Princeton University press, 2008), 173; Hans-Lukas Kieser, *Talaat Pasha: Father of Modern Turkey, Architect of Genocide* (Princeton: Princeton University Press, 2018), 154–56; Ümit Kurt and Doğan Gürpınar, 'The Balkan Wars and the Rise of the Reactionary Modernist Utopia in Young Turk Thought and the Journal *Türk Yurdu* [*Turkish Homeland*]', *Nations and Nationalism* 21, no. 2 (April 2015): 348–68.

The Land Question after the Outbreak of the Balkan Wars

4. Mustafa Aksakal, *The Ottoman Road to War in 1914: the Ottoman Empire and the First World War* (Cambridge: Cambridge University Press, 2008), chap. 3.
5. Bloxham, *Great Game of Genocide*, 64–65.
6. For the details of this reform debate, see Roderic H. Davison, 'The Armenian Crisis, 1912–1914', *The American Historical Review* 53, no. 3 (1948): 481–505; W. J. van der Dussen, 'The Question of Armenian Reforms in 1913–1914', *Armenian Review* 39, no. 1 (1986): 11–28; Hans-Lukas Kieser, Mehmet Polatel and Thomas Schmutz, 'Reform or Cataclysm? The Agreement of 8 February 1914 Regarding the Ottoman Eastern Provinces', *Journal of Genocide Research* 17, no. 3 (2015): 285–304; Yektan Türkyılmaz, 'Rethinking Genocide: Violence and Victimhood in Eastern Anatolia, 1913–1915' (PhD diss., Duke University, 2011).
7. Davison, 'Armenian Crisis', 486.
8. Michael A. Reynolds, *Shattering Empires: The Clash and Collapse of the Ottoman and Russian Empires, 1908–1918* (Cambridge: Cambridge University Press, 2011).
9. Sergei Dmitrievich Sazonov, *Fateful Years: 1909–1916* (New York: F. A. Stokes Company, 1928), 141.
10. This concern was clearly voiced by the Minister of Foreign Affairs of Russia, Sazonov, in a meeting with Turhan Pasha. BOA: BEO 4192/314360, Turhan Pasha, Ottoman Ambassador in St Petersburg, to the Ministry of Foreign Affairs, 2 July 1913.
11. Dussen, 'Question of Armenian', 15; Davison, 'Armenian Crisis', 482.
12. Zafer Toprak, *Türkiye'de Milli İktisat (1908–1918)* (Ankara: Yurt Yayınları, 1982).
13. For a detailed examination of Parvus' economic approach, see M. Asım Karaömerlioğlu, 'Alexander Helphand-Parvus and His Impact on Turkish Intellectual Life', *Middle Eastern Studies* 40, no. 6 (November 2004): 145–65.
14. Uğur Ümit Üngör and Mehmet Polatel, *Confiscation and Destruction: The Young Turk Seizure of Armenian Property* (London: Bloomsbury, 2011), 29.
15. Y. Doğan Çetinkaya, *Osmanlı'yı Müslümanlaştırmak: Kitle Siyaseti, Toplumsal Sınıflar, Boykotlar ve Milli İktisat, 1909–1914* (Istanbul: İletişim, 2015), 18.
16. For a detailed examination of the 1908 boycotts, see Y. Doğan Çetinkaya, *1908 Osmanlı Boykotu: Bir Toplumsal Hareketin Analizi* (Istanbul: İletisim, 2004).
17. Emre Erol, *The Ottoman Crisis in Western Anatolia: Turkey's Belle Epoque and the Transition to a Modern Nation State* (London: I. B. Tauris, 2016), 142. For an examination of the effects of the boycott of Greek products and traders on agricultural production in Western Anatolia, see Terzibaşoğlu, 'Land Disputes', 153–80.

18. Çetinkaya, *Osmanlı'yı Müslümanlaştırmak*, 198.
19. For the demographic policies of the CUP on the eve of the First World War, see Taner Akçam, *The Young Turks' Crime against Humanity: The Armenian Genocide and Ethnic Cleansing in the Ottoman Empire* (Princeton: Princeton University Press, 2012), 63–96; Fuat Dündar, *Modern Türkiye'nin Şifresi: İttihat ve Terakki'nin Etnisite Mühendisliği: (1913–1918)* (İstanbul: İletişim, 2008), 194–230.
20. BOA: BEO 3980/298468, the Minister of Foreign Affairs to the Grand Vizier's Office, 5 Kanun-ı Evvel 1328 (18 December 1912).
21. BOA: BEO 4107/308022, Tevfik Pasha, Ottoman Ambassador in London, to the Ministry of Foreign Affairs, 23 October 1912.
22. BOA: BEO 4107/308022, Tevfik Pasha, Ottoman Ambassador in London, to the Ministry of Foreign Affairs, 31 October 1912.
23. BOA: BEO 4107/308022, Nezaretlere müşavirler tayinine ve anların vezaifine müteallik kanun layihası müsveddesi, November 1912.
24. BOA: BEO 3980/298468, Van, Bitlis, Diyarbekir ve Mamüratülaziz Vilayetlerinde Tatbik Olunmak Üzere Kaleme Alınan Kanun-ı Muvakkat Lahiyası, 5 Kanun-ı Evvel 1328 (18 December 1912).
25. Ibid.
26. Ibid.
27. 'Hramanakir: Hoghayin Hartsi Aṛt'iw', *Haṛach*, 4 December 1912. For the official order in this regard, see BEO 4085/306347, Van, Bitlis, Mamuretülaziz vilayetlerine müteheyyi'-i azîmet bulunan valilere verilecek talimat, 5 Eylül 1328 (18 September 1912).
28. 'Bidi Kordzatriw', *Haṛach*, 6 December 1912.
29. Avagyan and Minassian, *Ermeniler ve İttihat*, 124.
30. TNA: FO 195/2449, M. Smith to Sir Gerard A. Lowther, 8 May 1913.
31. Papazian, *Im Husheri*, vol. 2, 178–79.
32. Ibid., 182; for the minutes of this meeting, see *Adenakrut'iwnk' Azkayin Ĕnthanur Zhoghov*, nist ZhĚ (session 18), 276–85.
33. Boghos Nubar Pasha was an important political actor who played a role in the emerging international public interest in the massacres committed against Armenians between 1894 and 1897. He prepared several reports on the matter. He also paved the way for the establishment of the Armenian General Benevolent Union (AGBU) in 1906.
34. Zaven Der Yeghiayan, *My Patriarchal Memoirs*, ed. Vatche Ghazarian, trans. Ared Misirliyan (Barrington: Mayreni, 2002), 22; Rober Koptaş, 'Zohrap, Papazyan ve Pastırmacıyan'ın Kalemlerinden 1914 Ermeni Reformu ve İttihatçı-Taşnak Müzakereleri', *Tarih ve Toplum Yeni Yaklaşımlar* 5 (2007): 166–67.
35. The memoirs of Papazian indicate that the Armenian political elite in the Ottoman Empire was uneasy regarding this situation. Papazian noted that 'what would be determined was our faith; we had specific problems and demands within our jurisdiction, and we knew (these problems and

The Land Question after the Outbreak of the Balkan Wars

demands) better'. Papazian, *Im Husheri*, vol. 2, 178–79. In his memoirs, the Armenian Patriarch Zaven Der Yeghiayan also pointed out that they had to keep their relationship with Nubar Pasha secret, as the Ottoman government was 'ill-disposed toward the Armenians and convinced that the Armenians served the interests of foreign powers'. *My Patriarchal Memoirs*, 24.

36. Babigian served as the deputy from Tekirdağ and a member of the investigation commission sent to Adana after the massacre of 1909. He returned to Istanbul and completed his report. Later, he was killed under suspicious circumstances. His report was first published in French, and the Armenian translation of this report was published in 1919. *Adanayi Eghernĕ: Deghegakir Hagob Babikeani*, trans. Hagop Barkisian (G. Bolis: Dbakr. G-Artskank, 1919); Hagop Babigyan, 'Adana Raporu', trans. Nıvart Taşçı, in *1909 Adana Katliamı: Üç Rapor*, ed. Ari Şekeryan (Istanbul: Aras Yayınları, 2015), 109–31; Matossian, *Horror of Adana*, 193–200.
37. The book was published in French in 1913. Marcel Léart, *La Question Arménienne à la lumière des documents* (Paris: A. Challamel, 1913); for the Turkish translation, see Marcel Léart (Krikor Zohrab), *Belgelerin Işığında Ermeni Meselesi*, trans. Renan Akman (Istanbul: İletişim Yayınları, 2015).
38. Zohrab, *Belgeler Işığında Ermeni Meselesi*, 51–57.
39. Ibid., 70.
40. Ibid., 70–71.
41. For copies of these pamphlets, see TNA: FO 371/1773, Sir G. Lowther to Sir Edward Grey, Constantinople, 6 April 1913, and Sir G. Lowther to Sir Edward Grey, Pera, 7 April 1913.
42. Koptaş, 'Zohrap, Papazyan', 167–69.
43. BOA: HR. SYS 2817/1, Hüseyin Hilmi, the Vienna ambassador to the Ministry of Foreign Affairs, 8 February 1913.
44. Yusuf Hikmet Bayur, *Türk İnkılâbı Tarihi*, vol. 2, no. 3 (Ankara: Türk Tarih Kurumu Basımevi, 1991), 42–43.
45. BOA: DH. SYS 118/13, the Ministry of Foreign Affairs to the Ministry of the Interior, 4 February 1913.
46. According to *Tanin*, the official newspaper of the CUP, the number of gendarmes in Van during the government of Mahmud Şevket Paşa increased from 1,265 to 1,345, in Diyarbekir from 1,180 to 1,265, in Erzurum from 1,115 to 1,465, in Bitlis from 1,190 to 1,490, in Mamuretülaziz from 980 to 1,330, and in Sivas from 1,235 to 1,555. 'Vilâyât-ı Şarkîyede Fa'âliyet-i Islâhiye', *Tanin*, 1 July 1913.
47. Bayur, *Türk İnkılâbı*, 43.
48. 'İdâre-i umûmiye-i vilâyât kânun-ı muvakkati', 13 Mart 1329/26 March 1913, *Düstur*, vol. 2, no. 5 (Dersaadet: Adliye Nezâreti İhsaiyat ve Müdevvenat-ı Kanuniniye Müdüriyeti, 1332), 186–216.
49. *Emvali Gayrimenkuleye Mütedâir Kâvanini Muvakkate* [Provisional Laws on the Statement of Properties] (Istanbul: Selanik Matbaası, 1329), 32–34. See also Mehmet Atılgan, Özgür Leman Eren, Nora Mildanoğlu

and Mehmet Polatel, *2012 Beyannamesi: İstanbul Ermeni Vakıflarının El Konan Mülkleri = 2012 Declaration: The Seized Properties of Armenian Foundations in Istanbul* (Istanbul: Hrant Dink Vakfı Yayınları, 2012), 32–39.
50. 'Sulh hâkimleri hakkında kânun-ı muvakkat', 11 Nisan 1329/24 April 1913, *Düstur*, vol. 2, no. 5, 322–48.
51. Bayur, *'Türk İnkılâbı'*, 44.
52. 'Islâhat Komisyonu', *Tanin*, 12 April 1913.
53. 'Heyet-i Islâhiye', *Tanin*, 4 May 1913. *Tanin* also announced that the programme and duties of the committee had been determined. 'Heyet-i Islâhiye', *Tanin*, 8 May 1913.
54. 'Ermeni Patrikinin Beyânâtı', *Tanin*, 10 May 1913.
55. Ibid.
56. İsmail Hakkı Babanzade, 'Ermeni Patrikinin Beyânâtı', *Tanin*, 11 May 1913.
57. Ibid.
58. Ibid.
59. 'Anadolu Islâhatı', *Tanin*, 13 May 1913.
60. 'Islâhat Hakkında', *Tanin*, 23 May 1913.
61. BOA: MV, 177/74, decision of the Council of Ministers, 14 Mayıs 1329 (27 May 1913).
62. The Council of Ministers specified ten problems that had led to the deterioration of relations between the communities and underscored that these problems were staining the image of the government. The problems specified by the Council of Ministers included lack of security, land disputes, the corruption of administrative and judicial officials, the kidnapping of girls and women, forced conversion of young girls, oppression by members of Tribal Regiments and illegal taxes (such as *hafirlik*) levied on Armenian peasants by *agha*s and tribal chiefs. The facts that Armenians were underrepresented in public service, that they were discriminately prohibited from carrying guns and that several notorious criminals had not been arrested and remained unpunished by the courts (Ibid.).
63. While the press referred to this commission as the reform commission, in official correspondence and decisions it was referred to as the investigation commission.
64. 'Talat Beyin Beyânâtı: Islâhat ve Hükümetin Nokta-i Nazarı', *Tanin*, 7 July 1913.
65. On Cavid Bey and his views on the Armenian issue, see Ozan Ozavcı, 'Honour and Shame: The Diaries of a Unionist and the "Armenian Question"', in *The End of the Ottomans: The Genocide of 1915 and the Politics of Turkish Nationalism*, ed. Hans-Lukas Kieser et al. (London: I. B. Tauris, 2019), 193–220.
66. 'Cavid Bey Efendinin Beyânâtı', *Tanin*, 16 July 1913.
67. Ibid.

68. 'Dâhiliye Nâzırı Patrikhânede', *Tanin*, 3 July 1913.
69. Ibid.
70. Ibid.
71. Papazian, *Im Husheri*, 190–91.
72. Koptaş, 'Zohrab, Papazyan', 172.
73. Halil Menteşe, *Osmanlı Mebusan Meclisi Reisi Halil Menteşe'nin Anıları*, ed. İsmail Arar (Istanbul: Hürriyet Vakfı Yayınları, 1986), 168.
74. BOA: MV 176/23, decision of the Council of Ministers, 2 Nisan 1329 (15 April 1913).
75. Ibid.
76. 'Communication from Tevfik Pasha', in *British Documents on the Origins of the War, 1898–1914*, vol. 10, pt. 1, ed. G. P. Gooch and Harold Temperley (New York: Johnson Reprint, 1967), 427–29.
77. Sir Edward Grey to Sir G. Lowther, 19 May 1913, no. 483, in *British Documents*, 433.
78. Sir G. Lowther to Sir Edward Grey, 9 May 1913, no. 481, in *British Documents*, 431. Britain also suggested the appointment of a French official as an adviser or general inspector and the assignment of another Frenchman as an advisor to the Ministry of Public Works. According to this reformulation, a German inspector would be assigned for forestry and agriculture.
79. Mr O'Beirne to Sir Edward Grey, 21 May 1913, no. 484, in *British Documents*, 433.
80. Sir Edward Grey to Tewfik Pasha, 24 May 1913, no. 491, in *British Documents*, 437.
81. Davison, 'Armenian Crisis', 494.
82. Mr O'Beirne to Sir Edward Grey, 26 May 1913, no. 492, in *British Documents*, 438.
83. Ibid.
84. Davison, 'Armenian Crisis', 494–95.
85. Sir Edward Grey to Sir E. Goshen, 2 June 1913, no. 499, in *British Documents*, 444–45.
86. Mr O'Beirne to Sir Edward Grey, 11 June 1913, no. 507, in *British Documents*, 449–50.
87. Sir G. Lowther to Sir Edward Grey, 6 June 1913, no. 503, in *British Documents*, 448.
88. Sir G. Lowther to Sir Edward Grey, 17 June 1913, no. 515, in *British Documents*, 454.
89. The Armenian actors and Mandelstam grounded this plan on the existing legislation, taking the Armenian reform scheme of 1895, the law of 1880 as revised by the International Commission for the European Provinces of Turkey, the Cretan and Lebanon Statutes, and the new Ottoman Law on the Vilayets of 1913 as reference points. *British Documents*, 454.
90. For the text of the Mandelstam plan, see Sir G. Lowther to Sir Edward Grey, 17 June 1913, in *British Documents*, 455–60; Bayur, *Türk İnkılâbı*, 108–11.

91. Ibid.
92. Aksakal, *Ottoman Road*, 73.
93. Sir Edward Grey to Sir E. Goschen, 3 July 1913, no. 537, in *British Documents*, 474.
94. Davison, 'Armenian Crisis', 497.
95. Ibid.
96. BOA: HR.SYS 1866-6/50-51, 25 June 1913, in Zekeriya Türkmen, *Vilayât-ı Şarkiye (Doğu Anadolu Vilayetleri) Islahat Müfettişliği, 1913–1914* (Ankara: Türk Tarih Kurumu, 2006), 133–34.
97. 'Additional Articles to the Law for the Administration of the Vilayets', in *British Documents*, 476; Bayur, *Türk İnkılâbı*, 117.
98. 'Instructions as to the Duties of the Inspectors-General', in *British Documents*, 477; Bayur, *Türk İnkılâbı*, 119–20.
99. Mr Marling to Sir Edward Grey, 3 July 1913, no. 538, in *British Documents*, 475–79.
100. Mr Marling to Sir Edward Grey, 4 July 1913, no. 540, in *British Documents*, 479–80.
101. Bayur, *Türk İnkılâbı*, 120.
102. Ibid., 121.
103. Davison, 'Armenian Crisis', 500.
104. Ibid.
105. Ibid., 501.
106. Mr Marling to Sir Edward Grey, 7 October 1913, no. 569, in *British Documents*, 518–20.
107. Koptaş, 'Zohrab, Papazyan', 172.
108. Ibid., 173.
109. Ibid., 174.
110. Davison, 'Armenian Crisis', 498–504; Dussen, 'Question of Armenian Reforms', 20–24; Sir L. Mallet to Sir Edward Grey, 9 February 1914, no. 591, in *British Documents*, 545–46.
111. Sir L. Mallet to Sir Edward Grey, 28 January 1914, no. 590, in *British Documents*, 542–46; Bayur, *Türk İnkılâbı*, 169–72.
112. Ibid.

Chapter 7

The Land Question on the Eve of the First World War

Negotiations were key to the reform process. Bureaucrats, diplomats and political elites from various backgrounds offered their suggestions and tried to shape the reform process in line with their interests. However, there were more layers to these negotiations, and a much wider array of negotiators. From the local officials whom the central government kept in the dark to the Kurdish notables who pressured the state representatives and diplomats in their regions, from Armenian intellectuals to Muslim religious authorities, people from a variety of backgrounds and with different capabilities attempted to influence the course of events as well as the content and scope of the resulting reform scheme. The issue of reform caused so much tension that it became the number-one topic of public debate in the Ottoman East, caused friction among different actors and the state and even contributed to the outbreak of revolts. In this chapter, I will explore these tensions and the unease which contributed to the widening gap between Armenians, Kurds and Turks on the eve of the First World War.

Moreover, this chapter will discuss the crystallisation of a decades-old process that has been traced throughout this book – that is, the transformation of land disputes into a key battleground for competing nationalisms and conflicting territorial aspirations and projections. This process, which had started in the nineteenth century with the territorialisation of Armenian nationalism, took a new turn in this period. As Turkish nationalism became dominant among the ranks of the bureaucrats and as Kurdish nationalism emerged as a political force, conflict over land gained an increasingly political character. At the end of this period, it was clear to all parties that what was at stake in these disputes was not only economic resources and a very critical means of production but also the key to establishing or maintaining political sovereignty and ethno-national dominance. As traced in this chapter, this awareness, along with the sense of urgency caused by the rise of reform debates at the international level, took the significance of the Armenian land question to new heights.

The Armenian Political and Religious Elite and the Land Question

The internationalisation of the reform question in the aftermath of the Balkan Wars increased the significance of the issues of population and land in the eyes of the Armenian political elite. This renewed significance reflected itself in Armenian newspapers and in discussions among the political elite in the Armenian National Assembly. Several Armenian actors worked to keep the land question on the agenda of the Ottoman, Armenian and international publics. As mentioned above, the first pamphlet prepared by the Patriarchate for submission to foreign consuls, public figures and politicians concerned the seizure of Armenian properties in the Hamidian period. The data provided in this pamphlet were widely used in the Armenian press, which published lists and articles to show the extent of the seizures and the significance of the land question. The Armenian press also raised the problem of new seizures carried out after the proclamation of the constitution.[1]

In a book published under the pseudonym Marcel Léart, Krikor Zohrab elaborated on socio-economic problems in general and the land question in particular. Zohrab claimed that, after the age of conquest had come to an end, Christians became the most productive population in the empire because they had to work hard. According to Zohrab, the government intervened to preserve the socio-economic dominance of Muslims by granting them privileges, jobs and status. It operated the state mechanism, including the courts and administration, in line with the Muslims' interests. He stated that most of the Kurdish chiefs who owned extensive land and flocks owed their fortunes to the impunity granted to them on account of their religious beliefs. According to Zohrab, neither the backing of the administration nor the partiality of the courts managed to raise Muslims above Christians in socio-economic terms:

> Thus, massacres were necessary to undermine the socio-economic activities of Christian elements and even to force them to leave the country and abandon their properties to Muslims. The land question in Turkish Armenia is a result of this. Thus, massacres in Turkey are socio-economic events that the Turkish government looks upon favourably rather than incidental tragedies.[2]

As illustrated in this quote, Zohrab emphasised the socio-economic background of the massacres of 1894–97 and underscored the importance of

The Land Question on the Eve of the First World War

competition over resources as explanation for mass violence. Another point that he underscored with respect to the massacres consisted of the Hamidian regime's demographic concerns. According to Zohrab, administrative re-organisation in the region was part of a policy of decimating the Armenian population by coercion, massacres, land seizure and the settlement of Kurds and Circassian immigrants.[3] Zohrab also argued that the Ottoman government had 'pulled the same trick' of administrative restructuring with the Bulgarians and Greeks on the Balkans.[4]

In this period, the emigration of Armenians became a pronounced problem in Armenian political circles.[5] On 19 June 1913, the Armenian National Administration wrote an official letter (*bashdonakir*) to the ANA, requesting that the assembly make an official declaration to prevent the emigration of the Armenian population 'from their motherland'.[6] The authors of this letter stated that the lack of security of life, property and honour as well as the forceful seizure of Armenian properties constituted the primary reasons for Armenians' emigration from Armenia. Emigration from the region was defined as a 'great disaster' (*medz aghēd*) causing serious political and economic damage. It was also noted that 'their staying in their lands is a requirement, especially at the present moment, for extraordinary reasons'.[7] What made 'the present moment' so special for the administration was the fact that the issue of Armenian reforms was to be discussed in the ambassadors' meeting two weeks later. One can only speculate about 'the extraordinary reasons' that required the prevention of emigration through the political action of Armenian institutions, but the administration was aware that a decline in the Armenian population in the region would weaken the claims that Armenian actors could possibly raise.

In the ANA session during which the letter of the Armenian National Administration was read, the deputies discussed the matter at length. The proceedings of this debate provide important insights into the approach of the Armenian political elite to the issues of population, demographic trends and land. In his speech, Papazian underscored that emigration was the 'greatest of great disasters' that the Armenians faced at the time.[8] He noted that …

> … if this continues for a couple of years, Armenians will become dispersed and [their numbers] will decrease in those places which are compact [in terms of Armenian population] in Armenia. There are several reasons for this, but the primary reasons are oppression and insecurity … This is not like the emigration of the past; they are taking their families with them now … Vacant lands of Armenia […] state lands are allocated to immigrants from Rumelia. This is a danger for Armenians.[9]

Papazian's speech placed great importance on demographics. He saw the increase of the Muslim population and the expansion of Muslim landholdings in the eastern provinces and Cilicia as a danger to Armenians.

Another deputy who delivered a speech on the matter was Teteyan Efendi; he emphasised the economic reasons for emigration. Teteyan Efendi stated that ...

> ... emigration is exactly like death [and] causes more evil than massacres. Presenting a decree will not be enough. After the Adana Massacre, manpower and material assistance was directed [to the region] and the danger began to be alleviated. This should be taken as an example. Emigration is not only political, [it is] especially economic. Without a doubt, those who emigrate also feel that there is now much to hope for in terms of politics, but there is no such hope in terms of economics.[10]

One of the most striking speeches in this debate was made by Hampartsum Boyadjian, who stated the following:

> I do not consider the massacres of the previous regime as something as evil as mass emigration. A massacre annihilates 10,000 or 100,000 at once, but emigration is a chronic disease that consumes a nation from within. My point is that life is sweet, and everyone is trying to escape from the troubles of this country, but they should be reminded of their ties to the fatherland and that there is no nationality without a fatherland.[11]

After several deputies had presented speeches on the issue, the assembly decided to send an order to the local branches to conduct meetings regarding the socio-economic conditions of the émigrés and to investigate what measures could be taken to curtail emigration.[12] These speeches and the correspondence among the Armenian institutions show that the Armenian political elite perceived the decline of the Armenian population in 'the fatherland' or 'Armenia', which included the eastern provinces and the region of Cilicia, as a national problem. The emigration of Armenians from the region and the increase of the Muslim population due to the settlement of Muslim immigrants were seen as threats.

Similar concerns were raised in *Harach* in the months following this debate in the assembly. On 17 October 1913, the newspaper published a summary of data presented in the first pamphlet prepared by the Patriarchate, regarding the number and characteristics of the seizures of Armenian properties.[13] *Harach* prepared a list based on these data and published this list to show the extent of such seizures. On the same page, *Harach* published an article titled 'Emigration and Land', stating that a fundamental way to prevent emigration was to resolve the land question immediately – 'because one cannot do anything without land'. According to the article, ...

... the land question should be solved, but it should be solved in a just manner, and in a way that is in line with our interests. Our interests are not necessarily against those of neighbouring national groups. This is the most important and urgent matter. Seized lands should be taken from the usurpers and given to the Armenians whose rights were violated. There cannot be any other settlement with regard to this question. And if they want to put an end to emigration from the country and prevent the disappearance of Armenia [*Hayasdan*], our official institutions and the Armenian people should follow a stronger and more decisive course of action.[14]

This article, along with the discussions in the ANA, supports the claim that, in the minds of the Armenian political elite, the land question was tied to the faith of the Armenians and the future of Armenia. The resolution of the land question was a matter of ethno-national existence for some Armenians in this period.

Kurdish Reactions to the Reform Plans

As analysed in Chapter 5, after 1910 a significant shift occurred in the approach of the Ottoman government to the issue of land disputes. The amendment to the order of 7 August – which introduced a limitation on the resolution of land disputes through arbitration by administrative councils – and the warm welcome of the Kurdish chiefs who had fled to Persia after having being pressured by local officials to return the seized properties were indicative of this change. These developments may function as indicators of a new agreement between the Ottoman state and the Kurdish chiefs, based on the recognition of the latter's rights to the seized Armenian lands. This rapprochement between the state and the Kurdish elite began to be threatened after 1912.

The internationalisation of the reform question after the outbreak of the Balkan Wars led to the escalation of tensions at the local level. Another issue intensifying these tensions rested in the fact that Russia was playing a double game in the region: while supporting the Armenians' demands for reform, Russia was equally giving support to several Kurdish power-holders and political elites who opposed these reforms. Kurdish chiefs, notables, sheikhs and political elites held several concerns regarding the prospect of reform. First, the reform debates brought out fears of being subject to Christian domination or rule. Another concern of the Kurdish elite was losing their privileges and positions. Reforms could compel them to return the properties which they had seized. Another related matter consisted of the rise of Kurdish nationalism, which had begun to develop in various Kurdish circles. With the rise of Kurdish nationalism making territorial claims to a geographical area overlapping with the territory claimed by Armenian political organisations, some Kurdish circles began to see land ownership as a means of ethno-national dominance.

Ömer Naci Bey, whom the CUP had sent to the eastern provinces along with Cavid Bey, described the situation there and analysed the reasons for conflict between Armenians and Kurds in an article published in *Tanin* on 16 August 1913.[15] This article reflects the observations of an important CUP member and provides significant insights into the question of how conflicts between Armenians and Kurds were perceived by the CUP at the height of the reform debates. In this article, Ömer Naci Bey accused the governors who had been appointed by the non-CUP government before the *Bâb-ı Âlî* coup of sowing discord between Armenians and Kurds. He said that these governors had agitated the Kurdish population, declaring that the 'Young Turks would sell you out; as they were allied with the Armenians, they would let them [Armenians] suppress you. We, on the other hand, will back you'.[16] According to Ömer Naci, this kind of declaration affected some Kurds. He also stated that Abdürrezzak Bey from the Bedirxan family was trying to provoke the Kurds by claiming that Russian was preferable to Armenian dominance. According to this account, the conflict was not between Kurds and Armenians, but between oppressor and oppressed. He argued that Armenians were not aiming at secession and that not only Armenians but also Kurds were complaining about the situation. Ömer Naci Bey noted that the same notables and tribal leaders who oppressed the Armenians committed similar crimes against the Kurdish population.

According to Ömer Naci, the government should pay attention to public works and education and put administrative operations, such as population registry and title deeds, in order. He underscored that the mistakes of low-ranking officials in the title deeds registry office could lead to great misdeeds, citing a case in Erciş in which seven title deeds had been issued for a small piece of land. He concluded that, if operations on the ground were not seen as significant administrative or political matters, the question of Eastern Anatolia would be reduced to a security issue.[17] Thus, in Ömer Naci Bey's account, the issues of population and the land registry were significant political matters rather than administrative procedures.

The expansion of Abdürrezzak Bedirxan's influence in the region emerged as one of the most important political developments in this period. As a member of the prestigious Bedirxan family, Abdürrezzak Bey possessed considerable social capital. In 1911, he was pardoned for his murder of Rıdvan Pasha and returned to the Ottoman East.[18] As a Kurdish nationalist, Abdürrezzak Bey tried to instigate a Kurdish nationalist movement in the region.[19] His campaigns and activities, which were supported by Russia, were linked to the issue of Armenian reforms. In the fall of 1913, when reform negotiations between Russia and the Ottoman Empire approached a conclusion, Abdürrezzak Bey published a manifesto about the prospective reforms. He protested the fact that the Kurds were not represented in the reform negotiations. Claiming that 'the population of the vilayets placed under the name Armenia, and those of other places [were] four-fifths Kurdish, and the Kurds [owned] most of the lands',[20] Abdürrezzak Bey argued that the rights and interests of the Kurds should have been given priority. It is important to note that he underscored the issues of land ownership and demographic majority to justify his claim that Kurdish interests in the region should take precedence over those of Armenians. This suggests that land ownership was seen as a means of ethno-national dominance in some Kurdish circles.

While this emphasis indicates that land disputes were taking on a new political character in some Kurdish nationalist circles, it is difficult to assess how widespread such an approach was among the general Kurdish population. Yet, the prospect of a resolution to the land question in favour of the Armenians provided a fertile ground for Abdürrezzak's mobilisation efforts directed at Kurdish chiefs. These developments were followed closely by the Ottoman authorities who were worried about the possibility that the discontent of Kurdish chiefs could lead them to join the movement instigated by Abdürrezzak Bey. This concern had been raised by the governor of Erzurum as early as 1912. According to the governor, land disputes could potentially lead to violence or to the establishment of an alliance between Kurdish tribal leaders and Russia via Abdürrezzak Bey.[21]

Rojî Kurd and the Land Question

Rojî Kurd was one of the most important periodicals of Kurdish nationalism in the second constitutional period. The monthly journal published articles in Ottoman Turkish and Kurdish.[22] Its articles promoted the idea that the Kurdish nation was a historical collectivity that had recently been awakened.[23] Examining the influence of this journal among the Kurdish elite and population is beyond the scope of this study; however, its articles provide important insights into the ways in which some Kurdish nationalists perceived the Armenian land question. The issue of the Armenian land question was examined in detail in a 1913 article titled 'The Land Question' and authored by Hüseyin Şükri;[24] its timing coincided with international reform debates. The issue featuring this article happened to be *Rojî Kurd*'s final issue.

Hüseyin Şükri identified the land question as one of the most important impediments to the improvement of relations between Kurds and Armenians. He used the term 'land question' in a limited way to denote land disputes between Armenians and Kurds. In his article, Şükri presented a case against the administrative resolution, without mentioning reform debates and debates over the inclusion of a resolution to the Armenian land question in the framework of international reforms. According to Şükri, administrative resolutions were bound to fail because those forced to return land would feel betrayed by the state authorities. If the land question were to be solved in an administrative fashion, one group of people would be deprived of their ownership rights. These people would not have peace of mind because they would also be deprived of a fair trial before the courts. Hüseyin Şükri's remarks regarding the potential implications of this lack of peace of mind and feeling of inequality can be interpreted as a covert threat to the central government:

> The sole purpose and actions of those who would be deprived would be directed at continuously compelling the government, which would accept these decisions, to resign and to force the government that would replace it into annulling the previous decision in an administrative fashion by making it tremble under the threat of a rebellion.[25]

According to Hüseyin Şükri, these feelings of inequality and unease would pave the way for agitators wanting to provoke those inclined towards rebellion. If the land question were solved in an administrative way, not only ignorant, common people but also the educated strata of society would question the central government's authority. Hüseyin Şükri argued that even the most educated with expert knowledge of the law would be moved by the questions raised by such agitators. This article indicates that some Kurdish nationalist intellectuals in this period saw the land question as a crucial Kurdish problem.

Musa Bey's Attempts at Receiving Pardon

Several Kurdish chiefs who had been involved in the murders of and depredations against Armenians tried to reconcile with the government in this period. The notorious Musa Bey and his brother Kasım Bey continued to oppress the Armenian peasants in Bitlis Province, even after the proclamation of the constitution. As noted in Chapter 5, even after 1908, Musa and his brother committed murder and plunder, levied illegal taxes (such as *hafir*) from the peasants, refused to return the lands which they had seized during the Hamidian period and continued to seize additional

The Land Question on the Eve of the First World War

lands, causing trouble in the region, especially in Huyt. However, in spite of these crimes and the Armenian peasants' complaints, the local government was unable to arrest Musa Bey, and he remained a fugitive.

By mid-1912, Musa Bey had started an initiative to obtain a pardon from the government. Musa Bey argued that some officials in the district of Muş were intent on creating a Kurdistan question, much like the Albanian question.[26] He declared that he was committed first to God and then to the sultan. According to his account, he was a victim of those who sought to create disorder in the region. Mazhar Bey, the governor of Bitlis, sent a telegram to the Ministry of the Interior regarding Musa Bey's situation and his request for amnesty. Mazhar Bey argued that Musa Bey was targeted as the perpetrator of a series of crimes due to his 'notorious reputation' (*gaddârâne şöhreti dolayısıyla*), but that he had not committed these crimes. According to Mazhar Bey, there were only a few cases of murder and cattle-rustling that concerned Musa Bey and his brother. The governor stated that several missions to capture him had failed because Musa Bey had a great number of men assisting him during his flight and period of hiding. He noted that ...

> ... since I was appointed to my post, he has been quiet and regretful of his previous acts, and he will pose a threat to the interests of the government and to security as long as he remains a fugitive. It is understood that he will be a loyal servant of the government if pardoned. His pardon will be an appropriate measure for this province.[27]

In another telegram to the Ministry of the Interior, Mazhar Bey claimed that Armenians not only targeted Musa Bey and his brother but made accusations about several influential individuals, exaggerating the situation. He repeated that Musa Bey's current position did not stand in conflict with the interests of the government and requested that he be employed or put on the government payroll.[28] In response, the Ministry of the Interior stated that, if Musa Bey and his brother moved to Istanbul, an appropriate salary would be provided. The ministry also wanted the governor to assure him that an imperial order could be issued to suspend the legal proceedings against them.[29] Unfortunately, I was not able to determine whether Musa Bey managed to receive an official pardon, although in December 1912 he 'made a public and even triumphal return to his own village'.[30] The rapprochement between Musa Bey and the Ottoman authorities indicates that some local powerholders in the region tried to benefit from the escalating tensions on the Balkans, by directly referring to the crisis in that region to escape from prosecution – and they succeeded in doing so.

Haydaranli Hüseyin Pasha's Situation

British Consul Monahan in Erzurum visited the provinces of Erzurum, Van and Bitlis in September 1913 and in his subsequent report described the situation in the eastern region in detail. The British consul stated that in the Pasinler and Eleşkird districts, there were no complaints from the Armenian population regarding the state of security, despite some petty cases of sheep theft and the abduction of girls. He noted that the local government was too weak to prevent these crimes. The consul also gave detailed information about Haydaranlı Hüseyin Pasha, noting that Hüseyin Pasha had neither made restitution to anyone nor returned any lands, despite his promise to give the lands that he had seized back to their real owners upon his return from Persia two years earlier. The consul stated that Hüseyin Pasha was carrying on with his sheep-raising business and had acquired a fortune. In Patnos, which twenty-five years earlier had been almost exclusively populated by Armenians, Hüseyin Pasha had seized land throughout the region, driving out the Armenians and replacing them with Kurds under his influence. After 1908, some Armenians – who had migrated due to Hüseyin Pasha's oppression – returned to Patnos and attempted to retake their lands but were unable to do so. The consul stated that ...

> ... Hüseyin Pasha so far as I heard does not seem to be just now an oppressive owner [...] Hüseyin Pasha is now seemingly an important political personage, courted by the Turkish government with whom he hesitates to cast his lot [...] That this old barbarian, though now calmed by age and changed circumstances, should rule a large region seems a state of things that cannot last.[31]

This report shows that, besides managing to keep the lands he had seized during the Hamidian period in his possession, Hüseyin Pasha had since established himself as a significant political actor in Van.

The Situation in the Eastern Provinces

British Consul Monahan's Visit to Muş

Muş continued to be problematic in terms of the oppression of Armenians in this period. In a petition submitted to the British Consul Monahan, the Armenian bishop in Muş presented a detailed picture of the situation and provided information regarding the murders and seizures committed by local Kurdish tribes. In this petition, the bishop claimed that some lands had been given to immigrants, that there existed severe oppression in

The Land Question on the Eve of the First World War

Sasun, Huyt and Mutki and that the Agricultural Bank had sold lands belonging to Armenian peasants who had been unable to pay their debts to third parties.[32] The petition stated that ...

> ... after the proclamation of the Ottoman Constitution, the Armenians were encouraged to apply to the Government to get back their lands, and during the first year of the Constitution some people succeeded in getting back their lands, but, little by little, things became quite different, the lands given back being again seized, while all who applied to the government were disappointed, many lost their lives, and the land question remained as before.[33]

Noting that the bishop's account might be exaggerated, the British consul suggested that the problem could be solved by appropriate measures, such as punishing the Kurdish oppressors of the likes of Hüseyin Pasha, Musa Bey, Mehmed Agha and Temo.[34] He argued that the punishment of Kurds for offences against persons or properties and the disbandment of tribal regiments could easily solve the problem. The consul also suggested measures for the resolution of land disputes concerning the seizures carried out after 1908, stating that 'it will not be practicable or even desirable to restore lands seized by Moslems to Armenians who have emigrated before the constitution but a commission, with some European members, should make careful inquiry in the villages concerned with a view to the restoration of seized lands whenever practicable'.[35]

THE SITUATION IN HUYT

In this period, the Armenian Patriarchate submitted another memorandum to the Ministry of Justice about the oppression and land seizures in the Bitlis region. Zaven Der Yeghiayan, the Armenian Patriarch, stated that he had investigated the situation in Bitlis himself during a visit to the region and that he had sent the Bishop of Muş to Huyt, tasking him with writing a report about the situation.[36] According to this investigation, the Kurds of the Balaklı tribe were demanding the buildings and half of the revenue from the lands and fields belonging to Armenians in the Huyt, Taghavank, Shenist (Erler) and Lordentzor (Beşevler) regions, in exchange for the value of goods (such as wheat) that they had given to the Armenians. They had seized several plots of land in the village of Taghavank. Despite the fact that the Armenians had managed to receive a decision in their favour from the court of Bitlis in 1911 (AH 1327), the situation did not change, and the usurpers did not return the lands. The Patriarchate noted that the Balaklı tribesmen had also murdered the village priest, Sarkis Efendi, and seven other persons. According to the Patriarchate, the offenders were not punished; therefore, other Kurds started to threaten the heirs of the victims and tried to seize their lands. The Patriarchate noted that the Ministry of the Interior had sent an order to the local government, and that the Bitlis government had sent a committee to investigate the situation in response. The Patriarchate claimed that this committee had forced the Armenians to sign contracts, putting them thousands of liras in debt. The Patriarchate contended that these contracts had been signed under duress, requesting that the Armenian peasants' rights be recognized.[37]

THE CASE OF NORDUZ: REFORM INITIATIVES IN VAN

The Armenian bishop of Van, Serob Efendi, also sent a petition to the Patriarchate, claiming that Kurdish immigrants had been settled in Armenian villages in the Hakkari region.[38] According to the British consul, the problem in Norduz was related to 'two thousand Manhoran Kurds who four months ago immigrated from Persia and settled in the Armenian villages'.[39] Although Tahsin Bey, the governor of Van, rejected this claim and said that 'there were no Kurdish immigrants in any Armenian houses', the British consul was of the opinion that a number of Kurdish immigrants were indeed staying in the Armenian villages.[40] The correspondence between Tahsin Bey and the Ministry of the Interior indicates that the findings of Tahsin Bey's inquiry differed from his public declarations. In a telegram sent on 21 June 1913, Tahsin Bey reported that the land dispute in Norduz was related to the lands of the Armenians who had fled from the region in the Hamidian period.[41] Tahsin Bey noted that the Armenians of Norduz were afraid to return and thus did not apply to the local government to reclaim their lands. According to Tahsin Bey, the land disputes in Norduz would be solved on their own once the administrative structure in the district was strengthened, telegraph lines extended to the region and a legion of soldiers dispatched.

British consular correspondence indicates that Tahsin Bey was carrying out some reform measures at the local level in this period. The British vice-consul in the region reported that some small-scale land disputes were resolved through these measures and that oppression by Kurdish tribes had stopped. The vice-consul also reported that the governor had organised a 'punitive expedition against the tribes of Norduz and Beytüşşebab'. This expedition was carried out in response to turmoil among the Kurds, which, according to the consul, was not 'the result of any organized plan, but merely the outcome of the belief that the Ottoman Empire [was] breaking up and that the moment [had] arrived when advantage [could] be taken of the Government's weakness'.[42] The vice-consul also stated that the land commission, which had been established by the former governor of Van, İzzet Bey, continued to operate, and that a few small-scale land disputes were solved administratively. Vice-Consul Molyneux-Seel pointed out that ...

> ... the suppression of the Kurds by spasmodic punitive expeditions, the forcible restitution of lands by the Kurds to the Armenians, the arming of the Armenian population by Taschnakists, the policing of the entire country by detachments of gendarmes or soldiers, none of these will bring about permanent good relations between Kurds and Armenians, since the source of the evil remains untouched. The source of the evil is the maintenance of feudal conditions among the Kurds and the influence exercised by the religious sheikhs.[43]

The account of the British vice-consul demonstrates that local authorities had taken several security measures at the local level after the internationalisation of the reform question and that Tahsin Bey, the governor of Van, was carrying out some reform measures in the province.

LOCAL REACTIONS TO THE REFORM PLANS

Correspondence between the central government and Ottoman officials at the local level shows that Kurdish chiefs and notables were raising objections to reform, through protests directed at the local officials. The governors' accounts indicate that the return of seized lands constituted a significant factor in the discontent of the local population with regard to the prospective reforms. A telegram sent by Tahsin Bey on 18 December 1913 to the Ministry of the Interior clearly reflects the pressure he felt. Tahsin Bey complained that he was not informed about developments regarding reforms being discussed between Russia and the central government of the Ottoman Empire, even though this was the most discussed topic in Van at that moment. Tahsin Bey also reported that newspaper coverage regarding reforms 'was stirring up the hearts of Muslims'.[44]

The escalating tension at the local level due to the internationalisation of the reform question is also apparent in a telegram that the governor of Diyarbekir, Hakkı Bey, sent to the central government on 26 January 1914. He complained that worried locals demanding the details of the reform plan frequented his office daily; the tone of the complaints of the locals coming to his office had changed in recent days. They had begun to claim that reforms 'would have an adverse effect on the Muslim population and might produce worrisome results in the future'.[45] In his account about the discontent and panic of the Muslim population, Hakkı Bey emphasised the role of the resolution of the land question in line with the reform scheme:

Especially publications [stating] that land matters and disputes would be settled and solved by general inspectors have driven the Muslim population into worry and panic, [and] it is clear that this panic and discontent will continue to be influential and harmful if the degree to which these rumours are true or false is not clarified.[46]

Hakkı Bey also noted that he followed developments in the press and requested to be informed by the central government regarding the content of the reform scheme. He furthermore demanded the exclusion of Diyarbekir from the reform scheme, underscoring that the Armenian population did not constitute a majority in the province. According to Hakkı Bey, Diyarbekir should not be considered an eastern province because of its geographic and demographic characteristics.

Tension at the local level also increased in Erzurum Province in the first months of 1914. In this province, the CUP club was 'employing interval in gaining adherents' against reform and foreign control and even planning a protest to mobilise Muslims.[47] This meeting was later cancelled.[48] Tensions in the city escalated because of articles in the local newspaper, *Al Bayrak*, which was run by prominent, local CUP members. The slogan of the newspaper indicates the position adopted with regard to reform debates and struggles for territorial sovereignty in the Ottoman East: 'The Eastern Provinces cannot be Armenia!' (*Vilayat-ı Şarkiye Ermenistan olamaz!*). According to the British consul in Erzurum, *Al Bayrak* had been publishing news targeting Armenians.[49] The news articles in *Al Bayrak* caused a diplomatic crisis because, while Hilmi Bey, the leader of the local CUP club, denied that the CUP was behind the publication, the British consuls were of the opinion that the CUP functioned as the principal actor causing the turmoil in the city.[50] The Russian consul took the matter to the grand vizier, underscoring his concern about the potential outbreak of mass violence against Armenians. The grand vizier reassured the Russian consul that the government was determined to maintain order.[51]

According to the British Vice-Consul Smith, there existed a significant difference in the approaches of higher and lower local officials when it came to international reform. The vice-consul reported that, although the Ottoman officials were hostile to foreign intervention, they admitted that 'everything in this part of Turkey is in a very backward and unsatisfactory state, and that this state of things cannot be allowed to continue'.[52] The vice-consul also noted that, while higher officials opposed the appointment of European inspectors and believed that this was the first step towards the region's secession from the empire, minor officials whose

The Land Question on the Eve of the First World War

salaries were not paid were inclined to support any measure that would improve their immediate conditions.

According to the vice-consul, landowners also supported international reform 'which would make for the material progress and development of the country', because they thought that the Ottoman officials were unable to protect their rights, property and security. The vice-consul noted that the reaction of the Kurdish population would depend on the position of their chiefs:

> The Kurdish tribesmen, who form some two-fifths of the population of the vilayet, live under almost feudal conditions, and follow the lead of their chiefs and sheikhs. The latter are quite ready to take advantage of a weak government, but respect a strong one which puts down brigandage and robbery with a firm hand.[53]

Another document that provides important insights regarding different provincial actors' approaches to the prospects of reform is Vice-Consul Smith's account of a meeting with Haydaranlı Hüseyin Pasha. This meeting was conducted after the conclusion of the reform agreement between Russia and the Ottoman Empire. In the meeting, Hüseyin Pasha harshly criticised the Ottoman government, claiming that 'the Kurds were dissatisfied with the government, not on account of the greater liberty and political importance which the Armenians' began to possess, 'but because the government treated the Kurds themselves with injustice'.[54] Hüseyin Pasha also complained that 'the government did nothing for the welfare of the Kurds'. Hüseyin Pasha's comments regarding the appointment of European inspectors shows that the anti-reform mission of the Kurdish chiefs was tied to the fear of being obliged to return the lands that they had seized. Vice-Consul Smith reported his observations on this point as follows:

> From what he said, Hussein Pasha seemed rather to welcome than otherwise the prospect of European Officials coming into the country to reorganize the administration, as it would mean a more settled policy on the part of the Local Government. What he feared was that when the Inspectors took in hand the adjustment of the lands which are in dispute between the Kurds and Armenians, the Kurds would be turned out without compensation.
>
> This is a point, the settlement of which will determine the attitude of many of the Kurdish Chiefs towards the proposed system of control, and as its success will depend in a large measure on their acquiescence, it is to be hoped that they will be given no justification for associating the presence of the European Inspectors with an adjustment of this question of lands, by which they may consider they are harshly treated. Their point of view is that under the old regime

they were encouraged to spread over the Armenian villages, and now that they have to restore the lands they occupied, it will be unjust for the Government to dispossess them after many years of possession without giving them compensation. If the European Inspectors are able to bring about a settlement on generous lines with due regard to the claims of the Kurdish Chiefs, the latter will feel that their interests have not suffered owing to the foreign control, and that will go far towards making them contented with the new order of things.[55]

Vice-Consul Smith's account of his meeting with Hüseyin Pasha indicates the extent to which tribal leaders in the Ottoman East were disturbed by the prospect of having to return the lands which they had seized. This account also indicates that some tribal chiefs were objecting to the return of seized properties, by underscoring the involvement and role of the central government in the processes of property transfer.

The Bitlis Rebellion
The outbreak of the Bitlis rebellion was another local development related to the anxieties and discontent of Kurdish powerholders, stemming from the prospect of reform in the eastern provinces. This rebellion, which started a few weeks after the Russo-Ottoman reform agreement had been concluded, was led by religious authorities, including Sheikh Selim, Sheikh Seyyid Ali and Sheikh Şahabettin.[56] The sheikhs mobilised the support of local Kurds, and two factors made mobilising the rebellion in Bitlis easy. First, popular opposition to the constitutional regime had shifted the legal basis of political life from sharia to civil law. According to the local Ottoman authorities, the correspondence of which is examined below, this fuelled much discontent. The second factor that facilitated the mobilisation effort can be found in the local notables and tribal leaders' discontent with the proposed reform scheme because it would require them to return the lands and properties that they had seized.

Tahsin Bey, the governor of Van, informed the central government that rebels were protesting the reforms, demanding the reinstatement of sharia law and considering an alliance with Russia.[57] Mr Maynard,[58] who was in Bitlis at the time, informed the British consulate that the prospect of reform and the 'severity with which the authorities of the adjacent vilayet of Van have been dealing with certain Kurdish chiefs' caused unrest and discontent in the region; these feelings brought about 'the importation of arms and their distribution among the Kurdish villagers'.[59] In a conversation with Sir Mallet, the British ambassador in Istanbul, Talat Pasha also declared that reactionaries among Kurdish tribes had engineered this rebellion due to their dislike of the reforms.[60] The governor of Van informed the British Vice-Consul that sheikhs in the Bitlis region

The Land Question on the Eve of the First World War

had been telling the people that 'the government of the country was to be handed over to the Armenians, and that it was necessary for the Kurds to show the Turkish authorities that they would not submit to being ruled by Christians'.[61]

While CUP members and local officials emphasised that the rebellion had a religious character and was fuelled by the Muslims' disgust with the prospect of equality, Armenians as a group were not the specific targets of violence in the Bitlis rebellion. The rebels committed no more than a few crimes against Christians and even reached out to Armenian community leaders to assure them that they intended no harm.[62] About 3,000 armed Kurds joined the rebellion. According to the British Vice-Consul, the objective of the armed movement was not to take over the city but to make an armed demonstration to 'force the government to agree to the demands put forward by the sheikhs'.[63] More than one hundred Kurds and twelve soldiers were killed during the suppression of the rebellion.[64] Around a hundred Kurds were arrested or exiled, and twenty were condemned to death in a court martial.[65]

The Bitlis rebellion may also have had a Kurdish nationalist aspect. According to British consular correspondence, Sheikh Seyyid Ali, in collaboration with Musa Bey, disseminated a declaration addressed to the Kurdish people in the fall of 1911. As early as in 1911, the Sheikh was promoting 'union among the Kurds' and exhorting them 'to combine and rise against the government demanding administrative autonomy for Kurds in the way in which the Albanians and the Arabs succeeded'.[66] While this leading organiser of the rebellion was known for his nationalist tendencies, the rebels' official demands did not include nationalist demands such as autonomy.[67]

It should be noted that the Bitlis rebellion also featured a material or socio-economic aspect that was related to the land question. In the beginning of 1914, the local authorities in the eastern provinces were notified that the procedure of arbitration through administrative councils was being re-introduced for the resolution of land disputes. This development, together with rumours that the general inspectors would have the authority to solve land disputes, might have contributed to the ease with which mobilisation for the rebellion was carried out. Another important point regarding the material aspect of the Bitlis rebellion is that its leaders were not only religious authorities but also powerholders who controlled agricultural production in a number of localities. Moreover, both Sheikh Seyyid Ali and Sheikh Selim had been involved in several cases of land seizure in Bitlis. Seyyid Ali's lodge (*tekke*) was in the Armenian village of Müşkünüs (Düzköy) in Tatig (Tanikdere). This tekke had been built over the shared threshing ground of the village in the late 1890s. Seyyid Ali had gained possession of half of the land belonging to the villagers, through an arrangement with the Agricultural Bank, and had subsequently usurped the other fields by force.[68]

As noted by the British consul, the forcefully seized lands had been restored to the original owners due to threats by the Tashnags, but Seyyid Ali kept the remaining lands, which he had acquired from the Agricultural Bank by nominally legal methods. Seyyid Ali had also seized other fields in the surrounding area, especially in the valley between Hizan Dere and Lake Van. According to the British consul, the villagers whose lands had been seized had not applied to the government due to their fear of the sheikh. After his arrest, the villagers wished to apply to the court for the return of their properties but were still afraid of what he might do to them if he were released.[69] Sheikh Selim was also involved in cases of land seizure. In the Hamidian period, he had seized by force a house, a hayloft, a cattle-shed and a plot of agricultural land belonging to Garo Yeghoyants in Çevlig, Bitlis. The total value of these properties amounted to 100 liras. Furthermore, he and several *beys* of the region had been involved in the forced seizure of four plots of land and a pasture belonging to Khachadur Bandoyan.[70] As these examples demonstrate, the sheikhs who instigated the rebellion had a vested interest in the non-resolution of the land question and had much to lose if reforms were to be implemented.

The Ottoman authorities restored security in Bitlis within a couple of weeks. Van's governor, Tahsin Bey, and the Bitlis governor, Abdülhalik Bey, who had been appointed upon Tahsin Bey's recommendation at the height of the rebellion, sent a telegram to the Ministry of the Interior on 4 April 1914, stating that extensive measures were required for the re-organisation of the region's political and social structure, which had 'feudal characteristics that were easily manipulated by Russia'. According to them, the central government had taken significant steps to suppress the Bedirxans and the Barzans, and it should continue in that direction. According to the governors, the government had to apprehend and punish those who hindered the development of the country, reward local powerholders who were loyal, return seized Armenian and Kurdish properties, capture murderers and brigands who had fled the country, establish smaller administrative units that would be more manageable and appoint a credible, strong, capable figure – like the earlier reformers Kurt İsmail Pasha and Topal/Hacı Osman – so as to promote civic conduct and proper religious activities among the Kurds. According to the governors, 'it was impossible to win in this region otherwise'.[71]

The Land Question on the Eve of the First World War

Michael A. Reynolds has pointed out that leading CUP members in Istanbul held a meeting to review the policies of the central government towards the eastern provinces and radically revised the CUP stance on the matter in the first weeks of April. Reynolds has stated that the CUP leaders 'resolved to win over the Kurds with a combination of methods, including financial subsidies, making leading Kurds senators, pressing the Kurds of Istanbul to use their influence over their brethren in Anatolia' after this meeting.[72]

Having established military and administrative control, the Ottoman authorities executed several leaders of the rebellion, including Sheikh Seyyid Ali, while exiling others. The severity of the punishment of the participants in the rebellion affected the Kurdish population and led to fear among them.[73] Aggravating the shock of the executions was that significant religious authorities were among those executed – a rare occurrence in the region. Correspondence among the Ottoman authorities indicates that the Ottoman government was concerned about the possibility of further uprisings in the region. Tahsin Bey's telegram to the Ministry of the Interior shows that some Kurdish actors under the influence of Russia were trying to capitalise on the discontent among the Kurdish population stemming from the execution of the sheikhs. Tahsin Bey reported that Abdürrezzak Bey had organised a congress in Hoy, presided over by the Russian ambassador Chirkov. Simko, Said Bey, Arusanlı Hasan Agha and Seyyid Taha's representative (*vekil*), Mecid, participated in this congress, among others. According to Tahsin Bey, the participants decided that, 'as the Bitlis incident presented the idea of revolution to Kurds and the execution of the sheikhs awakened the desire for revenge in the minds of Kurds, a general movement should be on the back of this incident'.[74]

According to Tahsin Bey, other decisions made in this congress included the elimination of pro-government Kurdish chiefs and the escalation of propaganda, which would include publications on the reasons behind the Bitlis rebellion, the execution of the chiefs and the reforms. The authors of these publications would refrain from targeting Armenians and Nestorians and instead directly target the government.[75] After the rebellion, Talat Pasha issued several complaints to the Russian ambassador, Giers, about the country's intrigues.[76] According to a report by the Commissioner of the Iranian Border (*Hudud-ı İraniye komiserliği*), Abdürrezzak Bey was put on Russia's payroll with a 16,000-ruble salary, in the function of chieftain of an Iranian tribe.[77] Despite Talat Pasha's complaints, Russia continued to pay a salary to Abdürrezzak, 'but now ordered him to keep a low profile and not undertake any actions against the Ottomans'.[78]

As stated above, several rebels were executed after the rebellion, while others were exiled. One group was exiled to the Black Sea region, and others were to be sent to Taif but later redirected to Medina.[79] Müftüzade Sadullah Bey, who was elected as deputy in the 1912 elections, also counted among those exiled. Sheikh Selim managed to take refuge in the Russian Consulate in Bitlis and stayed there under Russian protection until the outbreak of the First World War. Having first punished those involved, the government then rewarded the sheikhs and tribal leaders who had not participated in the rebellion and supported the military effort against the rebels. Among those receiving rewards counted Sheikh Ziyaeddin (Hazret), Sheikh Fethullah Alaeddin and Küfrevizade Sheikh Abdülbaki.[80] These local powerholders had also been involved in numerous seizures and had much to lose if a reform scheme including the resolution of land disputes were to be implemented. Nonetheless, they had not supported the rebellion. Later on, the exiled chiefs were invited back upon the advice of Sheikh Ziyaeddin and Alaeddin, and they were officially pardoned on 21 November 1914, after the Ottoman Empire had entered the First World War.[81]

Regulations and Policies Regarding the Resolution of Land Disputes on the Eve of the First World War

The following pages will examine the legislation and orders regarding the resolution of land disputes in the context of international reform negotiations, together with the activities and plans of the local authorities in the region. This examination shows that Ottoman authorities were concerned with controlling the outcomes of the reform plan at the local level. After the Russo-Ottoman Agreement regarding reforms, the central government re-introduced the use of arbitration procedures for land disputes and pressured the local governors in Van and Bitlis to resolve land disputes in their regions before the arrival of the general inspectors. In this correspondence, the resolution of the matter before the arrival of the general inspectors was deemed vitally important for the country's future.

As examined in Chapter 6, the Ottoman government lifted the limitation on the use of arbitration procedures through administrative councils. On 6 February 1912, an imperial order was issued regarding the re-introduction of arbitration procedures, and on 20 April 1912, an instruction was given to implement the imperial order dated 7 August 1909, which had introduced arbitration procedures through administrative councils in the first place. In the fall of 1912, the government ordered the establishment of special commissions for the resolution of land disputes, in line with the designated reform plans. British correspondence indicates that such a special commission established in Van by Governor İzzet Bey continued to operate after the *Bâb-ı Âlî* coup and after İzzet Bey's replacement with Tahsin Bey – at least until July 1913.[82] However, I was not able to find any other documents proving that such special commissions were established in other provinces. The correspondence between Mazhar Bey, the governor of Bitlis, and the Ministry of the Interior indicates that arbitration there continued to be carried out through the administrative council rather than a special commission. In this correspondence, it is also apparent that the local governors received an order to implement an administrative resolution in May 1913.

Yet, an important change in legislation occurred after the adoption of the decree-law on peace courts on 24 April 1913.[83] According to this law, the authority to decide land disputes lay with the peace courts. This change in legislation blocked the use of arbitration procedures through administrative councils. A telegram sent by Mazhar Bey shows that the change in the legislation was followed by an order stating that administrative councils did not have the authority to decide land disputes and to transfer these cases to the peace courts.[84] What complicated the matter further was the fact that no peace courts existed in many districts of the eastern provinces. When reform negotiations among Russia, Germany and the Ottoman Empire were at the point of being finalised, the Ottoman government re-introduced the use of arbitration procedures through administrative councils by adopting a decree-law. This decree-law was an addendum to the decree-law on peace courts dated 24 April 1913. According to this addendum, adopted on 5 January 1914, in regions where peace courts had not yet been established, administrative councils would resolve disputes concerning immovable properties, in line with the instruction of April 1912.[85] Thus, the central government re-introduced the use of administrative resolution procedures for the resolution of land disputes.

As analysed in the previous chapter, the Armenians had demanded an administrative approach to the resolution of land conflicts since the proclamation of the constitution. Changes to the legislation in this period indicate that an administrative resolution was seen as leverage by the Ottoman authorities, who blocked its use at the height of reform negotiations. During the reform negotiations between Russia and the Ottoman Empire, the Sublime Porte insisted on the resolution of land questions through the judiciary, while Russia insisted on their resolution through a special commission, to be presided over by the general inspector.[86] In the final agreement, it was decided that land disputes would be resolved under the supervision of the general inspector. The decree-law that re-introduced an administrative resolution on 5 January 1914 can be seen as an outcome of reform negotiations and strategies. Thus, these changes in the legislation constituted an important part of the reform debates.

Following the negotiations between the Ottoman Empire and the ambassadors of the Great Powers, the Sublime Porte decided to assign Major Nicolai Hoff of the Norwegian army and Louis C. Westenenk of the Dutch East Indian Service as general inspectors of the eastern provinces.[87] Major Hoff was assigned to the sector that included Van, Bitlis, Mamuretülaziz and Diyarbekir, while Mr Westenenk was assigned to the other sector, which included the Trabzon, Erzurum and Sivas provinces.[88] The contracts between the Sublime Porte and the two general inspectors were signed on 24 May 1914.[89] The Sublime Porte also adopted a regulation concerning the duties and authorities of the general inspectors.[90] Article 7 of this regulation specified the duties of the general inspectors regarding the resolution of land disputes. It was stipulated that 'general inspectors will have the authority to directly investigate and supervise the issue of the resolution and settlement of disputes and conflicts regarding the possession of lands which cause animosity between different elements of the population in some locations'.[91] Before going to the region to which he was assigned, General Inspector Hoff requested an annual fund from the government to carry out urgent reforms that included resolving land disputes, improving public works and conducting censuses.[92]

Correspondence among the Ottoman authorities indicates that they were concerned with resolving land disputes in several provinces, especially in Van and Bitlis, before the arrival of the general inspectors. On 25 January 1914, the Ministry of the Interior ordered Mazhar Bey, the governor of Bitlis, to provide information regarding the steps taken towards the resolution of land disputes, noting that civil inspectors (*mülkiye müfettişi*) had reported a great number of land disputes in the province. In his response, Mazhar Bey stated that the number of land disputes was the highest in Muş district, and those disputes which could be resolved administratively had already been so. The governor stated that 92 per cent of the cases in the town and its environs had been resolved by the administrative council, in line with the orders of the Ministry of the Interior, but the local government had received an order to transfer the remaining cases to the peace courts and had done so, transferring 257 cases. The governor noted that they had received the order to re-introduce administrative resolution procedures a week earlier and had begun work in this direction. He claimed that the new regulation lacked any articles that would make the decisions of the administrative council binding, underscoring that the new regulation did not prohibit the claimants' application to courts after the administrative council had reached a decision. He also argued that a new regulation was necessary to clarify the situation.[93] The order of the Ministry of the Interior to resolve the land disputes in Bitlis gives evidence that the central government placed significance on the resolution of land disputes in this province during this period.

PLANS FOR THE RESOLUTION OF LAND DISPUTES

As noted above, the Ottoman authorities saw the resolution of land disputes in Bitlis and Van before the arrival of general inspectors as an urgent and vital matter. The correspondence between Tahsin Bey, the governor of Van, and the Ministry of the Interior clearly shows the urgency and significance attached to this issue. In a telegram sent to the Ministry of the Interior on 8 July 1914, Tahsin Bey reported that he had attempted to resolve the land disputes in absolute terms before the arrival of the general inspectors. He noted that he had been somewhat successful, but the initiative remained inconclusive, as the central government did not grant the funds requested by the local authorities.[94] Upon this request for funds, Talat Pasha, the Minister of the Interior, stated that 'it is understood that, if these disputes were not completely and urgently resolved by a humble concession and if the issue was not settled immediately, the government will have to make great concessions in order to prevent trouble'.[95] Thus, the Ministry of the Interior applied to the Council of Ministers for the allocation of a fund of 2,000 liras to Van province.

Hakkari, Muradiye and Sasun
Articles in the Ottoman press show that, for the purposes of this first initiative, Tahsin Bey had limited his efforts to investigate and resolve the land conflicts in Van to the Hakkari district, which, even before the Hamidian period, housed an Armenian population smaller than in the rest of the province.

Tahsin Bey went to Hakkari at the beginning of 1914 and established a commission consisting of two Muslims, two Christians and a chair, who served as the director of the land registry. This commission examined cases of land disputes, identified different types of land disputes and determined the reasons for conflicts between parties. Tahsin Bey also prepared an instruction for the resolution of land disputes in Hakkari, based on the findings of this investigation. As a result of its investigation, the commission specified five types of land disputes. First were disputes related to lands that had been sold by the treasury due to tax arrears. The second type of dispute involved lands that the treasury considered vacant and allocated to third parties. According to the instruction for the resolution of land disputes in Hakkari, as prepared by Tahsin Bey, lands involved in these two types of disputes would be returned to their original owners, and if the lands had been allocated to immigrants, those immigrants would be settled in other villages.[96]

The third type of land dispute specified by the commission and Tahsin Bey concerned lands directly seized by third parties. According to the instructions, these lands would be returned to their original owners, and in the case that the original owners were not present in the region, they would be informed of the situation and given the opportunity to get their lands back within one year. The fourth type of disputes was related to lands held with unofficial sales documents (*adi senet*). According to the instructions, if such lands had been registered in the land registry by their current owners, then the value of the lands would be taken from their original owners and given to their current owners. The lands would then be registered in the names of the original owners. If there existed disputes among the parties regarding the land's value, then they would be directed to the peace courts. Finally, in cases of disputed lands where the current owner held official sales documents in hand, the commission would recognize the validity of the transfer if the parties agreed. If the parties disagreed, then the commission would compensate one of them.[97]

In the spring of 1914, Tahsin Bey launched an initiative to resolve the land problems in the Muradiye district of Van. To this end, he established a commission consisting of the mufti, the bishop and the title deeds officer (*tapu katibi*), under the chairmanship of the district governor. According to Tahsin Bey, the lands of those who had migrated from this district were mostly *mahlul*, and some had been usurped by third parties. Tahsin Bey prepared a 'land reform' plan in Muradiye, according to which every household would be given a piece of land of between 200 and 250 *dönüm*s, depending on the size of the family and the acreage of land that they held. As these lands were to be given to the people as if they were immigrants (*ahaliye muhacir namıyla arazi verileceğinden*), they would not be permitted to sell them for a period of ten years. Persons considered suspicious would be settled in the interior, while those considered reliable would be settled on the border zone. Muslims and non-Muslims would be settled separately. Finally, 'as lands in the possession of tribal chiefs had been registered as less valuable and smaller than their actual value and acreage', the records regarding these lands – which would stay in the hands of their current possessors – would be re-organised.[98]

The Land Question on the Eve of the First World War

Tahsin Bey stated that the local authorities had only spent 400 liras of the fund that had been provided for the resolution of land disputes, which amounted to 1,000 liras. He requested the remaining 600 liras from the central government, noting that, although the commission had arrived in Muradiye, they were not able to operate due to the lack of funds. Tahsin Bey sent several telegrams to the Ministry of the Interior regarding these funds, but the Ministry of Finance replied that the arrears of the previous year could not be transferred to the current year.[99]

Following this correspondence, the Ministry of the Interior asked the Sublime Porte to send these funds by making an addition to the new budget, and the Sublime Porte accepted the request on 19 September 1914.[100] This plan for 'land reform' in Muradiye indicates that the Ottoman authorities tried to control the implementation of the international reform plan in terms of the geographical distribution of the population in the Muradiye district. It also represents an accommodation among the demands of the various parties involved. The Ottoman government would settle 'reliable' people in the border zone. Some Armenians, together with local Muslims, would be given land. It is interesting that Tahsin Bey specifically mentioned problems in the registry records regarding the lands in the possession of tribal chiefs – that these lands were actually larger and more valuable than what was indicated in the records. This suggests that Tahsin Bey was also appealing to Kurdish powerholders, by legalising their ownership claims to lands which they had acquired by influence and coercion rather than through official property acquisition procedures.

Another region that concerned the Ottoman authorities in terms of the extent of land disputes was Sasun. On 24 June 1914, the Council of Ministers determined that there existed numerous land disputes in some villages of the Sasun district of Muş. The people had refrained from pursuing their cases, since the resolution of such cases in the *nizamiye* (regular) courts entailed a time-consuming and expensive process on the part of the claimants.[101] The Council of Ministers decided to establish a commission for the resolution of this matter through administrative channels. This commission would be able to compensate claimants by giving them money or lands from the treasury. The commission would be comprised of a Muslim and a non-Muslim and would work under the chairmanship of an official. If the commission failed to settle land disputes, the claimants would be directed to the peace courts. Thus, the Council of Ministers requested that the Ministry of the Interior provide a sum of 1,000 liras for the expenses of the commission and the compensation that it would dole out.[102]

Following this decision, Mustafa Abdülhalik Bey, the governor of Bitlis, sent a telegram to the Ministry of the Interior, proposing a different plan for the resolution of land disputes in Sasun. According to Abdülhalik Bey, the commission should include five members, four of them Muslim. Abdülhalik Bey also suggested that the commission should deal with the *hafirlik* problem. According to Abdülhalik Bey, 2,000 liras would be enough to settle the land disputes, but 5,000 liras would be necessary to solve the *hafirlik* problem.[103] *Hafirlik*, a tax levied on Christians by local powerholders, had already been illegal. Abdülhalik Bey's request for funds to solve the *hafirlik* problem shows that the Ottoman authorities were aware that the practice existed in the region. Arguably, Abdülhalik Bey requested this sum for the resolution of *hafirlik* to appease the Kurdish powerholders. The Ministry of the Interior replied that it would not be able to provide the funding requested by the governor, which exceeded the 1,000 liras that had been promised, due to a shortage of funds.[104] Correspondence regarding the resolution of land disputes and the *hafirlik* problem in Bitlis shows that the local governors tried to resolve those agrarian problems in which general inspectors might become involved before their arrival to their designated regions. Abdülhalik Bey's proposal, which included a programme to resolve the *hafirlik* issue, indicates that local governors tried to accommodate the interests of local powerholders while making plans to change agrarian structures.

A New Regulation for the Resolution of Land Disputes by Local Governors

In the summer of 1914, Tahsin Bey, the governor of Van, and Mustafa Abdülhalik Bey, the governor of Bitlis, prepared a regulation for the resolution of land disputes in Van and Bitlis. This regulation would not be implemented in the Sasun and Huyt regions of Bitlis. The governors argued that it was necessary to separate these regions because land disputes in these districts were 'commonplace and had a different form and character'.[105]

According to this regulation, a commission that would consist of two impartial Muslims, two non-Muslims and a chair – either the director of the land registry or another official – would be established. The director of the land registry would serve as member of this commission, and an official from the tax office might also be included. Thus, Armenian emigrants' or deserters' lands which had been seized without any documentation and were not registered in the title deeds office would be returned to their original owners. If the owners of such lands were not present, then the lands would be taken from the usurpers by the local government, which would keep them vacant for a period of one year (Article 1).[106]

The Land Question on the Eve of the First World War

Lands sold by the treasury for tax arrears and lands that were considered *mahlul* and given to Muslim immigrants or locals would be returned to their original owners after they had paid the value of the lands to the treasury. In this case, Muslim immigrants would be resettled on other lands or in other villages, in return for a sum (Article 2). Lands sold by unofficial sales documents would be returned to their owners after the latter had returned the sum of the value of the land. If the parties disputed the value recorded on the unofficial sales document, then the commission would resolve the dispute with the assistance of the treasury, through arbitration. If the occupier refused to settle in line with the arbitration decision, then they would be directed to the courts and the disputed land would be given to the original owner in the meantime (Article 3).[107]

Disputed lands had been sold with unofficial sales documents and registered in the title deeds office would be subject to the procedure specified in Article 3 of the regulation (Article 4). The commission would validate official sales procedures in cases where the parties agreed (Article 5). The commission would also keep records regarding land disputes (Article 6). The governors stated that all land disputes in Bitlis and Van could be resolved through this regulation in a period of two months and that all the lands of returnees would be restored to them (Article 7).[108] The governors requested funding of between 5,000 and 10,000 liras for the implementation of this regulation, but the Ministry of the Interior informed the governors on 6 September 1914 that it would be impossible to spare such sums.[109]

In a telegram sent to the British Ministry of Foreign Affairs on 25 September 1914, British Ambassador Sir Louis Mallet elaborated on developments regarding the resolution of the land question in the aftermath of the international reform plan, underscoring the difficulty of accommodating the interests of different groups involved in the matter:

All Turkish schemes for tinkering with the land question are indeed based on a principle unacceptable to the Armenians, that of monetary compensation. The Armenians wish for the actual land taken from them to be restored to its past owners and will accept nothing less. Their papers publish long list of communal lands and houses taken from them and to accept money in lieu of such property would in their view be to admit the legality of its transfer.

Recent disputes have in every case been decided against Armenians involved and more than once a local decision in their favour has been reversed at Constantinople. Their chief despoilers have been Kurds and Lazes and it is these races who predominate in the 'hamal' or stevedore calls in this city, from which Committee of Union and Progress recruits its mobs. The central Government dependent as it is on this kind of support is often more amenable to anti-Armenian influences than the Vilayet authorities. The Armenians cannot therefore appeal from local maladministration to Constantinople with any hope of success, nor can they believe in the possibility of any real effort on the part of the present Government to tackle questions outstanding.

[...] The Kurds are in a rather different position; they have no 'grievances' in the sense the modern politician would use the word; the land question for their Sheikhs is simply one of the keeping that which they have contrived to take from the Armenians; for their peasants it is one of finding money to pay these Sheikhs the exorbitant shares they demand in the lands' yield.[110]

The consul interpreted the reluctance of the government to resolve land disputes as a lack of will stemming from the CUP's reliance on the support of the usurpers. It is not possible to know the extent to which this concern affected the CUP leaders' approach to the matter. However, Tahsin Bey's reform plan for Muradiye proves that the Ottoman authorities took into consideration the cooperation of Kurdish chiefs.

In sum, the resolution of the land question in Bitlis and Van became a significant, urgent matter for the Ottoman authorities who attempted to take pre-emptive measures before the arrival of the general inspectors in the region. However, the outbreak of the world war and the declaration of a state of mobilisation (*seferberlik*) changed the course of events.[111] Plans prepared by the governors indicate that the Ottoman authorities tried to control the implementation of the reform programme in terms of land ownership and population distribution in the region. These documents also show that the local governors accommodated the demands of local powerholders in this process. Although the general inspector, Major Hoff, arrived in Erzurum on 6 August 1914, the Ottoman government ordered his return to Istanbul because of the declaration of the state of mobilisation.[112] The general inspector, Mr Westenenk, could not travel to the region to which he was assigned. After the Ottoman Empire's official entry to the war, the Council of Ministers decided to return the general inspectors to their countries of origin.[113]

Conclusion

Following the escalation of tensions on the Balkans and the outbreak of the Balkan Wars, significant changes occurred in the international and domestic context regarding the Armenian Question in general and the land question in particular. In this period, the most significant development regarding these two matters consisted of the issue of reform in the eastern provinces re-emerging on the agenda of international diplomacy. Debates in Armenian circles and in the press, as well as the actions and discourse

The Land Question on the Eve of the First World War

of the Armenian Patriarchate, the Armenian National Assembly and the Armenian political elite, demonstrate that demographic trends and the land question held a renewed significance at that time. Aware of the fact that demographics were crucially important for the success of territorial claims at the level of international diplomacy – and that land ownership was the tie that bound a people to a given territory – they began to consider maintaining the Armenian population in the eastern provinces and Cilicia as well as the resolution of land disputes as urgent matters. The Armenian political elite began to see Armenian land ownership and the resolution of land disputes concerning the Armenians as a matter of ethno-national existence.

The internationalisation of reform debates also affected the situation in the eastern provinces. Several documents examined in this chapter demonstrate that the prospect of an international reform plan that would oblige local powerholders to return the properties that they had seized caused discontent and panic in Kurdish circles. Another significant development lies in the rise of Kurdish nationalism with territorial claims to the Ottoman East. As indicated in Abdürrezzak Bedirxan's protests about the exclusion of Kurds from reform debates, some Kurdish nationalists began to consider land ownership as a means of ethno-national dominance.

As examined in the previous chapters, a number of Ottoman officials and CUP members equally started to see land ownership as a significant means of ethno-national dominance in the 1910s. After the Balkan Wars, concerns about the preservation of the empire's territorial integrity intensified. The central government's approach to the land question and the regulations and legislative changes concerning this matter indicate that the CUP saw the administrative resolution as political leverage. Therefore, it blocked the use of this procedure during international reform debates. Once the Russo-Ottoman accord had been signed, the central government re-opened the path to administrative resolution and launched initiatives in Van and Bitlis to control the implementation of reforms. As seen in the land reform plan prepared for the Muradiye district of Van, the Ottoman authorities tried to secure the settlement of 'reliable elements' in border zones, while settling 'suspicious people' in the interior.

When reform in the eastern provinces became a topic of international debate once again, the land question made for a massive social problem concerning thousands of persons. Competition for resources, subsistence concerns and objectives of enrichment were all influential in shaping this process and the debates around the issue. The political and territorial concerns and claims of the Armenian political actors, the Ottoman

Armenians and Land Disputes in the Ottoman Empire

government, the CUP and Kurdish political actors also effectively shaped this issue. The issues of land ownership and the resolution of land disputes featured an overtly political character in this period. By 1914, the issue was related not only to contested lands but also to contested territorialities.

Notes

1. For example, in a report titled 'The Situation of Armenians in Turkey', *Troshag* claimed that a significant number of Armenian properties had been seized in the constitutional period. Rober Koptaş, 'Sunuş: Fırtınadan Önce Bir Son Çırpınış', in Zohrab, *Belgeler Işığında*, 18.
2. Zohrab, *Belgeler Işığında*, 64.
3. Ibid., 52.
4. Ibid., 52.
5. Kévorkian, *Armenian Genocide*, 147–49.
6. *Adenakrut'iwnk' Azkayin Ĕnthanur Zhoghov*, nist Z (session 6), 21 June 1913, 108–9.
7. Ibid., 109.
8. Ibid., 109.
9. Ibid., 109.
10. Ibid., 110.
11. Ibid., 112.
12. Ibid., 116–17.
13. 'Vijagakrut'iwn mě', *Harach*, 17 October 1913.
14. 'Kaght'aganut'iwně ew Hoghayin Harts'ě', *Harach*, 17 October 1913.
15. 'Şarkî Anadolu Ahvâlî: Ömer Naci Bey'in Beyânâtı', *Tanin*, 16 August 1913. This article was also published under the title 'The Current Situation in Armenia' in *Harach*, 'Hayasdani Arti Vijagě', 17 August 1913.
16. Ibid.
17. Ibid.
18. Abdürrezzak Bedirxan was a grandson of Bedirxan Bey, the emir of Botan who had revolted against the Ottoman government after the proclamation of the Tanzimat. Due to his background, Abdürrezzak Bedirxan possessed a considerable network of affiliations. He is generally accepted as one of the first political actors to advocate for Kurdish nationalism. For detailed information about Abdürrezzak, see Michael A. Reynolds, 'Abdürrezzak Bedirhan: Ottoman Kurd and Russophile in the Twilight of Empire', *Kritika: Explorations in Russian and Eurasian History* 12, no. 2 (2011): 411–50.
19. For his activities to create a nationalist movement, see Bajalan, 'Between Accommodationism and Separatism', 275–82.
20. TNA: FO 195/2450, Consul Monahan to Sir Gerard Lowther, 31 October 1913. This was the summary translation of the pamphlet by Abdürrezzak from the Armenian newspaper *Harach*.

21. Yener Koç, 'Bedirxan Pashazades: Power Relations and Nationalism (1876–1914)' (Master's thesis, Boğaziçi University, 2012), 141–42.
22. For all issues of *Rojî Kurd* and their translations, see *Rojî Kurd 1913*, ed. Mesud Serfiraz and Serhat Bozkurt (Istanbul: Istanbul Kürt Enstitüsü Yayınları, 2013).
23. Bajalan, 'Between Accommodationism and Separatism', 224–39.
24. Hüseyin Şükri, 'Arâzi Meselesi', *Rojî Kurd* 4, 12 September 1913.
25. Ibid.
26. BOA: DH.H 16/3, telegram of Musa Bey to the Sublime Porte, 10 Teşrin-i Evvel 1328 (23 October 1912).
27. BOA: DH.H 16/3, Mazhar Bey, governor of Bitlis to the Ministry of the Interior, 12 Temmuz 1329 (25 July 1913).
28. BOA: DH.H 16/3, Mazhar Bey, governor of Bitlis to the Ministry of the Interior, 17 Temmuz 1329 (30 July 1913).
29. BOA: DH.H 16/3, the Ministry of the Interior to the governor of Bitlis, 20 Temmuz 1329 (2 August 1913).
30. TNA: FO 371/1781, Sir G. Lowther to Sir Edward Grey, Constantinople, 31 December 1912. See also Sedat Ulugana, *Kürt-Ermeni Coğrafyasının Sosyopolitik Dönüşümü (1908–1914): Halidiler, Hamidiyeliler, Bedirhaniler ve Taşnaklar* (Istanbul: İletişim, 2022), 238–40.
31. TNA: FO 371/1773, Mr Consul Monahan to Mr Marling, Erzurum, 29 September 1913.
32. The Armenian Patriarchate appealed to the Sublime Porte about the Agricultural Bank's sale of the lands of Armenian peasants. The Patriarchate submitted that an instalment plan should have been prepared for the payment of debts so that these peasants would not have lost their lands. BOA: BEO 4230/317147, the Armenian Patriarchate to the Sublime Porte, 16 Teşrin-i Evvel 1329 (29 October 1913).
33. TNA: FO 371/1773, Armenian Bishop of Moush to Consul Monahan, Moush, 2/15 August 1913.
34. TNA: FO 371/1773, Mr Consul Monahan to Mr Marling, Erzurum, 29 September 1913.
35. Ibid.
36. For his visit to the region, see Yeghiayan, *My Patriarchal Memoirs*, chap. 2.
37. BOA: DH.SYS 67/1-8, copy of the memorandum of the Armenian Patriarchate, 18 Teşrin-i Sani 1329 (1 December 1913).
38. BOA: DH.SYS 67/1-8, Bishop Serob to the Armenian Patriarchate, 15 Kanun-ı Evvel 1329 (28 December 1913).
39. TNA: FO 371/2130, Vice-Consul Smith to Sir L. Mallet, 10 January 1914.
40. BOA: DH.SYS 67/1-8, Tahsin Bey, governor of Van to the Ministry of the Interior, 23 Kanun-ı Evvel 1329 (5 January 1914); TNA: FO 371/2130, Vice-Consul Smith to Sir L. Mallet, 10 January 1914.
41. BOA: DH.SYS 67/1-8, cipher telegram from Tahsin Bey, governor of Van to the Ministry of the Interior, 8 Haziran 1329 (21 June 1913).

Armenians and Land Disputes in the Ottoman Empire

42. TNA: FO 371/1773, Vice-Consul Molyneux-Seel to Sir G. Lowther, 9 July 1913.
43. Ibid.
44. BOA: DH.KMS 2-2/5, the Governor of Van to the Ministry of the Interior, 5 Kanun-ı Evvel 1329 (18 December 1913).
45. BOA: DH.KMS 2-2/5, the Governor of Diyarbekir to the Ministry of the Interior, 13 Kanun-ı Sani 1329 (26 January 1913).
46. Ibid. On the rise of anti-Armenian sentiments among the Muslim population in Diyarbekir following the reform agreement, see also Uğur Ümit Üngör, *The Making of Modern Turkey: Nation and State in Eastern Anatolia, 1913–1950* (Oxford: Oxford University Press, 2011), 49–50.
47. TNA: FO 371/2124, Sir L. Mallet to Sir Edward Grey, Constantinople, 16 January 1914.
48. TNA: FO 371/ 2124, from Consul at Erzurum, 19 January 1914.
49. TNA: FO 371/2124, P. W Bulland to Sir L. Mallet, Erzurum, 17 January 1914.
50. Ibid.
51. TNA: FO 371/2124, Sir L. Mallet to Sir Edward Grey, Pera, 20 January 1914.
52. TNA: FO 371/2130, Vice-Consul Smith to Sir L. Mallet, Van, 10 January 1914.
53. Ibid.
54. TNA: FO 371/2130, Vice-Consul Smith to Sir L. Mallet, Van, 14 February 1914.
55. Ibid.
56. Sheikh Selim, who was seventy-five years old, was known in the region as the caliph. He was also a follower of the Gayda tekke and had influence over the Kurdish peasants. Sheikh Seyyid Ali, the son of Sheikh Celaleddin, was from the Gayda tekke in the Hizan district, where Sheikh Sıbgatullah from Baghdad was buried. This tekke held extensive influence in the area. At thirty-seven years old, Sheikh Seyyid Ali was a preponderant figure in the regions of Hizan, Bitlis, Gevaş, Garcikan, Varto and Mutki and commandeered about a hundred armed men. Sheikh Şahabettin was the brother of Seyyid Ali. 'Bitlis Vukû'âtı', *Tanin*, 5 April 1914. For the details of the Bitlis rebellion, see Reynolds, *Shattering Empires*, 78–81; Bajalan, 'Between Accommodationism and Separatism', 282–88; Mehmet Polatel, 'The State, Local Actors and Mass Violence in Bitlis Province', in Kieser et al. *The End of the Ottomans*, 124–28; Tibet Abak, 'Rus Arşiv Belgelerinde Bitlis İsyanı (1914)', *Toplumsal Tarih* 208 (April 2011): 2–11; Ulugana, *Kürt-Ermeni Coğrafyasının Sosyopolitik Dönüşümü*, chap. 3; Law Reşid, 'Bir Hikaye-i Tarih', *Jîn*, 10 Nisan 1335; Law Reşid, 'Bir Hikaye-i Tarih- Geçen Nüshadan Mabad ve Hitam', *Jîn*, 26 Nisan 1335, in *Jîn 1918–1919*, vol. 4, ed. M. Emin Bozarslan (Uppsala: Deng Yayınevi, 1987), 719–21, 752–57.

The Land Question on the Eve of the First World War

57. BOA: DH.KMS 16/30, Tahsin, governor of Van to the Ministry of the Interior, 6 Mart 1330 (19 March 1914).
58. Mr Maynard was an American missionary in charge of the H. M. Vice-Consulate at Bitlis.
59. TNA: FO 371/2130, P. W. Bulland to Sir L. Mallet. Erzurum, 25 March 1914.
60. TNA: FO 371/2130, Sir L. Mallet to Sir Edward Grey, Pera, 19 April 1914.
61. TNA: FO 371/2130, Vice-Consul Lieutenant Smith to Sir L. Mallet, Van, 22 March 1914.
62. For the letter of Sheikh Selim to the Armenian bishop of Bitlis, see BOA: DH.ŞFR 421/6, Mustafa, governor of Bitlis to the Ministry of the Interior, 21 Mart 1330 (3 April 1914). 'Mahommedan fedais have been assembled by us but we do this with the strict understanding that no harm will be done to your action. We request you on your part to order your people not to interfere or take part. Should your people meet mine in any of their villages let it be as if they did not see them, for that which we purpose to do is quite a separate guardion'. 2 March, Selim of Hizan, see TNA: FO 371/2130, Vice-Consul Lieutenant Smith to Sir L. Mallet, 16 April 1914. Kaligian has argued that the government provided rifles to the ARF, fearing that an attack on the Armenians could lead to foreign intervention. See Kaligian, *Armenian Organization*, 206. For the Armenian participation, see also Ulugana, *Kürt-Ermeni*, 326–30.
63. TNA: FO 371/2130, Vice-Consul Lieutenant Smith to Sir L. Mallet, 4 April 1914.
64. Ibid.
65. Fifteen to eighteen prisoners were executed. See TNA: FO 371/2130, Sir L. Mallet to Sir Edward Grey, 4 September 1914. Among the prisoners were Sheikh Seyyid Ali, his son Salahaddin, Fakir Halil of Hilit, Molla Muhiddin, Molla Haydar and Molla Halil, all from Hizan; Hacı Hüseyin Agha, brother-in-law of Seyyid Ali, and Cafer Agha, both from Garchigan; Ferid Agha, cousin of Seyyid Ali and Hasan Bey, of Gevaş; see TNA: FO 371/2130, Vice-Consul Lieutenant Smith to Sir L. Mallet, 3 May 1914.
66. TNA: FO 195/2375, Vice-Consul A. Safrastian to Consul P. J. McGregor, 25 September 1911.
67. Some Kurdish accounts of the Bitlis rebellion argue that it carried a Kurdish nationalist element. For example, in his evaluation of this rebellion in 1919, Law Reshid states that the Bitlis rebellion was an expression of the national cause in religious terms (*matalıb-ı diniye suretinde teselli eden âmâl-ı milliye*). Law Reşid, 'Bir Hikaye-i Tarih-Geçen Nüshadan Mabad', 757.
68. TNA: FO 371/2130, Vice-Consul Lieutenant Smith to Sir L. Mallet, 3 May 1914, 'Report on Journey through part of the Vilayets of Van and Bitlis'.
69. Ibid.
70. *Deghegakir*, vol. 2, 11.
71. BOA: DH.SFR 424/15, Tahsin, governor of Van and Mustafa, the governor of Bitlis, to the Ministry of the Interior, 2 Nisan 1330 (15 April 1914).

72. Reynolds, *Shattering Empires*, 80–81.
73. TNA: FO 371/2130, Vice-Consul Lieutenant Smith to Sir L. Mallet, 16 May 1914.
74. BOA: DH.EUM.EMN 74/21, copy of the cipher from the province of Van dated 8 Mayıs 1330 (21 May 1914).
75. Ibid.
76. Reynolds, 'Abdürrezzak Bedirhan', 446.
77. BOA: DH.EUM.EMN 74/21, the cipher telegram from Galip Pasha, 11th Corps Commander to the Ministry of War, 10 Mayıs 1330 (23 May 1914).
78. Reynolds, 'Abdürrezzak Bedirhan', 446.
79. BOA: DH.SFR 41/46, EUM to province of Hicaz, 8 Mayıs 1330 (21 May 1914); BOA: DH.ŞFR 43/130, EUM to province of Hicaz, 17 Temmuz 1330 (30 July 1914). According to the report of British consulate, about sixty Kurds would be exiled. See TNA: FO 371/2130, Vice-Consul Lieutenant Smith to Sir L. Mallet, 3 May 1914.
80. Erdal Aydoğan, *İttihat ve Terakki'nin Doğu Politikası, 1908–1918* (Istanbul: Ötüken Yayınları, 2005), 219.
81. BOA: DH.EUM.2.Şb 2/9, EUM to the Grand Vizier, 8 Teşrin-i Sani 1330 (21 November 1914).
82. TNA: FO 371/1773, Vice-Consul Molyneux-Seel to Sir G. Lowther, 9 July 1913.
83. 'Sulh hâkimleri hakkında kânun-ı muvakkat', 11 Nisan 1329/24 April 1913, *Düstur*, vol. 2, no. 5, 322–48.
84. BOA: DH.SYS 67/1-8, the Governor of Bitlis to the Ministry of the Interior, 3 Şubat 1329 (16 February 1914).
85. 'Sulh hâkimleri ta'yîn edilmemiş olan mahallerde emvali gayr-i menkûleye mute'allik men'-i tecâvüz da'vâlarının tâlîmat-ı mahsûsasına tevfîkan kemâfi's-sâbık mecâlis-i idârede fâsıl ve reviyetine dair sulh hâkimleri kânûn-ı muvakkatine müzeyyel madde hakkında kânûn-ı muvakkat'. Karakoç Sarkis, *Emval-i Gayr-i Menkûle Kanunları-Tahşiyeli* (Istanbul: Cihan, 1340/1342), 399. This law was published on 8 January 1914.
86. 'Mesele-i Islâhat: Rusya'nın Metâlibatı', *Tanin*, 14 January 1914.
87. Sir L. Mallet to Sir Edward Grey, 15 April 1914, no. 595, in *British Documents*, 548; Kieser et al., 'Reform or Cataclysm?' 298.
88. Bayur, *Türk İnkılâbı*, 186.
89. BOA: HR.SYS 2818-3/61-65, copy of the contract in French, 24 May 1914.
90. BOA: DH.HMŞ 28/44, 13 April 1914, in Türkmen, *Vilayat-ı Şarkiye*, 182.
91. Ibid.
92. BOA: DH.KMS 63/68, 16 June 1914, in Türkmen, *Vilayat-ı Şarkiye*, 153–54.
93. BOA: DH.SYS 67/1-8, the Governor of Bitlis to the Ministry of the Interior, 3 Şubat 1329 (16 February 1914).
94. BOA: BEO 4301/322568, copy of cipher telegram from the Governor of Van to the Ministry of the Interior, 25 Haziran 1330 (8 July 1914).

The Land Question on the Eve of the First World War

     Tahsin Bey later warned the Ottoman government that the general inspector Major Hoff was establishing close ties with the Armenians in Van. See Hilmar Kaiser, 'Tahsin Uzer: The CUP's Man in the East', in Kieser et al., *End of the Ottomans*, 98.
95. BOA: BEO 4301/322568, Talat, the Minister of the Interior to the Sublime Porte, 1 Temmuz 1330 (14 July 1914).
96. 'Van'da Arâzi Meselesi', *Tanin*, March 25, 1914.
97. Ibid.
98. BOA: DH.SYS 67/1-9, Tahsin Bey, governor of Van to the Ministry of the Interior, 16 Nisan 1330 (29 April 1914).
99. BOA: DH.SYS 67/1-9, Tahsin Bey, governor of Van to the Ministry of the Interior, 1 Mayıs 1330 (14 May 1914); BOA: DH.SYS 67/1-9, the Ministry of the Interior to the Sublime Porte, 18 Haziran 1330 (1 July 1914); BOA: DH.SYS 67/1-9, the Ministry of Finance to Ministry of the Interior, 15 Haziran 1330 (6 July 1914).
100. BOA: BEO 4311/323276, the Ministry of the Interior to the Sublime Porte, 19 Haziran 1330 (2 July 1914); BOA: DH.SYS 67/1-9, the Sublime Porte to the Ministry of the Interior, 6 Eylül 1330 (19 September 1914).
101. BOA: MV 189/78, decision of the Council of Ministers, 11 Haziran 1330 (24 June 1914).
102. Ibid.
103. BOA: BEO 4312/323358, copy of cipher telegram from the province of Bitlis to the Ministry of the Interior, 2 Temmuz 1330 (15 July 1914).
104. BOA: BEO 4316/323670, Minister of Finance to the Sublime Porte, 20 Ağustos 1330 (2 September 1914).
105. BOA: DH.SYS 67/1-9, Tahsin Bey, governor of Van and Mustafa Abdülhalik, governor of Bitlis to the Ministry of the Interior, 17 Temmuz 1330 (30 July 1914).
106. BOA: DH.SYS 67/1-9, copy of the regulation on the resolution of land disputes, no date.
107. Ibid.
108. Ibid.
109. BOA: DH.SYS 67/1-9, 24 Ağustos 1330 (6 September 1914).
110. TNA: FO 371/2137, Sir L. Mallet to Sir Edward Grey, Therapia, 25 September 1914.
111. On the Ottoman entry to the war, see Aksakal, *Ottoman Road*.
112. Türkmen, *Vilayat-ı Şarkiye*, 191.
113. Ibid., 203; BOA: DH.İD 186/72, the copy of the imperial order, 16 Kanun-ı Evvel 1330 (29 December 1914) and the Grand Vizierate to the Ministry of Interior, 17 Kanun-ı Evvel 1330 (30 December 1914).

Conclusion: The Armenian Genocide and the Land Question

On a hot summer day in 1915, a young man named Manaseh made one of the most challenging journeys imaginable. His travel companion was the son of a *bey*, the *bey* who had taken him as a servant and given him the name Ali. This was a journey that started in Kesrik, a village near the centre of Mamüretülaziz and ended on the banks of the Munzur River. In any other summer, this would have been a rather pleasurable six hours, because this area boasted some of the most fertile lands in the region, supplying fruit to places as far away as Baghdad.[1] In that year, however, the road was full of human remains. Manaseh and Küçük Bey (the little *bey*) drove their horses for hours, passing by piles of corpses.[2]

The destination of the travellers was the village of Munzuroğlu. There, they were welcomed by another Armenian youngster, an orphan called Hayo. Fifteen Armenian villages were located in the environs of Munzuroğlu. All their inhabitants, save for a handful like Hayo, who had been turned into servants, had been killed in the recent massacres.[3] It was their rotting bodies that Manaseh and Küçük Bey passed. Hayo, so the *bey* told Manaseh, knew everything about Munzuroğlu. Most importantly, he knew the borders of the lands in the village and which field belonged to which Armenian. And he would guide them and help them figure out which lands now belonged to the *bey* and which to his own master.[4] Thus, while the corpses of the original owners of these lands had not even started to disintegrate, the two Armenian youngsters were forced into helping the *bey*s share their lands among them. As illuminated by this instance, the land question constituted an integral part of the genocide. And it was a part of it from the start.

The genocide was a world-changing event for hundreds of thousands. It also changed the topic of this book on drastic terms. During the genocide, Armenians all over the country were dispossessed.[5] As shown in this

Conclusion

book, before the outbreak of the war, the Armenian land question had already been of an enormous extent. With the genocide, the extent of the seizures reached the level of almost the entire Armenian wealth in Asia Minor. Furthermore, the government utilised Armenian lands and properties as part of an ethno-religious policy of demographic engineering to resettle Muslim immigrants and refugees. This policy, akin to earlier practices of settling immigrants in Armenian villages, now involved the comprehensive deportation and killing of Armenians, with the aim of guaranteeing the dominance of Muslims.[6] Thus, the genocide led to a significant transformation in terms of land disputes involving Armenians.

There remains much to be explored in terms of the connections between the Armenian land question and the genocide. What did the usurpers do during the genocide? To what extent were the perpetrator networks established and populated by persons with a vested material interest in this issue? These questions can only be answered through further empirical research. However, this book has shown that, as it evolved into an unresolved social problem of great magnitude, the Armenian land question deepened the social cleavage among Muslims and Armenians, widening the distance between these two groups. Especially after the massacres of 1894–97, the Armenian question became a personal question for thousands of Muslims because the prospects of its resolution would now affect their prosperity and, for some, their subsistence. The social support for and mass participation in the genocide cannot be understood in isolation from this fact.

As might be expected, the regions where there happened massacres on site during the genocide – in other words, the areas where Armenians were killed within their own hometowns – featured a concentration of land disputes involving Armenians.[7] On-site massacres required local participation and approval.[8] Unsurprisingly, these were readily available or easy to procure in the Ottoman East, especially in places such as Muş or Van, where almost half of the arable land was contested between Armenians and Muslims.

The Armenian land question significantly contributed to the escalation of tensions between communities and to the poisoning of the relations between Armenians and the Ottoman state. However, I do not think that the genocide was an inevitable result of these tensions and disagreements. Undoubtedly, the land question presented one of the main factors that turned the Armenian question into a complicated problem. Yet, as shown through this book, there existed moments of opportunity and schemes of resolution that could have changed the course of events. For example, if the central government had accepted the local governors' proposals to carry out a radical reform scheme that would have entailed the *aghas*' repression, the land allocation to ordinary Kurds and the return of seized Armenian lands, then a different picture could have emerged. Or, had not the war broken out, events would have moved along different trajectory, which would have included at least a partial resolution of the Armenian land question under the auspices of the general inspectors.[9] In sum, there were instances when a different future seemed possible. The fact that the genocide followed this series of events does not mean that it was the only possible outcome.

One of the factors that shaped the transformation of the Armenian land question can be found in the new territorial turn that had started in the mid-nineteenth century. This turn, which led to changes in the terms in which land ownership and sovereignty were understood, affected land policies worldwide, turning rural land into a battleground for states and nationalist movements. With this new territorial turn, land questions erupted in various parts of the world and exclusivist approaches to land became dominant. The liberal understanding of land ownership was undermined by nationalist approaches which saw land as a means of establishing ethno-religious dominance. From the US to Russia, various states used land policies and dispossession to achieve demographic objectives and to target non-dominant groups within their borders. In this regard, the late Ottoman history concerning land disputes involving Armenians reflect a larger global current sweeping Europe and the colonies.

Starting with the Hamidian period, the Ottoman government began to see the Armenian presence in the Ottoman East, where Armenians comprised a significant portion of the population, as a problem. The changes in land policies, which also led to the practical barring of all Armenians from acquiring land in this region in the fin-de-siècle, reflect this change in the state's approach. However, as in many other places, such as Prussia, it was not only the state whose approach to land and land ownership changed at that time. Armenians, Kurds and Turks were all aware of the newly heightened political significance of owning land to establish and maintain political sovereignty and ethno-national dominance. This was why Armenians insisted on the return of the lands rather than compensation and saw this as a life-and-death matter for the Armenian nation's future. For the Kurds, too, land ownership became linked with political claims over the Ottoman East, and the land question became an important element of the Kurdish nationalist project and activism. By the mid-1910s, the Armenian land question had transformed the fields in the Ottoman East into a political (and at times literal) battleground among competing nationalist claims.

Conclusion

In addition to its political importance, land was also precious as a factor of production. In this agricultural economy, land constituted a very valuable thing. Especially in the east it was the key to subsistence and making a decent living. It was also the key to enrichment. Because of the agricultural nature of the economy, land-grabbing was the easiest form of accumulating capital. Land also held great value for the state because state revenues largely came from taxes imposed on agricultural production. The overwhelming economic significance of land ownership in the late Ottoman context made solving the Armenian land question difficult. This was so because the thousands involved in this debacle – including the Armenian peasants who had been dispossessed and reduced to serfdom, the Muslim refugees and former nomads who had been settled on these lands, the Kurdish notables and *agha*s who had amassed fortunes by seizing these lands – all had much to lose.

Land disputes concerning Armenians changed drastically between the mid-nineteenth century and the First World War. At first, there existed an apparent disparity between the parties involved. As far as can be traced from the Armenian Patriarchate's reports, all the usurpers of the Tanzimat period were people of power, such as local notables, *bey*s, *agha*s and religious authorities. The usurped lands belonged to Armenians of limited means, who did not have much beyond a small plot of land. The massacres of 1894–97 radically changed this situation. With the outbreak of this wave of mass violence, Armenians from all social backgrounds became targets, including large landowners. Moreover, Muslims with more diverse backgrounds took part in land seizures. While local powerholders took the lion's share, impoverished refugees or formerly nomadic tribespeople also counted among the beneficiaries of this seizure and allocation process.[10] Thus, in the transformation of land disputes involving Armenians into the Armenian land question, the main characteristic of the problem changed, and a class-based problem evolved into an ethno-national problem.

The massacres in the Hamidian period changed not only the characteristics but also the scale of the problem. In this period, when hundreds of thousands were killed or uprooted, the number of land disputes involving Armenians increased tremendously. In other words, mass violence brought about mass dispossession and mass property transfer. As noted, with the genocide, an even more significant expansion in terms of scale occurred. This transformative impact of mass violence on land ownership and disputes highlights the extent to which violence can affect socio-economic dynamics and structures.

The transformation of land disputes into such a crisis, deepening ethnic and religious differences and escalating social tensions, highlights the importance of competition over resources in shaping social life and relations. In the contemporary world, we do not feel our dependence on land as acutely as in the past. For most of us, there is a considerable distance between the agricultural production needed for our survival and our quotidian lives. However, we are still dependent on land. Land-grabbing, land disputes and other forms of competition over resources continue to shape lives and conflicts globally. The case examined in this book provides evidence for the claim that such disputes can be explosive and damaging. This is all the more critical today because the climate crisis has already started changing needs and available resources and heightened competitive struggles.[11] The Armenian land question and its long-term impact on the escalation of tensions should be seen as yet another warning sign for the dangers that lie ahead.

Notes

1. *Salname-i Vilayet-i Mamuretülaziz* (1310/1892), 57.
2. USC Shoah Foundation VHA, Hovannisian Oral History Collection, Manaseh Kaprileian interviewed in October 1982, no. 55874. Manaseh was born in 1893 in the village of Hoghe, Harput, and attended Euphrates College. After the First World War, he relocated to Aleppo, Syria, and a year later, in 1923, he settled in Beirut, Lebanon, where he worked as a pharmacist for more than four decades. When he left Harput, he also rescued some manuscripts from the library of the college by taking them with him. See Malina Zakian, 'The Journey of One Armenian Manuscript', Hill Museum and Manuscript Library, 5 August 2021, https://hmml.org/stories/series-travel-the-journey-of-one-armenian-manuscript/. For another story of a rescued manuscript, see Heghnar Zeitlian Watenpaugh, *The Missing Pages: The Modern Life of a Medieval Manuscript, from Genocide to Justice* (Palo Alto: Stanford University Press, 2019).
3. Hovsep Hayreni, *Yukarı Fırat Ermenileri 1915 ve Dersim* (Istanbul: Belge, 2015), 573.
4. Manaseh Kaprileian's interview. Another boy named Zohrab also witnessed corpses and human remains in mountains and streams in the surroundings of Munzuroğlu. Hayreni, *Yukarı Fırat*, 574. On the experiences of survivors, see Donald E. Miller and Lorna T. Miller, *Survivors: An Oral History of the Armenian Genocide* (Berkeley: University of California Press, 1999); Vahé Tachjian, *Daily Life in the Abyss: Genocide Diaries, 1915–1918*, trans. G. M. Goshgarian (New York: Berghahn, 2017); Khatchig Mouradian, *The Resistance Network: The Armenian Genocide and Humanitarianism in Ottoman Syria, 1915–1918* (East Lansing: Michigan State University Press, 2021); Elyse Semerdjian, *Remnants: Embodied Archives of the Armenian Genocide* (Palo Alto: Stanford University Press, 2023).

Conclusion

5. The literature on the confiscation and seizure of Armenian properties during the genocide has grown over the last two decades. See Kurt, *Armenians of Aintab*; Morack, *The Dowry of the State?*; Taner Akçam and Ümit Kurt, *The Spirit of the Laws: The Plunder of Wealth in the Armenian Genocide*, trans. Aram Arkun (New York: Berghahn, 2015); Hilmar Kaiser, *The Extermination of Armenians in the Diarbekir Region* (Istanbul: Istanbul Bilgi University Press, 2014); Oya Gözel, *A City Transformed: Great War, Deportation and Socio-Economic Change in Kayseri (1915–1920)* (Istanbul: Libra, 2019); Nevzat Onaran, *Osmanlı'da Ermeni ve Rum Mallarının Türkleştirilmesi (1914–1919)* (Istanbul: Evrensel Basım Yayın, 2013); Bedross Der Matossian, 'The Taboo within the Taboo: The Fate of "Armenian Capital" at the End of the Ottoman Empire', *European Journal of Turkish Studies* [online] (2011), http://journals.openedition.org/ejts/4411; Üngör and Polatel, *Confiscation and Destruction*.
6. On the demographic policies, see Nesim Şeker, 'Demographic Engineering in the Late Ottoman Empire and the Armenians', *Middle Eastern Studies* 43, no. 3 (May 2007): 461–74; Dündar, *İttihat ve Terakki*; Üngör, *Making of Modern Turkey*; Akçam, *The Young Turks' Crime*, chap. 2.
7. On-site massacres were concentrated in the Ottoman East. See Ara Sarafian, *Talaat Pasha's Report on the Armenian Genocide* (London: Gomidas, 2011); Kévorkian, *Armenian Genocide*, chap. 3–8. Mark Levene has defined the eastern part of the empire as the zone of genocide. See 'Creating a Modern "Zone of Genocide": The Impact of Nation- and State-Formation on Eastern Anatolia, 1878–1923', *Holocaust and Genocide Studies* 12, no. 3 (January 1998): 394.
8. Taner Akçam, 'Top-Down and Local Violence in the Late Ottoman Empire: The Role of Security Concerns and a Century of "Accumulated Experience"', *Journal of Genocide Research* (25 September 2022): 1–21.
9. For the impact of the war on the Armenian Genocide, see D. Bloxham, 'The Armenian Genocide of 1915–1916: Cumulative Radicalization and the Development of a Destruction Policy', *Past & Present* 181, no. 1 (1 November 2003): 141–91; Ronald Grigor Suny, 'Writing Genocide: The Fate of the Ottoman Armenians', in Suny et al., *Question of Genocide*, 15–41.
10. For the role of material motives in the Armenian Genocide, see Christian Gerlach, *Extremely Violent Societies: Mass Violence in the Twentieth-Century World* (Cambridge: Cambridge University Press, 2010), 92–120; Michael Mann, *The Dark Side of Democracy: Explaining Ethnic Cleansing* (Cambridge: Cambridge University Press, 2005), 27–32.
11. See the special issue of *The International Journal of Human Rights* 18, no. 3 (2014), on climate change, environmental violence and genocide.

Bibliography

Primary Sources

BAŞKANLIK OSMANLI ARŞIVI (BOA) – ISTANBUL

Bâb-ı Âlî Evrak Odası (BEO)
Bâb-ı Âsafî Dîvan-ı Hümâyun Sicilleri Nizâmat Defterleri (A.DVNS.NZAM.d)
Dâhiliye Emniyet-i Umumiye Emniyet Şubesi Evrakı (DH.EUM.EMN)
Dâhiliye Muhaberat-ı Umumiye İdaresi Evrakı (DH.MUİ)
Dâhiliye Nezâreti Dâhiliye Kalem-i Mahsus Evrakı (DH.KMS)
Dâhiliye Nezâreti Emniyet-i Umumiye İkinci Şube (DH.EUM.2.Şb)
Dâhiliye Nezâreti Hukuk Evrakı (DH.H)
Dâhiliye Nezâreti İdare Evrakı (DH.İD)
Dâhiliye Nezâreti Mektubi Kalemi (DH.MKT)
Dâhiliye Nezâreti Siyasî Kısım Belgeleri (DH.SYS)
Dâhiliye Nezâreti Şifre Kalemi Belgeleri (DH.ŞFR)
Dâhiliye Nezâreti Tesrî-i Muamelât ve Islahat Komisyonu–Muamelât (DH.TMIK.M)
Dâhiliye Nezâreti Tesrî-i Muamelât ve Islahat Komisyonu–Islahat (DH.TMIK.S)
Hariciye Nezâreti Siyasî Kısmı Belgeleri (HR.SYS)
İrade Dâhiliye (İ.DH)
Meclis-i Vâlâ (MVL)
Meclis-i Vükela (MV)
Sadâret Mektubî Kalemi Mühimme Kalemi (Odası) Belgeleri (A.MKT.MHM)
Şuray-ı Devlet (ŞD)
Yıldız Perakende Askerî Maruzât (Y.PRK.ASK)
Yıldız Perakende Dâhiliye Nezâreti Maruzâtı (Y.PRK.DH)
Yıldız Perakende Hariciye Nezâreti Maruzâtı (Y.PRK.HR)
Yıldız Perakende Mâbeyn Başkitâbeti (Y.PRK.BŞK)
Yıldız Perakende Sadâret Maruzâtı (Y.PRK.A)
Yıldız Perakende Umûm Vilâyetler Tahrirâtı (Y.PRK.UM)
Yıldız Sadâret Hususî Maruzât (Y.A.HUS)

Bibliography

THE NATIONAL ARCHIVES OF THE UNITED KINGDOM – LONDON
Foreign Office (FO)

AGBU NUBARIAN LIBRARY (LA BIBLIOTHÈQUE NUBARIAN) – PARIS
Adenakrut'iwnk'Azkayin Ĕnthanur Zhoghov, 1909–1914 (Minutes of National General Assembly).
Deghegakirk' Kawaṛagan Harsdaharut'eants'. G. Bolis: Dbakrut'iwn Aramean, 1876.
Deghegakir Hoghayin Krawmants Hantsnazhoghovoy. 4 vols. Istanbul: Doghramadjian Dbakragan, 1910–12.

USC SHOAH FOUNDATION VISUAL HISTORY ARCHIVE
Hovannisian Oral History Collection

Published Primary Sources

BOOKS, PUBLISHED DOCUMENTS AND REPORTS, ETC.

Adom. *Bedagan Veranorokut'iwnn u Hoghayin Harts'ĕ*. G. Bolis: Dbaran A. Shahēn, 1910.
Anadolu'nun Muhtelifesinde Emlak ve Arazi-i Magsube Hakkında Ermeni Patrikhanesince Teşkil Eden Komisyon-u Mahsusa Tarafından Tanzim Olunan Raporların Suret-i Mütercimesi. Dersaadet: Doğramacıyan Matbaası, 1327/1911.
Anadolu Vilayat-ı Osmaniyesindeki Arazi Meselesine Dair Ermeni Patrikhanesinden 7 Temmuz 327 Tarihiyle Makam-ı Sami-i Sadâret-i Uzmâ ile Dâhiliye ve Adliye ve Mezahib Nezaret-i Celilelerine Arz ve Takdim Kılınan Takririn Suretidir. Dersaadet: Dikran Doğramacıyan Matbaası, 1328.
A-Tō. *Vani, Pit'lisi ew Ērzrumi vilayēt'nerĕ: Usumnasirut'yan mi p'orts ayt yergri ashkharhakragan, vijagakragan, irawagan ew d'ndesagan trut'yan*. Yerewan: Dbaran Guldura, 1912.
British Documents on the Origins of the War, 1898–1914, vol. 10, pt. 1. Edited by G. P. Gooch and Harold Temperley. New York: Johnson Reprint, 1967.
Düstur, vol. 1, no. 1. Dersaadet: Matbaa-i Amire, 1289.
Düstur, vol. 1, no. 7. Dersaadet: Matbaa-i Amire, 1289.
Düstur, vol. 1, no. 3 (zeyl). Dersaadet: Matbaa-i Amire, 1300.
Düstur, vol. 2, no. 1. Dersaadet: Matbaa-i Osmaniye, 1329.
Düstur, vol. 2, no. 3. Dersaadet: Matbaa-i Osmaniye, 1330.
Düstur, vol. 2, no. 5. Dersaadet: Adliye Nezâreti İhsaiyat ve Müdevvenat-ı Kanuniniye Müdüriyeti, 1332.
Emvali Gayrimenkuleye Mütedair Kavanini Muvakkate. Istanbul: Selanik Matbaası, 1329.

Fisher, Sir Stanley. *Ottoman Land Laws: Containing the Ottoman Land Code and Later Legislation Affecting Land with Notes and an Appendix of Cyprus Laws and Rules Relating to Land.* London: Oxford University Press, 1919.

Garabedian, Kegham Der. *Hoghayin Harts'ĕ Hayap'nag Nahankneru Meç.* G. Bolis: H. Y. Taşnagtsutyan, Hradaragutyun, 1911.

İsmail Hakkı Bey. *Raporlarım.* Adana: Osmanlı Matbaası, 1328/1912.

Jîn 1918–1919, vol. 4. Edited by M. Emin Bozarslan. Uppsala: Deng Yayınevi, 1987.

Karakoç, Sarkis. *Arazi Kanunu ve Tapu Nizamnamesi, Tahşiyeli.* Istanbul: Cihan Biraderler Matbaası, 1340/42.

———. *Emval-i Gayr-i Menkûle Kanunları-Tahşiyeli.* Istanbul: Cihan, 1340/42.

———. *Kavanin-i Cedide Külliyatı*, no. 9. Istanbul: Matbaa ve Kütüphane-i Cihan, 1339–41.

Meclis-i Mebusan 1293–1877 Zabıt Ceridesi. Edited by Hakkı Tarık Us, vol. 2. Istanbul: Vakit Gazetesi Matbaa Kütüphanesi, 1954.

Meclis-i Mebusan Zabıt Ceridesi, period 1, vol. 1, session 1. 26 Kânun-ı sâni 1324/28 February 1909.

Osmanlı Belgelerinde Ermeni-Rus İlişkileri (1899–1906), vol. 2. Ankara: Başbakanlık Devlet Arşivleri Genel Müdürlüğü, 2006.

Reports on Provincial Oppressions. London: Gilbert and Rivington, 1877.

Roji Kurd 1913. Edited by Mesud Serfiraz and Serhat Bozkurt. Istanbul: Istanbul Kürt Enstitüsü Yayınları, 2013.

Tanzimat Sonrası Arazi ve Tapu. Istanbul: Osmanlı Arşivi Daire Başkanlığı, 2014.

The Ottoman Land Code. Translated by F. Ongley. London: William Clowes and Sons, 1892.

United States, *Capitulations of the Ottoman Empire: Report of Edward A. Van Dyck, Consular Clerk of the United States at Cairo, upon the Capitulations of the Ottoman Empire since the Year 1150*, 2 v. in 1. Washington DC: Govt. print. off., 1881.

United States Department of State. *Papers Relating to the Foreign Relations of the United States, with the Annual Message of the President Transmitted to Congress December 7, 1896, and the Annual Report of the Secretary of State. Washington DC:* U. S. Government Printing Office, 1896.

PARLIAMENTARY PAPERS

Correspondence Respecting the Condition of the Populations in Asia Minor and Syria. Turkey, no. 10 (1879). London: Harrison and Sons, 1879.

Correspondence Respecting the Condition of the Populations in Asia Minor and Syria. Turkey, no. 4 (1880). London: Harrison and Sons, 1880.

Correspondence Respecting the Introduction of Reforms in the Armenian Provinces of Asiatic Turkey. Turkey, no. 1 (1896). London: Harrison and Sons, 1896.

Bibliography

Further Correspondence Respecting the Condition of the Populations in Asia Minor and Syria. Turkey, no. 6 (1881). London: Harrison and Sons, 1881.

Reports by Her Majesty's Diplomatic and Consular Agents in Turkey Respecting the Condition of the Christian Subjects of the Porte: 1868–75. Turkey, no. 16 (1877). London: Harrison and Sons, 1877.

Reports from Her Majesty's Representatives Respecting the Tenure of Land in the Several Countries of Europe: 1869–70. London: Harrison and Sons, 1870.

NEWSPAPERS AND JOURNALS

Azadamart
Haṛach
Roji Kurd
Tanin
Tercüman-ı Hakikat

PROVINCIAL YEARBOOKS

Salname-i Vilayet-i Mamuretülaziz. 1310.

Secondary Sources

Abak, Tibet. 'Kürt Politikasında Hamidiye Siyasetine Dönüş ve Kör Hüseyin Paşa Olayı, 1910–1911'. In Adanır and Özel, *1915*, 277–92.

———. 'Rus Arşiv Belgelerin Bitlis İsyanı (1914)'. *Toplumsal Tarih* 208 (April 2011): 2–11.

Adanır, Fikret, and Oktay Özel, eds. *1915: Siyaset, Tehcir, Soykırım*. Istanbul: Tarih Vakfı Yurt Yayınları, 2015.

Ahmad, Feroz. *The Young Turks: The Committee of Union and Progress in Turkish Politics, 1908–1914*. London: Hurst, 2010.

Akarlı, Engin D. 'Abdülhamid II's Attempt to Integrate Arabs into the Ottoman System'. In *Palestine in the Late Ottoman Period: Political Social and Economic Transformation*, edited by David Kushner, 74–89. Jerusalem: Yad Izhak Ben Zvi Press, 1986.

Akçam, Taner. *A Shameful Act: The Armenian Genocide and the Question of Turkish Responsibility*. Trans. Paul Bessemer. New York: Holt Paperback; Metropolitan Books, 2007.

———. *The Young Turks' Crime against Humanity: The Armenian Genocide and Ethnic Cleansing in the Ottoman Empire*. Princeton: Princeton University Press, 2012.

———. 'Top-Down and Local Violence in the Late Ottoman Empire: The Role of Security Concerns and a Century of "Accumulated Experience"'. *Journal of Genocide Research* 25, no. 4 (September 2022): 1–21.

———. 'When Was the Decision to Annihilate the Armenians Taken?' *Journal of Genocide Research* 21, no. 4 (October 2019): 457–80.

Akçam, Taner, and Ümit Kurt. *The Spirit of the Laws: The Plunder of Wealth in the Armenian Genocide*. Translated by Aram Arkun. New York: Berghahn, 2015.

Akpınar, Alişan, and Eugene L. Rogan. *Aşiret, Mektep, Devlet: Osmanlı Devleti'nde Aşiret Mektebi*. Istanbul: Aram, 2001.

Akpınar, Özkan. 'Geographical Imagination in School Geography during the Late Ottoman Period, 1876–1908'. Master's thesis, Boğaziçi University, 2010.

Aksakal, Mustafa. *The Ottoman Road to War in 1914: the Ottoman Empire and the First World War*. Cambridge: Cambridge University Press, 2008.

Akşin, Sina. *31 Mart Olayı*. Ankara: Ankara Üniversitesi Siyasal Bilgiler Fakültesi, 1970.

Alanoğlu, Murat. 'Osmanlı Döneminde Muş (1515–1700)'. In *Muş Tarihi*, edited by Murat Alanoğlu, Mustafa Alican and Mehmet Özalper, 132–67. Istanbul: Ideal, 2021.

Anderson, Benedict R. *Imagined Communities: Reflections on the Origin and Spread of Nationalism*. Revised ed. London: Verso, 2006.

Antaramian, Richard E. *Brokers of Faith, Brokers of Empire: Armenians and the Politics of Reform in the Ottoman Empire*. Palo Alto: Stanford University Press, 2020.

Arat, Tuğrul. 'Türk Vatandaşlığından İskat Edilen Kişilerin Mülkiyet ve Miras Hakları'. *Ankara Üniversitesi Hukuk Fakültesi Dergisi* 31, no. 2 (1974): 279–360.

Arazi Kanunnamesi. Translated by Orhan Çeker. Istanbul: Ebru Yayınları, 1985.

Artinian, Vartan. *The Armenian National Constitutional System in the Ottoman Empire, 1839–1863: A Study of Its Historical Development*. Istanbul: The Isis Press, 1988.

Arvas, İbrahim. *Tarihi Hakikatler*. Ankara: Resimli Posta Matbaası, 1964.

Astourian, Stephan. 'On the Genealogy of the Armenian-Turkish Conflict, Sultan Abdülhamid and the Armenian Massacres'. In *Collective and State Violence in Turkey: The Construction of a National Identity from Empire to Nation-State*, edited by Stephan H. Astourian and Raymond H. Kévorkian, 13–55. New York: Berghahn, 2020.

———. 'Testing World-System Theory, Cilicia (1830s–1890s): Armenian-Turkish Polarization and the Ideology of Modern Ottoman Historiography'. PhD diss., University of California, 1996.

———. 'The Silence of Land: Agrarian Relations, Ethnicity, and Power'. In Suny, Göçek and Naimark, *Question of Genocide*, 55–81.

Ateş, Sabri. *The Ottoman-Iranian Borderlands: Making a Boundary, 1843–1914*. Cambridge: Cambridge University Press, 2013.

Atılgan, Mehmet, Özgür Leman Eren, Nora Mildanoğlu and Mehmet Polatel. *2012 Beyannamesi: İstanbul Ermeni Vakıflarının El Konan Mülkleri = 2012*

Bibliography

Declaration: The Seized Properties of Armenian Foundations in Istanbul. Istanbul: Hrant Dink Vakfı Yayınları, 2012.

Atmaca, Metin. 'Resistance to Centralisation in the Ottoman Periphery: The Kurdish Baban and Bohtan Emirates'. *Middle Eastern Studies* 55, no. 4 (July 2019): 519–39.

Avagyan, Arsen, and Gaidz F. Minassian. *Ermeniler ve İttihat Terakki: İşbirliğinden Çatışmaya.* Istanbul: Aras Yayınları, 2005.

Aydoğan, Erdal. *İttihat ve Terakki'nin Doğu Politikası, 1908–1918.* Istanbul: Ötüken Yayınları, 2005.

Aytekin, Erden Attila. 'Hukuk, Tarih ve Tarihyazı: 1858 Osmanlı Arazi Kanunnamesi'ne Yönelik Yaklaşımlar'. *Türkiye Araştırmaları Literatür Dergisi* 3, no. 5 (2005): 723–44.

———. 'Land, Rural Classes, and Law: Agrarian Conflict and State Regulation in the Ottoman Empire, 1830s–1860s'. PhD. diss., Binghamton University, 2006.

Babigian, Hagop. 'Adana Raporu', translated by Nıvart Taşçı. In *1909 Adana Katliamı: Üç Rapor*, edited by Ari Şekeryan, 109–31. Istanbul: Aras Yayınları, 2015.

———. *Adanayi Eghernĕ: Deghegakir Hagob Babikeani.* Translated by Hagop Barkisian. G. Bolis: Dbakr. G-Artskank, 1919.

Badem, Candan. *The Ottoman Crimean War (1853–1856).* Leiden: Brill, 2010.

Bajalan, Djene Rhys. 'Between Accommodationism and Separatism: Kurds, Ottomans and the Politics of Nationality (1839–1914)'. PhD diss., St Antony's College, University of Oxford, 2015.

Banner, Stuart. *How the Indians Lost Their Land: Law and Power on the Frontier.* Cambridge, MA: Belknap Press of Harvard University Press, 2005.

Barakat, Nora Elizabeth. 'An Empty Land? Nomads and Property Administration in Hamidian Syria'. PhD. diss., University of California, Berkeley, 2015.

———. *Bedouin Bureaucrats: Mobility and Property in the Ottoman Empire.* Palo Alto: Stanford University Press, 2023.

Barkan, Ömer Lütfü. *Türkiye'de Toprak Meselesi: Toplu Eserler 1.* Istanbul: Gözlem Yayınları, 1980.

Bayraktar, Uğur. 'Yurtluk-Ocaklıks: Land, Politics of Notables and Society in Ottoman Kurdistan, 1820–1890'. PhD diss., Boğaziçi University and École des Hautes Etudes en Sciences Sociales, 2015.

Bayur, Yusuf Hikmet. *Türk İnkılâbı Tarihi*, vol. 2, no. 3. Ankara: Türk Tarih Kurumu Basımevi, 1991.

Bebiroğlu, Murat. *Osmanlı Devleti'nde Gayrimüslim Nizamnameleri.* Edited by Cahit Külekçi. Istanbul: M. Bebiroğlu, 2008.

———. *Tanzimat'tan II. Meşrutiyet'e Ermeni Nizamnameleri.* Istanbul: M. Bebiroğlu, 2003.

Beinin, Joel. *Workers and Peasants in the Modern Middle East.* Cambridge: Cambridge University Press, 2004.

Ben-Bassat, Yuval. *Petitioning the Sultan: Protests and Justice in Late Ottoman Palestine, 1865–1908.* London: I. B. Tauris, 2013.

Ben-Bassat, Yuval, and Eyal Ginio, eds. *Late Ottoman Palestine: The Period of Young Turk Rule*. London: I. B. Tauris, 2011.

Berberian, Houri. *Roving Revolutionaries: Armenians and the Connected Revolutions in the Russian, Iranian, and Ottoman Worlds*. Oakland: University of California Press, 2019.

Beşiryan, Aylin. 'Hopes of Secularization in the Ottoman Empire: The Armenian National Constitution and the Armenian Newspaper *Masis*, 1856–1863'. Master's thesis, Boğaziçi University, 2007.

Billig, Michael. *Banal Nationalism*. London: Thousand Oaks, 1995.

Bloxham, Donald. 'The Armenian Genocide of 1915–1916: Cumulative Radicalization and the Development of a Destruction Policy'. *Past & Present* 181, no. 1 (November 2003): 141–91.

———. *The Great Game of Genocide: Imperialism, Nationalism, and the Destruction of the Ottoman Armenians*. Oxford: Oxford University Press, 2005.

Blumi, Isa. *Ottoman Refugees, 1878–1939: Migration in a Post-Imperial World*. London: Bloomsbury, 2013.

Branch, Jordan. *The Cartographic State: Maps, Territory, and the Origins of Sovereignty*. Cambridge: Cambridge University Press, 2014.

Breuilly, John. 'Modern Territoriality, the Nation-State, and Nationalism'. In *Spatial Formats under the Global Condition*, edited by Matthias Middell and Steffi Marung, 149–80. Berlin: De Gruyter, 2019.

Bruinessen, Martin van. *Agha, Shaikh and State: The Social and Political Structures of Kurdistan*. London: Zed Books Ltd, 1992.

Bull, Philip. 'Irish Land and British Politics'. In *The Land Question in Britain, 1750–1950*, edited by Matthew Cragoe and Paul Readman, 126–45. London: Palgrave Macmillan, 2010.

Caglioti, Daniela L. 'Property Rights in Time of War: Sequestration and Liquidation of Enemy Aliens' Assets in Western Europe during the First World War'. *Journal of Modern European History / Zeitschrift Für Moderne Europäische Geschichte / Revue d'histoire Européenne Contemporaine* 12, no. 4 (2014): 523–45.

———. 'Waging War on Civilians: The Expulsion of Aliens in the Franco-Prussian War'. *Past & Present* 221, no. 1 (November 2013): 161–95.

Campos, Michelle. *Ottoman Brothers: Muslims, Christians, and Jews in Early Twentieth-Century Palestine*. Palo Alto: Stanford University Press, 2011.

Can, Lâle. *Spiritual Subjects: Central Asian Pilgrims and the Ottoman Hajj at the End of Empire*. Palo Alto: Stanford University Press, 2020.

Can, Lâle, Michael Christopher Low, Kent F. Schull and Robert Zens, eds. *The Subjects of Ottoman International Law*. Bloomington: Indiana University Press, 2020.

Cemal Paşa. *Hatıralar*. Istanbul: Türkiye İş Bankası Kültür Yayınları, 2012.

Chang, David A. *The Color of the Land: Race, Nation, and the Politics of Landownership in Oklahoma, 1832–1929*. Chapel Hill: University of North Carolina Press, 2010.

Bibliography

Chochiev, Georgi, and Bekir Koç. 'Migrants from the North Caucasus in Eastern Anatolia: Some Notes on Their Settlement and Adaptation (Second Half of the 19th Century-Beginning of the 20th Century)'. *Journal of Asian History* 40, no. 1 (2006): 80–103.

Cin, Halil. *Mirî Arazi ve Bu Arazinin Özel Mülkiyete Dönüşümü*. Tarsus: Çağ Üniversitesi, 2005.

Clay, Christopher. 'Labour Migration and Economic Conditions in Nineteenth-Century Anatolia'. *Middle Eastern Studies* 34, no. 4 (1998): 1–32.

Cora, Yaşar Tolga. 'Doğu'da Kürt-Ermeni Çatışmasının Sosyoekonomik Arkaplanı'. In Adanır and Özel, *1915*, 126–39.

———. 'Osmanlı Taşrasındaki Ermeniler Üzerine Olan Tarihyazımında Sınıf Analizinin Eksikliği'. *Praksis* 39, no. 3 (2015): 23–44.

———. 'Transforming Erzurum/Karin: The Social and Economic History of a Multi-Ethnic Ottoman City in the Nineteenth Century'. PhD diss., University of Chicago, 2016.

Cora, Yaşar Tolga, Dzovinar Derderian and Ali Sipahi, eds. 'Introduction: Ottoman Historiography's Black Hole'. In Cora, Derderian and Sipahi, *Ottoman East*, 1–18.

———. *The Ottoman East in the Nineteenth Century: Societies, Identities and Politics*. London: I. B. Tauris, 2016.

Cuthell, David Cameron. 'The Muhacirin Komisyonu: An Agent in the Transformation of Ottoman Anatolia, 1860–1866'. PhD diss., Columbia University, 2005.

Çelik, Semih. 'Scarcity and Misery at the Time of "Abundance beyond Imagination": Climate Change, Famines and Empire-Building in Ottoman Anatolia (c. 1800–1850)'. PhD diss., European University Institute, 2017.

Çetinkaya, Y. Doğan. *1908 Osmanlı Boykotu: Bir Toplumsal Hareketin Analizi*. Istanbul: İletisim, 2004.

———. *Osmanlı'yı Müslümanlaştırmak: Kitle Siyaseti, Toplumsal Sınıflar, Boykotlar ve Milli İktisat: 1909–1914*. Istanbul: İletişim, 2015.

Çift, Salih. 'Bursa'da Bir Mısrî Dergâhı ve Son Postnişîni: Seyyid Baba Tekkesi ve Şeyh Sâbit Efendi'. *Uludağ Üniversitesi İlahiyat Fakültesi* 13, no. 2 (2004): 197–214.

Çiftçi, Erdal. 'Fragile Alliances in the Ottoman East: The Heyderan Tribe and the Empire, 1820–1929'. PhD diss., Bilkent University, 2018.

Çiftçi, Erdal, Veysel Gürhan and Mehmet Rezan Ekinci. *Osmanlı Devleti'nde Yurtluk-Ocaklık ve Hükümet Sancaklar*. Istanbul: Tarih Vakfı Yurt Yayınları, 2022.

Dadrian, Vahakn N. *The History of the Armenian Genocide: Ethnic Conflict from the Balkans to Anatolia to the Caucasus*. Providence: Berghahn Books, 1995.

———. *Warrant for Genocide: Key Elements of Turko-Armenian Conflict*. New Brunswick, NJ: Transaction, 2006.

Davison, Roderic H. *Reform in the Ottoman Empire, 1856–1876*. New York: Gordian Press, 1973.

———. 'The Armenian Crisis, 1912–1914'. *The American Historical Review* 53, no. 3 (1948): 481–505.
Derderian, Dzovinar. 'Mapping the Fatherland: Artzvi Vaspurakan's Reforms through the Memory of the Past'. *Houshamadyan* (16 December 2014). http://www.houshamadyan.org/en/mapottomanempire/vilayet-of-van/kaza-of-van/miscellaneous-scholarly-articles.html.
———. 'Nation-Making and the Language of Colonialism: Voices from Ottoman Van in Armenian Print Media and Handwritten Petitions (1820s to 1870s)'. PhD diss., University of Michigan, Ann Arbor, 2019.
———. 'Shaping Subjectivities and Contesting Power through the Image of Kurds, 1860s'. In Cora, Derderian and Sipahi, *Ottoman East*, 91–108.
Deringil, Selim. *Conversion and Apostasy in the Late Ottoman Empire*. Cambridge: Cambridge University Press, 2012.
———. 'From Ottoman to Turk: Self-image and Social Engineering in Turkey'. In *The Ottomans, the Turks and World Power Politics: Collected Studies*, Istanbul: The Isis Press, 2000.
———. '"The Armenian Question Is Finally Closed": Mass Conversions of Armenians in Anatolia during the Hamidian Massacres of 1895–1897'. *Comparative Studies in Society and History* 51, no. 2 (2009): 344–71.
———. *The Well-Protected Domains: Ideology and the Legitimation of Power in the Ottoman Empire, 1876–1909*. London: I. B. Tauris, 1998.
Devereux, Robert. *The First Ottoman Constitutional Period: A Study of the Midhat Constitution and Parliament*. Baltimore: The Johns Hopkins Press, 1963.
Dinçer, Sinan. 'Osmanlı'dan Dışarıya Ermeni Göçü ve Tabiiyyet Politikaları'. In Adanır and Özel, *1915*, 210–28.
———. '"Ya Sev Ya Terket"in Ermenicesi: Osmanlı Devletinde Tabiiyet ve Sınırdışı Uygulamalarından bir Fasıl'. In *Sınır ve Sınırdışı: Türkiye'de Yabancılar, Göç ve Devlete Disiplinlerarası Bakışlar*, edited by Didem Danış and İbrahim Soysüren, 322–54. Istanbul: Notabene Publications, 2014.
Dooley, Terence. 'Land and the People'. In *The Oxford Handbook of Modern Irish History*, edited by Alvin Jackson, 106–25. Oxford University Press, 2014.
Duguid, Stephen. 'Centralization and Localism, Aspects of Ottoman Policy in Eastern Anatolia, 1878–1908'. Master's thesis, Simon Fraser University, 1970.
———. 'The Politics of Unity: Hamidian Policy in Eastern Anatolia'. *Middle Eastern Studies* 9, no. 2 (1973): 139–55.
Duman, Gülseren. 'Reformları Müzakere Etmek: 19. Yüzyıl Muş Sancağı'nda Eski Elitler, Yeni Düzen'. In *Osmanlı Devleti'nde Yurtluk-Ocaklık ve Hükümet Sancaklar*, edited by Erdal Çiftçi, Veysel Gürhan and Mehmet Rezan Ekinci, 353–76. Istanbul: Tarih Vakfı Yurt Yayınları, 2022.
———. 'The Formations of the Kurdish Movement(s), 1908–1914: Exploring the Footprints of Kurdish Nationalism'. Master's thesis, Boğaziçi University, 2010.
Dussen, W. J. van der. 'The Question of Armenian Reforms in 1913–1914'. *Armenian Review* 39, no. 1 (1986): 11–28.

Bibliography

Dündar, Fuat. *Crime of Numbers: The Role of Statistics in the Armenian Question (1878–1918)*. New Brunswick, NJ: Transaction, 2010.

——. *İttihat ve Terakki'nin Müslümanları İskân Politikası (1913–1918)*. 3rd ed. Istanbul: İletişim Yayınları, 2002.

——. *Kahir Ekseriyet: Ermeni Nüfus Meselesi (1878–1923)*. Istanbul: Tarih Vakfı Yurt Yayınları, 2013.

——. *Modern Türkiye'nin Şifresi: İttihat ve Terakki'nin Etnisite Mühendisliği: (1913–1918)*. İstanbul: İletişim, 2008.

Eddie, Scott M. 'The Prussian Settlement Commission and Its Activities in the Land Market, 1886–1918'. In *Germans, Poland, and Colonial Expansion to the East: 1850 through the Present*, edited by Robert L. Nelson, 39–63. New York: Palgrave Macmillan US, 2009.

Eldem, Edhem. '26 Ağustos 1896 "Banka Vakası" ve 1896 "Ermeni Olayları"'. *Tarih ve Toplum: Yeni Yaklaşımlar* 5 (2007): 113–46.

Eldem, Vedat. *Osmanlı İmparatorluğu'nun İktisadi Şartları Hakkında Bir Tetkik*. Ankara: Türk Tarih Kurumu Basımevi, 1994.

Engerman, Stanley L., and Jacob Metzer, eds. *Land Rights, Ethno-Nationality, and Sovereignty in History*. London: Routledge, 2004.

Enh, Azlizan Mat. 'The Phantom of Bosnia-Herzegovina Revolt, 1875–1878'. *Journal of International Studies* 4 (2008): 91–101.

Eppel, Michael. 'The Demise of the Kurdish Emirates: The Impact of Ottoman Reforms and International Relations on Kurdistan during the First Half of the Nineteenth Century'. *Middle Eastern Studies* 44, no. 2 (2008): 237–58.

Erol, Emre. *The Ottoman Crisis in Western Anatolia: Turkey's Belle Epoque and the Transition to a Modern Nation State*. London: I. B. Tauris, 2016.

Ertem, Özge. 'British Views on the Indian and Ottoman Famines: Politics, Culture, and Morality'. *RCC Perspectives* 2 (2015): 17–27.

——. 'Sick Men of Asia Minor in an Ailing Empire: Famine, Villagers and Government in Missionary Accounts (1873–75)'. *International Review of Turkish Studies* 2, no. 1 (2012): 72–94.

Etmekjian, James. 'The Tanzimat Reforms and Their Effect on the Armenians in Turkey'. *The Armenian Review* 25, no. 1 (Spring 1972): 10–23.

Etmekjian, Lillian. 'The Armenian National Assembly of Turkey and Reform'. *Armenian Review* 29, no. 1 (1976): 38–52.

Farhi, David. 'The Şeriat as a Political Slogan: Or the "Incident of the 31st Mart"'. *Middle Eastern Studies* 7, no. 3 (1971): 275–99.

Fisher, Alan W. 'Emigration of Muslims from the Russian Empire in the Years after the Crimean War'. *Jahrbücher für Geschichte Osteuropas* 35, no. 3 (1987): 356–71.

Fishman, Louis A. *Jews and Palestinians in the Late Ottoman Era, 1908–1914: Claiming the Homeland*. Edinburgh: Edinburgh University Press, 2020.

Fortna, Benjamin C. 'Change in the School Maps of the Late Ottoman Empire'. *Imago Mundi* 57, no: 1 (2005): 23–34.

———. 'Sovereignty in the Ottoman Empire and After'. In *Sovereignty after Empire: Comparing the Middle East and Central Asia*, edited by Sally N. Cummings and Raymond Hinnebusch, 92–103. Edinburg: Edinburgh University Press, 2011.

Fratantuono, Ella. 'Producing Ottomans: Internal Colonization and Social Engineering in Ottoman Immigrant Settlement'. *Journal of Genocide Research* 21, no. 1 (2 January 2019): 1–24.

Frymer, Paul. '"A Rush and a Push and the Land Is Ours": Territorial Expansion, Land Policy, and US State Formation'. *Perspectives on Politics* 12, no. 1 (March 2014): 119–44.

Fuchs, Christian. 'Critical Globalization Studies: An Empirical and Theoretical Analysis of the New Imperialism'. *Science and Society* 74, no. 2 (2010): 215–47.

Gellner, Ernest. *Nations and Nationalism*. Oxford: Blackwell Publishers, 1983.

Gerber, Haim. *The Social Origins of the Modern Middle East*. Boulder: Lynne Rienner, 1987.

Gerlach, Christian. *Extremely Violent Societies: Mass Violence in the Twentieth-Century World*. Cambridge: Cambridge University Press, 2010.

Georgeon, François. *Sultan Abdülhamid*. Translated by Ali Berktay. Istanbul: Homer Kitabevi, 2006.

Ghazarian, Matthew. 'Ghost Rations: Empire, Ecology, and Community in the Ottoman East, 1839–94'. PhD diss., Columbia University, 2020.

Göçek, Fatma Müge. *Denial of Violence: Ottoman Past, Turkish Present, and Collective Violence against the Armenians, 1789–2009*. Oxford: Oxford University Press, 2015.

Gölbaşı, Edip. '1895–1896 Katliamları: Doğu Vilayetlerinde Cemaatler Arası "Şiddet İklimi" ve Ermeni Karşıtı Ayaklanmalar'. In Adanır and Özel, *1915*, 140–63.

———. 'Hamidiye Alayları: Bir Değerlendirme'. In Adanır and Özel, *1915*, 164–75.

———. 'The Anti-Armenian Riots of 1895–1897: The "Climate of Violence" and Intercommunal Conflict in Istanbul and the Eastern Anatolian Provinces of the Ottoman Empire'. PhD diss., Simon Fraser University, 2018.

Gözel, Oya. *A City Transformed: Great War, Deportation and Socio-Economic Change in Kayseri (1915–1920)*. Istanbul: Libra, 2019.

———. 'The Implementation of the Ottoman Land Code of 1858 in Eastern Anatolia'. Master's thesis, Middle East Technical University, 2007.

Gratien, Chris. *The Unsettled Plain: An Environmental History of the Late Ottoman Frontier*. Palo Alto: Stanford University Press, 2022.

Gutman, David. 'The Political Economy of Armenian Migration from the Harput Region to North America in the Hamidian Era, 1885–1908'. In Cora, Derderian and Sipahi, *Ottoman East*, 42–61.

———. *The Politics of Armenian Migration to North America, 1885–1915: Migrants, Smugglers and Dubious Citizens*. Edinburgh: Edinburgh University Press, 2019.

Bibliography

Güran, Tevfik. *19. Yüzyıl Osmanlı Tarımı*. Istanbul: Eren Yayınları, 1998.

Gürsel, Zeynep Devrim. 'Looking Together as Method: Encounters with Ottoman Armenian Expatriation Photographs'. *Visual Anthropology Review* 39, no. 1 (March 2023): 200–29.

Halaçoğlu, Ahmet. *Balkan Harbi Sırasında Rumeli'den Türk Göçleri (1912–1913)*. Ankara: Türk Tarih Kurumu Basımevi, 1994.

Hamed-Troyansky, Vladimir. *Empire of Refugees: North Caucasian Muslims and the Late Ottoman State*. Palo Alto: Stanford University Press, 2024.

——. 'Imperial Refuge: Resettlement of Muslims from Russia in the Ottoman Empire, 1860–1914'. PhD diss., Stanford University, 2018.

Hamparyan, A. S. *Akrarayin Haraperut'yunnerĕ Arevm'dyan Hayasdanum*. Yerewan: Haygagan Soṛ Kidut'yunneri Agatemiayi Hradaragch'ut'yun, 1965.

Hanioğlu, M. Şükrü. *A Brief History of the Late Ottoman Empire*. Princeton: Princeton University Press, 2008.

——. *Preparation for a Revolution: The Young Turks, 1902–1908*. Oxford: Oxford University Press, 2001.

——. *The Young Turks in Opposition*. Oxford: Oxford University Press, 1995.

Hanley, Will. 'What Ottoman Nationality Was and Was Not'. In Can, Low, Schull and Zens, *The Subjects of Ottoman International Law*, 55–75.

Harootunian, Harry D. *The Unspoken as Heritage: The Armenian Genocide and Its Unaccounted Lives*. Durham: Duke University Press, 2019.

Havemann, Axel. 'The Impact of Peasant Resistance on Nineteenth-Century Mount Lebanon'. In Kazemi and Waterbury, *Peasants and Politics*, 85–100.

Hayreni, Hovsep. *Yukarı Fırat Ermenileri 1915 ve Dersim*. Istanbul: Belge, 2015.

Healy, Róisín. 'From Commonwealth to Colony? Poland under Prussia'. In *The Shadow of Colonialism on Europe's Modern Past*, edited by Róisín Healy and Enrico Dal Lago, 109–25. London: Palgrave Macmillan, 2014.

Hobsbawm, Eric J. *The Age of Empire, 1875–1914*. New York: Vintage Books. 1989.

——. 'Mass-Producing Traditions: Europe, 1870–1914'. In *The Invention of Tradition*, edited by Eric Hobsbawm and Terence Ranger, 263–307. Cambridge: Cambridge University Press, 1992.

——. *Nations and Nationalism since 1780: Programme, Myth, Reality*. 2nd ed. Cambridge: Cambridge University Press, 2012.

Hourani, Albert. 'Ottoman Reform and the Politics of Notables'. In *The Emergence of the Modern Middle East*, 36–66. Berkeley: University of California Press, 1981.

Hovannisian, Richard G. 'The Armenian Question in the Ottoman Empire, 1876–1914'. In *The Armenian People from Ancient to Modern Times, vol. II: Foreign Dominion to Statehood: The Fifteenth Century to the Twentieth Century*, 203–38. New York: St Martin's Press, 2004.

Issawi, Charles, ed. *The Economic History of Turkey, 1800–1914*. Chicago: University of Chicago Press, 1980.

İnal, Onur. 'A Port and Its Hinterland: An Environmental History of Izmir in the Late Ottoman Period'. PhD diss., University of Arizona, 2015.

İnalcık, Halil. 'Filāha'. In *Encyclopaedia of Islam, Second Edition*, edited by P. Bearman, Th. Bianquis, C. E. Bosworth, E. van Donzel and W. P. Heinrichs. http://dx.doi.org/10.1163/1573-3912_islam_COM_0222.

——. 'Land Problems in Turkish History'. *The Muslim World* 45, no. 3 (July 1955): 221–28.

——. *Tanzimat ve Bulgar Meselesi (Doktora Tezi'nin 50. Yılı), 1942–1992*. Istanbul: Eren, 1992.

——. 'Tanzimat'ın Uygulanması ve Sosyal Tepkileri'. *Belleten* 27 (1964): 624–90.

——. 'The Emergence of Big Farms, *Çiftlik*s: State, Landlords, and Tenants'. In Keyder and Tabak, *Landholding*, 17–34.

——. 'The Socio-Political Effects of the Diffusion of Fire-Arms in the Middle East'. In *War, Technology and Society in the Middle East*, edited by V. J. Parry and M. E. Yapp, 195–217. London: Oxford University Press, 1975.

İnce, Onur Ulaş. 'Between Equal Rights: Primitive Accumulation and Capital's Violence'. *Political Theory* 46, no. 6 (December 2018): 885–914.

İpek, Nedim. *Rumeli'den Anadolu'ya Türk Göçleri (1877–1890)*. Ankara: Türk Tarih Kurumu Basımevi, 1994.

İslamoğlu, Huri. 'Politics of Administering Property: Law and Statistics in the Nineteenth-Century Ottoman Empire'. In *Constituting Modernity: Private Property in the East and West*, 276–319. London: I. B. Tauris, 2004.

——. 'Property as a Contested Domain: A Reevaluation of the Ottoman Land Code of 1858'. In *New Perspectives on Property and Land in the Middle East*, edited by Roger Owen, 3–62. Cambridge, MA: Harvard University Press, 2000.

İslamoğlu-İnan, Huri. 'Peasants, Commercialization, and Legitimation of State Power in Sixteenth-Century Anatolia'. In Keyder and Tabak, *Landholding*, 57–76.

Işık, Ayhan. 'Kurdish and Armenian Relations in the Ottoman-Kurdish Press'. Master's thesis, Bilgi University, 2014.

Jelavich, Barbara. *History of the Balkans: Eighteenth and Nineteenth Centuries*, vol. 1. Cambridge: Cambridge University Press, 1983.

Jwaideh, Wadie. *The Kurdish National Movement: Its Origins and Development*. Syracuse: Syracuse University Press, 2006.

Kadercan, Burak. *Shifting Grounds: The Social Origins of Territorial Conflict*. New York: Oxford University Press, 2023.

Kaiser, Hilmar. 'Tahsin Uzer: The CUP's Man in the East'. In Kieser et al., *The End of the Ottomans*, 93–118.

——. *The Extermination of Armenians in the Diyarbekir Region*. Istanbul: Istanbul Bilgi University Publications, 2014.

Kale, Başak. 'Transforming an Empire: The Ottoman Empire's Immigration and Settlement Policies in the Nineteenth and Early Twentieth Centuries'. *Middle Eastern Studies* 50, no. 2 (March 2014): 252–71.

Bibliography

Kaligian, Dikran. 'Agrarian Land Reform and the Armenians in the Ottoman Empire'. *Armenian Review* 48, no. 3–4 (2003): 22–45.

——. *Armenian Organization and Ideology under Ottoman Rule, 1908–1914*. London: Transaction, 2009.

Kaloosdian, Robert Aram. *Tadem, My Father's Village: Extinguished during the 1915 Armenian Genocide*. Portsmouth: Peter E. Randall, 2015.

Kansu, Aykut. *1908 Devrimi*. Istanbul: İletişim, 1995.

Karamustafa, Ahmet T. 'Introduction to Islamic Maps'. In *The History of Cartography, volume 2, book 1: Cartography in the Traditional Islamic and South Asian Societies*, edited by J. B. Harley and David Woodward, 3–11. Chicago: University of Chicago Press, 1992.

Karaömerlioğlu, M. Asım. 'Alexander Helphand-Parvus and His Impact on Turkish Intellectual Life'. *Middle Eastern Studies* 40, no. 6 (November 2004): 145–65.

Karekin Vartabed Sırvantsdyants. 'Toros Ahpar Ermenistan Yolcusu'. In *Palu-Harput 1878: Çarsancak, Çemişgezek, Çapakçur, Erzincan, Hizan ve Civar Bölgeler*, edited by Arsen Yarman, translated by Sirvart Malhasyan and Arsen Yarman, 470–87. Istanbul: Derlem Yayınları, 2010.

Karpat, Kemal. *Ottoman Population, 1830–1914: Demographic and Social Characteristics*. Madison: University of Wisconsin Press, 1985.

——. 'Ottoman Population Records and the Census of 1881/82–1893'. *International Journal of Middle East Studies* 9, no. 3 (October 1978): 237–74.

——. 'The Land Regime, Social Structure, and Modernization in the Ottoman Empire'. In *Beginnings of Modernization in the Middle East: The Nineteenth Century*, edited by William R. Polk and Richard L. Chambers, 69–93. Chicago: The University of Chicago Press, 1968.

——. 'The Status of the Muslim under European Rule: The Eviction and Settlement of Cerkes'. *Institute of Muslim Minority Affairs Journal* 1, no. 2 (1979): 7–27.

Kasaba, Reşat. *A Moveable Empire: Ottoman Nomads, Migrants, and Refugees*. Seattle: University of Washington Press, 2009.

——. *The Ottoman Empire and the World Economy: The Nineteenth Century*. Albany: State University of New York Press, 1988.

Kasaba, Reşat, Immanuel Wallerstein and Hale Decdeli. 'The Incorporation of the Ottoman Empire into the World-Economy'. In *The Ottoman Empire and the World-Economy*, edited by Huri İslamoglu-İnan, 88–97. Cambridge: Cambridge University Press, 1987.

Kaya, Alp Yücel, and Yücel Terzibaşoğlu. 'Tahrir'den Kadastro'ya: 1874 Istanbul Emlak Tahriri ve Vergisi: "Kadastro Tabir Olunur Tahrir-i Emlak"'. *Tarih ve Toplum Yeni Yaklaşımlar* 9 (2009): 9–58.

Kayalı, Hasan. *Arabs and Young Turks: Ottomanism, Arabism, and Islamism in the Ottoman Empire, 1908–1918*. Berkeley: California University Press, 1997.

Kazemi, Farhad, and John Waterbury, eds. *Peasants and Politics in the Modern Middle East*. Miami: Florida International University Press, 1991.

Kévorkian, Raymond. *The Armenian Genocide: A Complete History*. London: I. B. Tauris, 2011.

———. 'The Property Law and the Spoliation of Ottoman Armenians'. In *Documenting the Armenian Genocide: Essays in Honor of Taner Akçam*, edited by Thomas Kühne, Mary Jane Rein and Marc A. Mamigonian, 159–85. Cham: Palgrave Macmillan, 2024.

Keyder, Çağlar. *State and Class in Turkey: A Study in Capitalist Development*. London: Verso, 1987.

Keyder, Çağlar, and Şevket Pamuk. '1945 Çiftçiyi Topraklandırma Kanunu Üzerine Tezler'. *Yapıt* 8 (December/January 1984–85): 52–63.

Keyder, Çağlar, and Faruk Tabak, eds. *Landholding and Commercial Agriculture in the Middle East*. New York: State University of New York Press, 1991.

Khoury, Dina Rizk. *State and Provincial Society in the Ottoman Empire: Mosul, 1540–1834*. Cambridge: Cambridge University Press, 1997.

———. 'The Introduction of Commercial Agriculture in the Province of Mosul and its Effects on the Peasantry, 1750–1850'. In Keyder and Tabak, *Landholding*, 155–71.

———. 'The Ottoman Centre versus Provincial Power-Holders: An Analysis of the Historiography'. In *The Cambridge History of Turkey, vol. 3: The Later Ottoman Empire, 1603–1839*, edited by Suraiya N. Faroqhi, 135–56. Cambridge: Cambridge University Press, 2006.

Kılıçdağı, Ohannes. 'Ermeni Aydınlanması: Yeniden Doğuştan Yokoluşa'. In Adanır and Özel, *1915*, 44–61.

———. 'Socio-Political Reflections and Expectations of the Ottoman Armenians after the 1908 Revolution: Between Hope and Despair'. PhD diss., Boğaziçi University, 2014.

Kıran, İsmail. 'Aristokrat Kürt Aileler: Arvasiler'. *Kurdiyat* 3 (2021): 119–44.

Kırlı, Cengiz. 'Tyranny Illustrated: From Petition to Rebellion in Ottoman Vranje'. *New Perspectives on Turkey* 53 (November 2015): 3–36.

Kieser, Hans-Lukas. *Iskalanmış Barış: Doğu Vilayetleri'nde Misyonerlik, Etnik Kimlik ve Devlet, 1839–1938*. Translated by Atilla Dirim. Istanbul: İletişim, 2005.

———. *Talaat Pasha: Father of Modern Turkey, Architect of Genocide*. Princeton: Princeton University Press, 2018.

Kieser, Hans-Lukas, Margaret Lavinia Anderson, Seyhan Bayraktar and Thomas Schmutz, eds. *The End of the Ottomans: The Genocide of 1915 and the Politics of Turkish Nationalism*. London: I. B. Tauris, 2019.

Kieser, Hans-Lukas, Mehmet Polatel and Thomas Schmutz. 'Reform or Cataclysm? The Agreement of 8 February 1914 Regarding the Ottoman Eastern Provinces'. *Journal of Genocide Research* 17, no. 3 (2015): 285–304.

Kirakossian, Arman J. *British Diplomacy and the Armenian Question*. London: Gomidas Institute Books, 2003.

Klein, Janet. 'Kurdish Nationalists and Non-nationalist Kurdists: Rethinking Minority Nationalism and the Dissolution of the Ottoman Empire, 1908–1909'. *Nations and Nationalism* 13, no. 1 (January 2007): 135–53.

Bibliography

———. 'The Kurds and the Territorialization of Minorityhood'. *Journal of Contemporary Iraq and the Arab World* 14, no. 1 (1 June 2020): 13–30.

———. *The Margins of Empire: Kurdish Militias in the Ottoman Tribal Zone*. Palo Alto: Stanford University Press, 2011.

Koç, Yener. 'Bedirxan Pashazades: Power Relations and Nationalism (1876–1914)'. Master's thesis, Boğaziçi University, 2012.

———. 'Celali Aşireti: Üç İmparatorluğun Sınırında'. In *Kürt Aşiretleri: Aktör, Müttefik, Şakî*, edited by Tuncay Şur and Yalçın Çakmak, 299–316. Istanbul: İletişim, 2022.

Koptaş, Rober. 'Sunuş: Fırtınadan Önce Bir Son Çırpınış'. In Zohrab, *Belgeler Işığında*, 7–41.

———. 'Zohrap, Papazyan ve Pastırmacıyan'ın Kalemlerinden 1914 Ermeni Reformu ve İttihatçı- Taşnak Müzakereleri'. *Tarih ve Toplum: Yeni Yaklaşımlar* 5 (2007): 159–78.

Köksal, Yonca. 'Coercion and Mediation: Centralization and Sedentarization of Tribes in the Ottoman Empire'. *Middle Eastern Studies* 42, no. 3 (2006): 469–91.

———. '19. Yüzyılda Kuzeybatı Bulgaristan: Sessiz Toprak Reformu'. *Toplumsal Tarih* 170 (February 2008): 24–30.

Köksal, Yonca, and Mehmet Polatel. 'A Tribe as an Economic Actor: The Cihanbeyli Tribe and the Meat Provisioning of İstanbul in the Early Tanzimat Era'. *New Perspectives on Turkey* 61 (November 2019): 97–123.

Kurkjian, Vahan M. *A History of Armenia*. New York: Armenian General Benevolent Union New York, 1958.

Kurt, Burcu. 'II. Meşrutiyet Döneminde Basra Vilayeti (1908–1914)'. PhD diss., Marmara University, 2012.

Kurt, Ümit. 'Reform and Violence in the Hamidian Era: The Political Context of the 1895 Armenian Massacres in Aintab'. *Holocaust and Genocide Studies* 32, no. 3 (December 2018): 404–23.

———. *The Armenians of Aintab: The Economics of Genocide in an Ottoman Province*. Cambridge, MA: Harvard University Press, 2021.

Kurt, Ümit, and Doğan Gürpınar. 'The Balkan Wars and the Rise of the Reactionary Modernist Utopia in Young Turk Thought and the Journal *Türk Yurdu* [*Turkish Homeland*]'. *Nations and Nationalism* 21, no. 2 (April 2015): 348–68.

Kutlay, Naci. *İttihat Terakki ve Kürtler*. Ankara: Beybun Yayınları, 1992.

Léart, Marcel (Krikor Zohrab). *Belgelerin Işığında Ermeni Meselesi*. Translated by Renan Akman. Istanbul: İletişim Yayınları, 2015.

Léart, Marcel, *La Question Arménienne à la lumière des documents*. Paris: A. Challamel, 1913.

Levene, Mark. 'Creating a Modern "Zone of Genocide": The Impact of Nation- and State-Formation on Eastern Anatolia, 1878–1923'. *Holocaust and Genocide Studies* 12, no. 3 (January 1998): 393–433.

Li, Andy Hanlun. 'From Alien Land to Inalienable Parts of China: How Qing Imperial Possessions Became the Chinese Frontiers'. *European Journal of International Relations* 28, no. 2 (June 2022): 237–62.

Libaridian, Gerard. *Modern Armenia: People, Nation, State*. New Brunswick, NJ: Transaction, 2011.

——. 'The Ideology of Armenian Liberation. The Development of Armenian Political Thought Before the Revolutionary Movement (1639–1885)'. PhD diss., University of California, 1987.

——. 'What was Revolutionary about Armenian Revolutionary Parties in the Ottoman Empire'. In Suny, Göçek and Naimark, *Question of Genocide*, 82–112.

Low, Michael Christopher. *Imperial Mecca: Ottoman Arabia and the Indian Ocean Hajj*. New York: Columbia University Press, 2020.

MacPherson, Crawford B., ed. *Property: Mainstream and Critical Positions*. Oxford: Blackwell, 1978.

Maier, Charles S. 'Consigning the Twentieth Century to History: Alternative Narratives for the Modern Era'. *The American Historical Review* 105, no. 3 (June 2000): 807–31.

——. *Once within Borders: Territories of Power, Wealth, and Belonging since 1500*. Cambridge, MA: The Belknap Press of Harvard University Press, 2016.

Makdisi, Ussama Samir. *The Culture of Sectarianism: Community, History, and Violence in Nineteenth-Century Ottoman Lebanon*. Berkeley: University of California Press, 2000.

Mandel, Neville J. 'Ottoman Policy and Restrictions on Jewish Settlement in Palestine, 1881–1908: Part I'. *Middle Eastern Studies* 10, no. 3 (October 1974): 312–32.

Mann, Michael. *The Dark Side of Democracy: Explaining Ethnic Cleansing*. Cambridge: Cambridge University Press, 2005.

Mardin, Şerif. *Jön Türklerin Siyasi Fikirleri, 1895–1908*, 15th edition. Istanbul: İletişim Yayınları, 2008.

Marx, Karl. *Capital: A Critique of Political Economy*. Reprinted in Penguin Classics. London: Penguin, 1992.

Matossian, Bedross Der. *Shattered Dreams of Revolution: From Liberty to Violence in the Late Ottoman Empire*. Palo Alto: Stanford University Press, 2014.

——. *The Horrors of Adana: Revolution and Violence in the Early Twentieth Century*. Palo Alto: Stanford University Press, 2022.

——. 'The Ottoman Massacres of Armenians, 1894–1896 and 1909'. In *Cambridge World History of Genocide*, edited by Ned Backhawk, Ben Kiernan, Benjamin Madley and Rebe Taylor, vol. 2:609–33. Cambridge: Cambridge University Press, 2023.

——. 'The Taboo within the Taboo: The Fate of "Armenian Capital" at the End of the Ottoman Empire'. *European Journal of Turkish Studies*, 6 October 2011. https://doi.org/10.4000/ejts.4411.

——, ed. *The Armenian Social Democrat Hunchakian Party: Politics, Ideology and Transnational History*. London: I. B. Tauris, 2023.

Bibliography

McDowall, David. *A Modern History of the Kurds*. London: I. B. Tauris, 2004.

McGowan, Bruce. 'The Age of the *Ayan*s, 1699–1812'. In *An Economic and Social History of the Ottoman Empire, vol. 2: 1600–1914*, edited by Suraiya Faroqhi, Bruce McGowan, Donal Quataert and Şevket Pamuk, 639–758. Cambridge: Cambridge University Press, 1997.

Menteşe, Halil. *Osmanlı Mebusan Meclisi Reisi Halil Menteşe'nin Anıları*. Edited by İsmail Arar. Istanbul: Hürriyet Vakfı Yayınları, 1986.

Metzer, Jacob. 'Jewish Land – Israel Lands: Ethno-Nationality and Land Regime in Zionism and in Israel, 1897–1967'. In Engerman and Metzer, *Land Rights*, 87–110.

Metzer, Jacob, and Stanley L. Engerman. 'Some Considerations of Ethno-Nationality (and Other Distinctions), Property Rights in Land, and Territorial Sovereignty'. In Engerman and Metzer, *Land Rights*, 7–28.

Miller, Donald E., and Lorna T. Miller. *Survivors: An Oral History of the Armenian Genocide*. Berkeley: University of California Press, 1999.

Miller, Owen. 'Sasun 1894: Mountains, Missionaries and Massacres at the End of the Ottoman Empire'. PhD diss. Columbia University, 2015.

Minassian, Anaide Ter. *Ermeni Devrimci Hareketi'nde Milliyetçilik ve Sosyalizm (1887–1912)*. Translated by Mete Tunçay. Istanbul: İletişim, 2012.

Minassian, Gaidz F. 'Birinci Dünya Savaşı Öncesinde İttihat ve Terakki Cemiyeti ile Ermeni Devrimci Federasyonu Arasındaki İlişkiler'. In Avagyan and Minassian, *Ermeniler ve İttihat Terakki*, 145–208.

Mirkova, Anna M. *Muslim Land, Christian Labor: Transforming Ottoman Imperial Subjects into Bulgarian National Citizens, 1878–1939*. Budapest: Central European University Press, 2017.

———. '"Population Politics" at the End of Empire: Migration and Sovereignty in Ottoman Eastern Rumelia, 1877–1886'. *Comparative Studies in Society and History* 55, no. 4 (2013): 955–85.

Morack, Ellinor. *The Dowry of the State? The Politics of Abandoned Property and the Population Exchange in Turkey, 1921–1945*. Bamberg: University of Bamberg Press, 2017.

Moses, A. Dirk. *The Problems of Genocide: Permanent Security and the Language of Transgression*. Cambridge: Cambridge University Press, 2021.

Mouradian, Khatchig. *The Resistance Network: The Armenian Genocide and Humanitarianism in Ottoman Syria, 1915–1918*. East Lansing: Michigan State University Press, 2021.

Mundy, Martha. 'The State of Property: Late Ottoman Syria, the Kaza of 'Ajlun (1875–1918)'. In *Constituting Modernity: Private Property in the East and West*, edited by Huri İslamoğlu, 214–47. London: I. B. Tauris, 2004.

———. 'Village Authority and the Legal Order of Property (The Southern Hawran 1876–1922)'. In *New Perspectives on Property and Land in the Middle East*, edited by Roger Owen, 63–92. Cambridge: Harvard University Press, 2000.

Mundy, Martha, and Richard Saumarez Smith. *Governing Property, Making the Modern State: Law, Administration and Production in Ottoman Syria*. London: I. B. Tauris, 2007.

Nalbandian, Louise. *The Armenian Revolutionary Movement: The Development of Armenian Political Parties through the Nineteenth Century*. Berkeley: University of California Press, 1967.

Nichols, Robert. *Theft Is Property! Dispossession and Critical Theory*. Durham: Duke University Press, 2020.

Nizri, Michael. 'Defining Village Boundaries at the Time of the Introduction of the *Malikane* System: The Struggle of the Ottoman State for Reaffirming Ownership of the Land'. *Journal of the Ottoman and Turkish Studies Association* 2, no. 1 (2015): 37–57.

MacQueen, Norrie. *Colonialism*. London: Pearson, 2007.

Minawi, Mostafa. *The Ottoman Scramble for Africa: Empire and Diplomacy in the Sahara and the Hijaz*. Palo Alto: Stanford University Press, 2016.

Olson, Robert. *The Emergence of Kurdish Nationalism and the Sheikh Said Rebellion, 1880–1925*. Austin: University of Texas Press, 1989.

Onaran, Nevzat. *Osmanlı'da Ermeni ve Rum Mallarının Türkleştirilmesi (1914–1919)*. Istanbul: Evrensel Basım Yayın, 2013.

Ortaylı, İlber. *İmparatorluğun En Uzun Yüzyılı*. Istanbul: Hil Yayın, 1983.

Owen, Roger. 'The 1838 Anglo-Turkish Convention: An Overview'. *New Perspectives on Turkey* 7 (1992): 7–14.

Ozavcı, Ozan. *Dangerous Gifts: Imperialism, Security, and Civil Wars in the Levant, 1798–1864*. Oxford: Oxford University Press, 2021.

——. 'Honour and Shame: The Diaries of a Unionist and the "Armenian Question"'. In Kieser et al., *The End of the Ottomans*, 193–220.

Özbek, Nadir. *İmparatorluğun Bedeli: Osmanlı'da Vergi, Siyaset ve Toplumsal Adalet (1839–1908)*. Istanbul: Boğaziçi University Publications, 2015.

——. 'The Politics of Taxation and the "Armenian Question" during the Late Ottoman Empire, 1876–1908'. *Comparative Studies in Society and History* 54, no. 4 (2012): 770–97.

Özdemir, Hazal. 'Osmanlı Ermenilerinin Göçünün Fotoğrafını Çekmek: Terk-i Tâbiiyet ve Pasaport Politikaları'. *Toplumsal Tarih* 304 (April 2019): 82–90.

Özkan, Fulya. 'A Road in Rebellion, a History on the Move: The Social History of the Trabzon-Bayezıd Road and the Formation of the Modern State in the Late Ottoman World'. PhD diss., Binghamton University, 2012.

Özoğlu, Hakan. *Kurdish Notables and the Ottoman State: Evolving Identities, Competing Loyalties, and Shifting Boundaries*. Albany: State University of New York Press, 2004.

Özok-Gündoğan, Nilay. 'A "Peripheral" Approach to the 1908 Revolution in the Ottoman Empire: Land Disputes in Peasant Petitions in Post-Revolutionary Diyarbekir'. In *Social Relations in Ottoman Diyarbekir, 1870–1915*, edited by Joost Jongerden and Jelle Verheij, 179–215. Leiden: Brill, 2012.

Bibliography

———. *The Kurdish Nobility in the Ottoman Empire: Loyalty, Autonomy and Privilege*. Edinburgh: Edinburgh University Press, 2022.

———. 'The Making of the Modern Ottoman State in the Kurdish Periphery: The Politics of Land and Taxation, 1840–1870'. PhD diss., Binghamton University, 2011.

Özyüksel, Murat. *The Berlin-Baghdad Railway and the Ottoman Empire: Industrialization, Imperial Germany and the Middle East*. London: I. B. Tauris, 2016.

Pamuk, Şevket. 'Agriculture and Economic Development in Turkey, 1870–2000'. In *Agriculture and Economic Development in Europe since 1870*, edited by P. Lains and V. Pinilla, 375–96. London: Routledge Publishers, 2008.

———. *Osmanlı'dan Cumhuriyet'e Küreselleşme, İktisat Politikaları ve Büyüme: Seçme Eserleri II*. Istanbul: İş Bankası Yayınları, 2008.

———. *The Ottoman Empire and European Capitalism, 1820–1913: Trade, Investment, and Production*. Cambridge: Cambridge University Press, 2010.

———. *Türkiye'nin 200 Yıllık İktisadi Tarihi: Büyüme, Kurumlar ve Bölüşüm*. Istanbul: Türkiye İş Bankası Yayınları, 2014.

Panossian, Razmik. *The Armenians: From Kings and Priests to Merchants and Commissars*. London: Hurst and Company, 2006.

Papazian, Vahan. *Im Husherĕ*, vol. 2. Beyrut: Hamazkayin Dbaran, 1952.

Pehlivan, Zozan. 'Abandoned Villages in Diyarbekir Province at the End of the "Little Ice Age", 1800–50'. In Cora, Derderian and Sipahi, *Ottoman East*, 223–46.

———. 'Beyond "the Desert and the Sown": Peasants, Pastoralists, and Climate Crises in Ottoman Diyarbekir, 1840–1890'. PhD diss., Queen's University, 2016.

———. 'El Niño and the Nomads: Global Climate, Local Environment, and the Crisis of Pastoralism in Late Ottoman Kurdistan'. *Journal of the Economic and Social History of the Orient* 63, no. 3 (April 2020): 316–56.

Philliou, Christine May. *Biography of an Empire: Governing Ottomans in an Age of Revolution*. Berkeley: University of California Press, 2011.

Pinson, Mark. 'Ottoman Bulgaria in the First Tanzimat Period: The Revolts in Nish (1841) and Vidin (1850)'. *Middle Eastern Studies* 11, no. 2 (May 1975): 103–46.

———. 'Russian Policy and the Emigration of the Crimean Tatars to the Ottoman Empire, 1854–1862'. *Güney-Doğu Avrupa Araştırmaları Dergisi* 2–3 (1974): 101–14.

Polanyi, Karl. *The Great Transformation*. Boston: Beacon Press Boston, 1957.

Polatel, Mehmet. 'Köylüler "Senyör"e Karşı: Zomik Köyü Ahalisi ile Haydaranlı Hüseyin Paşa'nın Arazi Davası'. *Kürt Tarihi Dergisi* 47 (April 2022): 22–27.

———. 'The Armenian Massacre of 1895 in Bitlis Town'. *Kurdish Studies* 9, no. 1 (9 May 2021): 59–76.

———. 'The Complete Ruin of a District: The Sasun Massacre of 1894'. In Cora, Derderian and Sipahi, *Ottoman East*, 179–98.

———. 'The State, Local Actors and Mass Violence in Bitlis Province'. In Kieser et al., *The End of the Ottomans*, 119–40.

Quataert, Donald. *Osmanlı İmparatorluğu, 1700–1922*. Istanbul: İletişim Yayınları, 2000.

———. 'Ottoman Reform and Agriculture in Anatolia, 1876–1908'. PhD diss., University of California, 1973.

———. 'The Age of Reforms, 1812–1914'. In *An Economic and Social History of the Ottoman Empire, vol. 2: 1600–1914*, edited by Suraiya Faroqhi, Bruce McGowan, Donald Quataert and Şevket Pamuk, 759–943. Cambridge: Cambridge University Press, 1997.

Rafeq, Abdul-Karim. 'Land Tenure Problems and their Social Impact in Syria around the Middle of the Nineteenth Century'. In *Land Tenure and Social Transformation in the Middle East*, edited by Tarif Khalidi, 371–96. Beirut: American University of Beirut, 1984.

Raffi. *Tajkahayk*. Translated by Ara Stepan Melkonian. London: Taderon Press, 2008.

Reynolds, Michael A. 'Abdürrezzak Bedirhan: Ottoman Kurd and Russophile in the Twilight of Empire'. *Kritika: Explorations in Russian and Eurasian History* 12, no. 2 (2011): 411–50.

———. *Shattering Empires: The Clash and Collapse of the Ottoman and Russian Empires, 1908–1918*. Cambridge: Cambridge University Press, 2011.

Riedler, Florian. 'The City as a Stage for a Violent Spectacle: The Massacres of Armenians in Istanbul in 1895–96'. In *Urban Violence in the Middle East: Changing Cityscapes in the Transformation from Empire to Nation State*, edited by Ulrike Freitag, Nelida Fuccaro, Nora Lafi and Claudia Ghrawi, 164–78. New York: Berghahn Books, 2015.

Robson, Laura. *The Politics of Mass Violence in the Middle East*. Oxford: Oxford University Press, 2020.

Rogan, Eugene L. *Frontiers of the State in the Late Ottoman Empire: Transjordan, 1850–1921*. Cambridge: Cambridge University Press, 1999.

Rogger, Hans. 'Government, Jews, Peasants, and Land in Post-Emancipation Russia: The Pre-Emancipation Background; Stirrings and Limits of Reform'. *Cahiers Du Monde Russe et Soviétique* 17, no. 1 (1976): 5–25.

Sack, Robert D. 'Human Territoriality: A Theory'. *Annals of the Association of American Geographers* 73, no. 1 (1983): 55–74.

Saraçoğlu, M. Safa. *Nineteenth-Century Local Governance in Ottoman Bulgaria: Politics in Provincial Councils*. Edinburgh: Edinburgh University Press, 2018.

Sarafian, Ara. *Talaat Pasha's Report on the Armenian Genocide*. London: Gomidas, 2011.

Sasuni, Garo. *Kürt Ulusal Hareketleri ve 15. yy'dan Günümüze Ermeni Kürt İlişkileri*. Translated by Bedros Zartaryan and Memo Yetkin. Istanbul: Med Yayınları, 1992.

Sazonov, Sergei Dmitrievich. *Fateful Years: 1909–1916*. New York: F. A. Stokes Company, 1928.

Bibliography

Schaller, Dominik J. 'From Conquest to Genocide: Colonial Rule in German Southwest Africa and German East Africa'. In *Empire, Colony, Genocide*, edited by A. Dirk Moses, 296–324. New York: Berghahn, 2022.

Schatkowski Schilcher, Linda. 'The Grain Economy of Late Ottoman Syria and the Issue of Large-Scale Commercialization'. In Keyder and Tabak, *Landholding*, 173–95.

——. 'Violence in Rural Syria in the 1880s and 1890s: State Centralization, Rural Integration, and the World Market'. In Kazemi and Waterbury, *Peasants and Politics*, 50–84.

Semerdjian, Elyse. *Remnants: Embodied Archives of the Armenian Genocide*. Palo Alto: Stanford University Press, 2023.

Sheehan, J. James. 'The Problem of Sovereignty in European History'. *The American Historical Review* 111, no. 1 (February 2006): 1–15.

Shmavonian, Sarkis. 'Mikayel Nalbandian and Non-Territorial Armenian Nationalism'. *Armenian Review* 36, no. 3 (1983): 35–56.

Singer, Joseph William. *Property*. 3rd ed. New York: Aspen Publishers, 2010.

Sipahi, Ali. 'At Arm's Length: Historical Ethnography of Proximity in Harput'. PhD diss., University of Michigan, 2015.

Smith, David M. 'Introduction: The Sharing and Dividing of Geographical Space'. In *Shared Space, Divided Space: Essays on Conflict and Territorial Organization*, edited by Michael Chisholm and David M. Smith, 1–21. London: Unwin Hyman, 1990.

Snyder, Timothy. 'Ukrainians and Poles'. In *The Cambridge History of Russia, Vol. 2: Imperial Russia, 1689–1917*, edited by Dominic Lieven, 163–83. Cambridge: Cambridge University Press, 2006.

Sohrabi, Nader. *Revolution and Constitutionalism in the Ottoman Empire and Iran*. Cambridge: Cambridge Univ. Press, 2011.

Soja, Edward W. 'The Political Organization of Space'. *Association of American Geographers*, research paper no. 8 (1971): 1–54.

Suciyan, Talin. *Outcasting Armenians: Tanzimat of the Provinces* (Syracuse: Syracuse University Press, 2023).

Suny, Ronald Grigor. *Looking toward Ararat: Armenia in Modern History*. Bloomington: Indiana University Press, 1993.

——. 'The Empire Strikes Out: Imperial Russia, "National" Identity, and Theories of Empire'. In *A State of Nations: Empire and Nation-Making in the Age of Lenin and Stalin*, edited by Ronald Grigor Suny and Terry Martin, 23–66. Oxford: Oxford University Press, 2001.

——. *'They Can Live in the Desert but Nowhere Else': A History of the Armenian Genocide*. Princeton: Princeton University Press, 2015.

——. 'Writing Genocide: The Fate of the Ottoman Armenians'. In Suny, Göçek and Naimark, *Question of Genocide*, 15–41.

Suny, Ronald Grigor, Fatma Müge Göçek and Norman M. Naimark, eds. *A Question of Genocide: Armenians and Turks at the End of the Ottoman Empire*. Oxford: Oxford University Press, 2011.

Şaşmaz, Musa. *British Policy and the Application of Reforms for the Armenians in Eastern Anatolia*. Ankara: Turkish Historical Society Printing House, 2000.

——. 'Immigration and Settlement of Circassians in the Ottoman Empire on British Documents, 1857–1864'. *OTAM* 9 (1998): 331–66.

Şeker, Nesim. 'Demographic Engineering in the Late Ottoman Empire and the Armenians'. *Middle Eastern Studies* 43, no. 3 (2007): 461–74.

Tachjian, Vahé. 'Building the 'Model Ottoman Citizen': Life and Death in the Region of Harput-Mamüretülaziz (1908–1915)'. In *World War I and the End of the Ottomans: From the Balkan Wars to the Armenian Genocide*, edited by Hans-Lukas Kieser, Kerem Öktem and Maurus Reinkowski, 210–39. London: I. B. Tauris, 2015.

——. *Daily Life in the Abyss: Genocide Diaries, 1915–1918*. Translated by G. M. Goshgarian. New York: Berghahn, 2017.

Ternon, Yves. *Ermeni Tabusu*. Translated by Emirhan Oğuz. Istanbul: Belge Yayınları, 1993.

Terzibaşoğlu, Yücel. 'Eleni Hatun'un Zeytin Bahçeleri: 19. Yüzyılda Anadolu'da Mülkiyet Hakları Nasıl İnşa Edildi?' *Tarih ve Toplum Yeni Yaklaşımlar* 4 (2006): 121–47.

——. 'Land Disputes and Ethno-Politics: Northwestern Anatolia, 1877–1912'. In Engerman and Metzer, *Land Rights*, 153–80.

Terzibaşoğlu, Yücel, and Alp Yücel Kaya. '19. Yüzyılda Balkanlar'da Toprak Rejimi ve Emek İlişkileri'. In *İktisat Tarihinin Dönüşü: Yeni Yaklaşımlar ve Tartışmalar*, edited by Ulaş Karakoç and Alp Yücel Kaya, 49–106. Istanbul: İletişim, 2021.

'The Preliminary Treaty of Peace, signed at San Stefano'. http://pages.uoregon.edu/kimball/1878mr17.SanStef.trt.htm

Thompson, E. P. *Whigs and Hunters: The Origin of the Black Act*. London: Allen Lane, 1975.

Tilly, Charles. *Coercion, Capital, and European States, AD 990–1992*. Cambridge, MA: Blackwell, 1992.

Toksöz, Meltem. 'Adana Ermenileri ve 1909 "İğtişaşatı"'. *Tarih ve Toplum Yeni Yaklaşımlar* 5 (2007): 147–57.

——. 'The Çukurova: From Nomadic Life to Commercial Agriculture, 1800–1908'. PhD diss., State University of New York at Binghamton, 2000.

Toprak, Zafer. *Türkiye'de Milli İktisat (1908–1918)*. Ankara: Yurt Yayınları, 1982.

'Treaty of Berlin'. http://archive.thetablet.co.uk/article/20th-july-1878/11/the-treaty-of-berlin.

Tunaya, Tarık Zafer. *Türkiye'de Siyasi Partiler, cilt I: İkinci Meşrutiyet Dönemi*. Istanbul: Hürriyet Vakfı Yayınları, 1988.

——. *Türkiye'de Siyasal Partiler, cilt 3: İttihat ve Terakki, Bir Çağın, Bir Kuşağın, Bir Partinin Tarihi*, 3rd ed. Istanbul: İletişim, 2007.

Türkmen, Zekeriya. *Vilayât-ı Şarkiye (Doğu Anadolu Vilayetleri) Islahat Müfettişliği, 1913–1914*. Ankara: Türk Tarih Kurumu, 2006.

Bibliography

Türkyılmaz, Yektan. 'Devrim İçinde Devrim: Ermeni Örgütleri ve İttihat-Terakki İlişkileri, 1908–1915'. In Adanır and Oktay, *1915*, 324–53.

——. 'Rethinking Genocide: Violence and Victimhood in Eastern Anatolia, 1913–1915'. PhD diss., Duke University, 2011.

Ueno, Masayuki. '"For the Fatherland and the State": Armenians Negotiate the Tanzimat Reforms'. *International Journal of Middle East Studies* 45 (2013): 93–109.

Ulugana, Sedat. *Kürt-Ermeni Coğrafyasının Sosyopolitik Dönüşümü (1908–1914): Halidiler, Hamidiyeliler, Bedirhaniler ve Taşnaklar*. Istanbul: İletişim, 2022.

Unat, İlhan. *Türk Vatandaşlık Kanunu*. Ankara: Ankara Üniversitesi Siyasal Bilgiler Fakültesi, 1966.

Üngör, Uğur Ümit. *The Making of Modern Turkey: Nation and State in Eastern Anatolia, 1913–1950*. Oxford: Oxford University Press, 2011.

Üngör, Uğur Ümit, and Eric Lohr. 'Economic Nationalism, Confiscation, and Genocide: A Comparison of the Ottoman and Russian Empires during World War I'. *Journal of Modern European History / Zeitschrift Für Moderne Europäische Geschichte / Revue d'histoire Européenne Contemporaine* 12, no. 4 (2014): 500–22.

Üngör, Uğur Ümit, and Mehmet Polatel. *Confiscation and Destruction: The Young Turk Seizure of Armenian Property*. London: Bloomsbury, 2011.

Veinstein, Gilles. 'On the *Çiftlik* Debate'. In Keyder and Tabak, *Landholding*, 35–56.

Verheij, Jelle. 'Diyarbekir and the Armenian Crisis of 1895'. In Verheij and Jongerden, *Social Relations*, 85–146.

Verheij, Jelle, and Joost Jongerden, eds. *Social Relations in Ottoman Diyarbekir, 1870–1915*. Leiden: Brill, 2012.

Walker, Christopher J. *Armenia: The Survival of a Nation*. Revised 2nd ed. London: Routledge, 1991.

Walsh, Rachael, and Lorna Fox O'Mahony. 'Land Law, Property Ideologies and the British-Irish Relationship'. *Common Law World Review* 47, no. 1 (March 2018): 7–34.

Warriner, Doreen. 'Land Tenure in the Fertile Crescent' in the Nineteenth and Twentieth Centuries'. In *The Economic History of the Middle East, 1800–1914: A Book of Readings*, edited by Charles Issawi, 71–78. Chicago: University of Chicago Press, 1966.

Watenpaugh, Heghnar Zeitlian. *The Missing Pages: The Modern Life of a Medieval Manuscript, from Genocide to Justice*. Palo Alto: Stanford University Press, 2019.

Weeks, Theodore. 'Managing Empire: Tsarist Nationalities Policy'. In Lieven, *The Cambridge History of Russia*, 2:27–38.

Werner, Wolfgang. 'A Brief History of Land Dispossession in Namibia'. *Journal of Southern African Studies* 19, no. 1 (March 1993): 135–46.

Williams, Colin, and Anthony D. Smith. 'The National Construction of Social Space'. *Progress in Human Geography* 7, no. 4 (1983): 502–18.

Winchester, Simon. *Land: How the Hunger for the Ownership Shaped the Modern World*. New York: HarperCollins, 2021.
Winstanley, Michael J. *Ireland and the Land Question, 1800–1922*. London: Methuen, 1984.
Yadırgı, Veli. *The Political Economy of the Kurds of Turkey: From the Ottoman Empire to the Turkish Republic*. Cambridge: Cambridge University Press, 2017.
Yasamee, F. A. K. *Ottoman Diplomacy: Abdülhamid II and the Great Powers, 1878–1888*. Istanbul: The Isis Press, 1996.
Yavuz, Hakan, and Peter Sluglett, eds. *The Political and Social Implications for the Ottoman Empire and Its Successor States of the Treaty of Berlin, 1878*. Salt Lake City: University of Utah Press, 2011.
Yaycıoğlu, Ali. *Partners of the Empire: The Crisis of the Ottoman Order in the Age of Revolutions*. Palo Alto: Stanford University Press, 2016.
Yeghiayan, Zaven Der. *My Patriarchal Memoirs*. Edited by Vatche Ghazarian. Translated by Ared Misirliyan. Barrington, RI: Mayreni, 2002.
Yerevanian, Kevork A. *Badmutyun Charsanjaki Hayots*. Beyrut: Donigian, 1956.
Yılmaz, İlkay. 'Governing the Armenian Question through Passports in the Late Ottoman Empire (1876–1908)'. *Journal of Historical Sociology* 32, no. 4 (December 2019): 388–403.
———. *Ottoman Passports: Security and Geographic Mobility, 1876–1908*. Syracuse: Syracuse University Press, 2023.
Yosmaoğlu, İpek. *Blood Ties: Religion, Violence, and the Politics of Nationhood in Ottoman Macedonia, 1878–1908*. Ithaca: Cornell University Press, 2014.
Yücel, Naz. 'On Ottoman, British, and Belgian Monarchs' Ownership of Private Property in the Late Nineteenth Century'. *Comparative Studies of South Asia, Africa and the Middle East* 43, no. 2 (August 2023): 208–23.
Zakian, Malina. 'The Journey of One Armenian Manuscript'. Hill Museum and Manuscript Library, 5 August 2021. https://hmml.org/stories/series-travel-the-journey-of-one-armenian-manuscript/
Zandi-Sayek, Sibel. *Ottoman Izmir: xThe Rise of a Cosmopolitan Port, 1840/1880*. Minneapolis, London: University of Minnesota Press, 2012.
Zekiyan, Boğos Levon. *Ermeniler ve Modernite*. Istanbul: Aras, 2002.
Zimmerer, Jürgen. *From Windhoek to Auschwitz? Reflections on the Relationship between Colonialism and National Socialism*. Berlin: De Gruyter, 2024.
Zürcher, Eric Jan. *Turkey: A Modern History*. 4th ed. London: I. B. Tauris, 2017.
———. *Unionist Factor: The Role of the Committee of Union and Progress in the Turkish National Movement, 1905–1926*. Leiden: Brill, 1984.

Index

Abdülhalik Bey (governor of Bitlis), 238, 245–6
Abdülhamid II (sultan), 2, 9, 36–7, 47n, 69, 71, 84–5, 93, 128–32, 135
Abdürrezzak Bedirxan, 11, 162, 192, 226–7, 239, 249, 250n
Abidin Pasha, 70–1
Abraham, 1–2, 54; *see also* Dağ Marnik
Adana Massacre(s) (1909), 147, 198–9, 217n, 224
Adom (Harutiun Shahrikian), 10, 168–9, 177–9
administrative council(s), 119, 126, 145, 147–8, 152–4, 161, 178–9, 181
  arbitration by, 195, 205, 213, 225, 237, 240–1
  Bitlis, 149–50, 164, 242–3
  Damascene, 32
  Erzurum, 161–3
  Muş, 1
  provincial, 118
administrative resolution, 148–50, 152–4, 158, 167, 174, 178, 181–2, 205, 228, 241–2, 249
Agricultural Bank (*Ziraat Bank*), 77n, 101, 115n, 174, 231, 238, 251n
Akpınar, Özkan, 36

Al Bayrak (Erzurum), 234
Ali Seydi Bey (inspector), 167
Ambassadors' Conference *see* Yeniköy
Antaramian, Richard E., 48n, 67
Armenakan Party, 84
Armenian Civil Assembly, 85
Armenian Civil Council, 58
Armenian National Administration, 223
Armenian National Assembly (ANA), 9, 52–3, 56, 60, 67–8, 70, 147, 169, 179–80, 197, 222–3, 225, 249
Armenian political organization(s), 10, 82–5, 95, 133, 147, 158, 196–7, 226
Armenian Revolutionary Federation (ARF), 84, 143–5, 147, 158, 166, 172–4, 180–1, 189n, 197, 205–6, 212, 238, 253n
A-Tō (Hovhannes Der-Mardirossian), 10, 169
ayan (provincial notables), 20–1, 33, 57
Aytekin, Atilla, 34
Azadamart, 144–5, 157–8, 204

Bâb-ı Âlî Baskını (coup) 196, 226, 241
Babigian, Hagob, 198–9, 217n

Balaklı tribe, 95, 231
Balkan Crisis, 66, 84
Balkan Wars (1912–13), 11, 23, 51, 180, 182, 191–2, 194, 196, 198, 200, 214, 222, 225, 248–9
Barakat, Nora Elizabeth, 39
Barkan, Ömer Lütfü, 19, 27–8
Bayraktar, Uğur Bahadır, 20, 33
Bekir Sami Bey (governor of Van), 111n, 158
Black Sea, 4, 125, 139n, 141n, 240
Bloxham, Donald, 132
Boyadjian, Hampartsum, 171, 180, 224
boycotts, 155, 194
British inspectors, 193, 195, 206, 212

Çarsancak, 56–7, 63, 65, 180
Cavid Bey, 162, 204, 226
Celal Bey (governor of Erzurum), 163, 165–6
Central Anatolia, 5, 23, 41, 91–2
Cilicia, 3, 37–8, 43n, 70, 83, 89, 130, 224, 249
Circassian immigrants, 55, 70, 77n, 91, 99, 134, 141n, 160–1, 223
commission
  inquiry, 56, 172
  investigation, 65, 91, 98, 161, 178–9, 203–4, 217n, 218n
  on Seized Lands, 85
  property, 120
  reform, 70–2, 74, 118, 177, 179, 182, 194, 202–3, 218n
  special, 52, 55, 59, 70, 93, 118, 153, 164, 174, 195, 203–4, 209, 240–1
committee of inquiry, 145, 147
Committee of Union and Progress (CUP), 161–2, 191, 202–3, 210, 226, 250
  after Salonica congress, 155
  approach to land disputes, 157, 248
  ARF and, 145, 147, 172–3, 180, 189, 205

Armenians' distrust of, 212
  club in Erzurum, 234
  concerns regarding internationalisation of the reform, 199–200
  coup d'état, 196
  ethno-national politics of, 181, 194, 249
  Kurdish rapproachment, 11
  policies towards the eastern provinces, 239
  and reform, 204, 206, 208, 213
  socio-economic understanding of, 193
  view on Bitlis rebellion, 237
competition over resources, 2, 3, 223, 260
Congress of Berlin (1878), 66–9, 73
Crimean War (1854), 22, 51, 73, 79n, 132
Çukur 134, 150–1, 163

Dağ Marnik (Çubuklu), 1–2, 54
Davison, Roderic H., 193, 208, 210–12
Deringil, Selim, 84–5
Dinçer, Sinan, 62, 121–2, 137n

Eastern Anatolia, 23, 141n, 226; *see also* Ottoman East
Eastern Rumelia Administration, 38–9
Emin Pasha (Haydaranlı tribe), 92–3, 96, 110n, 152
emir(s), 4, 19, 21, 33, 52, 250n; *see also* ayan
Engerman, Stanley L., 7
ethno-religious
  classification, 137n
  differences, 35, 83, 105, 117
  dominance, 38, 155–6, 258
  policy of demographic engineering, 257
Etmekjian, Lillian, 53, 67
European inspectors, 234–6

Index

First World War, 2, 8, 11, 21, 38, 221, 240, 259, 260n
Fortna, Benjamin C., 36
Franco-Prussian War (1870), 8

Garabedian, Kegham Der, 10, 98–9, 102, 168–9, 171
Gellner, Ernest, 6
general inspector(s), 204–5, 206–7, 209–13, 219n, 234, 237, 240–3, 246, 248, 255n, 258
 appointment of, 195
Gerber, Haim, 20–1, 45n
Ghazarian, Matthew, 85, 115n
Giers, Mikhail Nikolayevich von (Russian ambassador), 211, 239; *see also* reform: Giers-Wangenheim plan
gospodarlık, 35, 64
Greek Patriarchate, 34

Hacı Necmeddin Efendi, 150–1, 163
hafir(lik) (illegal protection tax), 160, 218n, 228, 246
Halil Bey (Menteşe), 205–6, 212
Hamed-Troyansky, Vladimir, 13n, 77n, 88n, 132
Hamidian massacres *see* massacres of 1894–97
Hamidian Regiments, 37, 82–5, 91–2, 104, 113n, 133, 140n, 151, 209
Hamidian Tribal School, 38, 85
Harach (Erzurum), 172–3, 177, 196, 224, 250n
Hasenanlı tribe, 63, 95–6, 98
Hayri Bey (minister), 174, 179, 202
Hobsbawm, Eric J., 6
Hoff, Nicolai (general inspector), 242, 248, 255n
Hunchakian Revolutionary Party (Hunchaks), 84, 106n, 143, 147, 166, 197, 212
Hüseyin Efendi (mufti of Muş), 1–2, 54

Hüseyin Pasha (Haydaranlı), 11, 92–3, 95–6, 109n, 143, 148, 152, 161–3, 165, 169, 230–1, 235–6
Hüseyin Pasha (Karapapak Major in Sivas), 91–2
Hüseyin Şükri, 227–8
Huyt, 150, 159, 180, 229, 231, 246

İbrahim Efendi (head of administrative council, Bitlis), 150, 163
iltizam system (tax-farming), 20–2
İnalcık, Halil, 18
Inspection Commission (*Tesrî'-i Muamelât Komisyonu*), 92, 101, 103, 126–9, 138n
Ireland, 2, 8
İshak Bey, 56; *see also* Çarsancak
İslamoğlu, Huri, 18–19, 32, 64
İsmail Hakkı Babanzade, 203
İsmail Hakkı Bey (governor of Bitlis), 142, 151, 163–5
İsmail Pasha, (governor of Erzurum), 1–2, 54
İzzet Bey, (governor of Van), 233, 241

Kaprileian, Manaseh, 256, 260n
Karpat, Kemal, 20
Kaya, Alp Yücel, 35
Keyder, Çağlar, 18, 98
Khoury, Dina R., 20–1, 25
Khrimian, Mgrdich (Patriarch), 53, 67–8, 70
Kiğı, 71–2, 74, 101
Klein, Janet, 98
Koptaş, Rober, 206, 212
Kürt Teavün ve Terakki Cemiyeti (SKMAP), 146, 148, 183n

La Turquie, 202–3
land
 bank, 8
 commodification of, 22, 30, 51, 98–9, 102, 105

land (*cont.*)
　conflict(s), 34, 51, 53, 59–60, 63, 74, 143, 154, 162, 164, 167, 174, 177, 203–4, 241, 243
　grabbing, 259–60
　individual and exclusionary rights to, 22, 26, 30
　liberal conception, 7
　liberalisation of, 7, 29–30, 40, 136, 157
　market, 3, 7–8, 39, 118, 129–32, 136
　mevkufe, 28, 104
　miri, 18–20, 26–33, 55, 104, 123, 167
　mülk (freehold), 19–20, 27, 30, 123
　nationalisation of, 7, 17, 60
　policies, 7–8, 38–41, 127, 156, 258
　reform, 165, 244–5, 249
　regime, 5, 8, 17–23, 25, 28–31, 35, 51, 62, 64, 73, 135–6, 157
　registry, 172, 178, 204, 226, 243–4, 246
　survey, 166–7
　tenure, 18, 22, 24–5, 35, 64, 99
　waqf, 19–20, 25, 123
Land Code of 1858, 5, 21–2, 26, 28–31, 51, 54, 61–2, 71, 73, 104, 123, 144, 169–70
land ownership
　absolute, 19, 26, 30, 32, 55
　conflicts over, 35, 41
　disputes over, 32, 34
　economic importance of, 4, 52, 259
　ethno-demographic significance of, 132
　impact of mass violence on, 259
　liberal understanding of, 258
　matter of, 155–7
　means of establishing ethno-religious dominance, 38, 40, 226–7, 249
　nationalist approaches to, 7
　patterns of, 20–1, 39, 117, 128
　political significance of, 17, 39–40, 52
　rush, 2, 8
Léart, Marcel *see* Zohrab, Krikor
Lebanon, 33, 39, 41, 206, 209, 219n, 260n
Li, Andy Hanlun, 6
Libaridian, Gerard J., 53, 70, 84
List, Friedrich, 193
Lowther, Sir Gerard, 154, 180

Mahmud II (sultan), 21, 25
Mahmud Şevket Pasha, 151, 206
Mallet, Sir Louis (ambassador), 236, 247
Mandelstam, André, 199, 209, 219n
maraba(lık), 102, 135, 174
Marling, C. M. (consul), 148, 180, 184
mass violence, 2, 3, 41, 82, 85, 98, 102, 120, 223, 259
　against Armenians, 9, 130, 234
　and mass uprooting, 105
　outcomes of, 117
　perpetrators and organisers of, 135
　relationship between ethnoreligious tensions and competition over resources, 2
　transformative impact of, 259
massacres of 1894–97, 23, 57, 75, 77n, 82, 85, 98, 101–4, 129, 133, 142–3, 170, 222, 257, 259
Matossian, Bedross Der, 89
Mazhar Bey (governor of Bitlis), 229, 241–2
Mehmed Emin (governor of Erzurum), 163
Melkon, 1–2, 54; *see also* Dağ Marnik
Metzer, Jacob, 7
Milli İbrahim Pasha, 96
Mirkova, Anna M., 38
mobile courts (*seyyar mahkemeler*), 153, 176, 185n
Monahan, J. H. (consul), 230–1
Morack, Ellinor, 104

Index

Morgan, James (vice-consul), 148–50
Moses, A. Dirk, 8
Mundy, Martha, 19, 25, 29
Muradiye, 243–5, 248–9
Musa Bey, 11, 95, 114n, 159–60, 228–9, 231, 237
Mustafa Bey (inspector), 167

national economy (*millî iktisat*), 192–4
new imperialism, 7, 35
Nizri, Michael, 19–20
Nubar, Boghos, 197–200, 216n, 217n

Odian, Krikor, 53, 76n
Olson, Robert, 37
Ömer Naci Bey, 162, 226
Ottoman East
  agrarian relations, 87
  Armenian existence, 69, 120, 258
  Armenian peasants, 102, 158
  attacks on Armenians, 68
  autonomy of *emir*s, 21
  contestation over, 38
  demographics in, 85, 95, 132
  Kurdish territorial claims, 37, 249
  land ban, 135
  land disputes, 52, 64–5, 73, 167, 169
  land market, 118, 128–9, 131
  Muslim domination, 117, 133
  political life in, 4
  reforms, 200, 211, 213–14, 221
  refugee settlement, 5
  rural lands in, 3
  Russian intervention, 201
  security, 152
  territorial sovereignty, 234
Ottoman Nationality Law, 122–4, 126
Özbek, Nadir, 21, 140n
Özok-Gündoğan, Nilay, 33

Pamuk, Şevket, 23, 88, 98
Panossian, Razmik, 68
Papazian, Vahan, 171–3, 205, 216n, 223–4
Parvus (Israel Lazarevich Helphand), 193–4
Pehlivan, Zozan, 85
Persia, 3, 37, 120, 125, 225, 230, 232
  flight of Kurdish chiefs to, 152–3, 158, 162–3, 165, 181
  Ottoman border, 64
Philliou, Christine M., 129
Polanyi, Karl, 17
population
  decimating, 65, 117, 120–1, 135, 194, 223
  demographics, 191
  distribution, 23, 74, 245, 248
  exchange, 124
  and land, 3, 84, 130, 222, 226
  movement(s), 122, 125
Portukalian, Mgrdich, 68, 70, 84
prescriptive rights (*hakk-ı karar*), 28, 31, 33, 54–5, 104, 143–4, 152–4, 164, 169–70, 175–6
property
  alienable, 7, 29
  ban on sales to Armenians, 126, 128–31, 135
  market, 130
  rights, 7–8, 20, 40, 118, 130–2, 136, 170–1
  transfer(s), 38, 75, 82–3, 85–9, 91–3, 95–6, 98–9, 101–2, 117, 122, 128, 130, 135, 236, 259
  violation of, 53
  see also land market
Prussia, 8, 136, 258

Quataert, Donald, 23

Raffi, 9, 60–3, 78n, 95
Rauf Bey (governor of Erzurum), 96, 98

reform(s)
  commission *see under* commission
  domestic scheme, 200, 206, 212–13
  Giers-Wangenheim plan, 211, 213
  international guarantee for the implementation of, 199–200, 205, 212
  Mandelstam plan, 209–11, 213
  negotiations, 11, 191, 227, 240–2
  Ottoman plan, 210–11
  Russo-Ottoman agreement, 194, 213, 236, 240, 249
Reşkotan tribe, 95, 113n
Reynolds, Michael A., 239
Rojî Kurd, 227
Russo-Ottoman War of 1877–78, 23, 37–8, 51, 66–7, 73

Safrastian, A. (vice consul), 99, 151
Said Bey, Kurdish chief, 149, 151
Şakir Pasha (commissioner), 119, 127
Sasun
  land disputes in, 243, 245–6
  massacres in, 118
  oppression in, 231
Sasuni, Garo, 73
Sazonov, Sergei Dmitrievich (Russian Minister of Foreign Affairs), 201, 207–10
Schatkowski Schilcher, Linda, 31–2
Sectarian violence, 39
selef, 99, 101, 113n, 115n
Selim Bey (acting governor of Bitlis), 149–50
Şemseddin Efendi, 150, 163
Serengülian, Vartkes, 171, 179
Sheikh Abdulkadir, 148
Sheikh Hamid Paşa, 92–3, 111–12n
Sheikh Şahabettin, 111n, 236, 252n
Sheikh Selim, 11, 192, 236–8, 240, 250n
Sheikh Seyyid Ali, 95, 111n, 236–9, 252–53n
Sheikh Ubeydullah, 37

Smith, Richard Saumarez, 19, 25, 29
Smith, M. (vice consul), 234–6
statute of limitations, 152, 164, 170, 176
sulh hâkimleri kânunu (decree-law on peace court judges), 201, 241–2, 244
Suny, Ronald G., 7, 60, 84
Supreme Council (*Meclis-i Vâlâ*), 29, 56, 63
Syria, 23, 39

Taghavank (Uran), 150, 231
Tahsin Bey (governor of Van), 232–3, 236, 238–9, 241, 243–6, 248
Talat Pasha, (Minister of the Interior), 204–6, 236, 239, 243
Tanin, 200, 202, 204, 217–18n, 226
Tashnags *see* Armenian Revolutionary Federation
tax collection, 21, 70, 101, 105, 135
Taylor, J. G. (consul), 62, 64
Telan farm, 89
territorial
  integrity of Ottoman Empire, 193, 200, 208, 240
  sovereignty, 6, 36–9, 69, 84, 234
  turn, 3, 7, 9, 17, 37, 40, 51, 136, 258
territorialisation
  of Armenian nationalism, 37, 48n, 51, 68–9, 74, 83, 221
  of collective identity, 37
  of imperial power relations, 35
  of political power, 36
  of reform scheme, 206
territoriality 6, 36–40, 84, 135
  and nationalism, 35
  new conception of, 135–6
  Ottoman, 36, 40
  sovereignty and, 3, 7
Terzibaşoğlu, Yücel, 7, 31, 38, 51, 156
Tevfik Pasha (ambassador), 179, 206–7

Index

Thompson, E. P., 30
Toprak, Zafer, 193
Treaty of Berlin (1878), 13n, 66–70, 74, 84, 93, 132
Treaty of San Stefano, 66, 68–9, 74
tribal regiments (*aşiret alayları*), 196, 213, 218n, 231

Ueno, Masayuki, 67–8
Unionists *see* Committee of Union and Progress

Verheij, Jelle, 103
Vidin, 30, 34–5, 64, 79n

Wangenheim, Hans Baron von (ambassador), 211; *see also* reform: Giers-Wangenheim plan

Westenenk, Louis C. (general inspector), 242, 248
Western Anatolia, 4, 7, 24, 31, 38, 89, 156

Yeghiayan, Zaven Der, 217n, 231
Yeniköy Conference, 199, 208–11, 223, 242
Yıldız Palace, 119, 121, 124, 127–30, 132
Young Turks, 10, 142, 194, 226
yurtluk-ocaklık (hereditary estate), 19–20, 33, 58

Zeki Pasha (Fourth Army Commander), 85, 93, 124, 130–2
Zohrab, Krikor, 10, 147, 171–2, 174, 198–9, 212, 222–3
Zomik, 161–3

www.ingramcontent.com/pod-product-compliance
Lightning Source LLC
LaVergne TN
LVHW050050200525
811683LV00004B/111